"The Greatest Game
Ever Played in Dixie"

"The Greatest Game Ever Played in Dixie"

The Nashville Vols, Their 1908 Season, and the Championship Game

JOHN A. SIMPSON

McFarland & Company, Inc., Publishers
Jefferson, North Carolina, and London

LIBRARY OF CONGRESS CATALOGUING-IN-PUBLICATION DATA

Simpson, John A., 1949–
    "The greatest game ever played in Dixie" : the Nashville Vols, their 1908 season, and the championship game / John A Simpson.
        p.   cm.
    Includes bibliographical references and index.

    ISBN-13: 978-0-7864-3050-5
    softcover : 50# alkaline paper ∞

    1. Nashville Vols (Baseball team)—History. I. Title.
GV875.V65S56 2007
796.357'630976855—dc22
                                            2007017161

British Library cataloguing data are available

©2007 John A. Simpson. All rights reserved

No part of this book may be reproduced or transmitted in any form or by any means, electronic or mechanical, including photocopying or recording, or by any information storage and retrieval system, without permission in writing from the publisher.

On the cover: The 1908 Southern Association Champion Nashville Vols *(Nashville Banner)*

Manufactured in the United States of America

McFarland & Company, Inc., Publishers
    Box 611, Jefferson, North Carolina 28640
    www.mcfarlandpub.com

Acknowledgments

The research material needed to write a book about the 1908 Nashville Vols involved extensive travel and long distance communiques with many local experts. I would like to thank special people and institutions for their help in making this book possible. The staff at Kelso (WA) Public Library assisted with countless inter-library loan requests while Longview (WA) Public Library permitted me to tie up a microfilm machine for entire weekends at a time. The Inter-Library Loan department at Knight Library, University of Oregon filled more requests for books and microfilm than I can possibly remember. Jami Awalt, formerly of the Special Collections Room, Vanderbilt University, made available the Grantland Rice Collection for my inspection. Reference librarian Beth Odle at the Nashville Public Library was tremendously helpful with photographs as was Karina McDaniel at the Tennessee State Library and Archive, Nashville. The Society for American Baseball Research (SABR) lending library filled many long distance requests for microfilm. Comments from colleagues on the *SABR* Deadball Era Committee (DEC) list-serv also proved instructive. Thanks are due to both Heather Moore, photo historian for the U.S. Senate, and Lynn Ewbank of the Arkansas History Commission for their assistance in tracking down the photograph of William Marmaduke Kavanaugh. Genella Olker, former reference librarian at the TSLA, was instrumental in helping me learn and understand the history of Nashville over the past twenty-two years. She was like a personal tutor and her influence on my life as a scholar of Tennessee history has been profound. Thus, I dedicate this book in her memory.

Several individuals have offered encouragement and expertise throughout this project. Tim Wiles, director of research at the A. Bartlett Giamatti

Research Center, National Baseball Hall of Fame Library, Cooperstown, N.Y., has been prompt and energetic in answering all of my questions for specific details relating to players. Bill Burdick, director of photographic services at the same facility, cooperated fully in filling print orders. Steve Gietschier, senior managing editor for research at *The Sporting News* Archive, tracked down many files related to my topic during a brief visit to St. Louis. Genealogy societies from Miami to San Diego (and smaller communities in between) responded to direct requests for information, such as date of birth, date of death, and location of interment. One genealogist deserves special mention — Shirley DeBoer of Grand Rapids, MI.

I owe three former professors a tip of the cap as well. As a sophomore at Western Washington State College, August Radke introduced me to the joys of Civil War and Southern history which has consumed a major part of my professional life. But we also shared our love of sports — his in hockey and mine in baseball — in countless hours of discussion in Rad's office. When I moved on to graduate school at the University of Arkansas, I became the battery mate for my advisor, Tim Donovan, on the History Department fastpitch softball team. During earnest discussions about my search for a suitable thesis topic, Dr. Donovan suggested a team history of the Arkansas Travelers. The notion of conducting scholarly research on baseball in 1972 did not seem to command the same level of respect as other subfields of inquiry so I chose a more traditional subject which ultimately led to the publication of three books. Still, Dr. Donovan's advice stuck with me. When I arrived at the University of Oregon to work on a Ph.D., Professor Richard Maxwell Brown shaped my thinking in many significant directions. And, one of them was in baseball. Dr. Brown reminisced about his grad student days at Harvard where he took the subway to Fenway Park to root for the Red Sox. The message of these three learned men — Radke, Donovan, and Brown — finally dawned on me. Each scholar loved sports and understood the potential for an intellectual treatment of baseball. I thank each of them for gently guiding me to this realization.

I conducted two important interviews that were indispensable to the preparation of this book. First, I met Fred Russell in April, 1999. Russell, the dean of Nashville sports journalists, kindly accepted my overtures for an interview. Although he did not recall the '08 Vols, he did weave several related stories which are included in this book. The biggest face-to-face breakthrough, however, came when I tracked down the three children of Julius Augustus "Doc" Wiseman — a key player on the '08 Vols. In April, 2004, I spent an absolutely delightful weekend in Cincinnati interviewing Dr. James A. (and Helen) Wiseman, Dr. Donald E. Wiseman, and Jeanne (Wiseman) Groenke. Doc's grandsons, Tom and Andrew, were also present at the seven-hour session. I am deeply indebted to the friendship extended to me by the entire Wiseman clan. They supplied invaluable family history, which allowed me to better understand the character of Doc Wiseman, "the hero of the Dell." To

Jim, who passed away only three months after our meeting, I also dedicate this book.

I would like to extend three additional notes of appreciation — the first to my good friend (and former teaching and coaching colleague), Gordon B. Sargent. Gordy read the entire manuscript several times primarily to check for clarity and grammatical miscues. Second, Daniel Ross, director of the University of Alabama Press, gave the same kind of assessment. Dan spent more time "polishing this diamond" than either of us would care to admit, and I am deeply appreciative.

Finally, I would like to thank my family. My three children, Jamie, Annie, and Craig, were very patient over the years in allowing me to craft history out of notecards. Now fully grown up, Jamie and her husband, Kelly, prepared the monthly pocket schedules that appear in the text and offered technical assistance on computer issues. Annie compiled many of the statistics found in Chapter 9 and undertook occasional word processing chores. Craig turned into a fine player and student of the game and learned many of the more subtle nuances of baseball from his old man. If I have taught my grown children anything in life it is their genuine love of baseball. To my wife goes my deepest note of gratitude. Shirley has never read any of my finished books. She hasn't had to. She has heard all of them read aloud by me many times over. Thanks, dear, for lending an ear.

If there are errors to be found in "The Greatest Game Ever Played in Dixie," I accept them as matters of my own carelessness. I hope they are at a minimum.

John A. Simpson, Ph.D.
Kelso, Washington

To the memory of

Dr. James A. Wiseman (1928–2004),
son of Julius Augustus "Doc" Wiseman,

and

Genella Fitzgerald Nye Olker (1925–2006),
the best reference librarian ever

Table of Contents

Acknowledgments v
Preface 1

1. Nashville and the National Pastime in the Deadball Era 7
2. Going from Bad to ? 26
3. Play Ball 44
4. More of the Same 63
5. Month of Crises 83
6. In Search of Stability 100
7. Dog Days of Summer 119
8. Pennant Fever 142
9. The Greatest Game Ever Played in Dixie 159
10. Historic Legacy of the 1908 Nashville Vols 178
11. Life After Baseball 194

Appendix A: Players' Careers 229
Appendix B: Linescores for the Vols' 1908 Season 235
Appendix C: Should Jake Daubert Be in the Hall of Fame? 249
Chapter Notes 253
Bibliography 271
Index 277

Preface

In the early 1990s, I drove our church's van on Sunday mornings to pick up elderly members who resided in retirement homes to attend worship services, and this is where I first met Jack Love. Love had played professional baseball in the years before World War I, and we forged an instant friendship owing to our mutual interest in the game. His stories were delightful windows into a bygone era, as he told me how, as the leading hitter for the Fond du Lac club, he was awarded a black Labrador puppy for his accomplishment; how as a member of the St. Louis organization he barnstormed with the big leaguers through the South every spring only to be let go at the end of the preseason; and how he migrated to several minor league clubs in Texas and eventually to the Pennsylvania coal district where in the 1920s he managed a company team. He fondly recollected the strong spirit of community that existed between rivals on game day. He inspired me to learn more about his time, the roughly 30-year period that ended in 1920 and is now known as the Deadball Era.

A couple of years after Jack passed away, I was in Nashville conducting research at the Tennessee State Library and Archive on a post–Civil War subject when I uncovered a one-line reference to the 1908 championship game of the Southern Association. Being a lifelong baseball enthusiast, I jotted down the date of the contest, and as the library approached closing time I went to the microfilm room to read the newspaper coverage of the game. I was instantly hooked by the account: a full page, inning-by-inning description complete with box score and pictures underneath a headline that captured my imagination: "The Greatest Game Ever Played in Dixie." I estimated that there was at least enough information for a scholarly article about the finale and possibly a book about the entire Nashville season. I made a Xerox copy from the microfilm article and filed it away for several years.

The research process began in earnest in 1997. I prepared a reference sheet that most baseball coaches and scouts would recognize, color-coding a detailed scorecard white for home games and yellow for away games. On the front side, I created a line for the date of each game and a blank box score to record game data for both teams. I reserved the back of the card for the line score, pitching statistics, and plenty of space for notes about the game, my observations, quotations, and summaries. Since the Vols were covered by three local newspapers as well as two national tabloids there was no shortage of information from which to draw. Thus, I coded information with different colored pens—blue, black, red, green, and magenta—in order to distinguish between each source as I read through every game account.

Much about baseball as it was played one hundred years ago in the Southern Association would surprise fans today. It was the era of the deadball, when only one hardball was used for an entire game; when infielders juiced the ball with licorice or tobacco spittle, rubbed it down with dirt, and tossed it to the pitcher before a single pitch had been thrown; when one umpire worked the contest; when cost-conscious owners provided two sets of uniforms—one home white and one away gray—to last the entire season; when players were hardy and rough but their style of play, known as scientific baseball, was aggressive and intelligent; when managers strategized for one run at a time; when travel by train (often overnight), staying in third rate hotels, frequenting pool halls and saloons, and dining in substandard eateries challenged the civility of players; when the motivation of many bush leaguers was not necessarily predicated on making it to the Big Show but rather to return year after year to the same minor league circuit. Public enthusiasm for the game was fueled by sensational newspaper stories, and the presence of a professional baseball team conveyed a progressive community outlook that emphasized optimism and prosperity. Early twentieth-century Nashville, with its emerging baseball tradition, is a wonderful microcosm in which to view baseball as it was transforming into our national pastime.

Nashville and its league competitors captured the attention of a regional audience in the same manner that the major leagues were generating enthusiasm from a national audience, with drama. The last week of the 1908 season found three teams still very much in the Southern Association race, as Nashville, New Orleans, and Memphis battled fiercely for the top spot. In the American League, the hopes of Detroit, Cleveland, and Chicago were alive, and in the National League, Chicago, New York, and Pittsburgh were engaged in a pennant chase that is still written and talked about. None of the outcomes was decided until the final game of the season. One game separated the three contestants in both major leagues, and a playoff game determined the National League champion. The campaign in the South was decided by a .002 difference in winning percentage.

Many Southern baseball fans considered the Southern Association to be their major league. The eight-team league was peppered with former major leaguers as well as young talent on the way up. The level of play was sound, and the spirit of competition was fierce. Nashville, like its league counterparts, nevertheless struggled to operate a franchise in a small market and dealt with common ills that faced the sport then, including gambling, rowdyism, racism, and alcoholism. It also met strong resistance from Sabbatarianism, which opposed the playing games on Sunday.

I am hopeful that this monograph will make a significant contribution to the field of baseball history. Existing treatments of minor league teams more often cover the broad expanse of a franchise's history, which usually spans many decades. This story about the '08 Nashville Vols examines a single season, focusing on details of the deadball game—and specifically on the game in the minors and the South that cannot be touched on in works of broader scope. But if the reasons a book of this sort should be written appeal heavily to the historian, the reason it should be read is, I think, more compelling. The 1908 Vols are a great baseball story, and we are drawn to these men whose struggles to get past their own and their franchise's histories are the stuff of the best stories about sport.

The colorful prose of the Victorian Age lends charm to many of the articles quoted in the book. Among the terms that might be unfamiliar to some readers are: sphere or pill (ball); sack or pillow (base); dish (home plate); willow or stick (bat); hurler, twirler, spinner or slabman (pitcher); sackers (basemen); bingle (single); four-bagger (home run); scribes (sports writers); flag, rag or banner (pennant); mogul (owner or manager); dope (inside information); detail (scoreboard); slab or pitching box (mound); twirler (curve ball); fade away (screwball); floater or finger-nail (knuckleball); smoke ball (fastball); garden (outfield); kranks or bugs (fans); nines (baseball team); whip or soupbone (throwing arm); wickets, pins, or underpinnings (legs). Outside of the quotations, mostly the modern terms of baseball are used, but the text is lightly sprinkled with turn-of-the-century vernacular.

The book begins by tracing the connection between the city of Nashville and baseball from the Civil War to the creation of a second southern professional circuit in 1901. The organizational development of the game with its evolution of rule changes is reviewed to provide necessary background for the reader. Chapter 2 opens with the pathetic performance of Nashville in the final game in 1907, and follows with significant administrative changes in the offseason—new owners, stadium, and manager. This chapter provides an inside view of roster building as well as the role of Nashville's three energetic sports editors in drumming up public support for the revamped team. Preseason competition versus major league clubs, local amateur semi-pros, and a local university round out the third chapter. This chapter also documents the existence of an illegal farming relationship between Cleveland and Nashville, and concludes with the 1908 opener against defending league champion Atlanta. Chapter 4 relates the first quarter of the season when Nashville takes to the road against every league opponent, and builds toward the traditional doubleheader at the end of May. The month of June promised a favorable homestand, but Chapter 5 details a scandal that rocked the league as well as a devastating team crisis which threatened to derail the fragile Vols. Lethargic individual performances afflicted the squad as the midsummer doubleheader on the Fourth of July approached. The lackluster Vols found themselves at a crossroads: would they free fall into disarray or would the franchise stabilize? Next we examine the rise of several promising leaders as the team searched for a winning identity. In Chapter 7, the Vols have entered the dog days of summer, and the team is floundering in mediocrity with the rest of the league. Then a phenomenal resurgence began in early September — stellar pitching and solid defense combined with productive hitting to catapult the Vols into contention for the pennant. Chapter 9 examines the final three games of the season and play-by-play analysis of the winner-take-all finale against New Orleans is relived. The following chapter breaks down team statistics — offense, defense, and pitching — in order to evaluate key individual performances. This chapter looks at the disappointing 1909 campaign, assesses the historic legacy of the '08 season, and traces how the big game itself gradually faded from public memory. In the final chapter, the life stories of the former players are recounted. These vignettes about life after baseball are poignant reminders that time honored values such as teamwork, leadership, and commitment to excellence should always overcome selfishness, laziness, and disloyalty — an important lesson for all time. Two informative references are provided in the Appendices: a chronological list of each player's major and minor league career, and a complete season line score for every Nashville game in 1908. A final appendix examines the case for Jake Daubert's being inducted into the Hall of Fame.

Baseball is recognized as the great national game. The baseball fan should be recognized as the great national character.

Every branch of sport has its followers, but the baseball fan for loyalty and enthusiasm has them all played off the boards. For six months baseball holds the attention of the United States, and during that time it makes crazy rooters out of men from every walk of life. And, a number of the fair sex, of course, join in.... Baseball is truly the game of the masses.

> — Richard Hunter Yancey, Jr., sports editor of the *Nashville Banner*, on the eve of the 1908 Southern Association season.

CHAPTER 1

Nashville and the National Pastime in the Deadball Era

Baseball has a storied history in Nashville. The first known contest took place during the Civil War between bivouacked Union soldiers who occupied "the Athens of the South." Enamored by the new sport, Nashvillians organized into amateur nines in the decades following hostilities. By 1885, a professional circuit was formed and the city of Nashville eagerly fielded a team along with other growing urban municipalities in the South. By the late nineteenth and early twentieth centuries, the sport of baseball, as well as American society in general, encouraged a spirit of progressive and commercial reform that stressed the importance of leisure activities. Organized baseball reflected this positive attitude toward social change in the Deadball Era by adapting into a game style known as scientific baseball. This movement led to rule changes that ushered in the modern game as well as structural alterations, which defined the relationship between major and minor leagues. In 1901, as these modifications became codified into the modern rules and governance, Nashville applied for membership in a reorganized Southern Association and quickly established itself as a premiere baseball city for the next sixty years.

In 1862, a Union army of occupation under the command of General George Thomas camped north of the state house at a place known to locals as Sulphur Springs Bottom. By the early nineteenth century, this flat and wet canebrake had became a popular area for recreation, owing to an old North Carolina law mandating that all salt springs and salt licks must be preserved as a community resource.¹ Fifty years later, Northern soldiers spent their idle time playing baseball in the ideal flatlands of the Bottoms with an audience of Southern citizens observing firsthand this engaging new game.² "The coming of the Civil War did not portend the end of baseball," stated sports historian Allison Caveglia Barash. "In fact, it may have been the direct catalyst that caused it to flourish."³

When sectional hostilities came to an end in 1865, baseball had worked its way into the Nashville psyche. The natural playing surface at the Bottoms evolved into the Nashville Athletic Club Grounds, and the field attracted a steady flow of local participants. The *Nashville Republican Banner* reported the first organized club game on 12 September 1867.⁴ From this humble beginning, this Yankee game established itself as a vibrant and integral part of Nashville's urban landscape. One city sportswriter later commented, "Baseball was almost as much a part of Nashville's history as Fort Nashborough or the Public Square."⁵ Indeed, local businessmen and civic boosters anticipated the day when the sport would become professional in nature and Nashville might sponsor a team.

In 1885, with economic prosperity in full swing, the city of Nashville constructed an uncovered plank grandstand and playing diamond on the site of the historic Bottoms, and christened it Athletic Park. The wooden structure took up an entire city block between Cherry (Fourth Avenue North) and Summer Streets (Fifth Avenue North) and between Jackson and Harrison Streets. The tracks of the Tennessee Central Railroad ran parallel to the outfield palisade. Cap Anson opened the new ballyard with his major leaguers from Chicago, who trained for three weeks in the new facility and "took the [sulfur] waters." The presence of these professionals likely reinforced the efforts of the city fathers and leading entrepreneurs to secure a franchise of their own in the fledgling Southern League, which began organized play in April 1885.⁶

Henry W. Grady lent his stature to the new association. As the renowned managing editor of the *Atlanta Constitution,* the Georgian briefly presided over the new league that comprised eight teams from Nashville, Atlanta, Augusta, Macon, Columbus, Memphis, Chattanooga, and Birmingham. Shortly thereafter, John B. Nicklin of Chattanooga replaced the newspaper magnate as league president. The Nashville entry went by several different nicknames in the early years of the original Southern League—Americans, Blues, Tigers, and Seraphs.⁷ Two distinctions marked this new league: it was the first professional circuit to operate in the South, and the first minor league to launch a 100-game season. Financial troubles forced several cities to drop out but other cities were quickly added. Nashville slipped in and out of the association but maintained its charter membership in six of the league's ten full seasons.⁸ Sponsoring a minor league team filled a variety of business and social needs as Nashville expanded from a small city to a sprawling metropolis. "By providing urban dwellers with richer identities, the [baseball] teams helped satisfy deep yearnings for belonging and rootedness in an exceptionally mobile society," notes baseball scholar Benjamin G. Rader.[9] Local Nashville fans, or kranks as they were called in the 1880s, glowed with community pride and excitement as their team undertook a new campaign each spring at Athletic Park.

Minor league baseball spawned other forms of competition in the sprawling Nashville metropolitan area. "Baseball was the most important sport played by the middle classes in the period from 1870–1920," points out Steven A. Riess, "where its spirit of nationalism, wholesomeness, excitement, and drama made it the national pastime."[10] By the 1890s, competitive amateur nines sponsored by exclusive athletic clubs vied for supremacy on Nashville's baseball diamonds. Prep schools fielded squads and Vanderbilt University forged a deserved reputation of baseball excellence throughout the South.

Meanwhile, the structure and format of the game of baseball was undergoing broad changes beginning in the 1890s. The rules of play were still being established, the administrative hierarchy of league operations had not been refined, no set blueprint governed player-management conflicts, and fiscal problems infected all leagues as the national economy slid into a devastating depression in late 1893. Professional baseball would neither root itself in Nashville nor the South until the financial benefits of industrial development had filtered down to a growing urban population receptive to mass consumerism. Indeed, city folks would not adequately support commercial sports entertainment until they possessed both ample leisure time and an adequate income. Most of these necessary prerequisites had not taken root until after Nashville joined the Southern Association in the first decade of the new century. Then the ideals of the progressive age would contribute greatly to the public's acceptance of baseball as an integral part of Nashville society as a whole.[11]

When Nashville entered the Southern League in its inaugural season of 1885, the game operated under a pre-modern set of rules. Significant regulation changes in the decade between 1890–1900 helped to reshape the way the game would be played throughout the remainder of the Deadball Era — roughly from 1890 until 1920. Among the crucial procedural changes was the rule that the pitcher must deliver the ball with his back foot firmly anchored to the pitching rubber, rather than being allowed to take a running start from inside the 5' 4" pitcher's box. The distance between the pitcher's rubber (slab) to home plate was extended ten feet to 60' 6". Other new rules affected the batter as well. Now, it only took four called balls to earn a walk, down from the inconsistently enforced seven or nine errant throws that had been required to earn a free pass. Umpires also charged batters with a strike on the first two fouled balls in an effort to speed up the game. The upstart American Association, rival to the National League, impacted the game by ending the batter's privilege of calling for a particular pitch location (high or low), and began experimenting with a two-umpire system. The balk rule and batter's sacrifice (without being charged as an at-bat) also appeared at this time. As a result of these operational revisions, batting averages and runs scored soared in the 1890s. In order to counter the offensive explosion, home plate was enlarged from a 12" square to its current five-sided shape and to 17" across. The delicate balance between offense and defense was restored in the early 1900s when strikeouts increased and run production declined in the major leagues.[12]

The revamped rules helped to modernize the game as Nashvillians witnessed new and exciting methods of gamesmanship at Athletic Park. The new strategy was built around offensive speed to manufacture runs as well as defensive quickness that attempted to negate them. The Deadball Era (1890–1920) was the heyday of a "one-run-at-a-time" philosophy. The new style was most effectively displayed by John McGraw and his Baltimore squad, and it came to be known as scientific baseball.[13] On offense, the new thinking challenged managers to generate tallies by calling special plays such as the sacrifice bunt, hit-and-run, stolen base, double steal, and aggressive base running in general. This trademark placed a high priority on acquiring ballplayers who were intelligent, alert, and aggressive, and understood these new concepts that put added pressure on the defense. Adequate pre-game preparation became the norm as players now took batting practice and fielded ground balls. By 1900, the implementation of scientific baseball had revolutionized the game. Unquestionably, the speed of play at the professional level was noticeably quicker.[14]

The most fundamental tenet of scientific baseball, therefore, was designed to place tremendous pressure upon the defense to execute with errorless precision. In order to counter the advantages of cunning offense, the defense sought players with quick reactions, particularly at shortstop and second base. Catchers needed to be agile and possess strong throwing arms to go along with their tradition of physical toughness and pugnacious behavior. Indeed, "backstopper's" masks were still optional, shin guards had not yet been developed, and gloves of the day provided very little protection from hard throwing pitchers. Pitchers responded to the latest rules innovations by developing an entire repertoire of pitches—fastball, curve, slider, knuckleball, screwball, and the hallmark pitch of the day, the spitball. The ability of the pitcher to change the speed of delivery, then as well as now, remained the key to keeping a batter off balance.[15] Throughout the Deadball Era, managers expected their starters to throw a complete game even if the contest ran to extra innings. Rarely did a relief pitcher enter a game, and then he was not a specialist but a rested starter. Most teams customarily carried four pitchers, two catchers, and one utility player capable of providing several innings of pitching in an emergency.

The new philosophy of scientific baseball really appealed to managers who desired a more active role in the outcome of a game. Now, they could maneuver players in the field as well as put the offense into motion without uttering a single word. Thus, on-field decision-making passed from the players and into the hands of the manager as nonverbal signals keyed to the game situation became standard for both offense and defense.

This was the Deadball Era — a time of cavernous playing surfaces, flannel uniforms, tiny leather fielding gloves, and bats so heavy and awkward that they resembled cudgels. Only one ball was used to play an entire professional game; unsurprisingly, defenders quickly scuffed up and spat upon the game ball with either tobacco or licorice juice, rubbed it down with dirt, and tossed it irreverently around the infield before a single pitch had been thrown. Batters choked up on the hefty bat (willow) and tried to chop and slap at pitches. Foul balls that landed in the stands or outside the stadium were promptly retrieved by fans eager to see play resumed. Outfielders took a shallow position and dared batters to swing for the fences. Home runs, especially the outside-the-park variety, rarely occurred. Power hitters usually resorted to legging out long blasts that fell somewhere between the defenders and the outfield wall for inside-the-park round trippers.[16] Owners issued players only one gray and one white flannel suit, and in the case of Nashville a solitary "N" in Old English style was sewn over the left breast. Only the color of the socks and hats distinguished the teams competing in the Southern Association. Nashville wore black. Since each player was responsible for cleaning his uniform, their suits often appeared soiled, wrinkled, and dirty, as early photographs reveal.

The by-laws governing organized baseball were also in flux in the late nineteenth century, and these policies affected the way in which Nashville directors administered their club in the Southern Association. Dating back to 1858, the National Association of Base Ball Players (NABBP) attempted to standardize a set of rules that would govern amateur play. As the organization's title implies, the players operated it. There would be few problems as long as the game maintained its amateur status. However, pay-for-play had become standard practice by the early 1870s — a development that fostered disputes between amateur and professional players. Organized baseball changed forever with the formation of the first professional major league in 1871.[17]

With professionalization, the sport of baseball was transformed. Investors interested in turning a profit made the crucial personnel and scheduling decisions. Team owners, guided by capitalist motivation and driven by the financial considerations of individual stock holders, banded together to protect their interests by forming the National Association of Professional Base Ball Players. The NAPBBP declared itself the official mouthpiece for rule changes and labor arbitration. In the process, they designed an infrastructure that ushered in the modern professional game. By 1879, these captains of baseball had established the reserve clause — a phrase in a player's contract that effectively bound his services to the unilateral decisions of his employer. This thorny issue stood at the center of labor-management disagreements for nearly one hundred years.[18]

When Nashville entered its first full season in the Southern League in 1885, the American public, driven by Victorian principles of social morality, had grown to associate baseball players with gambling, drinking, corruption (fixing games), and other vices. Although the upstart American Association, also known as "the Beer and Whiskey League," refined some aspects of baseball's organization, it also contributed to a growing public perception that baseball attracted the most unsavory elements of society by serving inexpensive alcoholic beverages at its games. When the National League and American Association buried their rivalry and signed the National Agreement in 1883, both sides pledged to preserve the reserve clause. The potential of labor unrest surfaced two years later when John M. Ward formed the Brotherhood of Professional Base Ball Players. Union-related problems would plague the baseball industry and adversely affect several players on the 1908 Nashville team. Another change instituted by the American Association — the determination of the league's champion based upon winning percentage instead of number of wins — would also have a direct bearing upon the Southern Association race in 1908.[19]

When Nashville fielded its first professional team in 1885, there was no clear-cut policy governing the relationship between the major and minor leagues. Labor relations — the every day personnel matters between owner and player — had never been clearly spelled out in an official code. Rather, baseball's labor policy typified business practices commonly exercised in the industrial age. Baseball owners and directors looked upon the issue of players' salaries through the exact same lens as corporate moguls looked upon the issue of salaried workers. Gilded Age capitalists recognized the direct connection between employee wages and the overall amount of profits to be garnered in the market place.[20] The issues of player compensation and rights were complicated further in the mid–1880s by the birth and growth of the minor leagues. Absolutely no contract language existed at the lower rung to protect the players' interests. Without contractual protection through which to voice grievances to management, owners bounced minor leaguers around indiscriminately between both professional levels.

When the Southern League gained official minor league status, the Nashville franchise automatically inherited this maelstrom of labor ills that had plagued professional baseball since its debut. The central issue of the controversy — how to control player salaries and turn as large a profit as possible — worried the new owners. The public tended to share management's opinion that professional ballplayers were comparatively well paid. In 1885, Nashville's first year in the Southern League, major league owners signed a document which represented their solution to the difficulty. This Limited Agreement created a salary cap for team rosters. Although flagrantly broken by the more wealthy franchises, the plan governed baseball labor relations for the immediate future.[21]

Southern League owners also came to believe that on-the-field misbehaviors by players required some sort of consistent punishment. In the early 1890s, the patrons at minor league settings such as Nashville might witness advancing baserunners being restrained or tripped by infielders, intentional spiking of opponents, profane language, fist fights on the field and in the stands, verbal and physical assaults on umpires, and unruly, angry, or drunken fans throwing bottles onto the field.²² By the mid–1890s, standards geared to improving player and fan decorum were in the developmental stages. Continued acceptance of rowdyism was not in the best interest of the game since it did not appeal to middle-class families—the new audience baseball was wishing to attract.

In 1895, the final year of the original Southern League in its eight-team format and 135-game schedule, Nashville produced a quality team under the direction of player-manager George Stallings. The Seraphs, as they were known, notched 69 victories and shared the league crown with Atlanta. Yet, at season's end, the Seraphs folded while the league continued to operate for three more seasons with abbreviated schedules and fewer franchises.²³

The first decade of the twentieth century offered a fresh opportunity for baseball in Nashville as the sport recovered economically and was marked for a decade of unprecedented expansion. In 1900, Byron "Ban" Johnson, president of the Western League, sparked the growth when he established a second major circuit—the American League.²⁴ Johnson's move touched off a ferocious competition with the older National League for qualified players. This intense rivalry over talent trickled down to the minor leagues for a limited pool of quality players.

Amidst this revival of baseball interest in the fall of 1900, three former player-managers from the defunct Southern League met to organize the Southern Association—Abner Powell of New Orleans, Newt Fisher of Nashville, and Charley Frank of Memphis. In keeping with current minor league practice, league organizers agreed to 12-man rosters and a salary cap of $1,200 per player. They tendered franchises to cities originally in the circuit—New Orleans, Nashville, Memphis, Birmingham, Chattanooga, Little Rock, and Shreveport. Selma, Alabama, rounded out the eight-team league. Most of these cities would be affiliated with the Southern Association for more than a half-century.²⁵

Both the National and American Leagues signed players who were under contract with other leagues. This competition for talent led to a legal challenge to the reserve clause in 1901. Shortly before opening day, the Philadelphia (N.L.) club tried to prevent two of its star players from jumping to the upstart Philadelphia (A.L.) club. Napoleon Lajoie, a prized second baseman, and William "Strawberry Bill" Bernhard, a promising pitcher, had signed with Connie Mack's new Athletics. The National Leaguers promptly filed suit to prevent the two players from plying their trade anywhere in Pennsylvania. A.L.

President Johnson staved off a confrontation by convincing Mack to trade the players to the Cleveland (A.L.) team.[26] Lajoie went on to notch an outstanding twenty-one year career in the big leagues. The second sacker eventually entered the Hall of Fame in its first year of operation, 1937. Bernhard, a hard-throwing right-hander and workhorse of the pitching staff, posted 116 victories over a nine-year career ultimately cut short by arm trouble. In due time, Bernhard's baseball fortunes would lead him to Nashville.

The real loser in the formation of the American League and the subsequent baseball wars were the dozens of minor leagues whose team rosters were plundered indiscriminately, beginning in September, 1901. The minors had established an organization of their own in 1887 and rewritten their constitution in 1892 complete with the reserve clause. The major leagues, in turn, recognized two minor league classifications of play — Class A and B. An agreement between the majors and minors allowed the majors to draft promising players from both classes at fixed rates—$500 for Class B players and $1,000 for Class A players. The window for making such purchases fell between October 1 and February 1.[27]

In its search for talented players to replace those lost to the American League, the depleted National League abandoned the agreement and jeopardized the stability of the minor league system. To resolve the crisis, representatives from all of the beleaguered minor league circuits met in Chicago on 5–6 September 1901. Thomas J. Hickey, administrator of the Western League, presided over the gathering. Seven league presidents attended what turned out to be the most important show of solidarity in the history of minor league baseball.[28] President Nicklin of the Southern Association did not attend, but he did send a letter of support. The assemblage formed the National Association of Professional Baseball Leagues, and the document they produced laid out the procedure for minor league governance that would remain in operation for ten years; it created a new classification system for the minor leagues from Class A through D, usually arranged from larger to smaller cities respectively. They also set salary caps, endorsed the reserve clause, permitted upper tiers to draft from lower level teams, set reasonable compensation for player purchases, and established a Board of Arbitration empowered to issue suspensions, adjudicate violations of the reserve clause, reinstate suspended players, and review questionable trades.[29]

When play resumed in 1902, the Southern Association was assigned to Class B, and within three years rose to Class A along with the American Association, Pacific Coast League, Eastern League, and Western League. Arguably, the Southern Association was qualified to join the highest rung in 1908, Class AA, a testament to the flourishing population of Southern cities in the first decade of the twentieth century. Association by-laws contained several attractive innovations, including larger rosters and higher salary caps which enabled the S.A. to attract and retain talent, an advantage from the outset.[30]

1. Nashville and the National Pastime in the Deadball Era

In January, 1903, the feuding American and National Leagues settled their differences and ushered in a sustained period of cooperation and unprecedented prosperity for organized baseball at all professional levels. This National Agreement not only suspended the talent raids in professional baseball, it also approved the reforms set in place earlier at the minor league meetings. The major leagues recognized the sovereignty of the minors, and in return the minors agreed to fill the prescribed draft quotas of the big leagues. Two years later, the rules were amended so that major league teams could draft only one player from each minor league team. This provision delayed the development of the modern farm system for at least ten years. However, minor league baseball stabilized and flourished once peace had been established in the majors. By 1910, the number of minor leagues across America had swelled to an all-time high of 52.[31]

Another major accomplishment of baseball consolidation in the Deadball Era was the creation in 1903 of the National Commission — a fifty person body comprised of league presidents and team owners. The Commission took its direction from a ruling triumvirate — both major league presidents and Garry Herrmann, owner of the Cincinnati team. These leaders oversaw professional baseball prior to the advent of the commissioner system.

The Nashville team experienced immediate success in its first season in the Southern Association. The team fielded a top-notch 12-man roster led by manager and catcher Newt Fisher, and pitcher-outfielder Hugh Hill. They also landed an outstanding prospect from Cincinnati. Julius Augustus Wiseman traced his family's roots back to mid-nineteenth century Ohio.[32] Samuel Vinton Wiseman, born in Ohio in 1843, grew up on a farm in the southernmost district along the Ohio River and enlisted in the 91st Ohio Infantry shortly after the Civil War broke out. In 1863, the twenty-year-old Samuel joined Blazer's Scouts — an elite cavalry unit with special instructions to confront Confederate cavalryman John Singleton Mosby in northwestern Virginia. For much of the war, Samuel battled a variety of ailments, including pneumonia, typhoid fever, and malaria, and he spent a long convalescence in a field hospital near Fayetteville, West Virginia.

Mustered out of the army in June, 1865, near Cumberland, Maryland, Samuel returned to the family farm in feeble physical condition. For several years, he traveled out west to regain his health and dabble in livestock trading and land speculation. Returning to Ohio in the late 1860s, he attended college in nearby Athens (later Ohio University), and apprenticed to a physician in Gallia County. At the same time, he met a young woman with exceptional intellectual abilities, Barbara Rapp. The couple were wed in 1873 and relocated to Cincinnati, where Samuel enrolled in Miami Medical School (later University of Cincinnati). He graduated four years later.

Julius Augustus Wiseman was born on 26 May 1877, and twin brothers Cassius and Claudius joined him two years later. The latter did not survive childhood, but Julius and Cash became close siblings. Both boys were particularly fond to their mother, a woman whose appreciation of ancient Greek and Roman culture and language influenced the selection of their names. Homeschooled in the early years, Julius acquired a prodigious vocabulary and deep appreciation of words.[33]

By the early 1880s, Dr. Sam's "horse and buggy" medical practice had grown too large, so he contracted to have a house built in the new East End working class neighborhood on the outskirts of Cincinnati. The Delta Avenue dwelling was the grandest house in the neighborhood and was situated across from the trolley line, an ideal location with easy access to the city. A YMCA gym, drug store, police station, and saloon were soon erected within a block.[34]

The neighborhood had everything a growing boy could ask for, including plenty of playmates, a comfortable home, and a learning environment where the classics of western antiquity were appreciated. In his teenage years, Julius was taking the trolley five miles to Woodward High School in downtown Cincinnati, the oldest public high school west of the Allegheny Mountains. He earned solid grades in a rigorous curriculum that included Greek, Latin, chemistry, English literature, and composition, and received superior marks in deportment. Julius stood out on the school's athletic fields too — in particular, baseball. In his senior year (1895), he attracted attention for his exploits at shortstop on the Woodward and city league champion O.K. squads. It is rumored that he also moonlighted under a fictitious name at the University of Cincinnati before graduating high school.[35]

Julius finished his studies at Woodward in the top one-third of his class (81 percent average) and enrolled in the University of Cincinnati. But the lure of professional baseball proved too great for the 5' 7" infielder already known as "Little Doc." In 1896, Wiseman played a full season in the outfield for the Mobile Blackbirds, tied teammate Newt Fisher for most games played (100) and trailed only Fisher with a .288 batting average. Future Nashville manager Johnny Dobbs also played on that team.

In the off season, Wiseman returned to the university where he pursued a law degree. At the time, William Howard Taft served as dean of the law school — the fourth oldest program of its kind in the country. When the Southern League suspended operations in 1897, Julius returned as Cincinnati's shortstop and batted third in the lineup. In a testament to his athleticism, Little Doc pitched the first game of a doubleheader against the University of Indiana and collected a 12–11 victory. Then he led his team to a second victory with a two-run home run in a 17–13 win in the nightcap. The student newspaper, *The Burnet Woods Echo,* raved about the diamond heroics of "Doctorus Wiseman" in flowery prose popular in the day.[36]

Receiving an invitation in the spring of 1898 to play for Abner Powell's perennial Southern League powerhouse, New Orleans, Doc rushed to Dean Taft's office to beg for his release from spring classes. Taft, a baseball fanatic,

Doc Wiseman in University of Cincinnati uniform. (Collection of Dr. James A. Wiseman; courtesy Donald E. Wiseman, Reese, MI.)

consented. When the Spanish-American War abruptly interrupted the season, Doc resumed his class work and completed his law degree but not before passing the Ohio bar exam two weeks earlier. He then registered for postgraduate classes in accounting.

The lure of baseball had been too keen for Doc, however. When Newt Fisher organized and laid plans to manage Nashville's entry in the new Southern Association, Wiseman grabbed his glove and headed south. Over his next eleven seasons in Nashville, Doc's career came to personify the ancient virtues of hard work, loyalty, and dedication. In 1901, Wiseman responded well in his new surroundings in Nashville by hitting a robust .333 and helping his team to the first championship of the fledgling league. Nashville secured a back-to-back championship in 1902, but then fell into a five-season swoon marked by mediocrity.[37]

The Southern Association, like all professional baseball leagues, suffered three common problems in the first decade of the twentieth century: gambling, rowdyism, and Sabbatarianism (the moral opposition to playing games on Sunday).[38] Baseball, despite its growing popularity, could not shed its reputation as a haven for persons of dubious character. The Southern Association, then the only baseball circuit in the South, faced uniquely regional problems as well. A bastion of tradition, Southern culture stressed adherence to a strict set of mores regarding religious observance, public conduct and rigidly defined gender roles. Southern progressives as well as conservatives openly denounced public amusements in the growing urban communities, with both concerned about temperance and strict observance of the Sabbath.[39]

Southern baseball during the Deadball Era would put all of these scruples to the supreme test. New Orleans, with its large foreign-born population and tradition of Sunday amusements, often hosted weekend baseball during the original Southern League, and port cities like Memphis and Mobile experimented with the controversial practice beginning in the Southern Association.[40] Commercial amusement parks provided the religious public with yet another related social threat to Sabbatarianism, and baseball remained a close rival in this concern. Only saloons seemed a larger evil than amusement parks and ball games to these social watchdogs. One Tennessee critic of the new urban popular culture fumed: "How could we get farther from heaven and God than amidst the roaring shouts of a Base Ball contest?"[41] Nicklin, the first president of the Southern Association, was not able to balance the requirements of the game for social approval and popular patronage. The second president, William Marmaduke Kavanaugh, possessed the stature, vision, and integrity to pull it off.

William Marmaduke Kavanaugh was born on 3 March 1866, near Eutaw, Greene County, Alabama, the son of Reverend Hubbard Hinde Kavanaugh (chaplain of Kentucky's Orphan Brigade during the Civil War) and Anna Kimbrough Kavanaugh.[42] Young Kavanaugh received an academy education at Kentucky Military Institute. Following graduation in 1885, the twenty-year-old married Ida Floyd of Clarksville, Arkansas, and took a reporting job with the *Arkansas Gazette*. Kavanaugh possessed a dynamic personality and insatiable appetite for hard work. He quickly rose through the ranks to become managing editor in 1890. In 1896, Pulaski County (AR) voters elected Kavanaugh to serve as sheriff, and four years later chose him to sit on the county probate court. Some Arkansans speculated that the portly progressive harbored larger political ambitions.

Kavanaugh balanced his public service with a successful business career. In 1905, he organized and presided over the Southern Trust Company and Southern Construction Company in Little Rock. One year later he erected the first modern office building in the city. He was in politics as chairman of the Pulaski County Democratic Party and a member of the state's national delegation. Kavanaugh spurred calls to run for the Arkansas governorship in 1908, but filled the unexpired term of deceased Senator Jeff Davis in 1913. Venturing into public utilities, Kavanaugh managed the Natural Gas Supply Company, Consumer's Coal Company, and Little Rock Railway and Electric Company. In private life, Kavanaugh joined fraternal organizations such as the Elks and Masons, sat on the Little Rock School Board for twelve years, and belonged to the local McCarthy Light Guards.[43] By either measure — public or private — Kavanaugh was a successful man.

Keeping with his progressive activism and entrepreneurial successes, Kavanaugh accepted the directorship of the Little Rock baseball franchise in the reformed Southern Association in 1901. The following year, he agreed to serve as league vice president under Nicklin, and advanced to the presidency in 1903. Kavanaugh "did much to shape the destiny of the league" through its early tumultuous history, and remained its executive until 1915."[44] As league president, Kavanaugh represented the Southern Association on the powerful board of the National Association of Professional Baseball Clubs. In this capacity, he worked tirelessly to present a more acceptable baseball product to a national and regional middle-class market ready to embrace it. Later called "the sage of Dixie" and "the squarest [most honest] man in baseball," Kavanaugh reflected the Victorian and progressive values of the age in which he lived.[45]

Kavanaugh inherited a league full of problems symptomatic of the game itself as well as an array of colorful characters when he became president in 1903. He had to confront several recurring issues never completely addressed by his predecessor: teams in the league robbed each other's rosters without administrative sanction, suspended players ignored disciplinary suspensions and were permitted to play, and verbal and physical abuse by players and managers against umpires was endemic.

The New Orleans club served as a catalyst of these ills, and the principal culprit was its hard-nosed manager, Charlie Frank. His team routinely cheated on the salary cap, stole players outright from other teams, and resorted to unethical on-field antics such as umpire-baiting, profanity directed at fans, intimidation of opposing players, and fist-fighting in order to win games. One of the ongoing complaints by opponents of the New Orleans nine centered on "juicing the baseball." In May, 1906, Montgomery had come to the Crescent City for a three-game series, and there were reports of fly balls hit exceptionally well.[46] At the conclusion of one of the contests, the Montgomery manager confiscated the game ball, took it to his hotel room, and performed surgery on the suspicious ball. He claimed to have found rubber bands wound tightly around the inner core instead of the customary yarn. A cloud of suspicion hung over the Pelicans as the next visitor, Atlanta, arrived in the Crescent City.

Atlanta manager William "Tobacco Billy" Smith had been apprised of the juiced ball controversy, and also confiscated a game ball for closer examination.[47] He carried the questionable ball to Little Rock to be personally inspected by President Kavanaugh. There the league administrator split the ball open but found only tightly knit yarn encircling the core. Undeterred by this finding, Smith awaited his next visit to New Orleans.

When Atlanta arrived in New Orleans on 15 June 1906, both teams were on edge. Tobacco Billy aggravated the situation when he accused New Orleans pitching ace Moxey Manuel of throwing bean balls. Fans and players alike were incensed at Smith's allegation.[48] Newspaper accounts claimed that the ball used for that particular contest had "a good deal of elasticity in it."[49] Late in the game, Atlanta's captain and second baseman, Otto Jordan, had been called out on a close play at first base. The angry Jordan then wrestled the ball away from the first baseman and threw it over to his manager on the bench. Indignant Pelican players and angry fans immediately swarmed around the visiting skipper. Known for his short temper, Smith launched the ball clear out of the stadium and a fan had to retrieve it before play was resumed.

President William Marmaduke Kavanaugh of the Southern Association. (Courtesy Arkansas History Commission.)

Mutual hostilities reached a fever pitch in the bottom of the 8th inning with the home team behind by a score of 5–3. With one out, New Orleans recorded three runs on two outside-the-park home runs, a rarity in the Deadball Era. One of the blasts came from the bat of pitcher Moxey Manuel.

When the umpire tossed a new ball to the Atlanta pitcher, Jordan rushed in from second base, grabbed the ball, and proclaimed, "That ball's on the queer!" The umpire ignored him, whereupon Jordan announced that his team would not complete the game. The angry team captain thereupon kicked the official for good measure. Angry fans leaped from the stands and attacked the feisty second baseman. It took ten police officers to restore order and escort Jordan to the ballpark office. When Jordan refused to turn over the game ball, New Orleans manager Charlie Frank had him arrested for petty larceny, and the umpire declared the game a forfeit.[50]

Less than one month later, on 20 July 1906, the New Orleans contingent was involved in a similar brouhaha in Memphis. The scheduled umpire neglected to appear so it was mutually agreed that New Orleans pitching ace Ted Breitenstein would call balls and strikes. When Memphis first baseman George Carey proceeded to complain about the liberal strike zone, Breitenstein proceeded to hurl obscenities and punches at his critic. The chief of police happened to be in attendance and ordered the volatile substitute umpire to the local police station, where he was charged with assault and assessed a $25 fine for disturbing the peace.[51] These on-field shenanigans did not amuse President Kavanaugh.

At the turn of the century, the game of baseball had been thrust into a reform frenzy in part because the entire nation had entered a new and modern age predicated on new ideals forged by industrialization, urbanization, mass transportation and communication, and consumerism. Population increases, however, brought about the most significant changes to the urban landscape.[52] Northeastern cities absorbed large numbers of new immigrants while southern cities experienced similar growth through a shift in regional demographics from rural to urban living. In the three decades beginning in 1880, the cities in Dixie experienced nothing short of a population explosion. The chart below compares population figures in cities belonging to the Southern Association.[53]

SOUTHERN URBAN GROWTH, 1880–1910

City	Population in 1910	Increase
New Orleans	339,000	57%
Atlanta	155,000	314%
Birmingham	132,000	4,200%
Memphis	131,000	290%
Nashville	110,000	155%
Mobile	52,000	75%
Little Rock	46,000	250%
Montgomery	39,000	128%

As more and more Southerners left the farm to find new opportunities in the cities of the South, they also adapted to the new forms of urban commercial entertainment — vaudeville, wild west shows, circuses, motion pictures, and music halls. But, it was the national pastime that captured the imagination (and dollars) of many urbanites. A typical blue collar worker at the turn of the century worked a sixty-hour week and earned about $10, but admission to the bleachers at most baseball games was an affordable 25 cents. Large white-collar crowds filled the grandstands owing to increased leisure time afforded them by employers. Easier access to the ballparks through public transportation such as streetcars contributed to rising attendance by fans representing all social classes.[54]

Cities in the Southern Association discovered that sponsoring a professional baseball team added to their progressive status within the region. Civic boosterism, a hallmark of the era, encouraged economic rivalry between metropolitan areas competing for business and investment. One of the most visible manifestations of a city's activity and success was the community's baseball team. Professional baseball also added to the public's perception of, and identification with, their home town. "Uncertain about their city's status but hopeful for its future," observed one historian, "local newspapermen, merchants, and manufacturers frequently resorted to strident boosterism."[55] Nashville and Memphis were the bitterest of sports rivals throughout the early years of the Southern Association as they also battled intensely in Tennessee's commercial marketplace. A successful baseball franchise was one accepted measure of a city's worth within the region.[56]

Baseball franchises, whether major or minor league affiliates, received mutual blessings from local politicians, entrepreneurs, citizens, and newspapers. These connections with local government officials translated into countless favors. The Nashville Base Ball Club was no different. Its team owners were well known and respected community businessmen. They knew the civic power brokers intimately, and lobbied to influence and shape public policy that would be beneficial to their professional baseball franchise. That they also hoped to profit themselves as well as the community was not considered unethical. Many merchants and financiers viewed partial or total ownership of a baseball franchise as a wise investment as well as an opportunity to achieve even greater prestige and respectability within the community. Indeed, such "new men of influence" in Nashville harbored motivations beyond athletics.[57]

The growing popularity of baseball in Nashville and elsewhere during the progressive era owed much to the massive growth of print communication industries. The coverage allotted to baseball games once tucked away in remote corners of daily newspapers now found a new vehicle — the sports section — which provided sports enthusiasts with ample reports of game details through box scores, narrative columns, and editorial commentaries. In 1908, Nashville boasted three broadsheets — the *American, Banner,* and *Tennessean.* Each rag boasted its own sports page and sports editor, beginning in 1907. These dailies cost an affordable one penny. On the national level, weeklies like *The Sporting News* (since 1886) from St. Louis and *Sporting Life* (since 1883) from Philadelphia devoted extensive space to the coverage of major and minor league baseball and cost only a nickel. The first issue of *Baseball Magazine*, edited by F. C. Lane, rolled off the press in 1908 to meet the public's insatiable appetite for news from the diamond. In addition, comprehensive pocket-sized baseball references—*Spalding's Guide* and *Reach Guide*—became popular with an increasingly knowledgeable fan base thirsting to learn more about the game. This explosion in sports journalism translated into an inexpensive source of information for the dedicated Nashvillian who wanted to keep abreast of the most recent sporting news.[58]

Baseball afforded many Americans a leisure environment that replicated the slower pace of their previous agrarian existence in stark contrast to the busier flow of city life in which they now found themselves. The game was played in a green pastoral setting apart from the surrounding drabness of smoking factories and encroaching skylines. The game held additional appeal to the typical factory worker because its tempo was not dictated by a clock. The nine-inning contests held a timeless charm for urbanites driven by the demands of industrialization. The ballpark, an open-aired edifice, offered people accustomed to working indoors an afternoon out in the fresh air. There they could watch young athletes perform — also a component to the progressive ideal which stressed the importance of physical culture.[59]

On an even more esthetic level, the national pastime strengthened beliefs deemed fundamental to the progressives outlook about America. The baseball creed invoked traditional nineteenth century attributes stressing courage, honesty, individualism, patience, and an extremely relevant contemporary value: teamwork.[60] While baseball satisfied the entertainment appetite of the urban working class, it simultaneously reinforced the mores of middle-class Americans. Both classes were welcomed, and found reassurance in a ballpark.

The Nashville community would come to accept the diverse ethnic composition of the players on the '08 Vols just as the nation had eventually accepted the old immigrants who had come predominantly from Ireland and Germany as opposed to the more recent arrivals from Russia and Italy. Men of German extraction like Bernhard, Hardy, Siegle, Hess, and Hunter; French backgrounds like Daubert and Sitton; the Scots-Irish lineage of Wiseman, McElveen, McCormick, Bay, and Kellum were not evaluated by Nashville fans for their ethnicity, but rather for their ballplaying abilities. Ethnic backgrounds were not publicized, and perhaps the use of nicknames played a part to anglicize the true origins of the some players in the league. One can only speculate on the meaning of nicknames like Joe "The Frenchman" Pepe of Montgomery, Will "The Cuban" Cranston, and Joe "Chief" Eastman of Little Rock. What is clear, however, is that Jim Crow was deeply entrenched in southern society, and the possibility of Negro or mulatto athletes performing on the same field with white men would have been viewed as unacceptable. The diverse ethnic composition of the '08 Vols, a southern team, cannot be ignored or understated for its significance, and their presence opened economic avenues that ultimately led to middle-class livelihoods later in life.

The Union army had introduced the city of Nashville to baseball during the Civil War. Local athletic clubs eagerly picked up the game and continued to play at Sulphur Springs Bottom in the immediate postwar years. It is not too far-fetched to consider the role baseball played in Nashville's move toward sectional reconciliation. After all, this post–Civil War generation of Southerners that were welcoming the sport had recently spent four bloody years trying to separate from Yankee institutions. Now, through baseball, Nashvillians were actually embracing Northern sporting culture. This phenomenon is highly significant. As the game evolved into the national pastime, with its implicit reference to nationalism, the game itself served to lessen sectional animosities. While the game continued to be largely Northern in its player representation in Nashville with a disproportionate number of Ohioans (Hardy, East, Wiseman, and Siegle) and Pennsylvanians (Butler, Daubert, and Hunter) on the roster, a growing number of Southerners were beginning to appear — like Tennesseans McElveen and Perdue, and Sitton, a South Carolinian.

By the mid–1880s, the city accepted professional baseball, and maintained its affiliation with the original Southern League until the circuit folded. The sport underwent rule changes and organizational reforms during the Deadball Era. Nashville, one of the minor league markets, was privy to incorporating these reforms and witnessed the advent of scientific baseball. The title of this brand of baseball appealed to progressive thinkers who saw the future of a New South in modern terms synonymous with northern industrial capitalism.

When the Southern Association reopened under a more sound financial footing at the turn of the century, the sport blossomed in Nashville. It became the good fortune of the Nashville Base Ball Club to reappear at the very moment when professional baseball was achieving "a new institutional prominence and permanency in American life."[61] Indeed, the sport was undergoing unprecedented expansion and prosperity when it earned its moniker as the national pastime.

Americans and Nashvillians alike were in the midst of a significant shift — a modern progressive mindset was in the process of replacing an outmoded Victorian way of thinking. Most of the people living through this transitional era did not recognize the impact of such socio-cultural changes upon their lives. The fans came out to the ballpark in increasingly greater numbers not to philosophize, but simply to enjoy the sport for its entertainment value. A nineteen-year veteran of the Deadball Era, Tommy Leach, grasped the essence of baseball in his times:

I really believe baseball was a more exciting game back in those times. It was more rugged, first of all. Take the equipment. We had little gloves that would just fit over your hand... And the fields. Now the lowest minor leagues have better fields to play on than we did in the major leagues. You never knew how a ball was going to bounce in those days. Lots of times we'd get a rake and go out and rake the ground around our own positions. The style of play is very different now, too. We used to play a running game, a lot of bunting and base stealing.[62]

As these factors combined to propel the game to a central place in the life of this growing southern city, to Southerners and Nashvillians, the Southern Association was no different from the major leagues; indeed, it was the southern major league. Although attendance figures in the South did not rival the majors, neither did the size of the fan base, industrial capacity, or workers with leisure time nor the large amounts of disposable income.

In 1908, the commercial entertainment industry was growing in Nashville. But, no one foresaw that the city was going to host the championship contest — a game that Grantland Rice described as "the greatest game ever played in Dixie."[63]

Chapter 2

Going from Bad to ?

The year was 1907, and the seventh campaign of the Southern Association had been long and disappointing for Nashville. The final game of the season found the team entrenched in the league cellar; indeed, lackluster play and questionable attitudes had infected the team since its second-half tailspin in midsummer. The off-season hinted at new possibilities for success, however. New ownership willing to spend money inspired hope through promises to build a new stadium, hire a new manager, and pursue better players. These winter developments excited local kranks, and the energized sportswriters on Nashville's three daily newspapers—Rice, Ewing, and Yancey—kept the community abreast of every detail concerning the revamped franchise. By 1 March, after the Southern Association meetings, Nashville was a new team in every respect except player personnel.

The final game of 1907 found last-place Nashville playing a meaningless doubleheader in New Orleans. The Southern Association flag had already been sewn up by Atlanta, which held a comfortable four-game margin over second-place Memphis. Nashville languished twenty-one games behind the league leader.[1]

Southern Association Final Standings, 1907

	W	L	.Pct	GB
Atlanta	78	54	.591	—
Memphis	74	57	.565	3½
New Orleans	68	66	.507	11
Little Rock	66	66	.500	12
Birmingham	64	71	.474	15½

(continued)	W	L	.Pct	GB
Shreveport	62	70	.470	16
Montgomery	62	61	.466	16½
Nashville	59	78	.431	21½

In the first game, a promising 20-year-old pitcher from Gallatin, Tennessee, took the slab. Herbert, or Hub, Perdue could not keep New Orleans in check as the home team pounded out eleven hits in a lopsided 6–1 victory. The victors also stole six bases off Nashville catcher Robert "Kid" Wells. The game took one hour and thirty-five minutes to play — a standard length of time for Southern Association action.[2] The second game, a seven-inning affair, took even less time to play despite Nashville's fourteen runs on twenty base hits. Led by another Tennessean, Pryor Mynatt "Humpy" McElveen, four Nashville batters notched at least three hits. The outcome was even more surprising considering that pitcher Bill Sorrell had lost twelve of his last fourteen starts. New Orleans opted for their left-handed ace, Ted Breitenstein, who would be an important figure in Nashville's 1908 season.[3] The *Tennessean* and *Banner* both used the term "farce" to describe the level of play in the '07 season finale.

Henry Grantland Rice attained columnist status on the sports page of the *Tennessean* in 1907, and led the way in recounting, analyzing, and offering opinions about Nashville's dismal baseball team. Born in Murfreesboro on 1 November 1880, Rice's maternal grandparents had been wealthy cotton merchants, and when Grantland was five years old, the family moved to Nashville where he grew up playing sandlot baseball and football at Tarbox School. Later he attended Wallace School in West Nashville — an exclusive academy that prepared students for entrance into Vanderbilt University. An agile athlete, Rice was a natural shortstop and tight end in the Commodore baseball and football programs. In his senior year, Rice was selected captain of the baseball team and his skills caught the eye of Newt Fisher.

Discouraged by his father and grandfather from turning out for the Fishermen, the recent college graduate turned to his writing skills to obtain a position on Jere Baxter's new *Nashville Daily News*. Earning a salary of only $7.50 per week, the impoverished cub reporter worked very hard and often put in fifteen-hour work days. His stories were always thoroughly researched. Rice later acknowledged that his family upbringing had shaped his old-fashioned work ethic. When Baxter's newspaper folded, the young reporter turned to writing freelance articles in *The Forester Magazine*.

In late 1902, the *Atlanta Journal* wooed Grant, or Granny, away from middle Tennessee with a hefty raise as well as promotion to sports editor — a position practically unknown in the turn-of-the-century South. He pulled up stakes less than three years later for another advancement with the *Cleveland News*. In May 1907, Luke Lea enticed Rice to return to Nashville to establish

1907 Nashville Vols. *From left (first name given when known)*: Bill Sorrel, John Duggan, Hub Perdue, Pryor McElveen, Michael McCormick, Johnny Dobbs, Jack Hardy, Archie Persons, Wall, John Ely, Robert Wells, Smith, Whitey Morse, Hackett, Mills, Julius Wiseman, Cliff Latimer. (Courtesy National Baseball Hall of Fame Library, Cooperstown, N.Y.)

Grantland Rice (far right) and the 1908 Vanderbilt University team. (Courtesy *Nashville Banner*.)

a sports department in his new *Tennessean*. In addition to overseeing the sports room, Lea expected Rice to contribute to the editorial page and supply poems to add flavor to the news and sports stories. His baseball byline — SPORTSVILLE ECHOES — frequently preceded the editorial and society page.[4] Rice also served as theater critic, and he thrived under the stressful workload. Rice's office overlooked the new Tulane Hotel — a stylish establishment that housed several of Nashville's professional ballplayers. He befriended Vanderbilt's new football coach, Dan McGugin, who would later become a legend. In addition, Rice's alma mater turned over its baseball program to him — a coaching assignment he kept out of his sports column. His '08 Commodores posted a respectable 11–8–1 record.

Rice believed in the Protestant work ethic, and his analysis of the 1907 season revealed deep concern over the direction of the Nashville franchise. Final league statistics showed Nashville topped the league in team batting (.249), runs scored (514), and hits (1,179).[5] Catcher John "Scrappy Jack" Hardy hit a robust .312, third-best in the league. On the other hand, the Nashvillians fielded an abysmal .957 (seventh in league), and committed the most fielding errors (246). The sore spot was the pitching staff where no one threw with any degree of consistency. Rice chided the four starters and described them as a Class D act in a Class A conference. He seemed unsure as well about the ability of first-year player-manager Johnny Dobbs. Disharmony had beset the team since a midsummer swoon, and players argued with the manager and fought openly among themselves on the bench during games. One report stated that Dobbs had "no control whatsoever."[6]

Rice set forth his three-part plan for the team's success in 1908: One, build a "new accommodation" (stadium) similar to the ballyards in Atlanta, New Orleans, and Memphis. Two, find four new pitchers, three infielders, and one outfielder. Three, the players must train in the offseason to stay in shape.[7]

Rice's suggestions appear prophetic as half of the men who started the last doubleheader in 1907 would not be listed on the opening day roster in 1908. He also anticipated the all-star mentality of sports media by preparing a list of the league's top players. He placed three Nashvillians on his select team — Jack Hardy, Doc Wiseman, and first baseman Pete Lister. "It's bad form, they say, to knock or otherwise speak ill of the dead," said the sportswriter in reference to Nashville's recently concluded season, "so ... we'll chop the dope and let it go at that."[8]

It must have been frustrating for loyal Nashville baseball fans to support such a lackluster team because the 1907 season had been a stellar one. Attendance at most minor league parks ran at an all-time high, and the Southern Association reflected this increase at the turnstiles. Rice noted that the local fan base appeared solid as even "the tail-end brigade" [Nashville] drew over 95,000.[9]

Many of the Nashville players likely felt relief when the 1907 season finally

The 1907 Nashville team in a Shreveport tally-ho. (Courtesy National Baseball Hall of Fame Library, Cooperstown, N.Y.)

came to a close. The Southern Association season had begun in mid–April, and the 135-game schedule nearly matched the major league total of 154 games. The day-to-day life of minor league players did not emphasize comfort. Conditions for bush leaguers had not improved much since the 1890s. Travel was rough, dirty, and uncomfortable. Trains hauled the men from city to city, and management did not offer the luxury of sleeper cars. Southern Association teams normally began their journey to the next city immediately following the last out in the final game of a three-game series. Trips often required a night spent in hot, stuffy, and cramped railcars. The men customarily stayed in third-rate hotels located in the downtown district and close to the stadium. On game day, ballplayers would dress in their hotel room — usually shared by three or four teammates — and were transported to the ballpark in a tally-ho, or open aired horse-drawn wagon. Colorful interaction took place between the visible visitors and people walking along the street on the way to the ballyard.[10]

Once the visiting team arrived at the ball park, they did not find a clubhouse, locker room, or showers. Instead, they went directly to their bench, which was set up against the stadium wall in full view of the grandstands. Dugouts would not appear until 1910. After the game, many players chose to frequent saloons or billiard parlors in the vicinity of their hotel. Drinking, gambling, and smoking were occupational hazards of the day.[11]

The investment group that had owned the Nashville Base Ball Club since

1905 typified the business class of capitalists and civic boosters who recognized the value to Nashville in fielding a baseball team. Trustees H. N. McTyeire (bishop), W.E. Jordan (sheriff), William James Ewing, Sr. (newspaperman), William H. Bordeiser (businessman), and Bradley Walker (attorney) announced creation of a joint stock company and attempted to sell 100 shares of stock at $100 per share in order to raise $10,000. Falling short of its ambitious goal, the owners cut corners on salaries and stadium facilities to remain solvent. By the end of 1907, the group washed its hands of the operation and placed the team up for sale. At the same time, beleaguered Johnny Dobbs resigned as player-manager and went back to his dairy farm in Chattanooga.[12]

Mayor James S. Brown, a baseball fan, hoped new ownership of the Nashville club would establish a more solid financial base. Early in the winter of 1907, a group of investors stepped forward. The entrepreneurs included James B. Carr (president of B. H. Stief Jewelry Co.), Thomas James Tyne (lawyer and state legislator), J. T. Connor (real estate), James A. Bowling (contractor), Robert L. Bolling (lawyer), Rufus E. Fort (physician), William G. Hirsig (automobile and tire dealer), and Ferdinand E. Kuhn (shoe merchant). Well-known attorney S. A. Champion agreed to supply legal services to the new corporation. These men of wealth coughed up capital of $50,000, and picked Kuhn to preside over the board of directors.[13]

Ferd Kuhn had opened Kuhn-Cooper-Geary and Company shoe store in 1903. The business, located at 217 North Summer Street (5th Avenue North), did a brisk trade and Kuhn doubled his floor space. The storefront window displayed shoes on revolving pedestals. Inside, marble lined the walls and inlayed mirrors trimmed the back wall. Kuhn separated men's and women's departments as well as those for boys and girls. The latest in electric lighting and holophone reflectors lit the establishment, which earned a reputation as the premiere footwear store in downtown Nashville.[14]

The first order of business for President Kuhn was to restructure the team's on-field management. Rice recommended that the job go to catcher Jack Hardy as a reward for his exemplary offensive display in 1907, or to one of the recently retired major leaguers like Bill Bernhard or Lave Cross.[15] *The Sporting News* reported that the Nashville board of directors had pored over dozens of applications, including ones from Otis Stockdale and several other current Southern Association players.[16] The least likely Nashville newspaper to deliver a sports scoop, the *American,* did so on 29 December in announcing an agreement with Bill Bernhard to manage Nashville in 1908. Nashville anxiously awaited the arrival of its baseball savior.

William Henry Bernhard was born to Peter and Mary Seyfang Bernhard on 16 March 1871 in Clarence, New York. "Strawberry Bill," or "Berny," possessed big-time baseball credentials. He started his minor league career in the 1890s in the New York State League and Buffalo in the Eastern League. His imposing figure at 6' 2" and 200 lbs. and blazing fastball soon attracted

Manager Bill Bernhard at Sulphur Dell. (Courtesy National Baseball Hall of Fame Library, Cooperstown, N.Y.)

attention. Breaking into the majors with Philadelphia in 1899, he is best remembered for his years in Cleveland and close friendship with Nap Lajoie. He posted a 116–82 record over nine years until arm trouble forced him from the game in 1907. Now unemployed, Bernhard was looking for work.

Bernhard signed his Nashville contract for $3,000 in the law office of Thomas James Tyne on New Year's Eve, 1907. "Practically the hope of Nashville as a baseball town is now in his [Bernhard's] hands," reported Richard Hunter Yancey, Jr., the new sports editor at the *Banner*. Rice chimed in and warned that Bernhard should be wary of "boozers or loafers," a reference to the most glaring problems of the 1907 team. "With a man in charge who knows where to get men and make them work," said Rice, "there seems to be a lock on something better than the cellar championship."[17] Additional words of caution came from one of Bernhard's former teammates: "The trouble with many minor league managers," groused Henry "Cy" Voorhees, "is that they are not given absolute control. To succeed the man in charge should be held responsible [but] ... by no means should the stockholders and others do any dictating."[18] Bernhard's ambition was to reach upper management and own a club in the Eastern League.[19]

The hiring of Bernhard was cause for celebration in the Nashville press. Rice informed his readers that the new manager possessed a strong character and did not shy away from hard work. Furthermore, Bernhard was respected in baseball circles and deserved the Nashville "mogulship."[20] *Sporting Life* concurred: "Bill is also a great student of the game and his personality is such that he should be able to get good work out of his men."[21]

Rice predicted that big league clubs would soon be releasing young talent to the minor leagues, and Bernhard had solid contacts with them. Yancey agreed that the Nashville club should be in a good position to pick up discarded major leaguers.[22] The *American* eventually succumbed to competitive pressure from the *Tennessean* and *Banner* at the end of March, 1908, and appointed its own sports writer, William James Ewing, Jr., son of the editor-in-chief.[23]

A confident Bernhard confirmed the expectations everyone had placed upon him in his first interview. "Berny," as the national and local press called him, appeared in high spirits as he laid out a simple plan for Nashville. "I'm looking to give every man a square deal," said the new manager in language reminiscent of another strong leader — President Theodore Roosevelt. "There will be no boozers or loafers on the club I manage, and the man that tries to get away with anything like this will be up against a jolt from the start."[24] Berny cautioned in the *Tennessean* that "picking up a team after the rest have all cleaned up the field isn't as easy as smoking a good pipe. When a bunch winds up in the cellar it takes an awful struggle to even pull out again, no matter what money you spend or how hard you work."[25] The main task confronting Berny in January and February was to restock his team with personnel ready to play competitive baseball.

Meanwhile, Ferd Kuhn and the board of directors faced a dilemma in how to upgrade Athletic Park to the standards set by the elite programs in the Southern Association. The ideal location of the stadium was the envy of some franchises for its proximity to the business and residential districts and easy access by streetcar service. But clearly the wooden edifice needed substantial repairs or demolition. Yancey's editorial column in the *Banner* covered renovation plans under consideration by Kuhn. At first only cosmetic improvements such as the purchase of tarpaulins to cover the infield during inclement weather were discussed. Then, the president scheduled a visit to Atlanta in early January to tour its new facility, Ponce de Leon Park.[26]

Kuhn made a wise decision to check out Atlanta's new ballyard. Known as "Poncey" to the locals, the field boasted the latest innovations in wooden stadium design. The Georgia Railway and Electric had purchased the team in 1906, and broke ground for the new stadium at the end of a trolley route on the city limits about three miles from downtown. Indeed, traction companies played a large part in ownership of Southern Association franchises in Birmingham, Mobile, Montgomery and New Orleans.[27]

When completed, Poncey was considered the most state-of-the-art ballyard in the South. The stadium seated 6,800 fans with segregated bleachers for African-Americans. After all, this was the Jim Crow South. Its left field wall, a hedge, became a trademark as well as a minor league fielding oddity. The new site was located across the street from a large amusement park. The facility cost approximately $60,000 to build, and it opened in May 1907.[23] New stadiums, such as Poncey, quickly became urban symbols for residents proud of their city's commercial expansion, importance, and achievement. Atlanta ran away with the league pennant in 1907, and the Crackers' blueprint for success included a new stadium. The connection did not elude the observant Kuhn.

When Kuhn returned from his fact-finding junket, he asked Berny for advice. The new field general, in turn, contacted the secretary of the Cleveland club who was an apparent expert in the construction of grandstands. Berny received a detailed reply which called for the complete renovation of Athletic Park, including reconfiguration of the infield by putting home plate where first base currently sat. In doing so, the patrons would not be forced to gaze upon the smoldering garbage dump located just beyond the present outfield wall. Another suggestion called for special box seating in a new lower section of the grandstand similar to the kind found in some major league parks.

Although Kuhn and his board disregarded the first suggestion made by Cleveland's secretary, they adopted the second plan and contracted J.A.G. Sloan to design and build a brand new facility. The board budgeted $20,000 for the preliminary phase of construction. The accepted reconfiguration called for home plate to be moved slightly toward third base and the erection of two new covered grandstands to run parallel to the base lines as far as the bases. Bleachers would extend past the grandstand on the third base side, nearly to the spring house, to increase available seating by 600. The installation of 1,400 opera chairs with arm rests permitted maximum comfort for viewing the game at field level for the most affluent fans. The ticket office would be placed in the northeast corner of the ballyard. All told, the new stadium would seat over 3,000 patrons.[29]

The architect's sketches incorporated player needs with a clubhouse including eighteen lockers and two showers for the home team. Kuhn and the board of directors ordered new soil scattered on the infield to improve the playing surface and drainage. Late in the construction phase, the three sports editors—Rice, Yancey and Ewing—petitioned management to have a small wooden press box erected on the grandstand roof behind home plate, a unique innovation in the Southern Association. Previously, sports reporters sat in the stands among the fans. Nashville's new stadium, just like Poncey, promised to be state of the art.

Kuhn's vision of a modern baseball facility for Nashville was significantly out of step with renovations underway at the major league level, because the art of stadium construction was undergoing a radical change. Before 1908, baseball parks had been erected entirely out of wood. Normally, a roof covered the grandstand area down both lines as far as the bases, and an uncovered area extended the rest of the way to the outfield wall. These less expensive, sun-blanched seats became known as bleachers. While wooden stadiums still appealed to minor league owners because they were relatively inexpensive, they were also known fire traps. Between 1894 and 1911, there were sixteen fires in major league parks. Beginning in 1908, as part of a growing progressive desire for safer public buildings, new major league ballparks were made of fireproof materials like concrete and steel.[30]

In a broader sense, these new ballyards contributed to the city beautification movement which sought a higher quality of life for people in urban America. Municipal government also played a role in revising building codes in an effort to establish safer conditions in public places. Since the baseball industry was undergoing an economic boom in the first decade of the twentieth century, club owners could afford such improvements. "The decision to build modern fire-resistant parks symbolized a recognition of the maturity and stability of the baseball business," notes Steven Riess.[31] The new stadium in Nashville would not take the same form as structures in New York, Boston, or Chicago because Kuhn was forced to work within a more limited budget dictated by his smaller minor league market. Therefore, Nashville's new baseball temple would resemble the familiar nineteenth century models.

As work crews began to dismantle sections of Nashville's historic stadium in January, 1908, newspapermen Rice and Yancey felt the need to rename Athletic Park with a fresh, new label. Rice had first suggested "Sulphur Dell" on 14 January in order to make closer connection with the most unique feature that adorned the Bottoms — a sulphur spring house in the left field corner. Equally important, Rice believed that "dell" would provide more rhyming possibilities in his poetic articles. Likewise, Yancey referred to the field as "sulphur spring bottom diamond."[32] One week later, Rice's first poem appeared on a Nashville sports page — *"In Sulphur Dell."*

> There as a sound of revelry by day
> In Sulphur Dell with axes swinging free —
> And every fan there passed, yelled "Hip-Hooray —
> Lay on McDuff, and give one punch for me."
> And from afar the echo rolled in glee —
> "The Nashville grandstand's being torn away."
>
> Sweet are the songs which Madame Calve sings
> But not so sweet as that of falling axe
> In Sulphur Dell where every echo rings
> With timbers falling under mighty whacks
> Keep up the good work — break your blooming backs;
> "Keep up the good work — break your blooming necks
> We'll give a cheer each time the axlet swings.[33]

Rice's desire to give the new stadium a pastoral name allowed the field to take on a distinctive rural character.[34]

The conception of the new ballyard in Nashville, ambitious by Southern Association standards, began to materialize by early March. The palisades took up almost one city block. The trolley car line extended from downtown and ran past the stadium gate to a new residential district known as North Nashville, which started at Jackson Street. The Cumberland River, located only four blocks to the east and less than a quarter-mile away, posed a potential threat to the facility with its annual spring floods. Lying twenty-two-feet below street level, the playing surface and seating area formed a natural amphitheater, and resembled a large pond during spring floods.

The physical plant of the new park was impressive. A sixteen-foot high wooden palisade enclosed the property, and crowds sat on the steep grassy slope in right and left fields during overflow (sellout) games. The covered grandstand was wedged into the northeast corner behind home plate and ran parallel to the field of play. A hand-operated scoreboard protruded from the right field wall and uncovered bleachers ran part way along the left field line toward the famous landmark in the left field corner. Outside the stadium, the Atlantic Ice House towered over the diamond on Cherry Street. Occasionally, fans without a ticket watched games through the top-story windows or gazed out from the rooftop. Young boys carried tin buckets filled with soda pop or beer covered by shaved ice and wooden trays layered with bags of peanuts to hawk to seated fans. Chris Haury's saloon on Jackson Street became a popular watering hole for thirsty revelers prior to and following each game.

One of the charms of minor league parks was their sometimes odd field configurations, and the new ball park in Nashville was no exception. Surface dimensions were peculiar and several natural obstacles made fielding quite a challenge. The pancake-shaped infield was especially close to the spectators: third base was only twenty-six feet away from the stands, and first base was only forty-two-feet away. The measurements down the lines and straight-away center field were equally cozy:

left field: 334 feet
center field: 421 feet
right field: 262 feet (or 235 feet when fans sat behind the roped off area)

The tight corners and cavernous power alleys posed particular difficulties for visiting outfielders. Opposing pitchers wryly nicknamed the park "suffer hell." The outfield shape turned Sulphur Dell into a left-handed hitter's dream, but defending in right field became a nightmare and not simply because of the short porch. Right field became the stadium's hallmark oddity; stadium authority Philip Lowry calls it "the craziest right field in history" in referring to the contour of the land itself. Beginning at 225 feet from home plate, the ground rose 10–12 feet at a 45-degree angle and leveled off at a flat ten-foot terrace which gave the appearance of a step. From that point the angled slope resumed all the way to the right field wall. In all, the playing surface rose approximately twenty-five feet. A gradual, but much more playable rise also existed in left field. Right field at Sulphur Dell received the nickname "the Dump" partly because of the city landfill located just beyond the outfield wall and also because attempts to defend the position were an extreme challenge. Montgomery outfielder Casey Stengel once joked that he had laid a perfect bunt down the right field line for a home run.[35]

Doc Wiseman became a local legend in Nashville because of his efficiency in patrolling the Dump for eleven years. Rice particularly admired the career minor leaguer's skill and longevity in a Nashville uniform. "Any time an athlete sticks to a minor league town over three seasons," said the sportswriter, "you can put it down as a safe bet that he is delivering the stuff from year to year."[36] Doc earned the admiration of Nashville fans as well as a lesser-used second nickname because he had mastered the idiosyncrasies of defending the Dump so well. "The Goat" positioned himself at the base of the first incline, turned his back on fly balls and carefully raced uphill, picked up the flight of the ball and made the catch. Occasionally Wiseman could throw out a runner at first base on hard-hit ground balls. Such defensive prowess earned Wiseman mention in Edward Michael Ashenback's 1911 book, *Humor Among the Minors*.[37]

As Sulphur Dell began to take shape, president Kuhn and manager Bernhard attended the annual meeting of the Southern Association in mid–February. League president Kavanaugh convened the two-day conference in his Little Rock office at the Southern Trust Company. First, he told the attendees to dispel the unfounded rumor that he planned to run for governor of Arkansas, and then announced the agenda: the proposed schedule, retention of umpires, and an open debate on the problem of fan and player rowdyism. Kavanaugh also welcomed the newest member to the Southern Association family before settling down to business. Mobile had replaced the Shreveport franchise for the coming season.[38]

Scheduling was always a headache. Every year the biggest attendance gates occurred on the major summer holidays, Memorial (Decoration) Day, Independence Day, and Labor Day. It had been the custom to schedule doubleheaders on these three dates and allow each team to host at least one of them.[39] These were not revenue-sharing times, and big gates were important. Little Rock manager Mike Finn had assisted President Kavanaugh in drawing up the 1908 pairings, and not everyone was pleased. New Orleans and (strangely enough) Little Rock were on the road for all three of the coveted engagements while Birmingham and Atlanta were slated to play at home on all three dates. In addition, New Orleans was slated to play its last thirteen games of the season on the road while Nashville would play its last thirteen games at home. Despite vociferous complaints from Pelican skipper Charlie Frank and Montgomery president R. J. Chambers went unanswered, the 132-game schedule was adopted without change.[40]

Reform-minded Kavanaugh wanted league owners to take a more vigilant stand against rowdyism both on the field and in the stands. He pushed for and secured a resolution that mandated that home teams would provide a police presence at all games and arrest any fan guilty of throwing bottles at the visiting squad or any player(s) fighting on the field. Kavanaugh also announced the hiring of four umpires, included holdover Dan Pfenninger, former player and major league official W.B. Carpenter, A. J. Fitzsimmons from the Cotton States League, and J. J. O'Brien from the Eastern League. Kavanaugh hoped to hire one additional umpire before league play commenced in April.[41]

Then Chambers dropped a bombshell in a proposal to realign the Southern Association into a northern and southern division with a championship series at the conclusion of the season. The Montgomery mogul suggested Nashville, Memphis, Birmingham and Little Rock for the northern tier, and New Orleans, Montgomery, Mobile, and Atlanta in the southern group. The novel idea precipitated "a very heated session" and ultimately went down to defeat. Not until 1920 would a similar plan inaugurate the Dixie Series. Then, prior to adjourning to a sumptuous dinner in the basement, the assembly voted to increase Kavanaugh's salary to $3,000 — a 25 percent raise.[42]

The second day of the league meeting was set aside for social interaction between the team owners, managers, and league president. The affable Kavanaugh enjoyed hosting these social gatherings. He understood the importance of allowing these men, who would become fierce competitors in the

Southern Association team presidents, 1908 (*The Spalding Guide*): 1. Ferdinand E. Kuhn (Nashville); 2. R. H. Baugh (Birmingham); 3. J. W. Heisman (Atlanta); 4. F. P. Coleman (Memphis); 5. R. C. Rather (Little Rock); 6. L. L. Stern (New Orleans); 7. W. R. Joyner (Director, Atlanta); 8. T. F. McCullough (Sec.-Treas., Memphis).

Southern Association Managers, 1908 (*The Spalding Guide*): 1. Billy Smith (Atlanta); 2. Charlie Frank (New Orleans); 3. Bill Bernhard (Nashville); 4. Charlie Babb (Memphis); 5. Mike Finn (Little Rock); 6. Harry Hartwell (Mobile); 7. Carleton Molesworth (Birmingham). Not pictured: Jimmy Ryan and Ed Gremminger (Montgomery); Tom Fisher (Mobile); Harry Vaughn (Birmingham).

months ahead, to enjoy each other's company. He arranged for a tally-ho to transport the sixteen-man entourage to the Arlington Hotel in Hot Springs to attend another lavish banquet. The hotel arranged the dining room table in the shape of a baseball diamond. Kavanaugh sat at home plate, flanked by his two invited guests—the governor of Arkansas and mayor of Atlanta. Nashville's Kuhn sat at shortstop.[43]

Consensus among the league powers had it that the 1908 crown would fall to either Memphis or returning champion Atlanta. Team administrators sidestepped the sensitive topic of enforcing salary caps even though they were flagrantly disregarded by several franchises. The Southern Association had fallen into a familiar pattern in which teams with strong financial backing (New Orleans and Atlanta) spent large sums of money on top players while small-market teams (Little Rock and Birmingham) tended to dwell in the lower rung every year because they could not afford competitive talent. Kavanaugh recognized this lack of parity and hoped to obtain a tighter rein on player acquisitions, but not in 1908.[44]

Several weeks before the February league meeting, Ewing noted in the *American:* "Baseball news, that *is* news, is pretty scarce in this burg just now."[45] Nashville's three sports editors were about to spice things up with an original idea. Rice reprinted an article entitled "Team Nicknames" by *Memphis Commercial-Appeal* sportswriter T. G. Scarbrough. The piece traced the nicknames employed by teams in the 1907 Southern Association. Scarbrough pointed out that the Nashville nines started out as the "Hustlers" and then changed to the "Boosters" before settling for the "Dobbers" in honor of their manager, Johnny Dobbs. In his *Sportograms* column, Rice remarked that "it took an awful lot of nerve to call them [Nashville] 'Hustlers' especially after the first of August [1907]." The idea of finding a more suitable and lasting nickname inspired the triumvirate to sponsor a contest.[46]

Ewing had originally invited Rice to assist him in picking a new team moniker for the Nashville Base Ball Club, but Yancey intervened and suggested that "the tagging" should be left to the "vox populi," or fans. "The cognomen of a baseball team usually is one of its most important assets," said Yancey, "and a nickname that is attractive helps the popularity of the club."[47] The sports editor of the *Banner* also appealed to sportswriters in each Southern Association city to remain uniform in their usage of names chosen for the various teams. He pointed, with aggravation, to the practice of the Montgomery, Little Rock, and Memphis clubs, who went by more than one name in 1907. Yancey curiously omitted Nashville from his list of offenders.[48]

On 15 February, the *Tennessean, Banner,* and *American* simultaneously announced a public contest to select a new name for the 1908 club. The sportswriters proposed to assist the public in narrowing its focus to several suitable titles. The self-appointed judges mulled over nicknames like Hermits, Politicians, Presidents, Beavers, Tigers, Sulphurites, and Hickorys. Meanwhile, Rice lobbied for a proper name "that would stick" like Pelicans for New Orleans and Barons for Birmingham. The three scribes settled on these finalists: Volunteers, Rocks, and Lime Rocks. Rice's choice, the Vols, was a reference to the spirit of volunteerism which had swept over the state during the War of 1812. Yancey agreed: "Volunteers is the appellation that makes the Tennessee heart swell with pride [because] the name suggests courage, and should prove a talisman of victory."[49] Rice, a master of baseball slang, told the bugs [fans] to mail their recommendation to manager Bernhard before the deadline of 28 February.[50]

The contest captured the public's imagination, and Nashvillians cast over one thousand votes. On the 29th, each newspaper carried bold type headlines announcing the winning "sobriquet." Vols copped top honors with over 950 tallies. "The days of Fishermen, Finnites, Boosters, and Dobbers' are over," proclaimed Rice.[51] Now the team even boasted a new nickname.

The finale of 1907 had illustrated beyond a doubt the poor condition of the Nashville franchise. The organization suffered from twin ills: lackluster play on the field and lack of financial resources in the front office. A turnaround occurred with the appearance of new ownership and a broader financial base. Presided over by Ferd Kuhn, the new owners were not reluctant to spend their resources and spared little expense in construction of a new ballpark that promised to be a show place in the Southern Association despite its odd dimensions. The new board also made a wise decision in hiring a manager who was respected by baseball people nationally. The structure of the league itself, administered by the dynamic and robust President Kavanaugh, promised tighter administrative controls in the months ahead in order to preserve the game's growing family atmosphere. Finally, the sports fans of Nashville were blessed with three quality sportswriters. Led by the eloquence of Rice, these scribes generated great enthusiasm for the 1908 season long before the first pitch was thrown.

By 1 March, the necessary pieces had been put into place for the coming season with one crucial exception — the players. Berny had been at work since the first week of January evaluating his returning talent and researching the abilities of players who were available. He would make his roster choices soon and test them from mid–March to the opening day of the Southern Association season. Rice sensed the rising anticipation in Nashville for the impending season in referencing Shakespeare's masterpiece, *King Richard the Third:* "The Winter of our Discontent is done."[52] All that remained was to play ball.

Chapter 3

Play Ball

As the 1908 preseason began, other forms of entertainment and a heated political environment in Nashville rivaled baseball for the public's attention in the early spring. Baseballist bugs, as Rice coined the fans, realized that recent efforts by management to improve the stadium and hire an effective manager fostered hope for the coming season. Manager Bernhard had inherited a cellar-dwelling outfit that had spent the last half of the previous season in a nose dive, so he went to work immediately assembling a new squad. Berny oversaw rigorous spring training workouts and scheduled a slate of "ante season" games against barnstorming major league clubs. The practices and exhibition games offered the rookie manager valuable insight into which fifteen men would best contribute to the club. Nashville's long-awaited season was finally underway.

Berny's efforts to put a team together were carried out in the midst of other entertainment venues in the first few months of 1908. Nashville attracted cultural events that appealed to the upper crust of society. In mid-January, *Madame Butterfly* played at the Vendome to sellout crowds. Several days later, internationally renowned vocalist Emma Calve performed at the Ryman Auditorium. Musical comedies *Buster Brown* and *Piff, Poff, Pauf* packed the Bijou, and traveling dramatists staged such fare as Ibsen's *A Doll's House* and Shakespeare's *Macbeth*. For audiences with more common tastes, Ringling Brothers Circus and then the Annie Oakley Show set up in Centennial Park, and Al G. Fields' minstrel show paid its annual visit to town. Technological marvels also captured local attention when three representatives of the American Automobile Club drove from New York City to Nashville in a thirty-horsepower White steamer in only two weeks.[1]

On the political front, the Democratic party primary for governor promised to heat up public passions as much as any event in Tennessee's recent history. Incumbent Malcolm R. Patterson faced a stiff challenge from former U.S. Senator Edward Ward Carmack. The central campaign issue — prohibition — made the struggle a volatile one. The city of Nashville became a key battleground. Carmack, the managing editor of the *Tennessean*, opposed the sale of whiskey while Duncan Brown Cooper, owner and editor of the *American*, supported the anti-prohibition position taken by Patterson. The debate gathered force when Jack Daniel began the manufacture and distribution of *Old Time No. 7* from his Lynchburg distillery. Carmack and Patterson squared off in no fewer than forty-two public debates across the state. Nashville hosted several engagements on the Public Square and in Ryman Auditorium that attracted overflow crowds. Both sides sponsored large parades and at one rally a crowd of children chanted, "Carmack, Carmack, he's our man. We can't vote, but daddy can!" One observer proclaimed Patterson's narrow victory in March "the highlight of political history in Tennessee."[2] The bitter campaign and the single issue that fueled it would later culminate in a bloody shootout on the streets of Nashville.

Meanwhile, manager Bernhard was working to acquire two quality outfielders to complement right fielder Wiseman, one or two middle infielders depending upon the return of players, a first baseman to replace the departed Pete Lister (one of Nashville's leading hitters), and two experienced pitchers. This shopping list would be difficult to fill completely. In addition, the manager was made aware of the poor attitude exhibited by a handful of '07 players.

Berny had no shortage of players from which to build his program. Pitchers under contract included Johnny and Elmer Duggan, Herbert "Buttons" Briggs, George Hunter, Jack Hess (recently signed from Springfield, Massachusetts), Hub Perdue, Stanley Yerkes, Bill Sorrell, and Clarence Nelson. If necessary, former Cleveland pitching ace and current manager Bernhard himself could provide some relief. Infielders included Whitey Morse, Bert Conn, Pryor M. McElveen, Mike McCormick, Henry Jansing, and Art Nichols. The catching duties seemed set with Jack Hardy (who had led the team in hitting and ranked third in the league with a .312 batting average in 1907) and J. Warren Seabough. Doc Wiseman was the lone returning outfielder. The Nashville sportswriters learned that Nichols and McCormick had demanded their release, and Sorrell's name surfaced in rumored trade talks.[3]

The sporting news triumvirate were not without their own favorites, doghouse players, and projected sleepers, and Rice was the most outspoken of the bunch. Rice saved his highest accolades for "the little doctor who roamed in right field. Take him from every angle, and there were few in Wiseman's class on this league's pay roll in 1907," he beamed. The editor fretted that McElveen was a risk because his glove [defense] was suspect. No one disputed the third baseman's batting skills, however. Rice concluded that Berny had enough pitchers under contract "to start in a couple of leagues." He recalled Johnny Duggan's great season in 1906 but lamented about "the kink in his whip" (sore arm) in 1907. Rice had nothing positive to say for Sorrell — an unpopular Texan with poor work habits and a sour disposition. He predicted that the arrival of Hess would result in the removal of either Duggan or Sorrell from the roster. Rice also lobbied for Cleveland to cut loose Jake Daubert, a promising rookie first baseman in need of offensive seasoning.

Jacob Ellsworth Daubert was born in Shamokin, Pennsylvania, on 7 April 1884, to Jacob and Sarah Hay Daubert. As a youngster, he worked as a breaker boy separating slate and other impurities from coal, and then became a mule driver in the Blackwood Coal Mine near his boyhood home. As a teenager, Daubert pitched on the company team, the W & L Baseball Club in the Williams Valley League. After an ornery mule kicked him in the head, Daubert decided to try professional baseball. In 1906, the 20-year-old Daubert began pitching for an independent team, Lykens in the Wyoming Valley (PA) League. A year later he signed with Kane (PA) in the Interstate League and transferred to Marion (OH) in the Ohio & Pennsylvania League after the Kane franchise folded. A left-hander who hit for power and average (.285), Daubert had dazzled fans with his quick glove and footwork around the bag. He had committed only eight errors in 709 chances at Marion. Rice speculated that the young Pennsylvanian would fit in nicely for the departed Lister.[4] Of course, Rice attached a disclaimer to his "dope"; it is "a fine thing to read and talk about, but a poor thing to bet real money on."[5]

Yancey supported some of Rice's analyses in the *Banner*. He shared faith in Wiseman's ability to play the Dump, and mirrored his worries about the sloppy infield play and suspect pitchers. He believed in Duggan's "first class" talent, however, and felt that the Hoosier deserved another shot at making the pitching staff despite his chronic shoulder problem. Rice's colleague did not extend such sympathy to shortstop Mike McCormick, who had played erratic defense, pouted, and jumped the team at a critical stage of the 1907 season. Nor did Yancey appreciate second sacker Art Nichols, who "caused considerable dissension" among the players. Yancey had little confidence in pitchers Elmer Duggan, thought Yerkes was replaceable, owing to constant illness, and urged a trade for the talented but unhappy Sorrell. He felt that Berny would provide a calming influence on the immature Perdue. A first baseman remained a top priority according to Yancey, but until a suitable replacement was found, he recommended that catcher Jack Hardy fill the spot. Yancey confided that he did not have much confidence in the team that Berny had on paper because it resembled the '07 lot: "He [Bernhard] already has on the Nashville roll quite an array of material, but most of it does not look like pennant winning talent."[6]

Ewing offered his thoughts of player personnel in the *American*. Not surprisingly, it began with accolades for Wiseman, whom management had recently rewarded with a modest raise. Ewing also liked reports from the Florida Everglades League where Johnny Duggan had wintered and rehabilitated his arm. Likewise, Ewing praised hard-swinging third baseman Swede Jansing for his offseason efforts in the California League. He thought the Louisville product was fast and dependable on defense, important attributes at the hot corner. Surprisingly, Ewing identified an unlikely source as the nemesis that stood between Nashville and a successful season — catcher Jack Hardy. According to the sportswriter, Scrappy Jack befriended no one in the previous season and had told manager Dobbs at one point, "I'll do as I please regardless of you." Ewing chastised the arrogant catcher as "the worst sulker in the business" and even suspected him of throwing a game against Memphis. Ewing concluded that "Hardy's kind is not wanted in Nashville."[7] Hamilton Love, the local Nashville contributor to *The Sporting News,* offered a mixed assessment of Hardy as well. Love concurred with Ewing that the catcher was "quick-tempered, disagreeable, and hard to manage," but added that Hardy was "the very best backstopper in the Southern Association." If Berny could only control the offensive standout, he [Hardy] might "be a tower of strength."[8]

John Dolittle Hardy was born on 23 June 1877, in Akron, Ohio.[9] His days before professional baseball had hardened Jack physically and mentally, and he learned to deal with adversity in an aggressive manner. He had grown up on the streets of Cleveland, played football for a season at Hiram College despite never having completed high school, and served in the Spanish-American War. Hardy apprenticed as a catcher with Ft. Wayne, Canton, Youngstown, and Los Angeles in the renegade California League prior to 1907, and he bore a distinctive scar on his chin sustained in a 1903 train derailment while traveling with the Cleveland Blues.

Ewing looked to Berny's connection with Cleveland for assistance in filling Nashville's roster needs. He astutely picked out Harry Bay, an outfielder with blazing speed but hobbled by a recurring knee injury, as a possible solution to Nashville's dilemma in the outfield. Bay, or "Deerfoot," was once reputed to be "the fastest man ever to put on a pair of spikes." Cleveland manager Nap Lajoie was seeking a rehabilitation assignment for his lame outfielder. Perhaps, Ewing hoped, Berny would call upon his good friend Lajoie for a favor.

Managers in the Southern Association worked under a strict salary cap (which was rarely enforced) of only $2,700. The National Association had recently granted the league's request to permit the addition of one player to its team rosters. The fifteenth player ruling extended the salary roof to $3,000. A decent ballplayer could fetch as much as $200 and an outstanding one might earn $300. Berny and Kuhn had carefully balanced Nashville's books so that they would not be out of compliance despite rumors that other teams like New Orleans and Atlanta flagrantly disregarded the rule. Furthermore, the Southern Association competed for talent against other minor leagues like the American Association and Eastern League, which did not operate under caps at all and reportedly had team budgets in excess of $4,500. Within these salary restrictions, Berny — the first minor league manager plucked from Ban Johnson's American League — set about to recruit as fine a team as possible.

Berny mailed contracts to all of his roster players on 23 January, and notified them that practice would begin, weather permitting, on 10 March. The only permanent local resident from the '07 team, Perdue, worked on his parents' farm in nearby Gallatin in the offseason. Several of the players had wintered in Nashville and other teammates began to drift back to town around 1 March. All of the returnees began to work out informally at the downtown Nashville Athletic Club. Yerkes, the ex–Buffalo Bison standout, signed and returned his contract in less than a week. Management agreed to pay for each player's travel expenses and enclosed a railroad ticket with the contract. In the meantime, Berny ordered thirty new uniforms—fifteen white and fifteen gray flannel suits with black hats, socks, and belts—in anticipation of the upcoming season.

President Kuhn released the preseason schedule to the press in early March. The Vols' first exhibition game was slated for 23 March against Connie Mack's Philadelphia Athletics. Then came Vanderbilt University, coached by baseball alum Grantland Rice, on 24–26 March. The Chicago White Sox, Chicago Cubs, Brooklyn Superbas, and the Milwaukee Brewers from the American Association filled out the rest of the schedule. Berny also planned to play local athletic clubs and semipro teams on an as-needed basis. "In Uncle Sam's great pastime Dixie takes the limelight first," noted Rice. "In another month the advance guard of 400 big league athletes will be on its way across the southern trail, and the 1908 lid will be formally lifted."[10] The Vols would open league play on 15 April on the road against the defending Southern Association champion, Atlanta.

As Nashville players returned signed contracts, the trade mill operated at full speed. In his first official transaction as manager, Berny shipped off disgruntled Art Nichols to Waterbury in the Connecticut League for an unidentified pitcher nicknamed "the human sunflower."[11] The deal satisfied local fans who did not wish to keep bad seed Nichols in Nashville. Berny also signed a pair of twins: George Kerr, a 19-year-old pitcher with a live arm, and his brother, catcher Harry. The new Nashville pilot was surprised in the amount of interest being shown around the league in his third baseman. Berny received inquiries about the availability of McElveen from Red Fisher (Mobile), Billy Smith (Atlanta), and Harry Vaughn (Birmingham). Each manager offered to exchange players and cash to acquire the services of the hard-hitting east Tennessean.

Pryor Mynatt McElveen was born in Atlanta, Georgia, on 5 November 1883, but grew up in the hills of Jefferson County in east Tennessee.[12] McElveen enrolled in nearby Carson-Newman College in 1904 where he displayed superior athleticism in three sports—football, basketball, and baseball. A college photograph shows the gangly youth, already known as "Humpy," awkwardly gripping a thick-handled baseball bat. In the summer of 1905, he began playing professional baseball under Frank Moffett at Knoxville. When Humpy arrived on the Nashville scene in 1907, he was considered a raw, talented country boy, or rube. First-year skipper Johnny Dobbs used the versatile Tennessean at third base (122 games) and shortstop (19 games), and he led Nashville with 148 hits and carried a robust .286 batting average.

Other trade rumors swirled in Nashville newspapers, too. Discussions about the possibility of winning the rights to Bay and Daubert became routine. Understanding the club's need for outfielders, several names surfaced in early March — Billy Lush of Cleveland and Jack McCarthy of Brooklyn. Shortly before the first practice, Berny signed three players who were destined to play important roles on the '08 team. He picked up a tall and speedy 20-year-old shortstop from the St. Louis Browns, Willis "Kid" Butler.

Then the manager nabbed Carl Vedder Sitton, a pitcher from Jacksonville in the South Atlantic League with an excellent spitball and lively fastball. These two last-minute signees, Butler and Sitton, were relatively untested long shots. If each player panned out, however, they would fill important defensive needs.[13] Berny also inked Winford "Win" Kellum, a switch-hitting southpaw, from the Louisville club.

Winford Ainsley Kellum was born in Waterford, Ontario, Canada, on 11 April 1876, to Newton and Cassie Kellum.[14] Seven years later the family immigrated to the United States and Win learned to play baseball in the streets of Cleveland. When the family purchased a livestock farm outside Big Rapids, Michigan, he continued to hone his baseball skills, and the 19-year-old was rewarded with a professional contract in 1895 with Quincy (IL) of the Western Association. "I was a green and uninformed kid then," reminisced Kellum in 1950, "and was easy prey for the pranks of the older boys. I was awed by the cities I had never seen."[15] Although he sustained a season-ending injury after being struck in the eye by a line drive, the Montgomery club signed the promising star in 1896. There, the southpaw posted a sensational 21–5 record in an abbreviated four-month season, threw a no-hitter against Mobile, and led the Gladiators to a second-place finish.

In 1897, the Southern League suspended play owing to financial difficulties, and Kellum turned up in Indianapolis flannels. Shipped to Mansfield at midseason and recalled in 1899, the southpaw emerged as the ace on the Indians' staff with his best pitching performance ever, 27–9. Kellum remained the cornerstone of Indianapolis for four seasons.

In 1900, Indianapolis joined the American League to challenge the National League's monopoly on major league baseball. Although official recognition of the upstart league remained one season away, Kellum shone in a 6–0 no-hitter against the Chicago White Sox. Only one ChiSox reached base on a fielding error; otherwise, Kellum would have tossed a perfect game. In 1901,

Kellum jumped to Boston and split time between the Red Sox (2–3) and New Orleans (10–2) in the Southern Association.

Kellum returned to Indianapolis in 1902 where he pieced together two outstanding seasons— 29–7 and 25–8. There he teamed up with future Vols teammate Johnny Duggan. In 1903, Cincinnati purchased the rights to Kellum and in his only complete season in the majors, he went 15–10 (2.60 ERA) and led the National League with two relief victories. However, arm trouble afflicted the southpaw along with a run-in with manager Joe Kelly. He was sold to the St. Louis Cardinals in 1905 but finished with a disappointing 3–3 record. The Cardinals were concerned about Kellum's sore arm and lofty salary (which overshadowed that of the manager), so they shipped him to Toledo. The Mud Hens exhausted Kellum in thirteen straight games. His arm was gone, but Hall of Famer Wee Willie Keeler later admitted that he hated to face Kellum in his prime. Destined to pitch the remainder of his career in the minors, Kellum returned to familiar surroundings— Indianapolis (1906–07).

In Cleveland, Nap Lajoie had already disclosed that he was sending Nashville's standout first baseman, Pete Lister, to Toledo. The decision dashed Berny's hope of reacquiring the popular slugger at the same moment he failed to sign a promising collegian from Wilkes-Barre, Jim Robertson. Robertson had voiced reservations about playing in the South, citing the region's muggy summer climate as the reason. The heat concern relative to southern baseball prevailed among ballplayers who hailed from the North. Under the headline, "SOUTH SLANDERED," an article in *The Sporting News* described this "debilitating misconception" that adversely affected recruiting non-southern ballplayers. The article supported ballplayers' concerns, concluded ominously, "the whole circuit [Southern Association] is not a health resort."[16] Memphis and New Orleans had recently dealt with bouts of yellow fever; the latter city played out the second half of its 1905 season on the road because of an outbreak of the dreaded disease.[17] It was not uncommon for players to be stricken with malaria during the long, hot summer. Robertson's refusal to sign with Nashville, and his opinion about southern climes, was shared by the Duggan brothers, who resided near Indianapolis, and only two hundred miles north of Nashville. Bert Conn, a Philadelphia product, refused to report for the same reason.

On the eve of spring training, Nashville's seven rivals in the Southern Association had made progress in shoring up their staffs. Rice and Yancey, who seemed joined at the journalistic hip, predicted that either New Orleans or Atlanta would walk away with the '08 crown, while Ewing liked Memphis to win the rag. These selections were not long shots since these three teams had led the league in total victories over the past seven years. Montgomery, the forecasters agreed, had helped itself the greatest in the offseason by signing hard-hitting third baseman Ed Gremminger away from Minneapolis and picking up left-handed pitcher Bill Cristall from Memphis.[18] No one went out on a limb to pick Nashville any higher than fourth place. It seemed understood that Little Rock, Birmingham, and newcomer Mobile would slug it out for the basement. Rice concluded that the league, from top to bottom, was exceptionally well balanced. Charlie Frank, manager of New Orleans, agreed. "All the teams in the league look strong to me," commented Frank, "but the team that wins the flag will know that it has been in a real race."[19]

Berny announced that the Nashville contingent of athletes would be put through two-a-day practices once camp opened on 10 March. However, cold temperatures, the unfinished clubhouse, and sloppy field conditions forced Berny to postpone the first workout by one week. It was a good decision, because two key players, Wiseman and McElveen, had not yet arrived. Yancey described the unfinished locker room as "a palace" with hot and cold running water, wash basins, shower stalls, and large lockers. The grandstand and bleachers were not scheduled for completion until mid–April, so the construction site was abuzz with an estimated two hundred workers. When Berny held his first practice on 16 March, several hundred fans watched both turnouts from the unfinished grandstand and grassy right field knoll. Alf Williams and Bob Phillips, two raucous fellows who organized a group of faithful supporters known as the "Loyal Brigade," led the onlookers. Some of the bystanders complained about the seventy-foot gap between the grandstand and the bleachers. Management later agreed to fill the void with seats at an intermediate price of 35 cents.[20]

The fans enjoyed the lively workout as Berny put sixteen of his new Vols through their paces. Every pitcher threw in batting practice, and the three newspapermen were particularly impressed with the velocity of Berny and Hess. Rice nicknamed the latter pitcher "the William Howard Taft of the squad." A hefty man, Hess had also been a college chum of Berny's. Every player took batting practice, and Hardy stroked several long drives to the outfield wall. In the afternoon session, the team went through an extensive defensive workout. Berny assigned Hardy to play first base until a regular could be acquired, and McElveen and Butler rotated at middle infield. After two days of practice, Rice spoke highly of Butler's performance: "If young Mr. Butler displays the proper goods ... there's a chance that McElveen will be shifted out to picket duty [the outfield]."[21] When McCormick and Morse reported two days late, Berny moved career infielder McElveen to "the garden." To no one's surprise, Jansing held down his familiar spot at third base. Clearly the manager was searching for infield combinations that might click. Butler, it was hoped, would fit into those plans.

Willis Everett Butler, the youngest member of the '08 Vols, was born on 9 August 1887, in Franklin, Pennsylvania.[22] The rangy 5' 11" Kid was taller than the average shortstop, but he showed exceptional promise with Augusta (1904) as a 17-year-old rookie. He advanced to Youngstown and Akron (1905–06), and at the end of his third professional season in the minors, the doormat St.

Kid Butler at bat in Sulphur Dell. (Courtesy National Baseball Hall of Fame Library, Cooperstown, N.Y.)

Louis Browns called him up. Donning a Brownie uniform for the first time on 30 April 1907, Butler was the fifth-youngest player in the American League. However, he saw limited action in 20 games — mostly at second base — and hit a paltry .220. Then, Berny had picked up his release.

By the end of the first full week of practice, in which temperatures hovered in the low to mid–40s with light rain, Berny faced several problems. First, McElveen threatened to bolt the team and go back to farming if Berny planned to leave him permanently in the outfield. Second, McCormick and Morse resumed their rebelliousness from last season by showing a definite lack of hustle. Third, the Vols desperately needed a first baseman. Only the timely arrival of Wiseman offered a glimmer of hope. Said Rice about the right fielder's historic eighth season with the same team: "It would be a waste of copy paper to suggest that Doc looked good. Mr. Wiseman always looks good, whether to the female eye or to the glaring eyeball of the Bug."[23] Ewing disagreed. He thought the Little Doctor was out of shape.[24] The team went through a lackluster five-inning inter-squad game to finish its first week in training camp. Berny was reportedly searching frantically for some new infielders. It was the worst-kept secret in town.

No time to rest. The Philadelphia Athletics were scheduled to play on the 23 March and Berny's Vols looked ill-prepared after only six practice sessions. Still, the arrival of a major league team filled the local fans with excitement. Ewing made an interesting observation on the importance of spring training to the major leaguers:

> These Southern trips are most interesting even to the layman, because they are so completely at variance with what the onlooker would expect of men in training for a long, arduous season of big league work. In the first place, in the strict acceptance of the word, there is really no training for the men on the squad. They do not do the work of an athlete ... The ballplayer has no compulsory hours of sleep and no certain diet and no particular muscles to cultivate or look after. Teamwork is what is sought, and this makes up 90 per cent of the work done in the South.[25]

Ewing was developing perceptive sportswriting skills.

Connie Mack's team did not even get off the train when they arrived at Union Station during a heavy downpour. Instead, the A's stayed aboard for their next scheduled engagement in Louisville. Rice offered to pick up the open date with his Vanderbilt squad, and Berny accepted. Yancey quipped that the Commodores had been practicing longer and harder than their professional counterparts.

Approximately eight hundred fans weathered cold temperatures at Sulphur Dell to watch the Vols' first practice game of the season, a contest won handily by the professionals, 8–0. Sitton threw the first five innings and Sorrell finished the final four frames. Both Vols pitchers combined to scatter six hits while the collegians committed six costly errors. Jansing committed two throwing errors at third base, a harbinger of things to come. In a post-game interview, Berny told the Nashville press that he was eagerly seeking a first baseman. The manager diplomatically kept other concerns to himself, but seven out of twelve Vols who took the field against the Commodores were destined to play elsewhere within two months. Berny was pleased with the performance of Sitton.[26]

Named for a renowned Charleston Presbyterian minister, Charles Vedder Sitton was born on 22 September 1881, in Pendleton, South Carolina, the second of five children to Henry Philip and Amy Wilkinson Sitton.[27] Later known on the sports page as "Carl" or "C.V.," the family called him Vedder. His family had deep roots in the South Carolina upcountry. Grandfather John B. Sitton was born in the Old Pendleton District in 1810 and built the first brick building on the town square. The small hamlet grew into a thriving trade center, and by 1830 Pendleton earned a reputation for social refinement and where the southern code of chivalry was highly regarded. Carl's father Henry and Uncle Augustus were Confederate veterans, and after the Civil War they went into partnership in a general mercantile store and inherited several buildings on the town square. Augustus later played a prominent role in the Red Shirt movement to topple Radical Reconstruction in the Carolina upcountry and restore conservative white government. At the same time, Henry purchased a large house on a wooded lot once owned by Mrs. John C. Calhoun, named the dwelling Belvedere in keeping with antebellum tradition, and made a lifelong commitment to the Pendleton Presbyterian Church, where he served as deacon and elder.

Owing to his family's social status, it is probable that young Vedder attended the exclusive Pendleton Male Academy. In 1901, he enrolled in Clemson College only four miles away, and played football and baseball for three years but did not graduate. It is possible that he pitched in the textile leagues that punctuated the South Carolina upcountry at the time. His first verified experience in professional baseball occurred in 1906, when he pitched for Spartanburg in the South Carolina League and proceeded to Jacksonville in the SALLY a year later. Without a doubt, Sitton's aristocratic background did not jive with his pursuit of a career in baseball.

There was no rest for the Vols as they hosted the visiting Chicago White Sox the next day. Berny fielded the same lineup and split pitching duties between Perdue and Hess. Tennessean Perdue gave up two runs in four innings' work, and the underhanded delivery of Berny's rotund friend fooled no one as Hess surrendered three more runs. The crucial play of the game occurred when McElveen dropped a routine pop fly in left field and opened the gates for two unearned runs. The ChiSox put on a fine display of scientific baseball with precision bunting and stealing bases. Seabough and Butler contributed two hits apiece, but it was not enough to overtake the big leaguers, who won handily, 5–2.

The White Sox returned the next day to administer another pasting of the hapless Vols by a score of 3–0. The most serious damage occurred when George Davis drove a triple over McElveen's head in left field, and Jansing tossed in three throwing errors at third base. He complained afterwards of a sore hand. Kellum started the game and gave up all three Chicago runs. Sorrell threw four innings in masterful relief and allowed only one hit.

On 28 March, Berny arranged a last-minute practice game against Vanderbilt. Despite the rain that fell throughout the game, the professionals won the sloppy seven inning affair, 12–6. Berny drew up an unorthodox lineup with Seabough and Sorrell splitting time at first base. Hardy, Jansing, and Butler had falsely assumed that the game had been called off, owing to inclement weather, and never reported to Sulphur Dell.

Rain fell for the next two days and provided Berny with a welcome respite to sort through his team's strengths and weaknesses. By league statute, the manager had until 15 May to whittle down the team roster to fifteen players.[28] Berny had crucial decisions to make regarding the seven pitchers he currently had in camp. Also, pitcher Johnny Duggan was technically assigned to Brooklyn, even though his release to Nashville was expected. The Duggan brothers, however, had remained in Indiana, reportedly resting from their winter stint in Florida. Their absence from Nashville hinted at an unforeseen problem. Berny also struggled with the inconsistent outfield play of McElveen. The east Tennessean had turned left field play into an unpleasant adventure, but he was also crushing the ball at the plate. Berny needed to catch a break in the major league castoff market as well. At this moment, Rice started a new feature on the *Tennessean* sports page—letters to the sports editor. Now, Berny would have all of the arm-chair assistance he needed.

On the last day of March, as torrential rain pounded the city, Berny received his first break. Nap Lajoie released the young first baseman that showed so much promise, Jake Daubert, to his friend in Nashville. Rice proclaimed the welcome news in a headline: "DAUBERT ON DECK!" The young Pennsylvania coal miner was a genuine rising star. Lajoie came close to sending the talented first sacker to Toledo, but decided to help his former teammate, Berny, instead. The 22-year-old Daubert demonstrated a mature attitude concerning his reassignment to Nashville: "It may be that I am not ready for the big league, but I think with what I have learned ... and what I should pick up under a care-taking minor league manager, I should get there within a short time."[29]

The next scheduled exhibition against a major league opponent was over a week away, so Berny arranged for back-to-back contests with Vanderbilt and two amateur city league teams. The Vols easily handled Vanderbilt for a third straight time, 9–0, behind the pitching of Perdue, Sorrell, and Sitton; the Commodore pitcher "was wilder than an amateur automobilist." Jansing continued his wildness at third base, and the club hired a masseur to "work the kinks out of his soup bone."[30] Then, the Vols played one of the local amateur teams, Cheek-Neal.[31] The professionals played uninspired baseball in their lopsided 11–2 victory. Shortstop Mike "Dude" McCormick was sulking and not putting forth much effort according to a number of complaining patrons. Berny defended McCormick, saying that he had pulled a groin muscle.

Michael J. McCormick was born in May, 1883, but sources differ on the location — either Scotland, Ireland, or Jersey City.[32] It is known that he grew up in a squalid Irish immigrant slum in Jersey City known as the Horseshoe.[33] As a youngster, Mike was one of the most sports-minded and athletically skilled baseball, soccer, and handball players in the neighborhood. In the late 1890s, Dude played semipro baseball for the Cable team in lower Jersey City, and then signed contracts to play with Waterbury (1901), Holyoke (1903), and Brooklyn (1904). Appearing in his first major league game at third base on 14 April 1904, McCormick struggled offensively (.184) for the entire season. Defensively, he turned more double plays (21) than any other third baseman in the National League and committed the second fewest number of errors. When McCormick was given his unconditional release on 31 August, he returned to Holyoke as player-manager for the next two seasons. Then Johnny Dobbs selected the 5' 3" Dude to cover shortstop for his Nashville team. His explosive temperament and ongoing battle with Nashville fans boiled over in the summer of 1907 when he briefly left the team, but was allowed to return unpunished. Berny would have to monitor the man he had selected team captain closely.

The Vols faced the strongest local amateur team, the Nashville Athletic Club (N.A.C.), three days later. As expected, the outmanned city team gave up monstrous hits, including a triple by McElveen, a blast that rocked the left field wall. The practice game also marked the appearance of Daubert in a Nashville uniform.

The Chicago Cubs arrived in Nashville on 6 April with aspirations of repeating their 1907 world championship performance. "Baseballically speaking," as Rice wrote, the Vols would be in for quite a tussle. The Windy City foe did not disappoint. Cub pitcher Chick Fraser spun a two-hit gem on the way to a commanding 7–0 victory. Only Wiseman reached base on a pair of harmless singles in the first and last innings. The Nashville infield played poorly, with each position player save Daubert giving up an error while the big leaguers roughed up Hess. McElveen supplied the only surprise by making a leaping catch in left field to prevent the Chicagoans from tallying even more runs.

Berny had seen enough. His squad had not performed well against any major league opponent. Following the game, he hopped on a train bound for Birmingham, where he met with his long-time friend Lajoie, whose team was in town to play a series with the Barons. Berny's visit was no clandestine operation. Rice and Yancey informed Nashville readers that the skipper was shopping for an outfielder. No details exist about the meeting, and Berny returned to Nashville with no immediate announcement.

The Cubs made quick work of the Vols in their final meeting on 7 April. Chicago's agile second baseman, Johnny Evers, provided the defensive gem of the game when he robbed Wiseman of a base hit with "a World Series leap" on a sharply hit line drive. The Chicago infield excited the local fans with one of its celebrated Tinker-to-Evers-to-Chance double plays. In contrast, the Nashville infield defended weakly as McCormick, Jansing, and Butler each committed errors. Ewing focused on the miscues at second and concluded that Butler did not "have the noodle [intelligence] to play the keystone sack."[34] An estimated four thousand patrons had packed into Sulphur Dell to watch the World Champions manhandle the Vols, 7–2.

Patsy Donovan then arrived with his Brooklyn Superbas for a couple of games against the Vols. Welcome news greeted Berny as Donovan formally handed over rookie pitcher George Hunter for the 1908 season. Berny immediately pressed the versatile, left-handed sidewinder into service. George Henry Hunter was born on 8 July 1887, in Buffalo, New York, the twin brother of William Hunter.[35] Like Butler, Hunter had signed a professional contract when he was still a teenager. He advanced through the ranks, from Buffalo to Wilkes-Barre to Brooklyn in 1907. While Hunter was a pitcher by trade, he was also an accomplished batter and fielder. He could fill the role of a utility player — an invaluable commodity at all levels of baseball.

Vols fans were not disappointed in Hunter's first appearance as he threw five innings of two-hit, shutout ball against his former teammates. Then, the newest Vols member retired to his alternate position in center field. Heavy rain brought the game to a sudden close in the eighth, but the 1–0 loss did not dampen Berny's spirits; the arrival of Hunter had filled two gapping holes in his roster by adding a starting pitcher and a fleet-footed, switch-hitting center fielder. Every team in the league sought one solid utility man for its roster, and Hunter showed great promise in filling that role for Nashville. The contest also coincided with the long overdue arrival of the Duggan brothers. Berny now had his complete pitching staff on hand. McElveen had impressed the Brooklynites, especially owner Charlie Ebbets, with two extra-base hits.

The Vols' preseason began to take a turn for the better in their final meeting with the Superbas. Berny's club scored three times in the first inning and unleashed an eleven-hit attack. Catcher Seabough led the onslaught with three hits and a home run that smashed off the right field scoreboard and rolled around in the Dump. Wiseman demonstrated his skill several innings later by playing a fly ball perfectly at the base of the incline in right field, and threw a runner out at the plate who had tagged from third and attempted to score. Should Wiseman eventually retire from the game, Rice quipped, the Vols would have to replace him with someone "half player and half goat."[36] Sorrell pitched six strong innings and the Nashville infield turned three double plays in the long-awaited victory over a major league outfit.

With the Southern Association opener less than a week away, Berny focused on solidifying his pitching staff. He announced that Sorrell, Duggan, and Hunter would throw the opening series against Atlanta. Berny did not anticipate pitching himself until after the mid–May roster deadline. He wanted to give every pitcher an opportunity to make the team before making the final cuts. Then, the Vols played two uninspired games against local amateurs on 10–11 April. Perdue manhandled Cheek-Neal, and Sitton and Kellum dominated Cumberland Telephone in a lame affair.

The Milwaukee Brewers of the American Association (a higher minor league) paid a visit to Sulphur Dell on 13 April to play the final exhibition contest for both teams. Berny's announced season starters— Sorrell, Duggan, and Hunter — tuned up by pitching three innings each in the 3–2 loss. The lone bright offensive spot was Wiseman's triple with two men aboard in the second, but a hard-throwing Brewer outfielder threw out the greedy Doctor trying to stretch his three-bagger into a home run. With the preseason officially over, the Vols had amassed a mediocre 7–6 record with only one victory against a professional squad. The next time Nashville took the field, it would be to compete in Southern Association action.

In a flurry of last-minute transactions, Berny shed three pitchers. He sold Nelson to Houston, returned Sitton to Jacksonville, and shipped Kerr to East Liverpool in the Ohio and Pennsylvania League. Kerr's brother was given his outright release. In an unexpected move, Berny purchased the contract of Louisville outfielder Johnny Siegle. Siegle promptly announced that he would not go south because his wife could not tolerate the heat. Then a rumor surfaced from Cleveland that Harry Bay would soon be shipped to Nashville. If the Siegle-Bay reports panned out, Berny's outfield would be set. Whitey Morse, the grumbling six-year veteran of the Southern Association, was said to be soon released to a team in either the Ohio and Pennsylvania League or the New England League. The steady improvement of Kid Butler at second base had convinced Berny to risk losing Morse.

In the early morning of 15 April, the Nashville Vols boarded a train for Atlanta to kick off the 1908 season. The local press listed the players making the journey: catchers Hardy and Seabough; pitchers Sorrell, Duggan, Hunter, Perdue, and Hess; infielders Daubert, Butler, McCormick, Morse, and Jansing; and outfielders Wiseman, Decker, and McElveen. Three pitchers, Yerkes, Kellum, and Elmer Duggan, stayed in Nashville to nurse arm ailments. In an era when managers also played, Berny's presence permitted some flexibility on the Vols pitching staff.

Among Bernhard's group there simmered a handful of angry fellows, each with his own grievance. The slugging catcher, Hardy, felt slighted by Nashville management for not receiving a pay raise as a reward for his exceptional

3. Play Ball

1908 Southern Association Champion Nashville Vols. *Back row, left to right:* Ferdinand E. Kuhn, president, Win Kellum (pitcher), Johnny Duggan (pitcher), Jack Hardy (catcher), Carl Vedder Sitton (pitcher), Julius Augustus Wiseman (right fielder), Claud Davis (Sec.-Treas.). *Middle Row, left to right:* George Hunter (pitcher-outfielder), Willis Butler (shortstop), Walter East (second baseman), Bill Bernhard (manager-pitcher), Jake Daubert (first baseman), Johnny Siegle (center fielder), Harry Bay (right fielder). *Front row, left to right:* Hub Perdue (pitcher), Pryor McElveen (third baseman), James Warren Seabough (catcher). Not pictured: Ed Hurlburt (catcher). (*Nashville Banner.*)

offensive performance in 1907. Hunter, too, sprouted ruffled feathers in his belief that Brooklyn had erred in lending him to Nashville. There remained the long-standing negative influences of McCormick, Morse, Sorrell, and Yerkes. Thrown into this mix was the weak defense by McElveen, a disgruntled third baseman who felt insulted when sent to play in the outfield. The Nashville Vols were a dysfunctional lot as they entered league play.

Approximately 6,000 fans crammed into beautiful Ponce de Leon Park in Atlanta for opening day ceremonies. The first day of the baseball season was a festive event. The grandstands were decorated with colorful bunting, and a brass band led a parade of players through the city and into the stadium. Local businessmen and political dignitaries were present and a public figure would toss out the ceremonial first ball.[37] On this special occasion, both teams marched to deep center field, where Atlanta manager Billy Smith hoisted the 1907 league championship banner up the flag pole to the delight of cheering spectators.

Prior to game time, Nashville team captain McCormick handed the Vols' lineup card to Dan Pfenninger, the dean of Southern Association umpires and arguably the best arbiter hired by President Kavanaugh.[38] The batting order reflected the thinking of the Nashville chief on the first day of the new season. It signified who currently commanded Berny's confidence and those who were out of favor:

1. Decker CF
2. Wiseman RF
3. Jansing 3B
4. McElveen LF
5. Seabough C
6. Daubert 1B
7. McCormick SS
8. Butler 2B
9. Sorrell P

Sorrell got off to a shaky start by giving up four runs on four extra-base hits in the first two innings. The Nashville hurler settled down and allowed only three more hits in the final seven frames, but the damage had been done. Nashville's lone tally came in the second when McElveen walked and promptly stole second base. Seabough struck out but Daubert advanced Humpy into scoring position on a ground out. McCormick singled McElveen home for the Vols' lone run. Meanwhile, the Atlanta "spit ball boy," Russell Ford, appeared very sharp and limited the Vols to only two singles all afternoon.[39]

Newspapermen rarely joined teams on the road, but Rice did accompany the Vols to Atlanta. He noted that the Vols infielders looked lethargic and insipid in comparison to the chattering Crackers. Back in Nashville, President Kuhn ordered construction of a "detail"— an inning-by-inning line score hung on a rectangular slate board outside Sulphur Dell — so local fans could follow the game's progress.[40]

There was an unspoken message in the starting lineup for the Vols who did not start the contest. Hardy, the team batting leader in 1907, rode the pines as did Whitey Morse and George Hunter. Late in the game Morse replaced the error-prone Jansing at third base and Hardy pinch-hit for Decker, who was in a horrible preseason slump. Berny also was eager to find out more about Johnny Duggan.

John Duggan was born on 3 October 1883, near Acton, Indiana, to Michael J. and Mary Dean Duggan.[41] He attended Franklin College (IN) from 1903–1905, and received a degree in English while pitching on the school's baseball team. He signed with Vincennes (1905), where he was a teammate of Hub Perdue. The New York Yankees reserved Duggan and released him to Nashville in 1906, where he amassed an unimpressive record: 9–19 (1906) and 8–10 (1907).

Berny sent Duggan to the slab for game two of the series. Bitter cold weather greeted player and spectator alike, but everyone was treated to a hot pitching duel between Duggan and Atlanta's sensation, Roy Castleton. Neither pitcher gave up a run until the fourth when Wiseman walked and stole second. Jansing bunted the little Doctor third. At this crucial moment the

3. Play Ball

April

Mon	Tue	Wed	Thu	Fri	Sat	Sun
		1	2	3	4	5
6	7	8	9	10	11	12
13	14	15 @Atl	16 @Atl	17 @Atl	18 @Atl	19
20 Mont	21 Mont	22 Mont	23 Mont	24 Birm	25 Birm	26
27 Birm	28 Birm	29 @Mont	30 @Mont			

Atl = Atlanta
Birm = Birmingham
L.R. = Little Rock
Mem = Memphis
Mob = Mobile
Mont = Montgomery
N.O. = New Orleans
Bold print= @ Nashville
(2) =Double Header

Atlanta infield erred twice, and combined with a clean single by Daubert, two Vols scored. Neither side hit the ball with authority, and both squads ragged incessantly on the umpire, "Old Dan" Pfenninger. In the final frame, the Vols pushed a security run across the plate, but the thrilling action came in the bottom half when Atlanta loaded the bases with only one out. Jansing — an unlikely defensive hero — turned in the gem of the afternoon when he snagged a hard-hit line drive and stepped on his base to complete a double play and end the game. In the contest, Daubert snared sixteen putouts at first base, and Hardy stole two bases — perhaps in an effort to showcase his hustle and win back Berny's favor.[42] The final game of the series was rained out, and the Vols returned home to open their new stadium in a brief homestand with Montgomery and Birmingham.

The 1908 Nashville Vols' baseball operation faced many challenges. The club not only competed for the commercial entertainment dollar, but it also battled for space in the local press with the gripping stories of the day, such as the Democratic gubernatorial race and prohibition. The Nashville Base Ball

Club was confronted with serious personnel obstacles as well. Berny inherited a team torn by dissension and selfishness. He sensed the disruptive attitudes of McCormick and Morse, and he was also unsure of Sorrell and Yerkes. Hardy was blatantly angry over his contract dispute, and it interfered with his ability to perform on the field. McElveen's unwillingness to convert to the outfield still festered and would have to be addressed. The only bright spot was the reliable performance of Wiseman.

Bernhard experienced considerable frustration in his attempt to attract competitive athletes to Nashville. He had filled three holes by finding a quality first baseman and a pitcher/utility man. Daubert appeared to be the answer to the first need, and Hunter took care of the second and third. Berny was not yet sure of newcomers Butler and Kellum, and Siegle continued to hold out.

Nashville sportswriters Rice, Yancey, and Ewing captured the spirit of the upcoming season for their readers. Each scribe enjoyed picking heroes, goats, and villains. They also contributed to the rumor mill by naming potential new acquisitions and generated excitement for the 1908 baseball campaign. Furthermore, the location of the sports page in all three daily newspapers had become standardized, and signified the growing priority given to sporting news. Prior to the onset of the season, the *Banner* put sports stories on the last page of each edition, whereas the *American* and *Tennessean* positioned their articles wherever space allowed (never on page one). With the hiring of Rice, the *Tennessean* placed its sports news on page six, after the national and local news and editorial page.

Spring training accomplished its main task; it had exposed glaring weaknesses in the Vols' lineup and defensive alignment. While the team beat university and athletic clubs with ease, they fared less successfully against professional talent, owing to a porous defense, inconsistent offense, unsettled pitching staff, and questionable team morale. These infirmities had not gone unnoticed by Berny, and the next month leading to the final roster cut on 15 May would reconfirm his worries and necessitate changes.

Chapter 4

More of the Same

The first quarter of the season, up to the weekend doubleheader at the end of May, would reveal whether the '08 Vols had improved themselves. In the thirty games to be played over these six weeks, the Vols would face every Southern Association opponent at least once. In the meantime, Berny assessed his player pool, adding and trading players before the roster deadline on 15 May. The early portion of the schedule did not favor Nashville as they played twenty games on the road. By the time the club returned to the familiar surroundings of Sulphur Dell in June, Berny had gone to great lengths to strengthen his team. To the manager's mounting frustration, however, his Nashville Vols continued to play at a break-even level.

The Vols returned from their season-opening road trip in Atlanta to a city eager to embrace its untested heroes. Manager Jimmy Ryan brought his Montgomery Senators to town for a four-game tilt riding high after a three-game sweep of the Birmingham Barons. The Senators fielded a revamped club with only one returning player from the 1907 team. An estimated 4,400 fans cheered as Nashville Mayor James S. Brown threw out the first ball at 3:30 p.m., the starting time for all Vols home games. Prior to the first pitch, Berny was forced to substitute Morse for second baseman Kid Butler, who sustained an injury in pregame warm-ups.

Nashville tallied three runs in the bottom of the second inning on doubles by Daubert, McCormick, and Hunter. Hunter, the Vols starter, kept the bases clear for seven innings, and did not allow a single Senator to hit the ball out of the infield. The southpaw faded in the late innings, however, and the visitors held a 3–2 lead going into the bottom of the ninth. In the Vols' last at-bat, Hunter led off with a base on balls and moved into scoring position following a sacrifice bunt by Wiseman. With two outs, Berny called upon Hardy to bat for the hitless Jansing. The catcher did not disappoint his teammates. He drove a single into left field to score Hunter and tie the game. The game then settled into a pitchers' duel for six scoreless innings. Montgomery mounted a threat in the fourteenth when Clayton Perry led off with a double, but Seabough threw out the fleet second baseman attempting to steal third. Umpire Brown called the game after three hours of play, owing to darkness. Neither pitcher received a decision despite fifteen innings of work. Offensively, Hunter and McCormick contributed three hits apiece in Nashville's fifteen-hit attack. Archie Persons, a former Nashville outfielder, collected half of the visitors' six safeties. The popular Persons was destined to wear out Nashville pitching over the course of the season.

In the second game, Nashville fielders contributed four errors to the ten hits surrendered by pitcher Sorrell. Persons went 4-for-4 at the plate, drove in two runs, stole three bases, and scored once. Montgomery's shortstop, Joe Pepe, provided additional excitement by stealing three bases, including home plate in the sixth inning. The exploits of the Little Frenchman caused the removal of Hardy for Seabough. In addition, the 19-year-old shortstop turned in three fielding gems to rob Vols batters of base hits.

James Warren Seabough was born 29 October 1879 near Springfield, Missouri, where he attended Greenwood Central High School and Southwest Missouri State College. His amateur baseball background is not known, but Seabough did establish a regional reputation in 1904 as a catcher with Pittsburg (KS) in the Missouri Valley League. In those days, the southwest corner of Missouri and southeast corner of Kansas was a hotbed of professional baseball, and dozens of teams sprung up in small towns. In 1905, Seabough moved to Springfield and played two seasons before advancing to Montgomery in the Southern Association. Forging a reputation as a reliable signal caller, batter, and teammate, Seabough would average eighty games per year beind the dish and bat a respectable .275 in his seven-year tenure in the South.[1]

In preparation for the third encounter with Montgomery, Berny shook up the Nashville lineup. First, McElveen replaced Jansing at third base. Perhaps, Swede was nursing a bruised ego as well as a sore hand, for his many throwing errors were becoming costly. Second, Berny inserted the switch-hitting Hunter in center field to test the versatility of his latest acquisition. Decker had batted a paltry 1-for-17 in the first three games of the season. Third, Berny employed a pinch batter, a relative novelty by Nashville standards. Finally, he inserted Hardy in left field in a continuing search for a player to tie down that corner of the outfield. The team desperately needed the catcher to break out of his funk.

Ryan's Montgomery boys played solid against the revamped Nashville lineup. Again, Persons collected three hits and stolen bases on the afternoon. Hardy's triple in the fourth paved the way for four Vols runs. The Nashville defense sputtered on three costly errors, including a two-run fielding guffaw

Nashville infielders Swede Jansing (l), Mike McCormick (c), P. M. McElveen (r). (Courtesy National Baseball Hall of Fame Library, Cooperstown, N.Y.)

by Scrappy Jack in the sixth that proved to be the margin of victory for the Senators. Duggan failed to duplicate his first outing, and, instead, surrendered twelve hits and six runs in a 6–5 loss. Only 1,500 spectators witnessed the contest that took little more than one hour to play.[2]

Berny sent "The untamed son of Sumner County" to pitch the finale against Montgomery on 23 April. Herbert Rodney (Hub) Perdue was born in the rural hamlet of Bethpage, Sumner County, Tennessee, on 7 June 1882.[3] He entered professional baseball in Vincennes (1905), and many observers considered him raw, undisciplined, and fun-loving. Perdue spent only two seasons in Indiana, and arrived in Nashville in 1907 where he completed an uninspiring 11–15 season. The surrounding cast of Sorrell and Yerkes did little to push Hub toward excellence. Without question, the homegrown Tennessean was a crowd favorite.

A hard-throwing right-hander, Perdue limited the powerful Montgomery lineup to three hits in a masterful performance. He mixed pitches well — a spitball to complement his blazing fastball. But Hub's sharp-breaking curve was his out pitch. Seabough stroked three hits, and McElveen, Daubert, and Hardy all doubled in the slugfest. Perdue even dropped down a bunt single to help his own cause. The Vols pushed across three runs to come from behind in the bottom of the eighth thanks to the timely hitting of Hunter and Daubert. Perdue limited the red-hot Persons to one single, and beat first-place Montgomery, 4–2.[4]

Harry "Dad" Vaughn brought his cellar-dwelling Birmingham Barons to town, but rain canceled the first of the four-game series. A large crowd attended the second game in part because the date coincided with a weekend throng of visitors who had arrived in town to hear the first gubernatorial debate between Patterson and Carmack at the Ryman Auditorium later that evening. The Barons boasted the 1907 league batting champion in first baseman Henry "Buttermilk" Meek, but other than center fielder Carlton Molesworth, the rest of the squad presented little threat.[5]

A large and enthusiastic crowd was treated to a pitchers duel between Jack Hess and Joseph "Chick" Robitaille. Neither hurler allowed a run through six innings and the visitor had thrown a no-hitter to that point. "The general impression that the Barons were a punk lot of wild-eyed ping-pongers was soon lost in the scuffle," noted Rice.[6] The Vols broke the game open in the bottom of the seventh with hits by Hunter, Butler, and McCormick. Submariner Hess helped his own cause by driving in a pair of runs and scoring once. A touch of concern occurred in the top of the ninth when Daubert chased a vagrant throw from McCormick into the basepath, where he was run over by the rotund Meek. The Nashville first baseman crumpled to the turf, but was quickly revived with a bucket of water thrown over his face. The dazed Daubert finished the contest, a Nashville win.[7]

The middle game of the series was practically the antithesis of the previous close encounter between the Vols and Barons. Neither the Vols Hunter nor the Barons' Harry McNeal were sharp on the chilly day. The Barons opened the scoring in the third when second baseman Lewis Walters tripled and was squeezed home by Molesworth. The visitors tacked on three more runs an inning later on two miscues by Jansing at third base. Trailing by a score of 6–1 in the bottom of the eighth, Elmer Duggan, in his first appearance of the season in center field, began the fireworks when he tripled off the left field wall to drive in two runs. With two outs, McElveen smashed a line drive down the right field line past the outstretched mitt of Meek and a diving outfielder, Pat Reagan. Hunter and McCormick scampered around the bases and McElveen ended up on third base. The ball had hit the chalk line, but several Birmingham infielders insisted that McElveen's ball had landed in foul territory. Umpire Tom Brown disagreed and booted out the incensed Walters. Ryan brought in Harvey "Ginger" Clark to slow the carnage, but the Vols had already plated six runs to stage a stunning come-from-behind victory.

The game underscored three of Berny's main concerns. First, leadoff batter Doc Wiseman was not hitting well. In the first seven games of the season, the popular little Doctor had collected only two hits. A notorious slow starter, Wiseman could be counted on to work the kinks out of his swing. Second, Berny decided to bench Decker for his horrendous slow start at the plate. As it turned out, Decker had played his final game in a Nashville uniform. Johnny Siegle decided to report for duty. Finally, in his first appearance in three games, Swede Jansing had committed two more errors at third base. The manager's principal concern now shifted to third base.

John Herbert Siegle shared Hunter's birth date — 8 July — but the Vols center fielder was born in 1874 in Columbus, Ohio.[8] As a young boy, Johnny moved to Urbana, Ohio. He broke into organized ball in 1899 with Dayton, Columbus, and Grand Rapids, but he made his mark in Ilion of the New York State League where he played tremendous defense in the outfield for the next five seasons. In 1904, Siegle accepted a coaching position at Columbia University. Then, Cincinnati invited the 31-year-old to fill in the last month of the 1905 season. He impressed management with a .304 batting average and .446 slugging percentage in seventeen appearances. The prospect of Siegle sticking with the Reds appeared bright, but disaster struck early in the 1906 season when he broke his left ankle. The injury sidelined the middle-aged speedster, but once it healed he was shipped to Indianapolis. He rejoined the Reds for the final 22 games, batted only .118, and played his last game in the Big Show on 7 October 1906. Afterwards, Johnny was sent down to Indianapolis.

In the final meeting between the two tail-enders, Birmingham and Nashville, Berny shook up the batting order to see which players would respond. He dropped Jansing from the clean-up spot and moved him to second base in hopes of reducing his mounting miscues in the field. Yancey had lobbied heavily for the outright removal of Swede in favor of the hard-hitting McElveen, and predicted that Hardy could fill the important fourth spot in the lineup, providing he played up to expectations behind the plate. Berny had settled on a potent combination at the top of the batting order with Wiseman, McCormick, and McElveen.

In the last game against Birmingham, starting pitcher Duggan was far from his best form. He surrendered three runs in the top of the first on four neatly bunched Senator hits. The Vols committed four errors throughout the contest, including two more by the jinxed Jansing from his new location at second base. Wild Swede had fielded six opportunities and Daubert made sensational digs on three of his throws, thus saving the errant one from committing five errors in the contest. The Vols outhit their opponent, led by McCormick's three safeties, but they also outbobbled the Barons on the way to a 4–1 loss. In a sidelight, Yancey and Ewing had each referred to the Vols' stadium by its former name (Athletic Park) in their newspaper coverage of the first homestand. Only Rice used his creation, Sulphur Dell. Apparently, the new moniker would take time to stick.

During the Birmingham series, Yancey printed a letter from a fan who wanted to know when the Vols planned to implement a Ladies Day similar to the program begun in Atlanta. Nashville management responded immediately and offered the fairer sex grandstand seating to twenty-five selected home games for only $1. Kuhn and his associates hoped that the presence of ladies would promote decorum. Ladies traditionally sat in the grandstands; they were seldom found in the bleachers where the harmful rays of the sun could damage their complexion and the presence of lower-class ruffians might cause injury to their reputation.[9]

The Vols had split their six-game homestand with two teams predicted to finish at the bottom of the league. Shaky defense had given up nine errors against Montgomery and ten mistakes against the lowly Barons. The approaching month of May did not bode well for the struggling Nashvillians, who would play twenty-one out of twenty-seven games on the road.[10] Berny was contemplating several drastic personnel changes.

Before the team boarded a train for Montgomery, Berny's ax fell. First, he left Yerkes behind in Nashville, dealt Morse to Dayton (OH) in the Central League, and shipped Decker to Augusta (GA) in the SALLY. The arrival of Siegle, the second-best defensive outfielder in the 1907 American Association, made these changes possible. A rumor circulated that Sorrell would soon be shipped to Kansas City for outfielder Hugh Hill. On the current swing through Montgomery and Birmingham, Berny planned to take a closer look at two pitchers who were potentially on the chopping block — Win Kellum and Elmer Duggan.

Montgomery played its home games at Crampton Bowl, an old wooden structure at the corner of Madison Avenue and Hilliard Street. When the Vols arrived for their four-game tilt on 29 April, Berny was still experimenting with his lineup. He pushed his top three batters back one slot in the order and moved Hardy to leadoff. Daubert dropped back to eighth, and the switch-hitting Hunter fell to seventh. Berny's shakeup worked. Wiseman delivered two singles from the second spot to double his season's output. McElveen provided two hits and played third base in place of Jansing. Inconsistent pitching continued to plague the team, though, as Perdue gave up fourteen hits in six innings. The Gallatin Squash had "lost the buffalo sign" against Montgomery, and absorbed a sobering defeat. Elmer Duggan made a rare relief appearance on the slab to close out the last two frames. Persons, as usual, went 3-for-4 at the plate in his merciless onslaught against Nashville.

The Vols struck quickly in the second game against the Senators. McCormick singled and stole second base in the top of the first, and McElveen clubbed a long double to score him. Thereafter the opposing pitcher held the Vols to

May

Mon	Tue	Wed	Thu	Fri	Sat	Sun
				1 @Mont	2 @Mont	3
4 @Birm	5 @Birm	6 @Birm	7 @Birm	8 **Atl**	9 **Atl**	10
11 **Atl**	12 **Atl**	13 @Mem	14 @Mem	15 @Mem	16 @Mem	17
18 @L.R.	19 @L.R.	20 @L.R.	21 @N.O.	22 @N.O.	23 @N.O.	24 @N.O.
25 @Mob	26 @Mob	27 @Mob	28	29 **Mem**	30 **Mem (2)**	31

Atl = Atlanta
Birm = Birmingham
L.R. = Little Rock
Mem = Memphis
Mob = Mobile
Mont = Montgomery
N.O. = New Orleans
Bold print= @ Nashville
(2) =Double Header

no runs and only three hits. Meanwhile, the Vols' power pitcher, Hess, allowed two runs in the bottom of the opening frame before settling into his rhythm. The crowd rewarded "Heinie" with a standing ovation when he struck out the side in the third inning. However, the Vols lost their second game in two days by an identical score, 4–1, ending the month of April with an unimpressive 4–6 record.

The first of May promised to be an important date for the Nashville club as it marked the long-awaited appearance of Kellum on the mound and Siegle in center. McElveen continued his torrid hitting with a double and a triple. But the game remained scoreless until the eighth inning when the Vols loaded the bases with two free passes and a hit batsman. Seabough drove in the first run on a bloop single that barely cleared the infield, and the newly acquired Siegle pushed two more runs across the plate with a long single to left field. Kellum, the side-wheeling left-hander, handcuffed the Senator batters in a masterful display of changing speeds and earned a 5–0 victory. The five-hit performance of Kellum was a welcome sign to a Nashville pitching staff desperately in need of a lift. The stellar outfield play of Siegle freed Berny to move McElveen permanently to third base and signaled the end of Jansing's services to the club.

In the third game, Berny started another left-hander, Hunter, and boldly penciled in the switch-hitter in the leadoff spot. To make room at the top, Berny dropped Hardy down to the last spot on the card, a decision sure to rankle the haughty catcher. These daily lineup changes were unsettling to the club, but they also illustrate Berny's displeasure with the team's paltry offense. Wiseman and Siegle collected a pair of hits, but the Vols committed three errors (nine for the series), and the Senators threw away four chances (ten for the series). Rice singled out the mental mistakes of Butler at second and the slow performance of McCormick at shortstop. Ewing suspected that the Nashville pitcher-outfielder needed to rest what appeared to be a sore arm. Rice suggested that Berny should drop Hunter from the pitching rotation and make him the everyday center fielder. Wiseman had had a good series at the plate (six hits), and was emerging from his slump. Yet, McCormick began to demonstrate a disturbing pattern — good bat (five hits), no glove (three errors), and lack of hustle. The Vols had dropped three games out of four to the surprisingly competitive Senators, and found themselves in sixth place. Montgomery, on the other hand, had risen to second place behind defending league champion Atlanta.

The bedraggled Vols arrived in Birmingham for four games against the last-place Barons. The Barons played their home games at a field most locals referred to as "the Slag Pile," referring to a steel foundry beyond the outfield wall. The management had worked to bring the ancient stadium, built in the mid–1880s, up to Southern Association standards during the off season. They used rolled sod to cover the bare infield, and added seating to the cramped 600-seat facility. Still, the best way for locals to view a game was to sit atop one of the slag heaps beyond the outfield fence. Rice derisively referred to the Barons as the Slagmen.[11]

In the opener, Duggan evened his record to 2–2 with a much-needed 3–1 victory. McCormick sparked the offense with three base hits and two runs batted in, but also contributed a fielding error. A heavy rain washed out the games set for the fifth and sixth. These canceled contests were rescheduled (by league policy) as doubleheaders after the Fourth of July.

The final game between the Vols and Barons was played on a muddy field in front of the smallest crowd of the year — only 450 fans. Perdue struggled to find his control for the entire game. In the end, he surrendered twelve hits, and Siegle tracked down nine putouts in center field. McCormick tossed in another error, which was becoming a routine occurrence. In the meantime, spitballer Tuck Turner silenced the Nashville batsmen and limited them to only two hits and one unearned run. The Vols ended their road trip with a loss and limped back to Nashville to open a tough homestand against Atlanta.

The Vols welcomed the defending league champions on a cloudy and frigid afternoon amidst much fanfare. The buzz was caused largely in response to the first Ladies Day of the season. Any woman accompanied with a male escort would receive a free ticket to the grandstand. Once the game was underway, the Vols continued to display an anemic offense. Berny failed to manufacture a quick score in the bottom of the first inning with a foiled hit-and-run and a poorly executed double steal. Nashville did generate one run on four walks, although Daubert then struck out with the bases loaded to end the rally. The Vols threatened again in the sixth after loading the bases with two outs. Butler came to the plate and managed only a slow roller to the Atlanta shortstop. In a close play at first base, umpire Brown called the sliding Butler out. A heated argument ensued in which Rice claims Berny employed "an outburst of oratory that would have made Carmack and Patterson look like bush leaguers."[12] The Vols loss marked their sixth one-run performance in the last eight contests.

On 9 May, Kellum and "Hoot Mon" McKenzie (known for his "Highland fling delivery") locked in a tight pitching battle, and both teams played solid defense. Catcher Big Ed Hurlburt threw out three Nashvillians attempting to swipe second base. Wiseman launched a spectacular heave from the base of the Dump in the fourth to cut down Atlanta captain Otto Jordan at the plate. Neither hurler had surrendered a run until the bottom of the fifth when the Vols started the scoring on a bunt single by Daubert with two outs. Hustling down the base path, Jake forced Atlanta shortstop Louis Castro to rush his throw, which cleared the head of 6' 5" first baseman Jim "Claudius" Fox and allowed Siegle to score from third base.

The contest nearly erupted into a brawl a half-inning later. With Nashville clinging to a 1–0 lead, Cracker center fielder George Winters was rounding third base and heading for home when McElveen stuck out his foot and tripped the stocky runner. Winters rolled to the ground, recovered, and scored the game-tying run. The Atlanta bench immediately erupted into a chorus of angry jeers. McElveen returned the barbs in kind, and only the timely end of the inning prevented a violent outburst. Siegle continued to demonstrate his value to the team by scoring again in the seventh on Daubert's second RBI single. Kellum was solid in his second victory of the season, and he seemed to answer one of Nashville's questions in the pitching department.

Berny selected the little-used Stanley Yerkes in the next game to see what he could do before the roster deadline. The New Englander responded with an excellent performance and limited Atlanta to two unearned runs on four hits. Offensively, "too much Hunter and McCormick" described the Vols' offense; the former walked twice and scored three runs while the latter collected three hits and three RBI. Dude and Kid were still shaky in the field, but neither impeded the team's 4–2 victory.

As the roster deadline approached, people began to wonder which Nashville players would be cut loose. The Vols skipper did not wait for 15 May. Three days before the deadline, Berny sent ill-tempered Sorrell, who had been demanding a trade, to his hometown of Ft. Worth, and released Elmer Duggan to New Haven in the Connecticut League. Jansing's release was forthcoming. "Bernhard's ax is falling unmercifully now," reported Hamilton Love in *The Sporting News*.[13]

The next meeting between Nashville and Atlanta promised to be a closely contested affair, and both managers sent their aces in to pitch. Duggan did not look sharp. In the top of the second, the Brooklyn castoff threw two wild pitches, gave up three hits, two bases on balls, and surrendered five runs. The biggest blow, a home run by Roy Moran, cleared Siegle's head in center field. Berny yanked his starter after the sixth hit in less than two innings. Perdue entered in relief and settled the Cracker batters down in six consecutive innings of no-hit ball. Meanwhile, the Vols mounted a comeback in the bottom of the fourth, highlighted by McElveen's bases-loaded triple off the left field wall. By the time the carnage was complete, the Vols had tied the game at 5–5. An appreciative audience began a collection of $50 to be presented to McElveen after the game. Manager Billy Smith removed starter Russell Ford in favor of Grant Schopp. Both Smith and Bernhard were managing as if it were a playoff.

The game calmed down for the next four innings with the score knotted at five runs apiece. In the twilight glow in the top of the ninth inning, Perdue began to fade almost as quickly as the sun. He gave up his first hit in seven innings of relief, followed by a sacrifice bunt and a game-winning single. A Vols threat fell one clutch hit short of tying the game. Lamenting the bitter 6–5 loss that took over two and one-half hours to play, Rice faulted the performances of Hardy and Seabough behind the plate. Neither Nashville catcher could contain the Atlanta baserunners.

The Vols now prepared to embark upon a fourteen-game swing through the Western Division—four games at Memphis, three at Little Rock, four at New Orleans, and three in Mobile. The team would not return until 28 May. President Kuhn offered his athletes a banquet if they could muster a .500 record during the road trip. In addition, Kuhn promised local fans another slate detail on the Sulphur Dell facade to keep track of the Vols' progress while out of town. Later the board was relocated to the east side of the stadium to take advantage of the afternoon shade. Eventually the portable scoreboard was hung inside the Lyric Theater on Cherry Street, where a wireless was set up on stage to receive play-by-play transmissions and fans could sit in comfort instead of standing outside the stadium.[14]

The Vols left on their extended journey with a significant acquisition from the major leagues; Cleveland had released Harry Bay to Nashville. At one time Deerfoot was considered "the fastest ball player in captivity," quipped Rice, and his talent had been sought by every manager in the Southern Association.[15] Once clocked on a stop watch from plate to first in 3.5 seconds, Harry Bay was considered by many contemporary baseball authorities to be the fastest man in the American League.[16] A photographer experimenting with a motion picture camera filmed Deerfoot in full stride, and newspaper reports commonly referred to the speedster as "a ten-second man in the 100 yard dash." Bay utilized this blazing foot speed to forge a reputation marked by splendid base running, spectacular catches, and acrobatic dives. At the plate, he mastered the chop swing and slash bunt to further exploit his natural talent. A left-hander, Bay played both sides of the game — offense and defense — with reckless abandon. He was especially adept at sliding headlong into first base on particularly close plays. One account mused that Bay was so slender — 5' 8" and 138 lbs.— that he didn't even cast a shadow on sunny days and merited a second nickname: "Sliver," which qualified him as one of the slightest men in professional baseball.

Harry Elbert Bay was born on 17 January 1878, in Pontiac, Illinois, to George and Martha Springer Bay. At age five, Harry's family relocated to Peoria, where he played sandlot baseball and developed into "an all-around high school athlete." Upon graduation, Bay barnstormed the Midwest on an all-star team that included a young pitching prospect from Rock Island and future Hall of Famer, Joe McGinnity. A stellar fielder and base stealer, Bay attracted professional attention, and he signed with independent Lincoln (IL) in 1898.

Bay rose rapidly through the minor circuits. Playing for Rock Island (Three-I League) and Troy (New York State League) in 1899, he moved on one year later to Detroit (minor American League) and Marion (Inter-State League). His break came in 1901 with an outstanding performance at Indianapolis (American Association), where he hit .303, stole 24 bases, and fielded .949, and Cincinnati inked the fleet-footed outfielder. Bay appeared in his first major league contest on 23 July 1901 against Pittsburgh. He batted leadoff and played center field in 41 games but hit a disappointing .217 and spent much of the next season on the bench, owing to his inability to hit southpaws.

Released by the Reds in May, 1902, Bay promptly jumped to the American League Cleveland Blues, who were desperately seeking a replacement for injured left fielder Jack McCarthy and right fielder Elmer Flick. Harry starred in his first game, collecting a pair of singles, a double and stolen base, and initiated a double play from the outfield. The following day he hit safely in three plate appearances. Although McCarthy and Flick soon returned to the Blues' lineup, Bay had earned a spot. Appearing in 108 games, he batted .290 and swiped 22 bases. At one point, Deerfoot had a 26-game hitting streak. Moreover, he led all American League center fielders with a .973 fielding percentage. A personable fellow, Bay made an impression on the Washington, D.C. police, who fined him $25 for autographing the Washington Monument.

Bay's breakout season was 1903. He was comfortable in the leadoff role (.292 average), and he pilfered 45 bases to lead the American League. He placed high in other offensive categories as well: 579 at-bats (second), 169 hits (fourth), 94 runs scored (fifth), 201 times on base (ninth), 18 sacrifice hits (ninth), and 12 triples (tenth). Bay's personal life also began to take off with his marriage to Lelia Ballinger. In the offseason, the newlyweds joined the vaudeville act of Guy Kibbee — an actor destined to stardom on the silent silver screen. Harry was an accomplished cornet player.

By his own admission, Bay suffered from running on hard base paths. Sustaining a major knee injury in 1904, he slumped to .241 but still managed to steal 38 bases and dazzle crowds with his athleticism in the outfield. On 19 July, Bay registered 12 outfield putouts in a 12-inning contest against Boston to set a major league record. Less than two weeks later, he tracked down a towering fly ball launched by a Washington batter to the deepest part of the park. Turning his back to the plate, Deerfoot made a spectacular over-the-shoulder grab bare-handed.

Bay recovered sufficiently in 1905 to post some of the most impressive numbers of his career. He clubbed a personal best .301, nabbed 36 bases, and banged out 166 hits (fifth in A.L.). Twice he tallied five hits in a single game. On the same day that he became the first American Leaguer that season to reach the coveted 100-hit mark (July 27), he jammed his left shoulder while diving into a bag. Several days later, he aggravated his knee after slipping and sliding for fly balls on a muddy field. The lame Deerfoot played sporadically for the remainder of the season, and the damaged knee would plague him for the remainder of his baseball life.

Sidelined for much of his last two years in Cleveland, the frustrated Bay asked to be traded to Boston on 14 June 1907. "Maybe there can be torture more acute to an ambitious ball player than sitting stock while his teammates are out there hustling for victory," revealed Bay, "but I've yet to learn what it can be."[17] A trade never materialized, and adoring fans sent Bay a loving cup in appreciation of his contributions to Cleveland baseball. He literally limped through his last major league game on 3 May 1908. His eight-year batting and fielding numbers (.277 and .968) are above-average. More significant was Bay's 169 stolen bases, largely accomplished over four healthy seasons. When Cleveland skipper Nap Lajoie shipped Bay to Nashville, the outfielder was reunited with his former Blues teammate, Berny and Hardy. The Bay announcement made front-page headlines in *The Sporting News*, but his presence increased the Vols roster to sixteen players.[18]

League president Kavanaugh immediately recognized the roster issue and sent a letter inquiring into Berny's status on the team. The Nashville field general assured the league mogul that he would remain inactive unless the team needed him, and then he would release one player. Every manager in the league manipulated their roster as a matter of common practice. At the end of the month, Kavanaugh meted out a stiff penalty to Montgomery for using sixteen players and the Senators forfeited two victories to Memphis.[19] All Southern Association clubs acted as watchdogs and carefully monitored each other's transactions. Charges of impropriety, whether legitimate or not, were common. Frustrated, Kavanaugh announced on 9 June that he would dispatch an auditor to every head office to examine club books to determine eligibility of rostered players.[20]

The Vols traveled to Memphis to face their instate rival, but rain washed out the first game. On 14 May, Berny inserted Bay in the lineup to lead off and

Harry Bay. (Courtesy National Baseball Hall of Fame Library, Cooperstown, N.Y.)

play left field. The Memphis Turtles were managed by Charlie Babb, a native of Portland, Oregon, and no stranger to Southern Association baseball. His nines played at Red Elm Park, a stadium built in 1896 and located on bottoms land near a bayou that emptied into the Mississippi River. The surface of the infield rose dramatically to the pitcher's slab in order to improve drainage. Consequently, the diamond resembled the back of a turtle, which directly influenced the team's nickname. Located between Jefferson and Madison avenues and Edgeway and Dunlaps streets, Red Elm Park seated 3,000 fans. Its left field wall stood 424 feet from home plate, and fans sat behind roped-off sections in the recesses of the cavernous outfield during overflow games.[21]

Over the years, an intense commercial rivalry had developed between Memphis and Nashville, and it carried over in baseball as well. "Nashville fans would rather beat Memphis than any other team on the whole circuit," proclaimed Yancey.[22] Berny, disappointed in Duggan's previous two-inning performance, tossed him right back in to pitch the series opener. Babb chose Bill Chappelle, a former body guard to President Theodore Roosevelt, to pitch for the Turtles. The contest marked the first time in Nashville's season where two umpires officiated the same game.

Babb demonstrated the importance of this game when he manufactured a run in the bottom of the first inning on a double steal. Duggan, however, settled down and shut down the Turtles for the next four innings. When the Nashville bats erupted in the fourth, eight Vols batters stepped to the plate and scored four runs. The bottom of the order supplied most of the firepower as the number four through eight batters (McElveen, Seabough, Siegle, Daubert, and Butler) each scored a run. Bay delivered a two-run single, but he appeared fatigued from his long train trip from Cleveland. Duggan handcuffed the Turtles on eight hits and earned a 6–2 victory.

Several days later, President Kavanaugh announced a plan to standardize the record-keeping by official scorers in league contests. His press release explained how to score the double steal, which had increasingly entered managerial strategy in 1908. Kavanaugh also clarified the difference between a fielder's choice and a sacrifice for the official scorers. Specifically, he did not want a batter to be credited with an at-bat in sacrifice situations. On the other hand, an at-bat should be recorded in a fielder's choice.[23]

The Memphii turned to Ralph Savidge, the "finger-nail artist," to pitch the second game against the Vols' Hess.[24] Brilliant defensive plays by both squads dominated the errorless game, although the Vols produced baserunners in every inning. Berny unleashed his speedster, Bay, who walked three times, stole three bases, and scored three runs. He attempted to steal third base twice, but was sent back due to fouls. Had Bay successfully swiped five bases, he would have set a single-game club record. Early in the game Turtles catcher Dan O'Leary had difficulty hanging onto the floating knuckleballs being thrown by "the Human Whipcord." The scorekeeper leveled two passed balls on O'Leary and two wild pitches on Savidge after only three innings, and the Vols coasted to a 5–1 victory behind Hess.

The moral of this game did not escape the astute Berny, as speed on the basepaths obviously disrupted the Turtles' defense. The Vols now possessed a fleet of quick players in the persons of Bay, Butler, Siegle, Hunter, Bay, and Wiseman. Wiseman and Daubert were proficient bunters, adding to the team's offensive arsenal. Daubert and McCormick showed improvement as contact hitters, especially with runners in scoring position. McElveen and Seabough supplied power. The immediate impact of Bay's arrival was the benching of Hardy, who had been playing uninspired baseball, mostly in left field. Scrappy Jack made no appearances in the Memphis series, and caught only the final game of the next road series in Little Rock. Now that the offense was beginning to gel, Berny turned his attention to the inconsistent pitching staff.

Memphis desperately sought a victory in the final game against Nashville, but it was a depleted squad. Every one of the regular infielders was stricken by fever and unavailable with the exception of their fine shortstop, Will "The Cuban" Cranston. Prior to the previous day's game, Berny released Jansing, who was immediately picked up by the short-handed Turtles. Swede played less than a month for Memphis and Little Rock, and then went west to play in the renegade California League. The Vols played solid defense behind Hunter. "The Volunteers displayed perfect work," lauded Rice, "that bordered on the sensational at times."[25] With the game knotted at 2–2 in the top of the ninth, Daubert singled and Butler sacrificed him to second base. Then Hunter, the hero of the game, slashed a base hit between first and second base to drive in the go-ahead run and produce his second RBI for the day. In the bottom of the last frame, Daubert rose to the occasion defensively by snaring a hard-hit line drive off the bat of O'Leary to squelch a Turtle rally and end the game.

The three-game sweep of the Turtles did a lot to improve the attitude of the Vols. The players recognized the psychological lift Bay had provided, and someone playfully nicknamed him "the Spider." After the game, Berny invited the team to a victory celebration at a newly opened soda fountain. Then it was off to Little Rock.

SOUTHERN ASSOCIATION STANDINGS, MAY 16, 1908

	W	L
Montgomery	14	8
Atlanta	13	8
Mobile	14	10
Memphis	12	10
Nashville	10	10
New Orleans	10	15
Little Rock	10	15
Birmingham	6	14

No one expected much from Mike Finn's Little Rock club before the season began. Then "the Little Irishman" picked up a young center fielder by the name of Tris Speaker. Speaker and his overachieving teammates had figured out the Vols, and they would give them all they could handle throughout the season. In the first encounter, Perdue silenced the home team bats at West End Park by mixing his pitches well between a blazing fastball and a spitter. Nashville pulled out a 5–3 win based largely on their new asset — superb base running. Due to Bay's disruptiveness as the leadoff batter, Wiseman started to see better pitches in the second slot. Doc responded by clubbing three hits off Joe Connelly to lead the Vols.

The second Little Rock contest spotlighted the efforts of two fine pitchers, the side-wheeling Kellum and Bill Hart. "Old Baldy," or "Uncle Billy," had started his professional career with Chattanooga in the Southern League back in 1885. He earned a reputation as the workhorse of the staff, and sometimes pitched four days in a row.[26] "Old Methuselah," as Rice called him, was forty-three years old and the oldest pitcher in the league. Although he had difficulty facing the left-handed bats of Bay, Daubert, and Kellum — who collected all of the Nashville hits except for one — Hart delivered the goods when it counted and struck out five Vols with runners in scoring position. Southpaw Kellum was not nearly as sharp. He issued four walks, committed two throwing errors, and gave up three hits to Speaker, who also scored twice. Indeed, the future Hall of Famer raced all the way from first base to home plate when Kellum fumbled a bunt off the bat of Traveler second baseman Walter East and then threw the ball into right field. The outfield kept busy as Bay climbed the left field wall to rob East of a long drive, and Wiseman made a similar play in right field to take extra bases away from Speaker. Little Rock's win ended the Vols' winning streak at four games.

Little Rock jumped all over Nashville in the final game of the series. Hess surrendered four singles and two runs in the first, and the game quickly turned into a laugher. When the home team rocked Heinie for seven runs in five innings, Berny turned to Yerkes for relief but the onslaught continued. The game was mercifully called after 6½ innings so the Vols could catch a train for New Orleans. Little Rock pounded out fifteen hits and cruised to a 10–1 win. Speaker and East combined for six hits and outhit the entire Nashville team.

The last Little Rock game saw the return of Hardy to the lineup. Scrappy Jack had not played in the previous five games and had not caught in over a week. Some believed that Berny was about to release another player. Yancey predicted that either Hess or Yerkes should fall victim "to the pruning knife." Others believed that Hardy was the leading candidate to be cut loose.[27]

The Vols arrived in the Crescent City to face the perennial favorite of Southern Association baseball. New Orleans played in refurbished Sportsman's Park, a downtown stadium that seated 5,000 fans.[28] Managed by the great intimidator, Charley Frank, the Pelicans had limped off to an uncharacteristic slow start in 1908. Still, their pitching staff—"Gulfport" Jack Ryan, Bill Bartley, Theodore "Whitey" Guese, and Ted Breitenstein—was the envy of the league, for each hurler had seen major league service.

Duggan faced Ryan in the opener, but neither team mounted an offensive threat or rally for thirteen scoreless innings. The crucial moment of the game occurred in the bottom of the tenth when Duggan intentionally walked outfielders Joe Rickert and Bristol Lord to load the bases with two outs. Rickert and Lord commanded respect from opposing pitchers with good reason. Both men were skilled hitters. The strategy worked in Nashville's favor when the next batter, third baseman George Rohe, grounded out to Duggan to end the threat. The marathon contest was called after 2½ hours on account of darkness. The playoff atmosphere of this first encounter between the two clubs would be an omen.

The second game on 22 May marked another tight pitching match-up between Hunter and Bill Bartley. The Vols pitched well enough to win by scattering six Pelican hits, but the defense behind him fell apart, committing five errors. Each infielder had a role in the collapse. The Vols were still in the game when they scored a run in the top of the seventh to close the gap to 2–1. Then McCormick ran them out of a potential rally when he was thrown out at the plate trying to score from first base on McElveen's double. Berny also fretted about Bay's condition; Deerfoot had been in a woeful 4-for-28 slump since his triumphant arrival, and he went hitless in the New Orleans series. The listless Vols dropped the game, 4–1, and slipped into seventh place, only one game above the lowly Barons.

Nashville duplicated its dismal fielding performance in the third encounter by running up five more errors. Perdue cruised through the first three innings untouched. Then, in the fourth, Pelican batters smashed everything Hub had to offer, and his defenders booted the ball all over the field. "In the seventh inning the diamond was turned into a miniature run-around," quipped Rice, "with the Pelicans doing the running."[29] The Pelicans scored seven runs in the final two at-bats to hand the Vols a 10–1 loss. Pitcher Whitey Guese looked phenomenal in allowing only two Vols hits.[30]

Ten errors in consecutive games! The two day marathon of miscues was evenly distributed among the entire team: Bay (1), McCormick (1), McElveen (2), Daubert (1), Butler (1), Hardy (1), Seabough (2), and Hunter (1). Then a report about a potentially serious injury surfaced. Bay re-strained his right knee while diving for a ball in the 10–1 shellacking and had been replaced by Hardy. Seabough and Hunter also nursed "bad whips" [sore arms].[31]

The New Orleans strategy in the final game against Nashville emphasized the finer points of scientific baseball: bunting and basestealing. The crafty Franks was taking advantage of two glaring weaknesses—the inability of Hess to defend his position, and the deep positioning of third baseman McElveen in deference to the Pelican sluggers. Hess threw a typical game for a power pitcher; he struck out six Pelicans but issued five bases on balls and seven hits in a 5–0 loss. The Nashville defense did not self-destruct as it had in the previous two games, although catcher Seabough gave up an unprecedented six stolen bases. The offense continued to sputter, and no one reached third base. The Pelicans had convincingly swept the Vols in three games and "smeared a beautiful coat of whitewash on the visitors from the banks of the Cumberland," noted Rice.[32] On a brighter note, Kid Butler exchanged wedding vows with his sweetheart while the team was in New Orleans.

Berny was in a foul mood at the conclusion of the three-game tilt in New Orleans. He complained that the performance of umpire Brown throughout the series had been "rotten" and implied that he was not an impartial arbiter. The Nashville manager also took exception to the new sod that had been laid in the infield at Sportsman's Park during the "ante season." Despite Charlie Frank's comment that the improvements would be the envy of some major league teams, Berny complained publicly that the playing surface was "awful." Frustrated by poor play by his Vols, Berny might also have been reaching for excuses.[33] He had viewed the New Orleans series as a test of just how much the 1908 Vols had improved over the previous season. The results were hardly flattering; the team owned a five-game losing streak and threatened to retake the cellar while the high-flying Pelicans soared to seven straight victories and moved atop the league standings. As the doubleheader weekend at the end of May approached, the New Orleans and Nashville clubs appeared headed in opposite directions.

The Vols were in desperate need of rejuvenation when they arrived in Mobile to complete their long road trip. The Sea Gulls, skippered by Tom, or "Red," Fisher, were another surprisingly successful team in the early stage of the campaign. In the opener, both teams struggled offensively and registered an unearned run apiece in the sixth inning in front of a sparse crowd at Monroe Park. The score remained deadlocked until the top of the tenth frame when Wiseman drew a walk and moved to second base on McCormick's second hit of the afternoon. With two outs, the little Doctor scurried home on Hardy's game-winning RBI single. Kellum earned his third win. Moreover, the former Cincinnati star was beginning to impress Berny.

The second game between Mobile and Nashville was not a pretty sight as both teams booted the ball for a total of ten errors. Berny had chosen Yerkes to throw and everything remained calm for four innings. Trailing by a score of 1–0, the Vols made a spirited move in the top of the fifth inning. With the bases loaded, McElveen tripled. The stocky third sacker amassed three hits, three runs scored, and four RBI on the afternoon. But the lead slipped away from the Vols in the bottom of the frame through poor pitching and fielding. Hardy was dinged up a couple of times from wild pitches, but the scrappy one stayed in the game. Berny, having seen enough of Yerkes, replaced him with Duggan, and the Sea Gulls were limited to one hit for the rest of the day. Mobile committed a ghastly seven errors in the seventh and eighth innings, which allowed the Vols to score six times and break open the game, 10–4.

Rain canceled the game on 27 May, and the Vols returned to open a twenty-one game homestand against every league opponent except Atlanta. President Kuhn offered to make good on his promise to host a banquet for the team because it had played .500 ball on the road trip. Berny squelched the idea, however. He felt it was too early in the season to celebrate anything. Indeed, the wounded warriors owned sixth place with an uninspiring 14–15 record. Something needed to change. And soon![34]

The first six weeks of the season had been instructive. The initial housecleaning had removed Sorrell, Morse, Decker, and Jansing. Then Berny added Daubert, Siegle, Kellum, and Bay. By the end of May, the Vols fielded a very quick outfield in Bay, Siegle, Wiseman, and utility player Hunter. The infielders were slow, but might be built around the reliable play of Daubert at first base. McElveen and McCormick played inconsistent defense but contributed solidly on offense. Butler remained a question mark because he played tentatively and seemed uncomfortable at second base. Berny did not doubt the instincts and skills of Kid as an infielder; perhaps he was simply out of position.

Not one of the pitchers had stepped forward to take command of the staff. Hunter (2–2) showed promise, but he pitched inconsistently, offering Berny more as a utility outfielder and batter. Perdue (2–3) looked sharp or dull on any given start. The hard-throwing Hess (2–4) had been the biggest disappointment, followed by Yerkes (1–1), who lacked either dedication or desire. Duggan (4–3) had thrown the most innings, but the workhorse seemed as mediocre as the rest of the herd. The genuine surprise in the pitching rotation was Kellum (3–1). Despite Win's sore arm and propensity to change speeds by throwing slow, slower, and slowest, he alone had produced positive results. Baffled over the pitching puzzle, Berny realized he might have to call upon himself to hurl a few innings in the near future.

The catching department posed more questions. To this point in the season, two players shared the responsibility. Seabough possessed a dependable bat but he could not make the long throw to second base to put out anyone attempting to steal. Hardy, on the other hand, kept opposing runners honest but had lost his eye at the plate. Moreover, Hardy continued to carry a grudge from his failure to receive a raise in salary. If only Berny could strap Seabough's head onto Hardy's body. Good catching, as always, was hard to find. Thus Berny kept on the lookout for a suitable replacement.

Nashville's relative ease in acquiring Daubert, Hess, and Bay from Cleveland was beginning to attract national attention. Members in the National Commission were beginning to suspect that Cleveland was using Nashville as a farm club, which was against the rules. Unless Hess's contract with Springfield was clarified, and the official status of Daubert and Bay with Cleveland was publicly disclosed, the body might be forced to levy fines against both major and minor league clubs. In the worst scenario, they would rescind Nashville's right to these players.[35]

Berny's leadership style had had a settling effect on the team as well. An imposing figure, Berny towered over his smaller players, yet he chose to command the team with quiet resolve. Defending his players on the field and in the press, Berny addressed personnel problems directly, and demonstrated an aptitude for evaluating talent. He understood who to keep and who to trade away. However, Berny also dealt with his lineup card in a most unconventional way. In the first month, he experimented with the batting order in order to find combinations that would work. But when it came to substitutions or last-minute lineup changes, the Vols manager usually inserted player-for-player without regard for batting prowess, thereby missing an opportunity to make his lineup more potent by constructing it on offensive ability. At times, the Nashville lineup lacked cohesion.

The Vols had just finished their longest road trip of the season — a two-week western swing through Memphis, Little Rock, New Orleans, and Mobile. Despite the team's current sixth-place position in the standings, the race from top to bottom was hotly contested as only five games separated the top seven teams. Thus far, the first-place Montgomery Senators emerged as the surprise, not Nashville.

Berny's patience was drawing to a close. He realized that time was running out and his Vols needed to improve. The twenty-one-game homestand presented an opportunity to reverse the current trend and compete successfully against the elite teams. The overriding question remained whether the Vols players would stay within their losing comfort zone or push each other to become champions of the Southern Association.

The month of June, filled with so much promise, would usher in several unforeseen crises that would shake the club to its very foundation.

Chapter 5

Month of Crises

June provided the Vols with an opportunity to turn their misfortunes around and live up to the lofty expectations set by management and their fans. Optimists viewed the coming twenty-one game homestand at Sulphur Dell as a hopeful turning point in the team's fortunes. As June unfolded, however, scandal rocked the Southern Association in incidents concerning player-umpire relations, Sabbatarianism, and allegations that players were fixing games. Job insecurity for managers and players alike affected all teams and fostered several roster changes for the Nashville Vols. While the anticipated doubleheader in late May (which marked the quarter-point in the season) against the Memphis Turtles promised to be exciting, the team continued to languish near the cellar. The Vols then suffered a serious setback that threatened to worsen the team's already bleak standing in the league. Indeed, the disappointment of the first part of the season paled in comparison to the crisis the Nashville team faced.

Inappropriate player deportment had always been a leading concern to President Kavanaugh. The Southern Association, like other minor league circuits, suffered from coarse, rowdy, and rough behavior on the field. As the Vols were wrapping up their road series in Memphis, an ugly incident occurred in New Orleans that served notice to Kavanaugh and team owners that some players preferred this rollicking brand of baseball. On 16 May, the Pelicans hosted the front-runners from Montgomery. In the contest, Montgomery first baseman John "Moose" Baxter took exception to the officiating of umpire John O'Brien. O'Brien, an ex-constable from the Bowery noted for his short temper, tossed the foul-mouthed Baxter out of the game for excessive arguing. The beefy first baseman refused to leave the field, and a shoving match ensued that resulted in a full-scale fistfight at home plate. Baxter got the upper hand, threw the official to the ground, and pummeled him relentlessly. People sitting in the crowd were so disgusted by the brutality of the attack that the stadium quickly emptied of most patrons. Police officers finally restored order on the diamond and hauled both parties off to jail. Although O'Brien admitted to throwing the first punch, the municipal judge released him. Baxter, on the other hand, spent the night behind bars.[1]

Montgomery manager Jimmy Ryan complained in the *New Orleans Times-Picayune* that O'Brien had the beating coming to him. The court agreed that Baxter had acted in self-defense, and released him. President Kavanaugh was not amused. He fined both combatants $25, and suspended each man for ten days. The editor of *The Sporting News* lobbied for the expulsion of both men from the game forever. O'Brien nursed two broken ribs, injured pride, and heard about threats from New Orleans players that he would receive a bigger beating the next time he officiated in the Crescent City. Within four weeks the arbiter resigned and returned to calling balls and strikes in the more familiar confines of the New England League. Baxter, a fan favorite in Montgomery, could not stay out of trouble, so Ryan dealt the second-year player to New Orleans less than one month after the incident.[2]

Repercussions from the Baxter episode reached a climax two months later when the Senators again squared off against New Orleans. Ironically, the second brouhaha erupted with Baxter wearing Pelican flannels. Two fans seated in the stands, so the story goes, had rained vulgar epithets on Baxter, who had been coaching first base. Late in the contest, Baxter snapped, climbed into the stands, dragged the obnoxious patrons onto the field and proceeded to mete out justice. New Orleans first baseman Charlie Dexter rushed to assist his teammate, and the melee was on. Again, it took the police to restore order, and the four brawlers were hauled off to jail and charged with disturbing the peace. President Kavanaugh called for stiffer penalties in Baxter's case, and Frank sold his troubled first baseman to Johnstown (PA) shortly thereafter.[3]

Kavanaugh faced another public relations matter that held moral overtones—playing games on the Sabbath. Sunday blue laws were strongly enforced in the evangelical South at the turn of the century. Yet, every Southern Association team was acutely aware of the potential large receipts that could be garnered by playing on many laborers' only day off. But, the ministerial associations of each Southern city in the league had effectively resisted. The Alabama Supreme Court muddied the debate in mid–April when it declared a state law forbidding Sunday baseball unconstitutional. The ruling appeared to open the way for Sunday contests in Mobile, Montgomery, and Birmingham. Yet when New Orleans met Mobile on 10 May for a Sunday encounter, all of the players, managers, and umpires were promptly arrested by the local constabulary. The situation repeated itself twice when Atlanta visited Mobile and when the Sea Gulls traveled to Montgomery for a Sunday tilt. Obviously the issue of playing baseball on Sunday in the state of Alabama was far from resolved. In Nashville, Kuhn strenuously lobbied Mayor Brown without success to permit Sunday baseball. Only New Orleans and Memphis permitted Sunday baseball by local ordinance.[4] Without an explanation, President Kavanaugh's office was silent on the controversial issue.

When Berny prepared his team to open the long homestead against rival Memphis, it came as no surprise that he was reported to be in the market for a quality infielder. Prior to the opening game with the Turtles, the Nashville manager sat down with each player and had a "heart-to-heart talk." The *American* noted that the team, in general, loafed on the bases and lacked overall aggressiveness. "It is very noticeable to the fans," pointed out sportswriter Ewing, "that there is an air of indifference in the playing of several on the roster."[5] Players presumed to be on their way to Nashville included second baseman George "Rabbit" Nill from Cleveland and an undisclosed middle infielder from Little Rock.

Understanding the nature of the baseball business, Berny realized that the Vols' fortunes would have to improve in order to keep his own job secure. Already, Birmingham skipper Harry Vaughn had been replaced by outfielder Carleton Molesworth. Molesworth, thought to be one of the oldest players in the league, had taken over a Barons team in the throes of a horrendous losing streak and buried in last place. Berny knew that Vaughn's fate awaited him too if his Vols did not reverse their losing ways.

Excitement permeated the city as the Vols returned to Sulphur Dell after a seventeen-day absence. Not only did the hated opponent, Memphis, heighten interest in the game, but it was also Ladies Day. In fact, President Kuhn had tabbed every Friday for the remainder of the season as a special promotion for the ladies. In addition, two hundred newsboys from the *American*, most of them black, were allowed to parade in the streets with the baseball band prior to the game and were given free admission in the segregated portion of the bleachers. The hype was intensified with the introduction of Harry Bay to local fandom.[6]

The Memphis squad was a banged up lot. Forced to play outfielders at catcher and third base, the undermanned Turtles offered little resistance to a Vols team eager to please its loyal rooters. Apparently, Berny's closed-door meeting with the individual players had had its effect. Vols bats erupted for sixteen hits, led by McElveen and Butler, who produced three hits apiece for the second game in a row. The hometown heroes treated the fans by hitting balls off the outfield palisade, beating out bunts for hits, and playing scientific baseball — a suicide squeeze, two delayed steals, and several double steals. Deerfoot proved to be an immediate fan favorite by beating out two slash bunts for base hits and taking part in a delayed and double steal. His presence added a major league brand of hustle that had been sorely missing from the Nashville lineup. The Vols won by a lopsided score, 9–1, but not before Wiseman squeezed the last run across the plate in the bottom of the eighth inning. This action clearly demonstrated that there was no love lost between these two teams.

An estimated 4,000 fans practically filled Sulphur Dell to watch the first twin bill of the season on 30 May — a date which later evolved into the traditional Memorial Day doubleheader. In the opener, the fans were treated to a fine thirteen-inning pitching performance between Johnny Duggan and Ralph Savidge.[7] The latter scattered seven hits and won his own game in the thirteenth with a double into the right-center field gap to score second baseman Harry Redmond for the game's only run. Nashville put McElveen and Siegle on base in the bottom of the frame, but failed to score. The game marked the second time Duggan had lost a thirteen-inning affair, and the first time he had been scored upon in thirty innings of work.

In the shortened second game, Hess assumed the pitching duties, but Ewing noted in the *American* that the starter was "wilder than a March hare." Groggy infield play by Butler at second (two errors) and two wild pitches by Hess allowed two uncontested runs, which supplied most of the damage in a 5–2 Vols loss. Bay continued to please the home crowd with a single, double, and stolen base. Then both teams boarded the same train at Union Station and headed for Memphis to make up the rained out game of 13 May. The Turtles did not wish to relinquish home-field advantage, although they had just taken three road games in a row from the Vols. The decision probably owed more to the Nashville municipal ordinance that banned Sunday baseball.

The second occasion for Sunday baseball in Memphis occurred on 31 May. Only three weeks earlier, Jim Buchanan, a Nashville castoff, led Little Rock in a Sunday no-hitter over the hapless Turtles.[8] A lively throng of Nashvillians had accompanied both teams on the train, but the Vols must have left their bats at home. Memphis left-hander Charlie Shields limited the visitors to only one run on four hits. The Vols had opportunities in the third, fourth, and fifth innings, but each time Memphis turned back Nashville with an outstanding defensive play. For example, second baseman Harry Redmond knocked down a hard-hit grounder with his bare hand in the third, picked up the ball, and forced the baserunner out at second base to end the Vols' bases-loaded threat. In the next inning, McElveen scored on Butler's double, but Kid was subsequently thrown out attempting to score on Seabough's double. In the sixth, Nashville put two runners on base, but center fielder Bill Donahue made a sensational diving catch on a lazy fly ball to rob Butler of two RBI and turn away the Vols again. At the conclusion of the game, both teams boarded an eastbound train and returned to Nashville to conclude the series the following day. The Vols, owners of a three-game skid to their west Tennessee foes, were now firmly entrenched in seventh place.

The final game of the series on 1 June featured fine defensive plays by both teams, but two timely Memphis mistakes on the same play opened the door for the Vols. In the fifth inning, with the score knotted at 1–1, Daubert lashed a drive that rolled all the way to the top of the Dump in right field. Butler then sacrificed his teammate to third base. In a rare appearance, catcher Hardy lashed a ground ball to the second baseman, player-manager Charlie Babb, who fielded the ball cleanly. Preoccupied with Daubert standing on third base, however, Babb tossed the ball wide of first baseman George "Scoops" Carey. Daubert scored with ease and Hardy raced around the bases while Carey tracked down the errant throw. Carey compounded the error with an overthrow of his own while attempting to nab Hardy at third, and the Nashville catcher scored. Hardy not only took honors for driving in the go-ahead run, but he also scored twice in Nashville's 3–1 victory. The Vols played snappy defense behind the foxy southpaw, Win Kellum.

The Vols were relieved to see the Turtles leave town. In four games, the locals had committed nine fielding errors, been outhit 39–22, generally outpitched, and absorbed three losses to their rivals. The future did not look any brighter with the New Orleans Pelicans coming to town. The Pelicans boasted fourteen wins in their last sixteen contests, and Rice viewed the upcoming four games the most crucial set of the entire season.

In a puzzling move, Berny selected seldom-used Yerkes to pitch against the streaking New Orleans club. The Vols batters lashed out eleven hits and placed runners in scoring position in almost every frame, but hard-throwing "Whitey" Guese, who would be traded to Montgomery in three days, stranded nine Vols baserunners; six of them died at third base. Hardy provided some fireworks from the coaching box when the umpire ejected him for arguing a close play at first base. The horseshoe the catcher kept in his hip pocket for good luck did him no service this day. The argumentative Hardy's removal signaled a disturbing trend; his expulsion marked the second such occurrence in two weeks. Yerkes faded in the eighth, but Berny pulled his struggling hurler without allowing Duggan enough time to properly warm up. Two insurance runs resulted. Starting pitchers were seldom removed from games in the Deadball Era, even in extra-inning affairs, and Berny usually followed the standard practice. Yet, he had yanked Yerkes twice within a span of six days. Did Berny's quick trigger signal his lack of confidence in the rarely used pitcher? "All in all," concluded Rice in the *Tennessean*, "it was a first class ball game."[9] Both squads played hard, and the nod went to New Orleans, 5–2.

On 3 June, a driving rain caused cancellation of the second game between Nashville and New Orleans. The occasion also marked the observance of Decoration Day on the Tennessee calendar, an important date in Nashville's ex–Confederate community because it commemorated the birth of former president Jefferson Davis. A contingent of Confederate veterans had planned to attend the Vols-Pelican game following their annual observance at the Frank B. Cheatham Bivouac # 1 meeting hall and decoration of graves at Mt. Olivet Cemetery. It appears that the game of baseball had not only lent itself to the growing spirit

June

Mon	Tue	Wed	Thu	Fri	Sat	Sun
1 Mem	2 N.O.	3 N.O.	4 N.O.	5 N.O.	6 Mob	7
8 Mob	9 Mob	10 Mob	11 L.R.	12 L.R.	13 L.R.	14
15 Birm	16 Birm	17 Birm	18 Mont	19 Mont	20 Mont	21
22 @Atl	23 @Atl	24 @Atl	25 @Mont	26 @Mont	27 @Mont	28
29 Atl	30 Atl					

Atl = Atlanta
Birm = Birmingham
L.R. = Little Rock
Mem = Memphis
Mob = Mobile
Mont = Montgomery
N.O. = New Orleans
Bold print= @ Nashville
(2) =Double Header

of nationalism, as represented by the moniker of "the national pastime," but it also served a regional purpose to honor those who fought for the "Lost Cause" — a very significant function in the white community throughout the South.

Perdue took the slab to pitch the second game against New Orleans. The fans interpreted Berny's decision as another surprise move since the Sumner County lad had been erratic so far this season. Unknown to the public, the brash Perdue had gone to Berny several days earlier and complained that he wasn't getting enough work. The lighthearted Hub faced "Ginger" Clark, a hurler just acquired the previous day in a trade with Birmingham. The Vols pounced on the newest Bird in the bottom of the first and scored two quick runs. Perdue proved masterful and scattered seven hits in eight innings. For the second day in a row, Berny called upon Duggan to finish the game. He delivered a perfect frame, and in the bottom of the ninth inning, the dependable Wiseman and McCormick led off with a pair of singles. With two outs, Siegle ripped a walk-off single to center field to win the game. The poetic Rice described Siegle's two-RBI performance in a limerick:

> There once was a player named Siegle
> With a batting eye keen as an eagle;
> When we needed a hit
> On the spheroid he lit
> In a manner most stylishly regal.[10]

Berny came to a heartfelt decision following the game when he released his friend, Jack Hess, to Springfield in the Connecticut League. The decision might have been in response to the National Board's earlier query into the legality of Hess's contract with Nashville. Regardless of the motivation for the move, it marked the final stage of Berny's house-clearing of non-performing athletes. Then manager Bernhard signed his own player contract. It would be a matter of days before the popular skipper took the mound. Berny was acutely aware that his Nashville pitching staff currently ranked dead last in hits-per-game (8.02), and fifth in runs-allowed-per-game (3.13).[11]

Berny wanted to push Duggan to perform up to his potential, and gave the ball to the Hoosier for the third consecutive day in the final game against New Orleans. The Pelicans aided Duggan when they uncharacteristically committed four errors in the opening frame. Bay started the attack by reaching base on a throwing error by third baseman George Rohe. Wiseman then beat out a sacrifice bunt. McCormick followed with a slicing line drive that hopped between the legs of right fielder Frank Delahanty. The ball rolled all the way up the Dump as Bay scurried around the bases and scored. McElveen drew a base on balls to load the bases for Daubert. The lanky lefty wasted no time in driving a Bill Bartley fastball deep into center field for a bases-emptying triple. By the time the dust had settled, Nashville commanded a 4–0 lead. In the fifth, McElveen smashed his trademark hit — a triple — off the clubhouse door on the left field wall. Then, Daubert, the star of the day, drove the third baseman home for his fourth RBI of the afternoon. Bay provided a major league caliber defensive gem in the eighth with one run in and the sacks full of Pelicans. On the crack of the bat, Deerfoot turned his back to home plate and raced to a miraculous over-the-shoulder catch before crashing into the left field wall to kill the New Orleans rally and preserve a 5–2 victory. The series with the favored Birds provided a tremendous lift for the struggling Vols and their fans. On the down side, utility man Hunter nursed a sore arm, missed the entire New Orleans series, and would not return to the Volunteer lineup for two weeks.

A shocking story hit the newspapers which rocked the Southern Association to its foundation — an allegation of thrown games. Back on 22 May, the Memphis Turtles had traded pitcher Otis Stockdale to the Mobile Sea Gulls. Stockdale, a former major leaguer with extensive southern circuit experience, had protested the trade and refused to report to his new team.[12] After a week of sulking, Stockdale finally connected with his new team on the road in Atlanta. Instead of making his debut on the field, however, the disgruntled pitcher granted separate on-field interviews with Atlanta sportswriters Walter Taylor and Percy Whiting. In the session he made several disparaging comments about his former player-manager, Charlie Babb. Stockdale told Taylor that, while pitching for Memphis in the final days of the heated 1907 pennant race, he was instructed by Babb to throw a crucial game against the front-running Atlanta Crackers. Supposedly, Babb had given the order in an effort to increase gate receipts, which would help to defray expenses caused by recent construction improvements made to the Turtles' stadium. What made Stockdale's claim even more shocking was that Memphis was then competing against Atlanta for the league crown. Stockdale implied that Babb had received a substantial bribe from an unknown source to fix it so that Atlanta would win the flag. He added that the player-manager had personally been involved in several suspicious defensive miscues while playing second base during the final road trip of 1907. He charged that Babb was presently cleaning house of many good players, including himself, in order to conceal his actions. The *Atlanta Journal* printed Stockdale's comments on 2 June, and public reaction around the league was immediate.[13]

Rice typified the moral tone of the Nashville press. He called on President Kavanaugh to convene an owners meeting immediately and launch a full investigation into Stockdale's charges. "It is our belief," stated Rice, "that baseball is the cleanest, straightest, professional sport ... [in the country]. Popularity of the game is based on this assumption and unless allegations of crookedness are answered, public suspicion will erode the foundation of the game." The scribe questioned why it had taken Stockdale nine months to step forward and reveal the alleged corruption. Did not his lengthy silence also implicate the pitcher in the purported dirty deed, he wondered? Rice called for swift justice and recommended the permanent expulsion from baseball of any guilty party.[14] Atlanta manager Billy Smith added, "The league will have to blacklist [either] Babb or Stockdale, and I don't think it will be Babb."[15]

The leading characters in the case all swung into action. Babb flatly denied the accusations. Even Stockdale backtracked in light of the strong public outcry and claimed that reporter Taylor had misquoted him. The pitcher hedged his earlier statement and said that he was merely blowing off steam in disappointment over his trade to Mobile. Stockdale's retraction came too late despite the fact that it received broad exposure in the Birmingham press and *Sporting Life*. The allegations had stirred up sentiment that would not abate until someone was punished. The event became politicized when the mayors of Atlanta, Nashville, and Memphis each telegraphed President Kavanaugh asking for an immediate inquiry.

Kavanaugh called an emergency meeting of the board of directors for Little Rock on 15 June and then changed to 18 June at the Gayoso Hotel in Memphis. Kavanaugh presided over the group that included W.T. Crawford of Montgomery, F.P. Coleman of Memphis, F. H. Kuhn of Nashville, R.H. Baugh of Birmingham, W.R. Joyner of Atlanta, and H.C. Rather of Little Rock. The moguls summoned as witnesses sportswriters Walter Taylor and Percey Whiting of Atlanta, and W.G. Byrne of Memphis. Babb and Stockdale were also present.[16]

The proceedings took on a courtroom atmosphere. Babb spoke first and indignantly demanded Stockdale's lifetime banishment from baseball. Then Stockdale reiterated that the columnists had taken many of his comments out of context and they had not used good sense in seeing that his opinions were made in anger after being let go by Memphis. The beleaguered Stockdale claimed naively that the conversation with Taylor and Whiting was private in nature; his opinions were not intended for publication. Then, he made a statement for the record: Babb did want to string out the 1907 pennant race for business reasons; Babb had not personally thrown any games during the pennant race; Babb told no one to lose intentionally and sat people because they were injured or sick.[17] Stockdale identified two witnesses who were prepared to testify in his defense — Jimmie Jones, a former Southern Association player, and Nick Carter, currently manager of Winston-Salem. Neither man attended the meeting.

It is likely that the board of directors sympathized with Stockdale's explanation that he was simply blowing off steam to the Atlanta reporters. Kavanaugh's associates, however, could not deny that Stockdale's statements were injurious to the reputation of the Southern Association. Furthermore, Stockdale had offered no evidence to corroborate his claims of corruption. In the end, the board voted unanimously to ban Stockdale from baseball for life. Reflecting on the delicate relationship between athletes and the press, *The Sporting News* said:

> The lesson inculcated by his [Stockdale's] banishment from base ball will serve to keep players careful in making false charges that shake the public's confidence in the integrity of professional base ball. The good name of professional base ball suffers more injury from malignant and mendacious newspaper writers in a season than from the most degraded of its players.[18]

The editorial concluded that the National Board and National Commission should develop a similar punishment to "banish the parasite publicist" in cases like the Stockdale scandal.

Stockdale was allowed to appeal his banishment to the National Board and the National Commission. However, these outlets offered him little hope of vindication since the Southern Association's president sat on the all-powerful Board of Arbitration. Stockdale did file for reinstatement, but his case would not be resolved until mid–1909.[19] Meanwhile, the player's intemperate comments had done immeasurable harm to the image of honesty that Kavanaugh had fought so earnestly to establish. As fate would have it, the Mobile Sea Gulls arrived in Nashville for a four-game set along with their notorious ace. Stockdale's suspension would not take effect for another two weeks.

Rice picked up on Berny's recent roster move and also believed that the Vols must move forward during the homestand. "While the race isn't decided yet one way or another," analyzed the sportswriter, "the crucial epoch of the campaign is about due when the sheep will begin to wander away from the goats." Into this moment stepped the Sea Gulls. Optimism ran high in the stands as Kellum, the most steady Vols pitcher to date, strode to the slab. Spirits quickly faded as Mobile loaded the bases in the opening frame, and the Sea Gulls took a quick 2–0 lead. Bay tossed out a runner at the plate to bring the inning to a close. The only bright spot in the entire afternoon for the Vols was the defensive play of the fleet-footed left fielder; Deerfoot made another spectacular over-the-shoulder catch near the left field wall to rob a Sea Gull of an extra-base hit. Uncharacteristically, Kellum was victimized for fifteen hits and five runs in the loss.

Nashville's three sportswriters, Rice, Ewing, and Yancey, took this moment to review three sore spots that continued to plague the Vols. First, all three agreed that the time had come for Berny to pitch. The departure of Hess had cleared the way for the Nashville manager to show his stuff and reenergize the inconsistent pitching staff. Second, they felt that rotating the catching position between Seabough and Hardy was not working out. Seabough produced at the plate but he could not throw out those attempting to steal. Hardy was in a prolonged funk at the plate, and his batting average dipped 100 points below the previous season; but he could nab base thieves at will. Berny clearly favored Seabough who started twice as many games as the irritable and moody Scrappy Jack. Could Berny somehow attach one man's talent to the other, wistfully queried Rice, and thereby produce a quality catcher? Third, the sportswriters all lamented the periodic loafing of two key Vols. They singled out Wiseman, a surprising target in light of his usual high quality of play and popularity with the fans, and McCormick, who had been the recipient of press barbs for most of the season. Each would respond differently on the playing field to this scathing public critique.

In the middle game against Mobile, Perdue returned to the pitching box, and his teammates supported him with a barrage of eight base hits and five runs in the first three innings. The onslaught continued until the Vols collected seventeen safeties. Berny had opted to play scientific baseball and forced Sea Gull pitcher Clarence Torrey and third baseman Tom Benson to field bunt after bunt. These two failed to do so successfully, and the Mobile defense served up five errors to contribute to their own demise. McElveen crushed another triple, which was becoming routine fare for the east Tennessean. Dude McCormick committed his fourth error in five games and continued to attract the ire of the Nashville sportswriters. Wiseman, however, made a sensational running catch in the Dump and immediately regained the confidence of the sports page triumvirate. Nashville pasted Mobile by a score of 8–1.

Still, the Vols seemed to be running in place. Since the beginning of the season, the club had never been more than three games below or one game over the break-even point. As the club languished in sixth place, the New Orleans Pelicans had put together a successful month of May and climbed into familiar territory—first place.

Both managers made surprising picks as the starting pitcher for the third encounter between the Vols and Sea Gulls. Manager Tom Fisher opted for Otis Stockdale, the beleaguered central figure in the whirlwind controversy on everyone's mind. Bernhard elected Yerkes to make his third start in two weeks. As the game unfolded, Mobile nibbled away at the Nashville defense and tallied solo runs in the second, fourth, and sixth innings. Meanwhile, Stockdale mystified Vols batters and limited them to one hit through eight innings. All told, the Nashvillians collected only three scratch singles and a RBI double by McCormick. No one gave Yerkes very high marks in the defeat, and all three newspapers advised Berny to send the ineffective hurler "to slower company." Bay exhibited great hustle in the outfield, but re-injured his tender knee while diving for a ball. McCormick turned in a sensational play at shortstop, but the sportswriters were unimpressed. Ewing noted in the *American* that the team captain displayed a knack for making grandiose stops but muffing routine grounders. Yancey agreed in the *Banner* that the Vols were beginning to play "scrappy" defense with the exception of one individual—"Little Mac."[20]

In the final match, the Vols would have to face the pitcher who had carved them up in the first meeting—Beale Beeker. Berny responded with Duggan, the emerging ace of the staff. Both Beeker and Duggan threw in a businesslike manner and put up zeroes on the linescore until in the bottom of the sixth inning when McElveen drove a curveball over the head of center fielder Woodie Thornton, who fell down. Humpy rounded the bases for an inside-the-park home run as Thornton collected himself and raced after the errant missile. Yancey observed afterward that McElveen was emerging as a fan favorite because of his power and clutch hitting abilities. As long as McElveen and Duggan were in top form, Rice stated that "the Mobile unit had no more chance than a fat June bug in the path of a rock crusher."[21] Ewing reminded fans that the Nashville shortstop from Jersey City made the lone error of the game in the ninth with a wild toss to Butler, covering second base on a force play. McCormick's mistake might have kept a Sea Gull rally alive had it not been for another sensational catch by the hobbled Bay in left field. The volatile Dude continued his remarkable pace of committing a fielding error in practically every game. In McCormick's defense, the middle infielders for both teams had been busy that afternoon with sixteen putouts and assists each.

The Vols could not have felt satisfied with their performance against Mobile, a second-rung outfit. Despite Nashville's inability to play better than break-even ball, the sixth-place Vols trailed the league leading Pelicans by only five games. Another disappointment was Berny's continued absence from the slab. The manager had submitted his player contract to Kavanaugh in early

June after the departure of Hess, but the president had not yet approved it. Kavanaugh suspected that the loss of Hess and addition of Bay had canceled each other out, and the Nashville roster remained unchanged at the league maximum of fifteen players. Violation of the player limit rule was one of Kavanaugh's greatest concerns and one that he believed managers in the Southern Association frequently ignored. On 10 June, Kavanaugh dispatched league secretary Mose Wormser to every team office in the league to conduct an investigation to determine if some were guilty of manipulating the fifteen player rule.[22] Kavanaugh tabled Berny's document until Wormser completed his inquiry.

Once satisfied that Nashville's roster contained no irregularities, Kavanaugh cleared the way for Berny to play. "Greeted with salvos of applause," Berny made his pitching debut in Nashville flannels on 11 June, and his first outing in almost two years. He faced a young but talented Little Rock lineup and the sage veteran the Travelers' staff, Elwood "Pop" Eyler. What Finn's team lacked in experience they made up for it in youth, speed, and natural talent. The visitors based their team's success on a pair of quality outfielders, former Vols member Archie Persons and skilled newcomer Tris Speaker. Persons and Speaker would wear down Volunteer pitching all season, and they started with a serving of Berny. The former Cleveland hurler gave up a pair of runs to the visiting Travelers in the first and third innings, and struggled to shed the rust caused by inactivity. Little Rock batsmen banged him unmercifully for thirteen hits over nine innings, led by first baseman Joe Connors who went 5-for-5 with the willow. Two triples by platooned second baseman Walter East probably did not escape Berny's attention. The humbled pilot met with a bit of success on the afternoon when he smashed a double to the Dump in right-center field. Berny tired in the last frame and the Travs scored four more times on their way to an 8–2 victory.

Confident due to the recent success of Perdue, Berny sent in the Tennessee native to pitch on 12 June. Rice noted that the Gallatin Squash had good movement on his fastball and his control was "well-nigh perfect." The Vols clung to a slender 1–0 lead going into the bottom of the sixth inning when McElveen smoked a double to center field. Daubert, Butler, and Seabough followed with consecutive safeties. Bay provided heroics with a perfectly executed suicide squeeze to score Butler, who collected three hits to lead an eleven-hit Vols attack. Moreover, Wiseman was returning to his 1907 bases-stealing form. Perdue scattered four harmless hits and shut out Little Rock. Billy Page, who split time with East at second base, slashed a pair of doubles. Page and East hit in the .270 range and played solid defense. Both men deserved to be in the lineup every day.

Ewing described the third, and final, game between Little Rock and Nashville as "a farce." "The baseball dictionary does not contain enough words to tell just what happened during the matinee," he sneered.[23] A steady drizzle fell throughout the contest, soaking the entire infield with puddles, and the sole game ball became quite slippery. Kellum discovered early the difficulties in pitching under such conditions. In the top of the first inning, he walked three men, hit Speaker, and gave up two hits. The Vols looked listless in the field and fell behind by six runs largely on two errors in the third inning by an indifferent McCormick at shortstop. The spectators began to ride Dude unmercifully on his twentieth error in forty-four games. "The fans had their hammers out before the game started and they never let up until the finish," reported Ewing, a notorious McCormick baiter himself.[24] Visibly shaken, McCormick directed an angry tirade of his own at his protagonists in the stands. The wet conditions did not impede the power-hitting visitors. Little Rock's clean-up hitter, East, stroked two hits and scored three runs, and led the Travs to a comfortable 8–1 drubbing of the Vols. Nashville's lone tally occurred when Wiseman connected with a ball that towered over Speaker's head in center field, and the little Doctor scurried around the base paths for an inside-the-park home run. Rice added: "There isn't any lingering doubt but that the game was by all odds the saddest one of the season and the most uninteresting...."[25]

Vols bats showed signs of coming to life during the first two series in the long homestand. Nashville outhit its opponents, and surprisingly led the league with a .251 team batting average. The main offensive concern boiled down to clutch hitting and consistency. Indeed, Vols batters either pulverized the ball for double digit hits-per-game, or they couldn't find the white sphere with a telescope. This disparity carried into the win-loss column, where the club had settled into a pattern of trading a win for a loss, not very productive for a team with hopes of contending for the pennant. Rice summarized the Vols situation: "They are never good for any lengthy period, nor bad."[26] Perhaps they might continue to feast on their next guest, the anemic Birmingham Barons.

Birmingham may have arrived to town in pathetic shape, but the Vols were about to discover ailments of their own. Bay showed up at Sulphur Dell on 15 June with a swollen knee, so Berny replaced him with Hunter, whose sore elbow had kept him sidelined for two weeks. Hunter could not reach the infield with a throw from left field during pre-game warmups—a harbinger of things to come. The Vols were optimistic as their pitching workhorse took the field, but Duggan faced an equally strong talent in "Chick" Robitaille. The former Pittsburgh pitcher handcuffed Vols batters, limiting them to only three hits and no base on balls. Only one Vols member reached second base all afternoon: Duggan, in the bottom of the ninth inning. One of the sparse hits came from an unlikely source, struggling Jack Hardy. Ewing joked that "no one was more surprised than he [Hardy]."[27] Duggan struggled to find his control, and tired late in the contest as Birmingham swatted five hits in the eighth and three more in the ninth inning to coast to a 6–0 victory. The shamed Vols were only three losses away from switching places with Birmingham in the league basement.

Hunter, in for Bay again, led off the next game in splendid fashion by sending a fly ball over the head of Ed Manning in right field. Manning, who did not know the peculiarities of the Dump, promptly fell down. The fleet-footed utility player scurried around the bases for an inside-the-park home run as the Barons' outfielder crawled after the ball on his hands and knees. Perdue pitched smartly by jamming Birmingham batters with his blazing fastball and using the outside corner to spot "twirlers" [curveballs], and coasted to his fourth straight victory, a 5–3 decision. Rice cautioned, however, that the Vols were "still several leagues from polite baseball society."[28]

As Nashvillians awakened to their morning newspapers on 16 June, a serious storm cloud was building over the Vols. All three local newspapers reported that Berny was combing several minor league circuits for an infielder. Those who followed the club closely suspected that management was looking to replace their troubled shortstop, McCormick. Based on events to follow, it was likely that Dude was aware of the rumor mill. The key editorial was written by the normally mild Yancey and stirred the emotions of fans and players alike. "What is the matter with the Volunteers?" pondered Yancey. "This is the question that every baseball enthusiast in Nashville is now asking." Then the sportswriter fashioned his own answer: "It appears that two of the players have not tried to come up to their best. It is evident that something is wrong and should be corrected!"[29] One of the players earning Yancey's censure was the team captain, Mike "Dude" McCormick.

Yancey went on to list a series of indiscretions that illustrated the recent descent of McCormick. Although Berny had named him team captain at the beginning of the season, and he was earning the largest salary on the club, McCormick frequently second-guessed his skipper and management in the presence of reporters. More important, the disgruntled shortstop made no secret of his contempt for pitchers Kellum and Perdue. He admitted that he did not play hard while they were in the game. The final straw for McCormick may have come during the game on 15 June when he had a heated verbal exchange with fans seated in Rooters Row. Clearly audible to the Nashville press corps atop the grandstand, Dude hollered to several Birmingham players that this would be his last game in a Nashville uniform.[30]

Ironically, Rice wrote a poem that same day celebrating Victorian virtues of sportsmanship and teamwork in his "Tennessee 'Uns" column, which appeared on the editorial page. The thirteen stanzas described a recent reunion of football players at Vanderbilt University. In it Rice coined a phrase that would forever be associated with his brand of sports journalism. It was "not that you won or lost — but how you played the Game." It is arguable whether McCormick's negative attitude had inspired the wording; it is unquestionable that its appearance was timely.[31]

Southern Association Standings, June 16, 1908

	W	L
New Orleans	29	23
Montgomery	27	23
Memphis	27	24
Atlanta	23	21
Mobile	26	24
Little Rock	25	27
Nashville	21	24
Birmingham	17	29

The Vols went through pregame drills at Sulphur Dell on 17 June without McCormick. The team captain had left a note for Berny stating that his days as a Volunteer were over. McCormick's decision to abandon the team was made all the more grave in light of it being the second time that the hot-tempered shortstop had taken French leave. When the Vols had entered a tailspin in August 1907, Dude had quit the team and thereby placed rookie manager Johnny Dobbs in a tenuous position. Now the Nashville press united and demanded that club President Kuhn and league President Kavanaugh suspend and blacklist McCormick from professional baseball. A similar reaction had occurred in 1907 but quickly blew over when Dude returned unpunished. This time, McCormick's desertion received national attention. The editors of *Sporting Life* and *The Sporting News* echoed the voices of Rice, Yancey, and Ewing. "Captain Mike McCormick has pulled off his usual gumshoe act again and jumped the team," noted *The Sporting News* in disgust.[32] Yancey called for the supreme penalty—banishment from baseball for life. "It does the game good to make an example of a man like McCormick," he concluded.[33]

Presidents Kuhn and Kavanaugh needed no prodding in reaching a decision regarding Nashville's moody shortstop—placement on the blacklist indefinitely. Although Kuhn received a swift offer of $700 for Dude's contract, the Nashville mogul steadfastly refused. Berny told the Nashville press that he would neither trade McCormick nor release him from his contract. A principle was at stake, and it revolved around the integrity of the game as well as the relationship between a player, his teammates, and the community.

The defection of McCormick placed Berny and the Vols in a quandary as they prepared for their final game against Birmingham. The immediate question was, who would replace the departed captain at shortstop? Berny responded with a player who had broken into the Southern League in 1896 as a college shortstop—Doc Wiseman. The eight-year Nashville veteran was a natural choice; he was wiry, possessed quick reflexes, and commanded respect from his teammates through a quiet demeanor and good work habits. Whether he still possessed the physical skills necessary to hold down such a pivotal position remained to be seen.[34]

Then Berny directed his attention to the resulting void in right field. With Bay disabled, the Nashville manager chose his valuable utility player, Hunter, to play left; so Berny turned to a less desirable choice, Hardy, for right. The time had come for Scrappy Jack to put his grousing aside and elevate his game to help the team. The six-foot catcher possessed a wonderful throwing arm, an aggressive attitude, and understood the game. Nashville baseball needed him in this moment of genuine crisis.

Never one to adjust his lineup for substitutions, Berny inserted the underachieving Hardy in McCormick's third spot on the card. Siegle and Daubert were making better contact and were suited for McCormick's slot, but Berny's system of substitution followed a distinctive pattern: whenever a player left the lineup for an extended absence, his replacement filled his vacant place on the card.

Berny's final response to McCormick's sudden departure was a stroke of genius; he selected McElveen as team captain. A better choice could not have been made. The power hitter had held down the clean-up spot in the batting order since early in the season, and his defensive prowess around third base was also improving. His college moniker, "Humpy," a nickname normally applied to an unproved or unskilled player, was gradually being erased in the minds of his teammates. Being a native east Tennessean undoubtedly contributed to McElveen's popularity with Nashville fans.[35]

Berny slated southpaw Kellum to pitch against the Barons on 17 June, in part because their lineup contained so many left-handed hitters. The newspapers did not abandon the major team story, however. The sports page in the *Tennessean* proclaimed: "MIKE McCORMICK KANGAROOS AGAIN."[36] Rice noted that Mac's defection was self-defeating, citing the rumor that Berny was trying to ship his shortstop off to Cleveland — a major league club in desperate need of a middle infielder. Rice also noted concern about Bay's health. Berny believed that the Illinois native might have contracted malaria, a northern player's worst fear about playing in the South. Indeed, Bay was hospitalized with symptoms of the disease the next day.

When the patched up Vols ran onto the field, no one knew exactly what to expect. Kellum silenced the worriers with a masterful pitching performance. The middle of the Vols order, Wiseman, Hardy, McElveen, and Siegle, delivered two hits apiece, and blew the game open with four runs in the bottom of the fourth inning. Wiseman started the action with a single, and was followed on base by Hardy, who was hit on the elbow by a pitch from a young college prospect. McElveen came up in a sacrifice situation and laid down a dandy bunt. The rookie pitcher fielded the bunt but his throw to first base was so off-line that it "came near dismantling the scoreboard in right field." Another Baron throwing error on the relay from first baseman Bill Douglas emptied the bases of Volunteers. The Vols had passed an important test; they had banded together, fielded a competitive team, and won the game. All associated with the club understood, however, that Wiseman at shortstop was only a temporary solution. Berny continued to hunt for a suitable middle infielder.

The month of June had opened on an optimistic note for the Vols. They had looked forward to twenty-one games in the friendly confines of Sulphur Dell. But the opportunity to make up ground on the league leaders quickly evaporated as the Vols played break-even ball against relatively weak opponents. Off-the-field distractions also presented themselves. Sunday blue laws and the Baxter-O'Brien incident reminded patrons that minor league baseball at the turn of the century had not yet fully become family entertainment. The Stockdale scandal also hovered like a dark cloud over the league for the rest of the year.

On-the-field player improvements offered a glimmer of hope for Vols fans. Perdue had thrown four consecutive quality starts, Kellum continued to find success with his change-of-speed fare, and Duggan had responded to Berny's challenge to emerge as the workhorse of the pitching staff. The departure of Hess and appearance of Berny on the mound also hinted at good things to come. Hunter's sore arm continued to limit the team, yet he possessed the skills to emerge as the top utility player in the league. In the outfield, the Nashville club definitely strengthened itself with the acquisitions of Bay and Siegle. Bay possessed the offensive and defensive skills necessary to make an immediate impact. Berny would not have to worry about center field, as Siegle boasted a strong throwing arm and excellent foot speed. Some observers argued that Nashville fielded the fastest outfield in the Southern Association in Bay, Siegle, and Wiseman. McElveen had made significant strides since the beginning of the season. His lively bat, improved defense, and quiet leadership were admirable qualities on a team in search of positives. Daubert and Butler showed that they could deliver the goods—the former with occasional power and the latter with excellent base running. Both infielders were accomplished at bunting and sacrificing runners into scoring position. Finally, what could be done with the catcher's position? That situation demanded resolution.

Team morale had suffered a blow as the Vols prepared to face the surprising Montgomery Senators in three games to bring closure to their disappointing homestand. After the season, Berny admitted that Dude's defection was hurtful. "I didn't believe the game had that kind of a man in it," said the stunned manager.[37] Although McCormick had damaged the team's spirit, enough good men of strong character still remained. Berny, Bay, McElveen, Daubert, and Wisemen—all quiet men—were capable of leading by example and providing a nucleus on which to build a winning attitude. At this moment, the Nashville Vols were a team desperately in search of a new identity. Would they weather the stormy crisis of June?

CHAPTER 6

In Search of Stability

The traditional Fourth of July doubleheader, a midsummer classic, lay less than two weeks away and the Nashville Vols were, to outward appearance, a team in disarray. They had squandered an opportunity to make up ground on the league leaders through victories during an extended homestand in June. Now the Vols faced an equally lengthy road trip. Berny's most urgent problem was to locate a replacement for the blacklisted McCormick. He also needed to address lingering personality issues that held the team back. Several players would have to contribute by playing new positions or assuming leadership roles. Although the month of July witnessed the continuation of challenges to both the Nashville Vols and the Southern Association in the form of gambling, rowdyism, and intimidation, from Nashville's perspective the most important issues were stabilizing the roster, molding a positive team attitude, and winning on the field. Without question, this period leading up to the middle of July would be a crucial test for the floundering Vols.

Engulfed in the McCormick quagmire, the Vols did not relish facing a rising opponent like Montgomery, thus far the most improved team in 1908, in the final series of their homestand. Berny viewed the current situation a personal challenge as well as an opportunity to rally his beleaguered troops, so he assigned himself the responsibility to open on the slab. The first game started on a shaky note as Wiseman coughed up two errors at shortstop. Berny did not let the miscues rattle him. Instead, he showed the poise of a professional, and snuffed out the threat by striking out four Senators in the first two frames. Wiseman, the guardian of the Dump, settled down and fielded several spectacular shots, and at the plate he added a triple and scored two runs. Berny pressed the ailing Hunter into service in right field rather than Hardy, and the fleet-footed athlete put on an excellent show. The switch-hitter collected three hits, scored twice, and drove in two runs. Despite five Nashville errors, Berny was able to notch his first win in a Volunteer uniform, 5–1. The victory also restored Nashville to the .500 mark for the first time in a month.

Team president Kuhn also received a telegram from league president Kavanaugh upholding the Nashville decision to suspend McCormick indefinitely. Despite tempting offers in the coming weeks from several minor league teams, Berny refused to release his troubled ex-shortstop.[1]

The Vols received back-to-back solid pitching performances when Duggan took a one-hitter into the ninth inning of the second meeting with Montgomery. Johnny showed "plenty of the old smoke" for the fans. Wiseman committed another infield error, but he clubbed another triple and scored three times. The first four batters in the lineup — Bay, Wiseman, Hunter, and McElveen — accounted for nine of the team's eleven hits. Ewing jested that Hunter had been given pointers from Wiseman on the nuances of his new position in the Dump. His extra practice paid off as the nimble outfielder plucked two towering fly balls down at the base of the right field wall. Butler also caught the attention of manager Bernhard, turning in two fine defensive plays in the final frame. The 7–2 victory, Nashville's fourth in a row, thrust the revitalized Vols into the first division (the top four teams in the league standings), which was considered the mark of a contender.

Berny selected his hottest pitcher to finish the Senators in the final game. Perdue rose to the occasion; only one Montgomery baserunner reached third base in the two-hour contest enjoyed by over 3,000 fans. Wiseman tripled in his third consecutive game, but the fireworks really began in the fourth when Daubert tripled and Butler followed with a rare outside-the-park home run. The clean stroke landed in a sewage ditch beyond the center field wall. Kid, an unlikely candidate for the long ball, was the first Nashville player to clear the palisade at Sulphur Dell. An appreciative crowd raised money to supply Butler with a complementary load of coal and a free shave for one year at Max Newman's barber shop on Church Street. Hunter contributed three stolen bases, and Wiseman's outstanding work at shortstop "could never have been achieved by McCormick in his best days," reported Rice.[2] On the other side, the normally reliable glove work of Montgomery shortstop Joe Pepe exploded for three miscues in the Senators 8–0 loss.

The victory marked the end of Nashville's twenty-one game homestand, as the club won its last five games and swept the hottest team in the league. The Vols outscored the Senators, 20–3, and climbed into sole possession of third place. The current streak would be tested, first in Atlanta, as Nashville embarked on a twenty-game road trip. The Crackers had been playing consistent ball all season. Other than one brief home series, the Vols would not return to the friendly confines of Sulphur Dell until 20 July.

As the train carried the visiting Vols to the Georgia capitol, Berny pondered two burning issues. Would he be able to find a replacement for McCormick, who was rumored to be lurking around Nashville and apologetically asking for his old job back? The Nashville press leaked a story that Berny was leaning heavily on his Cleveland buddy Nap Lajoie for the services of infielder George Nill. But such talks usually took time. Berny wanted resolution of his team's pitching woes as well. He hoped to solidify the rotation and not have to rely upon his own services. He turned to the seldom-used Stanley Yerkes to see whether the Bostonian could deliver the goods and earn a permanent spot on the staff.

Yerkes got off to a poor start in the opener against Atlanta. He surrendered three runs on three hits and three bases on balls in three innings of work, and Berny pulled him in favor of Kellum. The contest seesawed back and forth as the score was knotted twice and the lead changed hands three times. With the score tied 4–4 in the top of the ninth, Butler singled, Hardy sacrificed him to second base, and Kellum drove in the winning run with a sharp line-drive single to left field. The bottom of the Vols order delivered some timely base hits. The outfield corps of Bay, Siegle, and Hunter aided the soft-throwing Kellum by tracking down twelve lofty fly balls. At the conclusion of the game, Yancey called for the immediate release of Yerkes.[3]

On 24 June, Atlanta hosted Nashville in a rare midseason doubleheader. Vols batters picked up exactly where they had left off and pummeled the Crackers for three runs in the top of the first inning. Manager Billy Smith yanked his ineffective starter with only two outs and replaced him with Harry Johns. Perdue baffled the Atlanta hitters with a "lively fastball and sharp breaking curves" and earned his sixth win in a row.[4] The Vols had notched their seventh consecutive victory.

In the second game of the twin bill, the Vols winning streak came to an end. The Crackers threw their ace, Roy Castleton, and the hurler did not disappoint his fans. He scattered four harmless hits while his offense played an opportunistic brand of baseball. In the fourth inning, Roy Moran scored easily from third base as Hardy threw out a basestealer at second base. One inning later, Atlanta put the double steal into operation with the same results, as Wiseman botched the coverage. Tobacco Billy was taking advantage of Wiseman's lack of recent experience at shortstop, and the "Runnin'" Crackers defeated Duggan handily by a score of 5–1.

Following the doubleheader, Berny announced that the Vols had purchased a second baseman from the Little Rock Travelers for $600. Walter Rufus East was born in Coulterville, Illinois, on 29 March 1883, to Rufus and Lucinda Robinson East.[5] The youngest of six brothers, Walter's family moved to Barberton, Ohio, as a youth. There he developed a reputation as a fine high school and later college athlete at the University of Pittsburgh. He enjoyed the baseball diamond and football gridiron equally, and played some professional football for the famous Massillon Club. In 1904, East's notoriety soared when he earned a spot on the professional baseball club in nearby Akron, where he rose to player-manager. In the offseason, Walter attended law school.

East and Berny had been acquainted for several years, and the agreement promised to solve a glaring defensive problem for Nashville. As important, Kid Butler had played shortstop on East's 1907 Akron team. Now the reunited middle infield combo allowed Berny to shift Butler to his accustomed position. Management made room for East on the roster by giving Yerkes his unconditional release, who later surfaced in the Galveston roster in the Texas League. Near the end of the season, the disgruntled New England product sent a letter to Garry Herrmann demanding compensation for lost income and immediate reinstatement with Nashville after Berny ignored these claims.[6]

Atlanta salvaged a split with Nashville in the final game behind the masterful pitching of spitballer Russell Ford. The future major leaguer handcuffed the Volunteers and limited them to three base hits. The Vols attack had gone silent in two consecutive games. Bernhard threw for the visitors but his sore arm offered up eleven Cracker hits and five runs in his second consecutive rough start. It took real fortitude for Berny to throw while injured, a message not missed by his players. The pivotal play behind Berny occurred in the third inning when Hunter dropped a routine fly ball and opened the floodgates for three unearned Atlanta runs. In contrast, Bay turned in a marvelous catch two frames later when he outran a line drive hit to deep left field off the bat of first baseman Jim Fox. Deerfoot turned his back on the ball in a move that was becoming his trademark and, in a tremendous display of athleticism, made a spectacular diving over-the-shoulder catch. Although he tumbled to the ground and rolled over several times, Bay managed to hold onto the ball. His exploit thrilled the fans, but it was not enough to bring about a Vols victory.

The Vols opened a bizarre three-game series at Montgomery on 25 June. The slowball artist, Kellum, took the slab against Ted Guese, a recent retread from New Orleans and a proven Vols-killer. Playing close to the vest, Montgomery clung to a slender 1–0 lead through six innings. Wiseman's rustiness at shortstop reappeared when manager Jimmy "Pony" Ryan set the double steal and bunt in motion. A hard-charging Doctor overran the ball and found himself sheepishly standing alongside McElveen. Neither infielder had communicated with the other and third base was left uncovered. The mistake led to the first Senator tally. Rattled, Wiseman bobbled several other opportunities, and later his errant throw drew Daubert off the bag at first base and into the basepath. There, the unprotected fielder collided with Archie Persons, sprinting down the line. Jake fell to the ground writhing in pain, but recovered sufficiently to smash a two-run home run in the top of the ninth to narrow Montgomery's lead. Bay produced another defensive gem with a tumbling catch near the left field wall to rob Montgomery of an extra-base hit.

Bad luck found Scrappy Jack Hardy that afternoon; he had taken several vicious foul tips off his throwing hand and chest. In the bottom of the seventh inning, with the score knotted at one run apiece, he incurred an injury. With Pepe and Persons occupying the corners, Pony Ryan gave Persons the sign to steal second base. Hardy received the pitch and made a clean throw to Wiseman, wheeling into position behind the slab to set up the cutoff play. As soon as the ball left Hardy's hand, however, Pepe broke for the plate. Wiseman relayed the ball to Hardy, who had the dish blocked with his left knee. The baseball and baserunner arrived at the same time, and the sliding Pepe tore a deep gash in Hardy's unprotected thigh. The bleeding catcher was carried from the field and the Senators tacked on another run as Persons scampered to third base and later scored. The timely arrival of East from Little Rock during the contest meant that Berny could return Wiseman to his familiar position in right field and swing Butler to shortstop. This fielding realignment promised to solidify the Vols' defense.

After losing Hardy and the middle game, the Vols went with their six-game winner, Perdue. He faced a stiff challenge from Montgomery's workhorse, Forrest Thomas. Both pitchers threw well enough to win. Perdue scattered seven hits, but again, in the fourth straight game, Nashville batsmen could not find their hitting groove. Newcomer East smashed a double in the top of the sixth to score Bay all the way from first base, but it proved to be the lone Nashville tally off three paltry hits. Montgomery's scores, on the other hand, resulted from shoddy Nashville defense and more of Ryan's scientific baseball. In the bottom of the second frame, Ed Gremminger slashed a single to left field and the ball dribbled between the usually reliable Bay's legs. Had Battleship Ed not possessed "the speed of an ice-wagon," Rice claimed the portly first baseman would have scored. As it was, Gremminger sailed easily into second base. On the very next play, a frustrated Perdue attempted to pick off the full-figured Gremminger, but the ball caromed off the baserunner and rolled into the outfield. The Senator steamed into third base unchallenged. Several pitches later, Big Ed sailed home on a sacrifice fly for the first run of the contest. Montgomery completed the scoring in the bottom of the sixth inning, and walked away with its second consecutive one-run victory, 2–1. Perdue had absorbed his first loss in seven starts. On a more welcome note, East had paid immediate dividends as a contact hitter capable of holding down McCormick's number three slot in the batting order.

The final game in the Alabama capitol turned into the most unusual contest of the entire season. A large crowd jammed into Vandiver Park in hopes of witnessing a sweep of the visiting Volunteers. Disappointed through five innings, the fans watched the visitors protect a 3–1 lead when, in the bottom of the sixth inning, a Montgomery player was trapped in a heated rundown between third base and home. Seabough applied an aggressive tag in a close play at the plate, and umpire Fitzsimmons called the runner out to end the inning. Then, owing to considerable bench jockeying from the Montgomery players, Fitzsimmons inexplicably reversed his decision and allowed the run to score. Dismayed by the official's change of mind, Seabough argued his case to the point where Fitzsimmons ejected him from the game.

Berny charged up to Fitzsimmons. The Nashville manager pleaded that he had no other catcher available, owing to Hardy's spiking injury from two days ago. After a heated exchange, Berny was forced to call upon center fielder Siegle to catch and insert Hunter in the outfield. This switch should have placed Hunter in Seabough's number eight spot in the batting order. Meanwhile, Hardy watched the entire episode unfold from the grandstands, where he sat with a leg bandaged beneath his dress slacks.

Events worsened in the top of the seventh when Nashville sent its number three, four, and five batters to the plate — East, McElveen, and Siegle. As soon as Hunter stepped into the box in the fifth spot and took a pitch, the official scorer notified Fitzsimmons that the Volunteers had batted out of order. Siegle should have batted, and not Hunter. The umpire immediately called the batter out, and tossed Hunter from the game for batting out of turn. This placed Berny in a real bind because he now was forced to insert the injured Hardy. Less than thrilled with this decision, Scrappy Jack climbed out of the stands and arrogantly sauntered toward home plate. His body language suggested to everyone present that he was highly inconvenienced. Still wearing his suit and tan street shoes, he donned the catcher's mask and stooped behind the dish.

Now it was Jimmy Ryan's turn to react. The Mobile manager protested to Fitzsimmons that Hardy was ineligible to play because he was not wearing the Nashville team uniform. Seabough offered to exchange his game flannels with Hardy and the two catchers departed for the clubhouse beneath the grandstands. Ryan continued to vent, claiming that Hardy was not eligible to play at all because he had not been appropriately suited from the start of the game. When Hardy appeared after a ten-minute absence still wearing his street shoes, Ryan flew into a tirade. Equally frustrated, Fitzsimmons thought that Hardy was attempting to show him up. As a result, the official kicked Hardy from the game, announced a forfeit, and awarded a 9–0 victory to Montgomery.

Pandemonium broke loose on the Nashville bench. Berny argued that Fitzsimmons had been manipulated by Ryan and the situation had been blown out of proportion. Furthermore, he could not find a basis for Ryan's objections anywhere in the rule book. Finally, the Nashville manager did not understand how the game could be forfeited in light of the umpire's prior decision to allow Hardy to change clothes and enter the lineup. As fans shouted catcalls from the stands, the home team retired to its clubhouse and Berny protested the game.[7]

The implications surrounding the raucous finale in Montgomery were immediately apparent. Duggan had been cruising along with a 3–1 lead on five scattered hits and five strikeouts. Back in Nashville, Ewing labeled Fitzsimmons an "incapable official" and Rice compared the umpire's backbone to that of a shrimp. Looking ahead, Yancey pondered whether this defeat might come back to haunt the Vols at the end of the season.[8] The race for the 1908 flag was unfolding into a very tight affair. The sports editor of the *Banner* also chastised Hardy for his childish on-field behavior, charging that if Hardy had been playing up to his 1907 form, the Vols would likely be sitting in first place.[9] Scrappy Jack's mediocre performance was becoming a matter of public concern.

The Nashville contingent limped home only to be greeted by rain. When action resumed on 30 June against Atlanta, the Vols were thirsting for a victory. Hunter, whose sore elbow had sidelined him from pitching for a month, was driven from action after only one inning of work. Duggan came on in relief and he threw a masterful two-hitter. It marked the Hoosier's second victory in four days and seventeen innings of work. In the sixth, Daubert struck a ball to the center field wall, but as the first baseman rounded third base, coach Hub Perdue unwisely signaled him to go home. Caught in a rundown between third base and home, Jake eluded embarrassment by scoring, but only after a Cracker defender dropped the ball. Hunter's lingering injury coupled with Duggan's relief heroics illustrated Nashville's ongoing need for another starting pitcher. The game also marked the return of "Chewing Gum" Johnnie O'Brien to Sulphur Dell. O'Brien now served as an umpire in the Southern Association, but many local fans recalled the days when he used to cover second base for Nashville.[10]

The Gallatin Cyclone, Perdue, continued his mastery over opposing batters in the final contest against the Crackers. He changed speed on his pitches with baffling effectiveness, struck out nine batters, and gave up only three hits. Perdue allowed baserunners only in the first and sixth innings. In the latter frame, he issued two walks and a double and then proceeded to strike out the side. As further evidence of his farm boy toughness, Perdue plunked the opposing pitcher, southpaw Grant Schopp. Offensively, Siegle contributed two hits and three RBI while Bay, Siegle, and Butler collected five stolen bases against aging Atlanta catcher Big Ed Hurlburt. Perdue notched his seventh victory in eight starts, 5–0.[11]

The next day a jubilant Perdue sought out Grantland Rice at the sports desk of the *Tennessean*. Rice asked the affable Volunteer State native to what he attributed his recent success. Giving up cigarettes had bettered his physical condition, Perdue began. "As long as I was hitting those nails, I was never in good shape to work." He also praised Berny, who had set aside three days each week to offer instruction "on the mechanics of delivery." Perdue added that Berny was respected by all members of the team. "A fellow that wouldn't work for Bernhard wouldn't be willing to work for anybody," concluded Perdue.[12]

The Vols hit the road, where they would play their next fourteen games in five cities: Birmingham, New Orleans, Mobile, Little Rock, and Memphis. The traditional Fourth of July doubleheader slated for Birmingham approximated the midseason point for the Southern Association. Currently the Vols occupied fourth place, batted .230 (.233 league average), and fielded at .953 (.956 league average). Only five games separated the four teams in the first division. These statistics either reflected the averageness of the Vols or the overall parity that existed in the league.[13]

The Birmingham Barons had been reeling since opening day. They already fired their manager, and by midseason dropped 16½ games behind league leading New Orleans. In a desperate move, the Barons' new player-manager, Carleton Molesworth, signed two rookie pitchers—youngsters named Robinson from the South Atlantic League and Bauer from the Cotton States League. The move revealed Molesworth's youth movement in Birmingham, which would pay big dividends two years later. But now the Vols probably looked upon the Birmingham squad as a series of victories just waiting to happen.

In the opening game, Kellum started for Nashville. His off-speed sidearm pitches dropping from the southern side baffled the Barons as they pounded eighteen ground outs to Vols infielders. The former Cincinnati star threw a heavy, sinking ball that day, and while he did not overpower his opponent, he achieved satisfying results in allowing only two runs on four hits. Two timely hits combined with fielding errors by Bay and Butler resulted in the only Baron tallies in the sixth inning. The home-squad opener, Harry McNeal, did not look sharp. McNeal surrendered three hits and two runs to the visitors in the opening round, and when he issued two consecutive bases on balls to start the third, Molesworth pulled him in favor of the new talent, Robinson. The rookie held the Vols in check for four innings. Then Wiseman led off the seventh with a scorching triple off the outfield scoreboard and scored on Daubert's infield single. Butler completed the damage with a two-RBI single to capture the opener, 5–2. The home crowd hollered epithets throughout the game about the umpiring skills of O'Brien.

The next day, the Fourth of July, started under darkened skies, and a crowd of 1,500 filed into the stadium to watch the traditional twin bill. Berny threw Duggan into the fray and Molesworth countered with his other raw prospect, Bauer. The "lowly groundhogs," as Rice referred to the Barons, jumped to a quick 2–0 lead, but both pitchers remained locked in a close tussle. Trailing by a run in the top of the ninth, McElveen, Siegle, and Daubert beat out bunts. With the bases loaded, Butler drove in two runs on a single and Hardy accounted for a third tally with a sacrifice fly to right field. Butler then crossed the plate after Duggan reached base on an infielder's throwing error. When the dust had cleared in the last inning, the Vols had pushed across four runs to stage an exciting comeback.

Big Mole, a 200-pounder amply spread over a 5' 6" frame, was probably disappointed for a number of reasons—the Vols late-inning fireworks had stolen a victory from his young pitcher, the skies threatened to unleash a downpour at any moment, and the holiday gate was disappointingly sparse.

July

Mon	Tue	Wed	Thu	Fri	Sat	Sun
		1 Atl	2	3 @Birm	4 @Birm (2)	5
6 @N.O.	7 @N.O.	8 @N.O.	9 @Mob	10 @Mob	11 @Mob	12 @Mob
13 @L.R.	14 @L.R.	15 @L.R.	16 @L.R.	17 @Mont	18 @Mont	19 @Mont
20 **L.R.**	21 **L.R.**	22 **L.R.**	23 **Mob**	24 **Mob**	25 **Mob**	26
27 **N.O.**	28 **N.O.**	29 **N.O.**	30 **Mem**	31 **Mem**		

Atl = Atlanta
Birm = Birmingham
L.R. = Little Rock
Mem = Memphis
Mob = Mobile
Mont = Montgomery
N.O. = New Orleans
Bold print= @ Nashville
(2) =Double Header

To make matters worse, umpire O'Brien canceled the second game on account of the threatening weather despite the animated protests of Molesworth. The Vols stacked their bats and headed for the Crescent City.

The Vols knew that they faced a tough opponent in New Orleans, but they also realized that the series presented a marvelous opportunity to make up some ground on the league-leading Pelicans. Berny went with the healthiest arm, Perdue, and Frank selected "Ginger" Clark for the Birds. Recently acquired from Birmingham, Clark had broken in with the Barons back in 1902 and had presently demonstrated considerable success against Nashville in 1908. The game promised to be an interesting matchup between the young Perdue and the veteran Clark.

Under dark and foreboding clouds, both teams scored an early unearned run — Nashville in the first and New Orleans in the second inning. Then the pitchers took control of the game. After McElveen was cut down trying to steal second base in the second, the Vols produced no other baserunner. The bottom of the last frame opened with the score knotted at 1–1, and a steady drizzle began to fall accompanied by the rumble of distant thunder. With only one out and the bases crammed with Pelicans, pinch-hitter "Moose" Baxter drove in the winning run on a hard grounder that went between East's wickets. Perdue suffered a disappointing loss in which he had struck out nine batters, but his counterpart, Clarke, had thrown a two-hit gem. In every account, the game was heralded as the best contest of the season by both teams. Less than five minutes after the game ended, a torrential downpour ensued.

The second encounter between Nashville and New Orleans on 6 July promised to be as exciting as the opening tiff. If the Vols could not subdue the Pelicans with Perdue's blazing fastball and biting curve, perhaps the slow motion of Kellum could accomplish the task. New Orleans countered with Ted Breitenstein, "the $10,000 Beauty."

Born on 1 June 1869, Theodore P. Breitenstein never played for the Nashville Vols, but he contributed significantly to the club's '08 history as the premier pitcher of the New Orleans Pelicans.[14] Beer magnate Chris Von der Ahe owned the St. Louis Browns, and signed the young factory worker and left-handed star pitcher of the 1890 city league champion Home Comforts to a professional contract. Theo, or "Red," was assigned to pitch for the independent Brown Seconds, but Von der Ahe elevated him to the parent club on the final day of the 1891 season. Breitenstein established a record by tossing a no-hitter and walking only one Louisville batter in his major league debut. Throughout the Gay '90s, he was the only consistent Brownie pitcher and known to have plenty of stuff. Breit teamed up with catcher Heinie Peitz to form the famed pretzel battery in 1894.

Von der Ahe underpaid and overworked his homegrown southpaw. On one occasion, the feisty owner fined Breit because he refused to pitch both games in a doubleheader despite logging forty-three innings in nine days. Breit irritated "Der Boss" further with his excessive fondness for drink and wagering on the ponies. In 1897, Von der Ahe shipped the spirited Breit to Cincinnati over a salary dispute as well as the pitcher's outright refusal to quit the vaudeville circuit in the offseason. The deal established one of Breit's nicknames—"the $10,000 Beauty"—owing to Cincinnati's outlandish payment to Von der Ahe. Breit rewarded his new employer with a second major league no-hitter, where he faced the minimum of 27 batters.

Pitching statistics reflect Breitenstein's durability and longevity with St. Louis and Cincinnati. In eleven major league seasons, he posted a 164–169 record, completed 300 out of 314 starts, hurled 2,900 innings, issued 1,200 bases on balls, and struck out 900 batters. During his best season (1894), Breit led the league in appearances (56), starts (50), complete games (46), and innings pitched (447). The next season he led the league in losses (30) and bases on balls (178). Overall, Breitenstein was one of the top performing left-handers in the National League in the 1890s.

When Breit's major league career ended, he followed his friend and player-manager Charlie Frank first to Memphis and then to New Orleans, where he pitched for ten more seasons. In Breitenstein's combined twenty-one years in the National League and Southern Association (1891–1911), he took the slab in 830 games for a combined record of 322–258. He is credited with two no-hitters in both leagues, and played on four minor league championships. By 1908, Breit was no longer overpowering, but relied on a broad selection of pitches—a drop curve, "in shoot," rising fastball, and deceptive changeup.

Favorable comparisons abounded between Breitenstein and Kellum: both southpaws possessed major league credentials, changed speeds effectively, threw intelligently, and brought a high degree of professionalism to the slab. Kellum seemed to "hold the whammy" over New Orleans every time he faced the power-hitting lineup. The only scoring took place in the top of the first inning on singles by Wiseman, East, and Siegle, which accounted for two tallies. Kellum made both runs stand up as he tossed a stunning three-hitter against the most fearsome lineup in the Southern Association. The Vols pitcher, backed by impeccable defense that produced two inning-ending double plays, faced only twenty-eight Pelicans. Umpire O'Brien did not fare as well. His reputation as a pro-Nashville official preceded him from Birmingham, and riled fans encouraged Moose Baxter, a player with a reputation for fighting, to "break O'Brien's face."[15]

Unlike the first two contests between the Vols and Pelicans, the finale was wide open as both teams brought their bats into play. Duggan faced Bill Bartley, a pitcher with five year's experience in the Southern Association. Duggan got the better of his foe as his offense supplied him with 3–0 lead through six innings. Every Vols batter except Butler reached base via a base hit; East, McElveen, and Daubert had two hits apiece. Siegle, the Vols' underrated center fielder, scored two runs. Daubert's clutch double off the left field wall in the top of the sixth inning provided the big blow, which drove in a pair of runs. New Orleans threatened in the bottom of the seventh and scored one run, but were turned away by another inning-ending double play. Rain fell on 8 July and forced the cancellation of the fourth game, but the weather did not dampen the Vols' spirits. They had played well against the league leaders in three vigorously contested games and came away with a 2–1 split.

As the Vols departed for Mobile, a brouhaha was unfolding in Nashville's three sports pages over the most severe public relations issue facing baseball in the Deadball Era—gambling. Yancey opened the debate in the *Banner* with an allegation that several well-known Nashville saloons were involved in betting on Vols games. Yancey took a high moral stance when he warned that this activity was "an affront to the great national game," and his concern extended to a fear that such wagering might have corrupted several Vols players. Rice may have discussed this topic with Yancey as he notified his readers in the *Tennessean* that McCormick had openly consorted with known gamblers at

Sulphur Dell while serving as team captain. Rice supported President Kuhn's decision to blackball McCormick for the remainder of the season, and he would not remain silent as Dude continued to associate with gamblers within earshot of the stadium after his banishment.[16]

It was not unreasonable for Rice's white, middle-class readership to accept these conclusions and brand McCormick as an evil gambler type who was capable of fixing games. After all, Dude's lower class upbringing in a poor ethnic neighborhood in Jersey City was evidence enough that he might be susceptible to taking bribes and other illegal offers. Yet, McCormick's relationship with underworld characters in 1908 was not an isolated incident; indeed, the Southern Association was rocked by scandal on an annual basis. Even the major leagues were not impervious to tainted connections between ballplayers and con men. While McCormick should not be condoned for engaging in illegal bookmaking activities, it was prolific at all levels of professional baseball during the Deadball Era.

Yancey proposed that Nashville sports enthusiasts respond energetically to the fixing threat in order to thwart attempts to throw Vols games. He proposed a collection, or bonus fund, with the proceeds divided equally among Vols players at the end of the season. Several prominent businessmen backed Yancey's idea as a means to advertise the community of Nashville in a positive light to the rest of the South as well as prevent players from being tempted by bribes.[17]

The Vols moved on to Mobile to face the Sea Gulls in cavernous Monroe Park.[18] Berny had evolved a plan for the current road trip — start Perdue in game one, and if any series went to a fourth game he would pitch it himself. Perdue faced Clarence Torrey in the opener, and inning after inning, they produced goose eggs on the scoreboard. Neither team mustered much offense while both pitchers gained in strength as the contest went along. For their part, no Vols player reached base between the ninth and fourteenth innings, and only two reached third base in the entire game — Wiseman in the fourth and Bay in the seventeenth. The visitors squandered two marvelous scoring opportunities late in the contest. In the sixteenth, Butler launched a sharp single that the left fielder bobbled. Playing conservatively, Kid held up at first base. Witnesses claimed that the fleet-footed Volunteer shortstop could have reached second base easily. Batting next, Seabough sent a line drive into right field that should have scored Butler from the keystone pillow, but he ended up stranded on base. Then, Bay led off the seventeenth inning with a single and advanced to second base on Wiseman's groundout. A wild pitch sent Deerfoot to third base, but he died there when East struck out and McElveen grounded out weakly to the first baseman. During the contest, Bay was uncharacteristically picked off twice. In the bottom of the frame, Siegle made a sensational catch in center field to thwart an extra-base hit. Defensively, both first basemen were active all afternoon. Daubert registered twenty putouts while Mobile's Eddie

Sabrie tallied twenty-eight. As the marathon contest approached the three-hour mark and darkness enveloped the field, umpire Carpenter called the game a tie.

Pitchers Perdue and Torrey were hailed as iron men for their performances in the marathon affair. Hamilton Love wrote in *The Sporting News* that Perdue "has done more than any one man to hold up the [Vols] team."[19] Rice proclaimed it "the greatest game of baseball that has ever been witnessed." Perhaps Yancey said it best when he noted that this might have been the greatest game ever played in Dixie — an encomium that would be resurrected for another Vols game at the end of the season.[20] Regardless of all of the superlatives used to describe the contest, it would go down in Volunteer history as the second-longest game in franchise history, and the longest scoreless feature in Southern Association history.[21]

On 10 July, a scant Mobile crowd was treated to another nail-biting game. Despite a lingering sore arm, Hunter assumed the pitching duty and for the second day in a row, the Vols were involved in an extra-inning tussle. Unlike the previous day, Nashville's defense played poorly as the battery of Hunter and Hardy contributed two of the team's four errors. Mobile held on to a slender 2–0 lead going into the seventh inning when Siegle led off with a single and scored on a triple by Daubert. But Jake rounded third base too far, and the left fielder threw behind him and picked off the careless baserunner. Still, Siegle's run represented the first Volunteer score in twenty-six consecutive innings. The Vols tied the score in the eighth inning by executing small ball. Hunter singled, Bay sacrificed him to second base, and East drove him in on a sharp single. As the game entered its first extra inning, Mobile removed its starting pitcher, "Kitty" Beeker, and replaced him with a relatively unknown pitcher named Gaskill who had taken no warm-up pitches. The unprepared reliever promptly surrendered two base hits and a walk before Wiseman drove in Hardy for the winning run. The Vols were beginning to earn a reputation as a decent road team.

Nashville broke into the scoring column first in the third game with a lone run in the fifth inning. Mobile responded in the bottom of the sixth when Butler committed two errors at shortstop, and both free passes promptly scored on a bases-clearing triple. Bay committed another baserunning mistake when he was picked off of second base for the third time in three games. The mishap suggests that Deerfoot was either losing his concentration or that he might have aggravated his chronic sore knee. Kellum's "float ball" worked to perfection, but his two-hitter ended in a tough one-run loss. Owing to the limited number of available pitchers on both teams, the managers agreed to cancel the second game of the doubleheader despite the fact that they already needed to make up two contests.

In the series finale, Berny worked against the youngster who had been torched for the loss in relief two days earlier, Gaskill. Daubert supplied a single, double, triple, and three RBI to lead the Vols offensively, and Bernhard added a two-run double. As Nashville bunched its hits, Mobile accommodated them by committing seven fielding errors. The home team was probably relieved that the 6–3 loss had not been greater. As Berny's boys headed for Little Rock, they could take comfort in a road trip record of 6–2–1. The two losses came by identical close scores of 2–1.

Rice had noted as early as 28 June that major league scouts and owners were preparing for their annual swing through the South to assess talent. Charlie Ebbets was reportedly interested in examining several Nashville pitchers while the team played in Little Rock. The Brooklyn owner's release of Hunter and Hess at the beginning of the season had come with the unwritten stipulation that the Trolley Dodgers would draft Nashville's top pitching prospect at the end of the 1908 season. It was rumored that Ebbets coveted either Perdue or Duggan.

West Elm Park was home to the best hitter in the Southern Association, rookie outfielder Tris Speaker. As the Vols arrived in the Arkansas capitol for a four-game tilt with their second division opponent, they were amazed to learn about Speaker's most recent feat — the first player in the league to reach the 100-hit plateau. No pitcher could control the lightning quick swing of the left-hander. He was arguably the best prospect in the league and destined to hit over .350 in 1908. As usual, it fell upon Perdue to try to corral the future major league Hall of Famer and his associates in game one.

The Vols had arrived late after an all-night trip from Mobile, and were rushed directly from the train station to the ballpark. Rice quipped that southern railroads had run more efficiently during Confederate times than in the present. The pregame activities took a quirky twist when umpire O'Brien failed to take the field, reportedly due to an eye injury he had recently sustained. As a result, substitute umpires were used for a week. Managers Bernhard and Finn chose two of their injured catchers as arbiters, and after considerable arm-twisting, Scrappy Jack Hardy and Robert Wood agreed to officiate.

The Vols opened the scoring in the top of the first with consecutive singles by East, McElveen, Siegle, and the streaking Daubert, who collected two RBI. Butler's costly throwing error in the bottom of the second was compounded by two more throwing errors by Perdue and led to three Little Rock runs. The Vols evened the score in the top of the fourth, and the score remained tied for the next nine frames. Perdue pitched with special care to Speaker, who collected only two hits on the afternoon. In the twelfth inning, the Nashville pitcher intentionally walked the dangerous center fielder to load the bases with two outs rather than pitch to him. The strategy worked and the Travelers did not score. Darkness caused the game to be canceled after thirteen innings. Perdue may have been crestfallen as Charles Ebbets was in the stands watching him; plus, he had thrown thirty shutout innings in his last two starts without receiving a decision. In his last five games, the gritty

Gallatin Squash had thrown fifty-nine innings and surrendered only five runs (three earned).

Under a Brooklyn contract, Hunter received the nod from Berny to pitch in game two. A steady rain fell throughout the game as deep puddles and tacky mud surrounded all of the base sacks. Hunter and Bill Hart, the ancient Little Rock hurler, were locked in a scoreless tie when the Vols pushed across the first run in the top of the fifth after Butler singled and scored on Hardy's double. The soggy infield slowed Hardy in his attempt to stretch his hit, and the Scrappy One was thrown out at third base by a comfortable margin. Lately the Vols had been guilty of baserunning mistakes. When successful, such efforts were praised as aggressive, but when unsuccessful they were interpreted as foolish attempts. In the eighth inning, Siegle made an outstanding over-the-shoulder catch as he crashed into the outfield wall to rob Tris Speaker of a sure home run. The center fielder injured his back on the play, and afterwards Berny sent him to Nashville where he was briefly hospitalized. Following Siegle's circus catch, Hunter faded and gave up three runs on a hit batter, a fielding error, and two base hits to absorb a 4–1 loss. "For some queer reason," observed Rice, "those pop-eyed Travelers have had the Indian sign on Nashville all season."[22] Perhaps Little Rock's success had something to do with the fact that they led the league in many offensive categories.

Ebbets was neither impressed with Perdue's performance a day earlier nor Hunter's later collapse. The mogul confided to Berny that he considered Ralph Savidge to be the top pitching prospect in the Southern Association. Before he left Little Rock, however, Ebbets made an extravagant offer to purchase Speaker, effective immediately. Team owners rejected the offer, and Speaker remained in a Little Rock uniform, at least for the moment. Ebbets was also impressed with McElveen, and let it be known that the Dodgers were prepared to enter a bidding war with the Tigers and Cardinals for his services.[23] Hearsay eventually turned into reality when McElveen signed a contract with Brooklyn in late summer.

The Vols and Travelers met for a doubleheader on 15 July. The visitors squandered thirteen hits, led by Hunter (3-for-3) and Seabough (4-for-4) in the opener, and produced their lone run in the top of the eighth on consecutive singles by Hunter — the valuable utility player who replaced Siegle in center field — Daubert, and Seabough. Throughout the game, many players on both teams had reached third base only to die there owing to marvelous defensive plays in the field. According to Rice, Duggan completely outpitched "Chief" Eastman — a 200-lb. hurler and supposedly a full-blooded Cherokee Indian.[24] Thrown out at home plate while attempting to score in the seventh inning, Duggan carried a 1–0 lead on a six-hitter into the bottom of the final frame, but he had to face the heart of the Little Rock batting order. With one out, Speaker launched a triple over the head of Bay in left field. Then, McElveen misplayed a routine fly ball that would have been the second out of the inning.

Instead, the blooper scored Speaker and placed another Traveler on base. Perhaps distraught over the premature departure of Ebbets, his potential future boss, Duggan became visibly upset over McElveen's careless error. The next batter, outfielder Beals Becker, crushed one of Duggan's pitches deep over Hunter's head in center field to register the second triple of the inning and complete Little Rock's come-from-behind victory.

The second game of the twin bill required a bit of last-minute heroics on the part of the Volunteers to salvage a split. Kellum faced Jim Buchanan, owner of the league's first no-hitter earlier in the season. East provided most of the Vols' offense with three base hits against his former teammates, including a triple in the fourth inning to open the Nashville scoring. Later, the inspired East broke up a double play attempt at second base with a hard slide into shortstop Monroe Stark. For insurance, East held the defender's arm in order to prevent his throw to first base. Hardy provided the margin of victory with a rare home run that showcased a three-run Nashville eighth inning. Meanwhile, Kellum fooled none of the Little Rock batters who slugged fourteen hits in the game. However, four Traveler errors more than offset their team's impressive offense. Kellum held on to post a 5–4 win despite surrendering solo runs in the bottom of the eighth and ninth innings. League President Kavanaugh witnessed the doubleheader from his personal box seat.

SOUTHERN ASSOCIATION STANDINGS, JULY 16, 1908

	W	L
New Orleans	43	34
Memphis	42	34
Nashville	37	33
Mobile	40	36
Little Rock	41	39
Atlanta	36	33
Montgomery	34	41
Birmingham	25	46

The previous three games in Little Rock were officiated by a former major league umpire named Moran and a former Cotton States League pitcher named Hale. The umpire shortage reflected a larger concern which had recently arisen concerning on-the-field safety of officials. The issue quickly ballooned into a public debate about how player behavior should be controlled by the league. The discussion began following a game in early July when umpire Brown had officiated a game between New Orleans and Montgomery. During a heated moment, Pelican outfielder Frank Delahanty took exception to a call made by Brown and spat in the official's face. President Kavanaugh wasted no time and issued a one-month suspension to the uncouth player. Manager Frank objected to the president's decision and lobbied in the newspapers for the termination of three officials he deemed unfit for Southern Association duty — Brown, O'Brien, and Pfenninger. Frank claimed he had conducted a poll among team managers who unanimously agreed with his charges. When Kavanaugh refused to act on his suggestion, Frank attacked the integrity of the league president. "Too much attention to Arkansas politics and not enough to his league office makes the president's salary an unearned pension," stormed Frank.[25]

Frank's slanderous comment at Kavanaugh received an unfavorable response from the southern and national press. "Manager Frank of New Orleans has come forth with his annual attack on somebody connected with Southern Association baseball," commented *Sporting Life*. Beneath a bold print headline on the front page of *The Sporting News*—KAVANAUGH STILL BOSS— sportswriter Fanner came to the defense of the league mogul. He lauded Kavanaugh's esteemed character and integrity, and praised the league president for attempting to elevate the public perception of the heretofore rowdy league. Prior to Kavanaugh's administration, Fanner reported, the two senior and most intimidating managers, Charlie Frank and Newt Fisher, had manipulated the league's governance to suit their own purposes. They had bullied the executive branch with impunity. Moreover, the duo had terrorized game officials for years by using the home crowd and policemen to intimidate umpires, and successfully lobbied for the removal from league service of anyone who displeased them. "Frank will learn," stated Fanner, "that the period of the bushwhacking and bulldozing magnate has passed." The columnist concluded that Kavanaugh was one of the most capable executives at any level in the game — a lofty accolade from the most widely read sports weekly in the country. Fanner intimated that Frank and the New Orleans franchise ignored the salary cap established by the league, and wryly noted the ability of New Orleans to pay major league salaries to maintain a roster and pitching staff that insured a contender every year, yet never received official sanctions.[26]

Kavanaugh brought the confrontation with Frank to a head when he ordered umpire O'Brien to report for duty to New Orleans in mid–July in spite of manager Frank's unilateral banishment of the official from the Crescent City.[27] O'Brien felt physically threatened, however, and submitted his resignation to Kavanaugh prior to the Little Rock–Nashville series. Like Brown, O'Brien later turned up as an official in the New England League.[28]

Concern over rowdyism and intimidation of officials did not end with the Brown-O'Brien incidents. Less than ten days after O'Brien's resignation, another ugly episode occurred in Montgomery, where police were forced to send for reinforcements and provide an escort back to his hotel for umpire Fitzsimmons following an unpopular call. An unruly mob threatened violence and disregarded police orders to disperse. Instead, enraged fans boarded a trolley car and tailed the constables to Fitzsimmons' lodging. Designing a new plan, an official dressed the alarmed umpire in a disguise in an effort to fool the headstrong crowd and deliver him secretly to the train depot.[29] Kavanaugh had his work cut out to improve working conditions for officials in the Southern Association.

The end of the recent road trip brought the Vols to the home of state rival Memphis. Perdue had thrown a tremendous number of innings on the road swing, but Berny stuck with his strategy. Perdue faced a quality pitcher in Bill Chappelle — a 6' 2", 200-pounder with service in the major leagues and destined for a six-year stint in the Southern Association. Both hurlers stumbled momentarily out of the chute, but the Volunteers had grown accustomed to extra-inning affairs when Perdue pitched. Wiseman, East, and McElveen collected three hits apiece, but their effectiveness was scattered across eleven innings. In the top of the eleventh, McElveen ripped a triple, and Siegle lofted a sacrifice fly to drive in the go-ahead run. Then, in the bottom of the frame, Memphis shortstop Bill Cranston reached third base with only one out. Player-manager Babb then lined a shallow drive into center field. Hunter charged in, made a fine shoestring catch, and threw a strike to Seabough at the plate to nab Cranston (who had tagged up at third) in a cloud of dust for the final out of the game. Perdue had won for the first time in four starts, but his glee was tempered by a leg injury sustained by Bay. Now, the Vols were without two starting outfielders — Bay and Siegle.

Bernhard and Charlie Shields, a home-grown Memphian, were slated to tangle in the second game of the series. The Nashville manager also had picked Hardy to replace Bay in left field, and unimaginatively placed the sub-par hitter in Bay's leadoff slot in the lineup. This substitution highlighted one of Berny's few managerial weaknesses — his tendency to substitute new players in the same spot in the lineup as the departing player without consideration to such matters as foot speed, batting average, or contact versus power types.

Bernhard spun a marvelous five-hitter, and the outcome was never in doubt as five Vols struck for two hits — Hardy, Wiseman, East, Hunter, and Seabough. The visitors carried a 2–0 lead into the seventh inning when they added three additional tallies on an inside-the-park home run by East, who completed the drama with a slide at the plate. Nashville posted a 6–1 victory.

The game on 19 July was rained out after two scoreless innings, and the soggy Vols headed for home. The recent road swing had been hailed as a tremendous success in the local press. The club went 9–4–2 with series wins over Birmingham, New Orleans, Mobile, and Memphis. They lost only the match with Little Rock. In addition, the Vols played four extra-inning affairs in which they won twice and tied twice. Rice analyzed that the road trip had strengthened the Vols as a team. They had kept pace with the front-running Pelicans, five games back, but also leapt from fifth to second place. The season was shaping up as a real scramble between the first division teams who were seldom separated by more than five games: New Orleans, Memphis, Nashville, and Mobile. Atlanta and Montgomery had slipped dramatically in July, and Little Rock struggled, barely above Birmingham. The Volunteers were now returning to Nashville for their longest homestand of the season — twenty-one games through 12 August.

The Vols had started the July road trip with many unsettled issues. The month since McCormick's defection had tested the team's resolve on whether they would gel or not as an effective unit. Berny worked diligently to right the Volunteer's ship by stabilizing the roster. He made an immediate impact in selecting McElveen as team captain. Although the position was largely ceremonial — exchanging lineup cards with the home plate official prior to each game — McElveen's promotion sent a clear message to the rest of the men. It revealed exactly what kind of a player Berny valued — hard-working, competitive, and possessing professional respect for the game. Then, Berny removed the last non-contributor with the release of Yerkes, and strengthened the infield substantially by acquiring East, who was a solid contact hitter. Moreover, East's arrival allowed Butler to move back to his accustomed position at shortstop.

The team responded favorably to Berny's style of leadership; Perdue displayed his stamina pitching extra-inning games, and Hunter demonstrated courage despite injury. Kellum and Berny provided the stability and confidence expected of former major leaguers. Offensively, Daubert, McElveen, and Seabough were beginning to swing hot bats for extra-base hits, and Wiseman, Bay, and East were dependably getting on base. Butler and Siegle offered the club steady defensive play at the key positions of shortstop and center field. Offensive production on their part would be a bonus. Only Hardy remained an enigma. Scrappy Jack's attitude festered and presented a stumbling block to team morale as his haughty behavior in Montgomery illustrated. His skill behind the plate was never in doubt.

By late July, the Vols still faced an array of concerns. First, the team was still in need of another quality starting pitcher; no one knew how long the aging arms of Berny or Kellum would hold out. And injuries were beginning to take their toll on the team; there was no telling how long it would take Siegle (sore back), Bay (sore leg), Hunter (sore arm), and Hardy and Duggan (bruised egos) to mend. One thing was certain — the club could not sustain further injuries and compete for the 1908 championship.

The season was now heading into the dog days of summer when afternoon game temperatures consistently ranged in the low- to mid–90s. And the stifling humidity! Southern Association teams rarely put on big winning spurts at this point in the season, but hung on to play break-even baseball. Clubs that managed to avoid long losing streaks and stay healthy stood the greatest chance of making a successful pennant run in September.

Chapter 7

Dog Days of Summer

The hot and muggy summertime in the American South was guaranteed to sap energy from even the hardiest athlete. Berny had assembled his kind of team in a remarkably short period of time, but greater challenges were yet to come. Could the team rebound from nagging injuries, play as well at home as they had on the road, and overcome adversities like McCormick's defection? Between 20 July and the end of August, the Volunteers were slated to play thirty-six games. Berny's formula for success in these dog days of summer— dominate weak teams while splitting with more powerful clubs— seemed practical. The manner in which Berny reacted to unforeseen difficulties like injuries, substitutions, new talent, and the pitching rotation was equally important to the equation. If the Vols could endure these mental and physical hardships and cope with the climate, they would be in position to make a legitimate run at the league championship in September.

Berny's Vols were beginning to attract national and regional attention following the recent road trip. Correspondents for Birmingham and Memphis in *The Sporting News* complemented the Vols as "a smooth lot of ball players."[1] On the eve of the homestand Rice interviewed Berny. "We've got the gamest team I ever saw on a ball field," noted the Nashville manager. "They don't know what the word 'quit' means.... You can't beat that kind of ball playing.... I always think that a team of hustlers would beat any other kind of team on earth."[2] But not all kudos were reserved for the men on the field. Addressing Bernhard's style of leadership, the sports editor of the *Atlanta Journal* observed:

> Bill Bernhard, commander-in-chief of the Nashville Volunteers ... is a [strong] man who knows the game from the beginning to the end, and

because he knows how to lead his men. He is quiet and conservative at all times.... He maintains perfect discipline and does it in a way that does not make a display of his power as manager. He is getting the very best possible efforts out of all the players. One of the secrets of his success is that [he] never loses his temper.... He takes life in a rational manner and expects his players to do the same thing.[3]

Rice summarized Berny's attributes best: "The secret of it all is that Bernhard has stuck by his team and the team has stuck by Bernhard."[4] In the first half of the season, he had dealt with tough personnel changes and kept the Vols in contention despite injuries and pitching woes.

Evidence suggests that the Vols were poised to improve in the league standings. Not only was the twenty-one-game homestand justification for optimism, but the visitors in that stretch came mostly from the "eastern theater"— teams with the poorest records. At the same time, Nashville's stiffest competitors came from the West, and they all hit the road. The opportunity seemed ripe for the Vols to make a move.

On 20 July the largest home crowd of the season, an estimated 3,000 fans, jammed into Sulphur Dell to welcome the team home. The grandstands were packed, and many late-arriving rooters had to sit behind a roped-off area in the Dump. Showing appreciation for the team's recent road success, the fans gave the Vols a standing ovation as they warmed up. "The old town is baseball mad just now," scribbled Ewing in the *American*.[5]

Siegle returned to the Nashville lineup, and an attractive matchup featured Duggan versus Little Rock's John Neuer, a utilityman pressed into pitching for the first time this season. Neuer looked sharp in his debut. The southpaw did not allow a baserunner until the fourth, scattered nine hits, gave up only one run until the final frame, and notched nine strike outs. Duggan was even sharper. After surrendering a first-inning score, the Hoosier shut down the most potent offense in the league for the next thirteen innings. He allowed only four hits, and no Traveler reached base after the tenth inning. In the bottom of the fourteenth, Siegle and Butler "touched off the fuse to the powder magazine."[6] Siegle led off with a double that rolled up the incline in the Dump, and Daubert sacrificed him to third base, whereupon Butler delivered a walk-off RBI single to win the game. The two-hour contest was the Vols' fourth extra-inning game in two weeks.

The second game looked like an equally exciting pair of starters as Perdue squared off against hard-throwing Jim Buchanan. The Vols had opportunities early on, but Little Rock outfielders played stupendous defense and robbed Vols hitters on "drives that looked as safe as a Democratic nominee in Texas or a Republican machine in Vermont," said Rice.[7] Conversely, Nashville played sloppy defense and committed three infield errors. The only excitement occurred in the eighth when Perdue nailed John Connors on the elbow with a fastball. Rice quipped that the Trav first sacker "flopped around like a ten-pound fish hooked to a tortilla." The game was played at a brisk pace, and Perdue absorbed a loss, 3–0.[8]

The final meeting between Little Rock and Nashville consisted of enough offense to satisfy even the most complacent spectator as the game turned into an old-fashioned slugfest. Neither Hunter nor Elwood "Pop" Eyler were in command of their pitches. The Vols scored first in the second, and one frame later exploded for nine more tallies. In all, thirteen Vols went to the plate and stroked eight hits, including triples by East and Butler. Spotted a 10–0 lead, Hunter and the Nashville defense relaxed, but the Travelers mounted a steady comeback, beginning in the fifth inning. When the afternoon dust had settled, the Vols had scored fifteen runs on twenty hits and five errors. Every Vols hitter reached base safely, and everyone had scored except Butler. Bay returned to the lineup after spending two days in the hospital and responded with four hits, but limped noticeably. Little Rock finished with eight runs on thirteen hits and four errors. Hunter, Eyler, and reliever Buchanan issued ten bases on balls and allowed fifty-two runners to reach base. The game dragged on for almost 2½ hours, the longest of the entire season. "About as poorly played a contest as can be imagined," summarized Ewing in the *American*.[9]

Rice took backstage on the laugher to write insightful words on the unsung hero of the Vols: "Siegle has been a big card in the Volunteer's upward progress, for while there are no particular flourishes to his style of play he looms up as one of the most consistent actors in the league."[10] A nice tribute to a quiet everyday performer. On a more worrisome note, Duggan left the team, allegedly to be with his ailing brother Elmer in Indiana. In a conflicting news release, Berny stated that Duggan had been sent home to rest following his fourteen-inning victory over Little Rock three days earlier.[11]

Thomas "Red" Fisher brought his Sea Gulls to town on 23 July for three games at the Dell. The opener against Mobile contrasted sharply with the contest of a day earlier; it was a low-scoring contest dominated by good pitching. The game also brought attention to a growing trend in recent Nashville games—plenty of defensive mistakes. Butler muffed three grounders at shortstop to lead the team's five miscues. The Vols had misfired ten times in the field in the last two games, with Daubert and Butler accounting for four guffaws apiece.

The Volunteers had ample opportunities to reach Mobile hurler Gordon Hickman. They loaded the bases in the first and fifth innings, but stranded all six and left thirteen runners on base overall. Kellum tossed a six-hitter, but took a disappointing 2–0 loss. A rainout the following day allowed the local nines to rest and regroup. In the meantime, Nashville's gossip mill was discussing Berny's plan to recall Sitton, who was currently leading Jacksonville toward the SALLY pennant with a 17–5 record. The Clemson product had turned some heads when he recently won both ends of a doubleheader by throwing a three- and four-hitter. With Duggan unavailable to take his normal place in the rotation, Berny was desperate for another arm.[12]

In the final game of the Mobile series, Perdue faced Torrey and fans anticipated a repeat of their seventeen-inning, scoreless marathon on 9 July. The historic no decision would not be duplicated, however. The field was slippery and wet after nearly two days of thundershower activity. Berny had ordered several wagonloads of sawdust, which was sprinkled on the infield to absorb the moisture. The Perdue-Torrey billing did not live up to its advance hype as the pitchers gave up eight and thirteen hits respectively. With the score jammed at 1-1 in the top of the fourth, Paul Sentell shocked the crowd when he successfully stole home plate to give the visitors the lead. Then Daubert delivered a clutch two-run single with two outs in the bottom of the fifth inning. The home team tacked on an insurance run and cruised to a 4–2 victory, but Berny could not have been pleased. His team made thirteen hits but scored only four runs. More distressing was the continuation of fielding mistakes—three more—for a total of sixteen errors in the past four games.

Prior to departing for a single make-up game in Memphis on Sunday, 26 July, an interesting plea appeared in the *Tennessean* and *Banner*. Apparently, there had been growing complaints from male patrons at Sulphur Dell concerning female spectators who came to the ballpark wearing the fashion of the day—the merry widow hat. The gigantic bonnet obstructed the view of the field for anyone sitting directly behind one of them. Yancey requested that women should remove their hats as a courtesy to all patrons, a curious suggestion which defied southern feminine social custom of the day. One annoyed letter to the editor demanded Vols management to do away with Ladies Day altogether. Rice supported his colleague's concern about the tall headgear, but the issue went unresolved.[13]

Bernhard stepped up to fill in for Duggan until the Hoosier returned to active duty, but he faced a determined challenger in Joe Garrity. The feisty submariner struck out five Vols in the first three innings and did not surrender a hit between the second and eleventh innings. Berny threw smartly, and took a 1-0 lead into the bottom of the ninth when a passed ball by Hardy tied the score at one run apiece. The game remained deadlocked until the top of the thirteenth when Hardy tripled and Berny drove him in. Afterward, Berny complained about a sore shoulder, but the 2–1 victory in extra innings and his key hit must have relieved his pain. Approximately one hundred Nashville fans, including several women in their merry widow hats, and Alf Williams—the self-proclaimed leader of the Volunteer boosters—paid $5 to make the round trip to Memphis.

The Vols returned to Nashville for an important series against the league-leading New Orleans Pelicans, whom they trailed by only 1½ games. Berny opted to start Kellum, who had earned a reputation as a "bird killer." It was a humid afternoon with temperatures reaching 90 degrees. As predicted, Kellum throttled Pelican batters with masterful changes of speed, and allowed no baserunner between the second and eighth innings. Meanwhile, the Vols tallied three runs across eight frames, with East collecting three doubles and an RBI and Daubert going 2-for-3 with two RBI. Kellum tired in the last two innings, surrendered four singles and a lone run, but held onto a 3–1 victory.

Hunter took his ailing soupbone to the slab for the middle game against "Ginger" Clark. Both teams played exceptional defense for five innings. In the top of the sixth, Hunter fell apart, walking three batters in a row (four in all) and surrendering a bases-loaded triple to Charlie Dexter, which flew over Bay's bewildered replacement in left field — Scrappy Jack Hardy. In all, Hunter had faced eleven batters and given up six runs in the costly frame. Hunter's collapse underscored Nashville's pitching dilemma because there was no other hurler available to enter in relief; Berny nursed a sore shoulder, Kellum complained of stiffness from his start, Duggan was still gone, and Perdue had reported to the park with a fever. Despite his chronic soreness, Hunter would have to continue to pitch. "The southpaw blew into so many pieces that the fragments were still falling when the battle ended," chuckled Rice in reference to Hunter's performance.[14] The Vols were not offensively ineffective, however. Everyone except Hardy collected at least one safety in a twelve-hit attack. Wiseman, McElveen, and Daubert clubbed triples, and the Vols mounted a ferocious rally in the bottom of the eighth. Hunter opened the festivities with the team's fourth triple, and three runs pushed across the plate. Then, with two outs in the bottom of the ninth, the Vols loaded the bases only to see an impatient McElveen pop out on the first pitch to end the game in the Pelican's favor, 7–5.

Berny showed true professionalism in assuming the pitching duties for the final game against New Orleans on only two days of rest. He threw several wild pitches and hit a batter, but his wildness kept the Pelicans in check and resulted in an impressive five-hit shutout. New Orleans contributed to their own demise with five errors, including two in the first inning by new acquisition George Nill. One of the ex–Clevelander's miscues led to Nashville's first score when Berny signaled for a first-and-third delayed steal and Nill muffed the coverage. In contrast, Daubert stood out for his graceful handiwork around first base. Jake was emerging as a fan favorite: "The demon first sacker has handed out some ... plays that looked well nigh impossible," marveled Rice. "Time and again he figured in the center of a sensation, stretching his system until he looked like a snapshot of the Rubber Trust in action."[15]

The frustrated New Orleans bunch resorted to a tactic that had brought them success in the past — intimidation of the game official. In the second inning, Butler slapped a single and Hardy followed with a scorching drive down the third base line. The speedy shortstop scampered around the bases and scored. Angry Pelican infielders surrounded umpire Dan Pfenninger and argued that Scrappy Jack's blow had landed in foul territory. Second baseman Augie Dundon yelled vociferously and delivered a stiff-arm to Pfenninger's chest for added emphasis. The blow spun the official completely around, whereupon pitcher Charlie Fritz repeated the action. The visitors "evidently pooh-poohed Dan's ancestry with dire suggestions about his future," noted Rice.[16] Vinegar Dan, not the type of arbiter to be bullied, promptly threw Dundon out of the game and play resumed. The 2–0 lead stood as Berny collected his fourth straight victory; in his last twenty-two innings of work, the Nashville manager had given up only one earned run.

Julius Augustus Wiseman was considered by ardent Vols followers the dean of Southern Association players. Commenting on the outfielder's athleticism, Yancey observed: "The way Doc works the Dump is this: He goes up higher than necessary and then if the ball is below him he finds it much easier to race back down than it would have been to try and climb higher."[17] By 1908, Wiseman's steady play and longevity with Nashville earned him a degree of community respect tendered to no other Vol. Wiseman's boyish good looks, slender frame, and vigorous hustle made him a huge hit with the Nashville ladies. "Again, did you ever watch the ladies when Doc is to the bat?" questioned Ewing. "The ladies like Doc, that's all there is to it. They are all excitement when the Little Doctor marches to the plate with his trusty hickory. And, if he is lucky enough to cop a safety they squeal with delight."[18] Wiseman was arguably the most popular man in a Nashville uniform for the entire decade.

More than 9,000 fans had turned out for the three games with New Orleans. If any opponent raised the competitive hackles of Nashvillians more than the Pelicans, it was the next visitor from Memphis. Manager Babb had kept his hard-shellers in the hunt for the crown all season; the Turtles had not dropped lower than fourth place and were always in striking distance of the league leaders. The cross-state rivals arrived at Sulphur Dell on 30 July for an important showdown.

Still suffering the effects of a fever, Perdue pitched the opener, and his shaky condition probably affected his demeanor because he did not allow a hit until the sixth inning. Then the Turtles broke a 1–1 tie with four singles in the seventh to push two more runs across the plate. Berny came on in relief, but the Memphii had discovered an offensive groove and torched the Nashville player-manager for two additional runs. Some Vols appeared listless: Daubert committed a rare error at first base, and later fell victim to a mental mistake at the plate. While batting in the bottom of the seventh, Jake had taken a called third strike, but catcher Harry Matthews mishandled the pitch. The ball bounced off the face of the grandstand behind home plate, but Daubert merely watched as the catcher retrieved it and tagged him out. Did fatigue, heat, or illness play a role in Daubert's uncharacteristic blunder? No one ventured an opinion. Meanwhile, the first baseman's teammates had accomplished little offensively. The home team had loaded the bases twice, only to be turned away empty-handed. Trailing by a score of 5–2 in the bottom of the ninth, the Vols loaded the bases when Babb inserted renowned knuckleballer Ralph Savidge to face Berny with one down. The ex–Clevelander drove Savidge's first offering deep into the left field corner, but the ball hooked into foul territory and bounced off the sulphur spring house. Nashville's hopes were dashed as the player-manager then grounded into a double play to end the game.

Duggan's return to Nashville was greeted by hearsay, which insinuated his recent absence owed less to physical illness or family problems than to dissatisfaction with his teammates for not delivering enough run support in his recent starts. His return also coincided with speculation about the impending arrival of Sitton. Some reports said the South Carolinian would be wearing Nashville flannels by the end of the week.[19] In spite of the lack of answers surrounding Duggan's ten-day absence, Berny immediately inserted the Hoosier in the lineup.

Duggan opposed the tough Ralph Savidge, the relief savior of game one. At 6' 2", "The Human Whipcord" was considered one of the elite hurlers in the league. Despite his layoff, Duggan pitched effectively. In the top of the fourth, Turtle shortstop Bill Cranston drove a line drive to left field. Playing in place of the lame Bay, Hunter charged in aggressively but misjudged the ball, which bounced off the top of his foot. Cranston coasted into second base. Then Babb sacrificed Cranny to third base, and Cranston scored on a sacrifice fly by first baseman George Carey. The Memphii had executed little ball perfectly and made the lone run stand up despite the fact that the Vols had played flawless defense themselves. Doc Wiseman led the way with seven putouts as he roamed up and down the incline in the Dump. The best opportunity for a home team score occurred in the bottom of the eighth when Hunter led off and was struck by a pitch. He promptly stole second and third base, but such thievery went for naught when the middle of the Nashville order failed to deliver a key hit or sacrifice. The Vols ended on the short end of a heartbreaking 1–0 loss. More important, East sustained an ankle injury following an awkward slide. The second baseman had to be carried off the field with his playing status in doubt.

A large number of rooters passed through the Sulphur Dell turnstiles to witness the final game between the instate rivals. As expected, East sat out to nurse "a swollen ankle that resembled a cantaloupe." Berny replaced the Ohio native with fellow Buckeye Scrappy Jack Hardy, who also inherited East's critical third spot in the lineup despite his low batting average. The Vols jumped out quickly in the bottom of the first as Wiseman and Hardy singled and scored on Siegle's two-bagger to the Dump. Play was temporarily suspended in the second frame when Turtle second baseman Harry Redmond was hit square in the nose by a hard ground ball. The "spheroid had pecked him in the nostril, smearing that portion of his physical anatomy all over his features," reported Rice, "For about ten minutes, the stricken athlete oozed enough gore to float a battleship."[20] Teammates escorted the woozy Redmond to the bench, where a doctor set the broken beak. When action resumed, Hardy took advantage of his rare start by launching the first of two triples. Meanwhile, Kellum kept

August

Mon	Tue	Wed	Thu	Fri	Sat	Sun
					1 Mem	2
3 Birm	4 Birm	5 Birm	6 Atl	7 Atl	8 Atl	9
10 Mont	11 Mont	12 Mont	13 @Atl	14 @Atl	15 @Atl	16
17 @Mont	18 @Mont	19 @Mont	20 @Birm	21 @Birm	22 @Birm	23
24 @L.R.	25 @L.R.	26 @L.R.	27	28 @Mem	29 @Mem	30 @Mem
31 @N.O.						

Atl = Atlanta
Birm = Birmingham
L.R. = Little Rock
Mem = Memphis
Mob = Mobile
Mont = Montgomery
N.O. = New Orleans
Bold print= @ Nashville
(2) =Double Header

Memphis batters off balance with off-speed pitches. Trailing by three runs, the visitors posed a threat in the eighth inning when they loaded the bases, but Seabough squelched the Turtles' rally when he picked up a bunt in front of the dish and initiated a plate-to-first, inning-ending double play. Kellum coasted to a 3–0 victory in the well-played contest and salvaged the last game of the series. Nashville held onto second place by a slender margin.

Baseball fever had struck Nashville as over 16,000 patrons filed into Sulphur Dell to watch the six games versus the front-running Pelicans and third-place Turtles. Everyone anticipated the arrival of Birmingham—a team twenty-one games off the pace. Yancey warned that the Barons were playing more competitive baseball under the direction of new player-manager Carleton Molesworth. When Birmingham took the field on 3 August, it also marked the final appearance of every team visiting Sulphur Dell; the season had reached the two-thirds point.

Perdue had returned on the morning train from his home in Gallatin to a rumor that he was unhappy with Berny's decision to yank him in the eighth inning of his previous start against Memphis. In reality, Perdue's spate of extra-inning heroics were beginning to take a physical toll on his shoulder. The pitcher also believed his string of extraordinary performances were underappreciated by the locals, so thought the *Tennessean*. Hub acted indifferent as he worked on the slab, observed Yancey, "and fielded like an elephant."[21] Baron left fielder Noah Henline lit up Perdue for four hits and scored Birmingham's first three runs. When the mush-armed Squash surrendered a fourth run in the seventh inning, hecklers in the stands bantered that Berny should "take out the cheese." In all, the Barons unleashed fourteen hits, and the Vols did not record a solitary hit until the seventh inning. Playing out of position at second base, Hardy committed an error and neglected to cover first base twice when Daubert had left his sack to field bunts. Rice held Hardy personally responsible for three Birmingham tallies.[22] The Vols sustained a disappointing 6–2 loss to the lowly "slag men."

Despite a dismal performance in the opener, the Nashville club had reason for celebration. First, Bay returned to the lineup, and his presence permitted Hunter a brief rest. Second, president Kuhn confirmed that Sitton was en route to Nashville. Rice fanned local excitement, reporting that the former Clemson star had tossed a no-hitter in his final outing in Jacksonville, and had been instrumental in bringing the SALLY crown to the Florida city. The sports editor added that Sitton had thrown 67 consecutive innings without allowing a single run to score.[23]

The Vols were due for a break-out game, and one occurred in the second meeting with the Barons at the expense of pitcher "Chick" Robitaille. The sidewheeling Hunter pitched for the Vols and surrendered two early runs, but Nashville batters exploded on anything Robitaille served. Every Vols batter collected at least two hits except Hardy, who probably allowed two errors to affect his hitless plate performance. Bay lashed four hits, and Wiseman drove in six RBI on a pair of doubles that cleared the bases in the seventh and eighth. Nashville scored four times in the fifth, added five more in the seventh and eighth, and finished with fifteen runs, eighteen hits, and twenty-five baserunners. Shortstop Tom Downey added to the Barons' woes with four errors, and third baseman Andrew Larsen was handcuffed by the accuracy of Nashville's bunters—especially Hunter and Bay, who reached base safely five times. Hunter had been so overpowering on the slab that he asked for, and received, permission from Berny to throw the second game of the twin bill. The manager's decision was surprising not because pitching both ends of a doubleheader was a novelty in the Deadball Era; on the contrary, it was somewhat common. Rather, Hunter had nursed a sore arm from the day of his arrival in Nashville. Fortunately, a sudden thunderstorm forced cancellation of the second contest, and saved Hunter's fragile arm from further aggravation.

The Nashville club eagerly awaited the rescheduled doubleheader against Birmingham on 5 August. The steamy 84-degree day compared favorably to the heat generated by torrid Nashville batters as the hometowners picked up where they had left off. The Vols scored runs in the first five innings and spotted Kellum a comfortable 10–0 lead. One of the more exciting plays of the season occurred in the fifth with Wiseman at bat and Seabough on third, Kellum at second, and Bay at first base. The Little Doctor wasted no time and swatted a double in the outfield gap. A great cutoff and relay throw nailed Kellum sliding into home, but unknown to the catcher, the fleet-footed Deerfoot was right behind him. With a sweeping hook slide on the infield side of the plate, Bay scored to the chagrin of the Barons and glee of the fans. Both teams combined for twenty-eight hits and eight errors in the field. Nashville missed the services of East at second base as Hardy made his fifth error in only four games. The Vols notched their second eighteen-hit performance in a row, led by McElveen's four hits and three apiece for Daubert and Bay in the one-sided 13–1 win.

In the Barons' final appearance of the season, Nashville batters continued to sizzle. Duggan assumed the pitching responsibilities but Rice complained that he was "unsteady, wild, ineffective, and horribly weak."[24] He surrendered only five hits, but gave up five additional free passes. Ewing opined that the pitcher "virtually lost the best opportunity of the season by his liberality with bases on balls."[25] Both teams exchanged runs in the third, fifth, and sixth innings, and an outstanding defensive play was turned in by Molesworth to shut down a Vols rally in the third. With two outs, Bay and Wiseman were in scoring position as McElveen dug in at the plate. "At the crack of the bat the fleet Baron (Molesworth) wheeled and started for the trench beyond the signboard in center field. The ball whizzed over his bun just as he reached the edge of the tall grass, and with his back to the setting sun, still moving at full speed, the visiting leader flung out his bare talons and speared the near-triple as he wallowed into the morass. It was, without any doubt, the greatest catch ever made in Sulphur Dell," recounted Rice.[26]

Moley's fantastic grab frustrated a Vols team that squandered twelve hits in which every player reached base; Wiseman went 4-for-5. Baron right fielder Carlos "The Human Giraffe" Smith sealed victory with a home run that cleared the Dump and landed in the middle of cotton bales stacked along the railroad tracks. Smith's blast duplicated his 1906 feat by being the first visitor to hit a ball out of Sulphur Dell. The Vols took advantage of Birmingham's major weakness, pitching, accumulating sixty base hits. Wiseman led the way with eleven safeties and RBI for the series and McElveen chipped in nine hits, several for extra bases, in the last four outings. Despite splitting the doubleheader, the Vols slipped into first place by .003.

Nashville players hoped to increase their soaring batting averages against rookie sensation Roy Radabaugh and the slumping Atlanta Crackers on 6 August. The defending league champs had fallen upon hard times in the pitching department, and dropped into the second division of the standings. Young

"Rady" had every reason to be nervous in his first appearance as he faced the hottest-hitting team in the league—the Nashville Vols. The hometown nines jumped on the newcomer for three runs in the first two innings. Berny kept the Crackers off the bases and the Vols offense pounded eleven hits—the fourth game in a row in which the team had hit for double digits in base hits. Berny coasted to his second shutout, 6–0.

The middle game against Atlanta marked the long-anticipated debut of Sitton on the slab. The former Clemsonian had wrapped up business in Jacksonville a little more than a week earlier, and arrived in Nashville in time to watch the twin bill with the Barons. Berny wanted to see if the spitballer lived up to all the South Atlantic League hype, and inserted Sitton to work against Bert Maxwell, a promising 21-year-old rookie in his own right. A large crowd arrived to seek validation of Sitton's skills.

Player transactions went by a different set of rules in the Deadball Era. Minor league teams like Nashville might own the rights to other minor league players at lower classifications, and no other team above Nashville had the right to interfere with that privilege. Thus, when Nashville drafted Sitton in 1907 he could not be plucked from the roster by Toledo or Cleveland. In this manner, every classification in professional baseball could develop its own working relationship with individual players and/or teams in the lesser leagues without fear of being pirated from above. This is the relationship that was in operation prior to the creation of more formal working agreements, i.e., the farm system.

If any doubt existed about the talent of the sandy-haired Sitton prior to his first start in the Southern Association, it was dispelled by the end of the afternoon. The rookie weaved a masterful four-hitter and struck out eight Crackers to win a squeaker, 2–1. Daubert made fifteen putouts at first base, indicating that the stoop-shouldered right-hander had plenty of velocity on his fastball as well as movement on his spitter. The Crackers' lone score occurred when Sitton failed to cover first base as Daubert fielded a bunt. Without much offense of their own against Maxwell, the Vols scored the go-ahead run in the bottom of the fifth when Siegle singled to score McElveen. An unlikely offensive hero, Siegle posted two of Nashville's five hits. In the recent offensive juggernaut against Birmingham, the center fielder had struggled at the plate (4-for-19), but his defensive acumen kept him in the lineup. "Johnny is extremely popular with the fans," supported Ewing, "and always gives the best he has got. Nashville has a right to be proud of such a man."[27] Sitton's commanding performance provided hope that he might live up to his advanced billing as the savior of Nashville baseball.

A doubleheader was slated to conclude the Crackers-Vols series on 8 August, but the day was dreary and damp. During a first-inning drizzle, the Vols loaded the bases on three bases on balls issued by Atlanta twirler Bill Viebahn. With one out, Siegle hit a sacrifice fly to left field to drive in Wiseman, and contributed a second RBI in the sixth to cap the victory. For two days in a row, Siegle's offense carried the team. He turned in several fine defensive plays, too, and the rest of the Vols played errorless in back of Hunter. Owing to constant rainfall, Hunter later admitted that he threw only four curveballs in the 2–0 win. The second game of the twin bill was rained out, and Atlanta left town a discouraged lot, having scored only one run in three games.

Montgomery reported to Sulphur Dell sporting a new leader as Senator ownership had fired Manager Jimmie Ryan a week earlier and replaced him with first baseman Ed Gremminger. After jumping to a quick start in the first month of the season, Montgomery had slipped in the standings and languished in the middle of the pack. Team moguls hoped that "Battleship Ed" would restore the club to original form. The Alabama squad had actually begun a resurgence in the final days of Ryan, winning twelve of its last sixteen games.

A nice-sized crowd greeted Duggan in hopes of seeing him handcuff Montgomery. The Hoosier spotted the Senators a first-inning run, and then settled into a comfortable rhythm. Nashville scored twice in the third inning off Elmer Bliss, but a brouhaha nearly ensued when Butler spiked Clayton Perry in a close force-out play at third base. In the bottom of the next inning, former Baron Pat Reagan offered a lesson in how not to play the Dump when Daubert sent a towering fly ball to deep right field. Reagan twisted and turned several times while backpedaling up the incline, became dizzy, and fell down; the ball, nearly dinged him on the head. Gremminger ran all the way from first base to retrieve the ball which lay in the grass near the collapsed outfielder's feet. Meanwhile, Daubert sprinted to third base with a triple. Only McElveen and Butler failed to reach base in the game, and many fly ball putouts punctuated the contest. The Vols had captured their fifth consecutive win, 6–1.

The temperature climbed to 88 degrees at game time on 11 August, but Kellum, known as a nibbler, could not throw a strike. Rice said the sidewinder "heard the Call of the Wild," a reference to the popular adventure story written by Jack London and metaphor for the fact that Kellum had issued four bases on balls in key situations.[28] The Senators threw Ted Guese, a New Orleans castoff with a 3–0 record against the Vols. "Whitey" or "Old Man" Guese kept Nashville batters guessing all afternoon. The Vols produced only one run on a wild pitch, and fumbled the baseball for five errors in "moth-eaten support" of Kellum, who lost, 3–1. On a more ominous note, Perdue, who had not pitched since 4 August, had aggravated a tender shoulder. Berny announced that Sitton would fill in for the popular workhorse, who would not reappear for two weeks.

Berny faced Senator pitcher Forrest Thomas in the final game of the homestand. Both pitchers performed well, and baserunners were at a premium throughout the afternoon. In the bottom of the second, McElveen doubled and two bases on balls loaded the sacks with two outs. On the first pitch to Berny, McElveen noticed that the third baseman was in a deep defensive position and not holding him close to the bag. More important, the pitcher was ignoring Humpy, too. When the count reached 1–1, the aggressive team captain broke for home on the pitcher's delivery to the plate. "McElveen emerged from the cloud of dust to a noisy ovation," reported Rice in the *Tennessean*.[29] The daring stunt worked and Nashville took a 1–0 lead. Montgomery threw a scare into Vols fans when a runner reached scoring position in the top of the ninth, but Berny stranded him. The Nashville manager was able to protect the lead and preserve his third straight shutout.

The productive twenty-one-game homestand came to a satisfying conclusion with the Vols clinging to first place over the pesky Pelicans, who trailed by a slim two-game margin. The Nashvillians amassed an impressive 13–8 record and increased their overall record to 53–41. The crucial game in the homestand, the victory over Birmingham on 4 August, was the beginning of an important 7–2 run that catapulted the Vols into first place. In the homestand, Nashville lost only one series to Memphis while dominating Birmingham and Atlanta. In addition, the tough series against the Pelicans showed that the Vols could compete with the perennial contenders.

Halfway through the dog days of summer, the Vols prepared to go on the road. The longest trip of the season, twenty-four games between 13 August and 5 September, would surely test the team's newfound success. The Vols would not return to Sulphur Dell until the traditional Labor Day doubleheader against Memphis. In addition, the team might be forced to play as many as seven doubleheaders in order to make up games canceled earlier in the season. Thus, the Vols could conceivably take the field as much as thirty-one times in twenty-three days. Such a grueling pace would stretch the wounded pitching staff to its limit as well as pressure the defense and offense, which was prone to streaky production. The concluded homestand had been equally successful at the turnstiles as almost 40,000 spectators had crammed into Sulphur Dell to cheer for the Vols.

When the Vols pulled into the Georgia capital on 13 August, Atlanta was in a tailspin. The Crackers had recently lost two key players for the remainder of the season — pitcher Roy Castleton had contracted typhoid fever and leading hitter George Winters recently dislocated his shoulder. East returned to the Nashville lineup, greeted pitcher Bill Viebahn with a triple in his first at-bat to score Wiseman, and spotted the visitors a first-inning lead. Viebahn settled down and retired the Vols 1–2–3 in the next five innings, and helped himself with a game-tying home run in the bottom of the third inning. The righthander's overpowering performance would not be forgotten by Berny in the offseason. The sore-armed Hunter, on the other hand, relied heavily on breaking balls, and Cracker batters struck for two runs in the sixth and eighth innings on the way to a 5–2 victory. McElveen contributed to the opening loss with an error at third base — the Tennessean's sixth miscue in seven games. In the first pitch count ever published in a Nashville newspaper, Yancey reported that Hunter threw 108 pitches while the victorious Viebahn tossed only 85.[30]

The return of East cemented Berny's lineup for the remainder of the season. The manager followed this batting order with rare exception:

Bay	LF	Daubert	1st
Wiseman	RF	Butler	SS
East	2nd	Seabough	C
McElveen	3rd	(or Hardy)	
Siegle	CF	Pitcher	P

The Vols and Crackers squared off in a make-up doubleheader on 14 August, which featured Sitton's second start. The pugnacious South Carolinian matched up against cagey Russell Ford, and the spitballers kept the score low on a pair of four-hitters. In the final frame, Wiseman led off with a base on balls. East laid down a sacrifice bunt but the Crackers' catcher threw the ball into right field. When the dust settled, Wiseman had circled the bases to score and East stood on second base. McElveen advanced East, and Siegle doubled the second baseman home. Daubert ended the scoring with a mammoth home run to cavernous right-center field. The four-run ninth sealed a 5–1 victory for the visitors. In an interesting footnote, the Crackers had recently added Sitton's brother and Jacksonville teammate, Phil, to their depleted pitching staff.

The second game of the twin bill ended in spectacular fashion on a controversial call. The Vols spotted Duggan a 2–0 lead in the second, and the hard thrower made the score hold up until the bottom of the ninth inning. Then left fielder Roy Moran reached first base following a costly fielding error by Butler at shortstop. The Crackers proceeded to play little ball, and moved the runner into scoring position. Scrappy Jack Hardy, who was catching for the first time in sixteen games, served a two-base error, which led to Atlanta tying the score, much to the delight of the screaming fans in Ponce de Leon Park. With two outs, second baseman Otto Jordan danced up and down the third base line as the Crackers' pitcher stepped into the batter's box. Harry Johns promptly took two called strikes. The impatient Jordan was not about to stand idle and watch his hurler go down on strikes and kill the rally. As Duggan went into his pitching motion, Jordan broke for home plate. The anxious Johns waved ineffectively at the ball and the umpire pronounced "strike three" as Jordan crossed the dish. Hardy did not handle the ball cleanly, however. Dropping the ball, he picked it up, and rolled it to the pitcher's box. Meanwhile, Johns was walking toward the Atlanta bench as his relief, pitcher Bill Viebahn, strolled toward the slab. At that moment, pandemonium broke loose when first-base coach and shortstop Louis Castro shouted at Johns to run to first base. The Vols players stood dumbfounded along the bench; upon reaching first base, umpire Brown declared Johns safe, the run good, and the game over in Atlanta's favor.

A host of angry Nashville players surrounded the official and argued, but to no avail, and settled for a heartbreaking 3–2 loss. Hardy had single-handedly kept the Atlanta rally alive, and then cemented the loss with the grievous mental error by failing to throw the dropped third strike to first base. Writing in the *American,* Ewing praised the decision by Nashville management to pick up Seabough at the start of the season, and chided that "Hardy lacks a noodle in the pinches."[31]

Since both ends of the doubleheader had been decided in the last frame, the fourth and final encounter of the season between the Vols and Crackers promised to be a barn-burner. The Vols felt like the second game on 14 August had been stolen from them, and a degree of urgency surrounded their preparation for the series finale. The game turned into a scoreless duel between Kellum and Bert Maxwell, however. Atlanta scored a run in the bottom of the seventh, and the score held as the Vols took their final at-bat. East walked with one out and Berny inserted the newcomer, Sitton, as a pinch-runner. Maxwell had thrown brilliantly all afternoon, but drilled McElveen with the next pitch. Siegle grounded out to the right side of the infield and pushed both Vols baserunners into scoring position. Daubert was intentionally walked to load the bases for Butler. Seeing a golden opportunity to win the game, Berny made his second managerial decision of the inning and sent Hunter to pinch-hit for the light-hitting shortstop. On the second pitch, Hunter launched a bases-clearing triple to the outfield wall to give Nashville a stunning 3–1 lead. Atlanta brought the winning run to the plate in the bottom of the inning but failed to score. Wiseman, ever ready to be used wherever needed, filled in for Butler at shortstop. The come-from-behind win gave the Vols their second ninth-inning victory in three days.

As Nashville boarded a train for Montgomery, the squad was keenly aware of its current position in the standings. With only forty games left on the schedule, the race for the league crown was unbelievably tight. Seven games separated the first-place Vols from the seventh-place Crackers, and only the Barons were out of contention. As the championship hung in the balance, the Vols were about to face a formidable opponent in Montgomery. The Senators had played the Vols tough all season, holding a two-game advantage (and one tie) in sixteen previous encounters. Earlier in the season they had stuck several one-sided defeats on Nashville, and stellar center fielder Archie Persons always played his former team with extra fervor.

SOUTHERN ASSOCIATION STANDINGS, AUGUST 16, 1908

	W	L
Nashville	55	43
New Orleans	56	46
Memphis	54	49
Mobile	53	50
Montgomery	50	50
Little Rock	53	55
Atlanta	49	51
Birmingham	36	62

Berny chose Sitton to make his third start in ten days. The Vols drew the ace of the Montgomery pitching staff, Forrest Thomas. Sitton tricked no one, and the Alabamans scored five runs in the bottom of the third. Again, the newest Vols member failed to field his position in two sacrifice situations. Indeed, improper coverage of bunts seemed to be his main weakness. Senator baserunners also took advantage of catcher Seabough for seven stolen bases. Persons continued to torment Vols pitching with another two-hit performance and two runs scored. East drove in all three Nashville runs in a one-sided 8–3 loss. The defeat dropped the Vols out of first place for the first time in two weeks.

The second game marked the one-hundredth game of the season. With the game deadlocked at 1–1 in the top of the fifth, the weather grew windy and sent billowing clouds of dust across the diamond. The umpire stopped play several times, hoping that the blustery conditions would die down. Both teams took advantage of the elements when action resumed, as the Vols immediately tallied eight runs and the Senators added four of their own. Ewing described the twelve-run fifth inning as "a merry-go round."[32] Siegle had an all-star performance, reaching base five times on three singles, a base on balls, and hit-by-pitch. On the other hand, Daubert went 0-for-5 at the plate and struck out four times. Perdue and his pitching counterpart, Herb Juul, struggled, allowing twenty-four hits, but the Vols came out on top of the 11–6 slugfest.

Berny decided to pitch the final game of the season against a team in which he held a 2–0 record, but his counterpart, Ted Guese, owned a 4–0 mark against Nashville. Bay, whose batting productivity had been relatively silent over the past two weeks, drove in Bernhard for the first score with a triple in the third. Montgomery countered with a pair of runs in the bottom of the fifth, and the score seesawed back and forth. Understanding the strong similarities and relative equality of both teams, Guese and Bernhard each plunked two opposing batters. The Vols clung to a slender 3–2 lead in the ninth, and received an insurance run from a rather unlikely source. With East and McElveen on base, Butler blasted a line drive off the center field fence for an inside-the-park home run to seal Berny's sixth victory in a row. Owing to the Senators' forfeit victory over the Vols on 28 June and "no decision" on 20 April, they were the only club in 1908 to hold a season advantage over Nashville.[33]

Vols players felt a sense of elation as they traveled to Slagtown to take on the lowly Birmingham club. The press picked on the Barons, referring to them derisively as "groundhogs," owing to their season-long occupation of last place.[34] The Vols hoped to use this series to wrestle first place back from New Orleans. Spirits were high as the team took the field, but no one could have predicted what followed. Duggan allowed a solo run in the bottom of the third, and Montgomery pitcher L.J. Bauer held Nashville scoreless. With his team trailing, 1–0, Daubert led off the crucial last licks with an infield single. Butler's sacrifice and Seabough's groundout advanced the first baseman to third base. With the game on the line, Berny turned once again to Hunter to pinch-hit for the pitcher. The valuable utilityman delivered the goods with a sharp single to right field, scoring Daubert and knotting the score at one run apiece. Perdue entered in relief of Duggan as a gentle rain began to fall. The Gallatin Squash was in top form as he set down Birmingham batters 1–2–3 in five of the next six innings. As the weather worsened and the field became sloppy, the umpire called the contest in the fourteenth. The Vols settled for a disappointing tie.

The next day both managers agreed each game of the slated doubleheader would last only seven innings. Nashville spotted starting pitcher Kellum a 2–0 lead in the first inning, but the Michigander had difficulty locating his breaking ball over the plate. Birmingham came rushing back with a pair of runs the bottom of the second, tacking on three more scores in the next inning and an additional run in the fifth. Heavy rain began to fall two innings later, and the umpire called the first game with the Barons leading by a comfortable 6–2 margin. The defeat, in which Kellum issued five walks and was pummeled for nine hits by the worst offense in the league, shocked the Vols. Yancey called the game "a severe drubbing."[35]

After an hour delay, the Barons took the muddy field for game two. Nashville's hopes rested on the arm of Sitton. Again the Vols leaped to an early 1–0 lead, but the Barons quickly tied the score. Then Sitton lost command of his pitches, issuing three bases on balls and three hits in the bottom of the fifth. When the inning came to a close, Birmingham had tabbed the spitballer for three more runs. Trailing 5–2 in the top of the seventh, the Vols launched a desperate rally. Hunter pinch-hit for Sitton and slapped a single to start a comeback. Bay and Wiseman followed with singles of their own. With the sacks crammed, captain McElveen delivered a two-run double. But the rally died, and the Barons owned a sweep of the Vols. In the twinkill, Vols pitchers gave up eleven runs, seventeen hits, and eleven bases on balls.

On 22 August, the Vols and Barons were scheduled to play a back-to-back doubleheader that was sure to strain both pitching staffs. Berny was forced to go with the sore but reliable Hunter and Birmingham countered with workhorse "Chick" Robitaille. In the top of the seventh, Wiseman delivered a two-run single to break a 1–1 tie. Berny called Perdue to twirl the last three frames — the second time Hub had thrown relief in the Birmingham series, and he made the 3–1 score stand.

Then Berny made an unorthodox decision to start Perdue in the second game, owing to the Vols' thin pitching ranks. The result was immediate as Birmingham jumped all over the Tennessean for four runs in the bottom of the first, adding two more the next inning, and driving him from the game. Placed in a predicament, the Nashville manager turned to his lanky first baseman to perform a little relief magic. The choice of putting Daubert on the slab was not altogether unusual in that he had started his professional career as a pitcher in the coal mine leagues of Pennsylvania. Daubert inherited a 6–0 deficit, and the rusty hurler plunked the first two batters he faced and threw two wild pitches, but escaped the inning by giving up only one run. Then he shut down the Barons for the next four innings. Writing in *The Sporting News,* Hamilton Love opined that Daubert's intelligent and agile defense at first base was the biggest drawing card in Nashville, but accolades for his pitching abilities would have to wait.[36]

The sun began to set in the fifth inning, and by the seventh darkness had settled over the field. Birmingham shortstop Tom Downey ignited some loose papers in the pitching box to suggest to the official that it might be getting too dark to continue. Not to be shown up, umpire Brown fined Downey $5 for his antics. Minutes later, Perdue appeared in the third-base coach's box holding a flickering candle. Unamused, Brown tossed Perdue out of the game. Once decorum had been restored, the umpire ended the game on his terms after the Vols batted in the eighth inning. Birmingham had taken a 7–0 victory and thoroughly humiliated the Vols in the four-game series. Nashville's only salvation was that New Orleans had gone on a short losing streak of its own, and the Vols trailed the Pelicans by one game. Indeed, only five games separated the first seven teams. More than ever, the league crown availed itself to any team that could sustain a winning streak.

The Vols had arrived in Birmingham overconfident and left with doubts to face another second division opponent, but one that had played them very well — Tris Speaker and the Little Rock Travelers. "This benighted and blighted center of near-civilization [Little Rock]," quipped Rice, "has been a nightmare for the Vols squad all season."[37] Daubert's work on the slab in Birmingham sent mixed messages about the condition of the Nashville pitching staff. In previous moments of crisis, Berny had demonstrated leadership by taking the ball himself. So, in the first Little Rock encounter, Bernhard challenged the aging "Pop" Eyler.

The contest could best be described as one of missed opportunities as the Vols clubbed twelve hits and had runners aboard in every inning. Only Wiseman failed to connect with the bat. On the other hand, Berny successfully throttled most of the Little Rock lineup. Only outfielders Joe Collins and Hub Northen managed hits — three each. Northen, a recent acquisition from the Cotton States League, drove in both Traveler runs. Speaker had another amazing day in the field, throwing out two Vols baserunners at the plate. In all, five Nashville runners were gunned down at the dish. Nashville scored in the fifth when Hardy tumbled across home plate in an awkward slide, but the tally came at a cost; Berny was forced to remove the Scrappy One from the game, owing to a swollen knee. The Vols threw away a marvelous scoring opportunity with the bases loaded and only one out in the eighth. McElveen was forced out at the plate, and an overly aggressive Siegle rounded third base too far, was caught in a run down, and tagged out to end the threat. The Travelers rallied with two outs in the bottom of the ninth when Connors singled and stole second base. Then the lefty Northen scorched a grounder off Daubert's mitt. By the time the nimble first baseman retrieved the ball and fired it to Seabough, Connors had crossed the plate with the winning run. The official scorer tagged a game-losing error on Daubert.

Berny learned the next morning that Hardy's knee injury was actually broken ribs, and Scrappy Jack would likely miss the remainder of the season. Now the Nashville club was in its biggest bind of the year, having to rely entirely on Seabough as the team's sole catcher. The season had proven Doc to be a reliable hitter and solid teammate, but opponents had taken advantage of his weak arm and had stolen bases off him on a regular basis. Berny put out feelers for a replacement — no small order at this late stage in the season.

Duggan's sinker and a touch of wildness worked wonders in the second contest against Little Rock on 25 August. He forced Traveler batters into twenty-two infield outs and held them scoreless for eight innings. Meanwhile, Nashville's defense played errorless ball. Butler set the tone for inspired field work in the bottom of the first inning with an unassisted double play. Offensively, the Vols completed their second consecutive eleven-hit performance, this time at the expense of "Chief" Eastman, a pitcher acquired from Waterbury in the Connecticut League. Duggan surrendered two hits to Speaker, but carried a shutout into the bottom of the ninth, and held on to win the game, 5–3.

Vols fans received a welcome bit of news on 26 August — Ed Hurlburt, the ex–Atlanta and Memphis catcher, had signed a contract to finish out the year with Nashville. Edward Leroy Hurlburt was born 22 January 1875 in Illinois to English immigrants Thomas and Sarah (Guthrie) Hurlburt.[38] Big Ed had begun his professional career in the old Pacific Coast League and moved to Atlanta in the Southern Association in 1902, but soon transferred to Memphis, where he spent the next five seasons. Hurlburt established himself in the community as a thriving entrepreneur in the dry cleaning business. He began the '08 season back in Atlanta, but the Crackers released him at the roster deadline in May. The Hurlburt story was so significant to Nashville baseball that it made the front page in the *Banner*.[39] The article explained that Big Ed would not report until after the upcoming Nashville-Memphis series, however. It is likely the veteran catcher did not wish to compete against former teammates in his hometown. While Hurlburt had agreed to help Nashville for the final three weeks of the season, he did not wish to alienate his Turtle connections.

Perdue performed magnificently in the first game of the doubleheader on 26 August. He scattered four hits, three to 19-year-old shortstop Art Hess. The focused Tennessean contributed two hits and one RBI to his own cause. Every Vols batter connected off pitcher Jim Buchanan, and Manager Finn tore his hair out in frustration as the Vols slashed thirty-three base hits in the first three games. The Vols' offensive onslaught was a omen of things to come.

Nashville took game one handily, 4–0. Rice reported that the victory had been doubly sweet for Perdue because the pitcher had been suffering from illness for the past three weeks.[40]

In the Vols' final appearance in the Arkansas capital, Kellum squared off against ancient Bill Hart. Unlike Win's last start, his breaking ball and change-of-speed worked to perfection. He stymied Traveler batters, who pounded the ball into the ground for twenty-two infield outs. Butler shined, in particular, at shortstop where he made two sensational plays to rob batters of apparent base hits. East, who was enjoying a solid fielding series against his former teammates, put up good offensive numbers with a hit, run scored, and an RBI. Little Rock recorded two unearned runs when a towering pop fly to shallow right field landed between the colliding East and Wiseman, allowing Collins and Speaker to wind up in scoring position. Frustrated by the error, Kellum attempted a pickoff at third base, but his throw went array of McElveen and both Travelers raced around the bases to score. The deciding moment in the game occurred in the top of the seventh when Seabough hit a Texas League single to center field to score Siegle for the second time. Little Rock loaded the bases in the bottom of the eighth, but Kellum pitched out of the jam to preserve a 3–2 win. The doubleheader sweep of Little Rock came at a crucial time for Nashville. The Vols had combined forty-one hits with solid pitching performances from Bernhard, Duggan, Perdue, and Kellum.

Contests between interstate rivals like Nashville and Memphis are special events. Memphis had been nipping at the heels of Nashville and New Orleans since early August, and had never dropped more than three games off the pace. The Turtles appeared destined to play a major role in the outcome of the 1908 race either as champion or spoiler, but when the Vols arrived on 29 August, they faced a riddled Memphii squad. The club had released thirteen-game-winner Bill Chappelle for public drunkenness, traded outfielder Howard Murphy to Denver in the Western League, and lost second baseman Harry Redmond to the broken nose sustained earlier in Nashville. Furthermore, Babb had used four different shortstops throughout the season, and now catcher Frank Owens was injured. Although Memphis boasted the best pitcher in the league (Savidge), the Vols liked their chances against the Turtles.

Memphis batters had not faced Sitton's spitball, and apparently catcher Seabough had never seen the likes of it, either. The Missouri native experienced an off day behind the dish as he allowed three passed balls and failed to throw out four thieving Turtles. Memphis twirler Rudy "Iron Man" Schwenck silenced the hot Vols batters and surrendered only one run when Siegle doubled McElveen home in the seventh inning. Sitton absorbed a tough 2–1 loss, his third defeat in a row, owing largely to the difficulties experienced by his struggling batterymate.

A huge crowd filed into Red Elm Park for the second game of the series. Facing a must-win situation, Berny handed the ball to the Vols pitcher that he trusted the most — himself. This move was unexpected because the normal pitching rotation pointed to either Duggan or Perdue — Nashville's two steadiest performers. Perhaps Berny accepted the challenge to oppose ace Ralph Savidge in order to downplay the hype (pressure) associated with such a matchup. The Bernhard-Savidge confrontation up did not live up to its anticipated billing, however. Memphis treated Berny like he was the batting practice hurler, pouncing on him for thirteen hits. The Vols responded similarly with ten hits against Savidge. McElveen led the team with three safeties followed by Bay (two singles) and Butler (two doubles). In the field, Seabough went through another excoriating afternoon at catcher. In the second inning, he dropped a third-strike pitch that allowed Babb to reach first base; the player-manager moved to second on a sacrifice, proceeded to third on Seabough's second passed ball, and scored on a grounder bobbled by East. Memphis won its second game in a row, 5–1. Nashville's pennant hopes seemed to be setting in the west Tennessee sky.

The final game between Nashville and Memphis on 30 August had a playoff atmosphere. President Kavanaugh traveled from Little Rock to join the festivities along with 5,000 Turtle rooters in the stands. Berny picked Duggan to represent Nashville on the slab while Babb made an interesting decision in rookie E. Kieber, a recent signee from Savannah in the Cotton States League. The Vols had scoring opportunities in the first, third, and fourth innings, but ran themselves out of each chance as ailing catcher Frank Owens gunned down four Vols attempting to steal. On the other hand, the Turtles ran with reckless abandon as they pilfered four bases of their own off an ineffective Seabough. Duggan faded in the seventh, and Perdue entered in relief. The use of Perdue in relief situations on the current road trip had been paying huge dividends for Nashville; his two starts and four relief appearances carried the team's pitching load during the last twelve days of August. Perdue did not allow a baserunner in his first three innings, and both pitchers combined to limit the Memphii to only seven hits. As the game entered extra innings, Kieber gave way to another recent acquisition, Joe Garrity.

Dramatic moments occurred in the tenth and eleventh innings. In the top of the tenth, Butler bounced a triple off the outfield scoreboard. Then Seabough lofted a towering fly ball behind second base. Butler, not realizing there were two outs, stuck close to the bag. When the ball dropped to the ground, he broke for home but was thrown out to end the threat. In the eleventh, Siegle drove a double in the outfield gap, and Butler singled him in to give the Vols a 2–1 advantage. With two outs in the bottom of the inning, Butler committed a costly error at shortstop that allowed the Turtles to crawl back into a tie. It is not uncommon for a player to go from "goat to hero" or visa versa, but rarely does an athlete make the gamut from "goat-to-hero-to-goat." Butler managed the unflattering feat. After nearly 2½ hours and fourteen innings, umpire Brown called the game a tie on account of darkness.

The Vols stewed over the team's collapse in Memphis as their train lumbered toward the city of New Orleans for a crucial showdown with the Pelicans. While Nashville could not muster a single win against the Turtles, the front-running Pelicans had feasted on the inept Barons. As the month of September dawned, New Orleans opened a commanding four-game lead over Nashville, and Memphis had slipped into second place. With three weeks and fifteen games left on the docket, the Volunteer star was beginning to fade. Still, for the three teams, the race remained a mathematical possibility.

The Nashville Vols survived the first half of the dog days of summer at home. Between 20 July to 12 August, the Nashville Base Ball Club had dealt with several important personnel developments. First, the absence of East in the middle infield had an immediate impact. Hardy substituted at the keystone sack for eleven games, but in the process he'd committed six errors and batted a weak 11-for-43. Five of Scrappy Jack's hits came in his first eight at-bats. Second, Bay's recurring knee problem forced Berny to scramble to find a suitable outfield replacement as well as hold down the leadoff spot in the batting order. Hunter, the most versatile Vols player, filled the latter role admirably despite his own nagging arm issues caused by overwork. Third, summer fever also afflicted the club as Bay, Duggan, McElveen, and Perdue experienced bouts of illness at different times. Fourth, the shaky condition of the pitching staff continued to be a problem. Every pitcher had developed soreness, and only the arrival of Sitton promised some relief. Yet, Berny's personal work ethic and his handling of the pitching staff typified standard practice in an era when a great deal was expected physiologically from hurlers. At a time when baseball was just beginning to understand the importance of the bullpen, Berny demanded much from his starters, but no more than he expected from himself.

The first five stops of the August road trip — Atlanta, Montgomery, Birmingham, Little Rock, and Memphis — had produced discouraging numbers. In the games played between 13–30 August, the Vols went 8–9–3, and lost their grip on first and second place. An unimpressive pattern of one win and one loss was typical of the team's effort. The club neither won nor lost more than two games in any stretch. Instead of feasting on lower division teams as Berny had envisioned, the Vols played down to the level of their second-tier opponents. And two ties in Birmingham and Memphis did nothing to enhance their position in the standings. While the Vols won two surprisingly difficult series with Montgomery and Little Rock, they dropped shocking sets to Birmingham and Memphis. Furthermore, the club fared poorly in doubleheaders with a mediocre 8–8 split record. The New Orleans Pelicans started to distance themselves from the pack in late August, but it was still too early to predict who would win the coveted flag.

The second half of the dog days of August witnessed two important roster additions to the Nashville Base Ball Club. First, Carl Vedder Sitton promised to relieve a pitching staff already stretched to the limits, but while the

South Carolinian produced two quick victories, he struggled in his next three outings. Second, the season-ending injury to Hardy might have proved devastating as opposing baserunners lined up to steal bases off J. Warren Seabough. Ed Hurlburt proposed to solve that problem. Big Ed met the club at the Memphis train station as promised, but only after participating in a street brawl with several Turtle boosters, who objected to his defection. The clutch hitting of utilityman/pitcher Hunter, slugging of McElveen and Daubert, outstanding defense of Bay, Wiseman, and Siegle, and gutsy pitching of Duggan, Berny, and Perdue were the main accomplishments of the road trip. Overall the Vols had played just well enough to keep alive in the hunt for the pennant.

The first three weeks in September would decide where the 1908 championship flag would hang — in New Orleans, Memphis, or Nashville. The Vols controlled their own destiny with seven games against the Pelicans and Sea Gulls, four with the Travelers, and three with the Turtles. Out of these final twenty-one games, the last thirteen would be played in the friendly confines of Sulphur Dell, where pennant fever was building.

Chapter 8

Pennant Fever

No more talk about expectations for the season. The season boiled down to the first three weeks in September. On or before 19 September, the 1908 champion of the Southern Association would be crowned. Every manager, owner, player, and fan understood the league rule regarding the necessity to make up canceled games. But, these contests clogged the September slate with unwanted doubleheaders and placed tremendous strain on the pitchers. Yet, the club that could combine solid pitching with consistent defense and offense would emerge the least scathed from this barrage of twin bills and emerge as the leading contender for the pennant. The tight '08 race placed immense pressure on players, and sometimes the fiercest confrontations took place not on the field between opponents, but on the bench between teammates. Furthermore, avid fans started to realize that something special was taking place with the national pastime. The Southern Association race and several other minor circuits waged competitive battles that rivaled the close campaigns at the highest level of "baseballdom"— the American and National Leagues. "When 1908 slips into past history the annals of the fading campaign will more than likely indicate the best contested season among leading leagues in the recount of the game," observed Rice.[1] The baseball finale in Dixie boiled down to a three-way battle between New Orleans, Memphis, and Nashville.

On the verge of the New Orleans series, Rice informed his readers about an editorial change at the *Tennessean* that might impact the way he reported on baseball. On 31 August, Edward Ward Carmack, the unsuccessful Democratic nominee for governor and newspaper editor of the *Memphis Commercial-Appeal,* became editor-in-chief. Many Tennesseans suspected that Carmack planned to use the Nashville newspaper as a vehicle to promote his political aspirations for statewide office.² In keeping with his moral crusade for prohibition, Carmack asked Rice to stop embellishing his coverage of Vols games in his sports editorial column, *Sportograms*. Carmack particularly objected to Rice's penchant of predicting outcomes and analyzing team performances, something the manager associated with another social vice — gambling — and preferred that Rice stick to printing box scores.³ Fortunately, Carmack did not enforce his new policy, and Rice continued to report on Vols baseball in the style his readers had become accustomed.

Kellum had contained hard-hitting New Orleans on two earlier occasions, and he was primed to do it again. Berny assigned Big Ed Hurlburt to catch in what the press billed as the biggest game of the season for both teams. Patrons flooded Athletic Park to watch Bill Bartley match wits with Kellum. The Vols played sensational defense behind the slowballer. Deerfoot tracked down two fly balls in front of the left field wall, making signature over-the-shoulder catches. Although Hurlburt struggled to find his catcher's legs and gave up an early passed ball, no Pelican stole a bag despite the methodical wind-up of his side-wheeling batterymate. The game was scoreless until the top of the eighth inning when Kellum reached base on a line drive that caromed off the glove of third baseman George Rohe. With two outs, Wiseman delivered a clutch hit to right field, advancing Kellum to third base. Doc stretched his hit into a double, sliding safely under the tag at second base. New Orleans fans took exception to the call, and Pelican infielders tried unsuccessfully to persuade umpire Brown to reverse his decision. When order was restored, all eyes shifted to the next batter, East. The pudgy second baseman blooped a single into right field to drive in both baserunners. The Pelicans mounted a rally in the bottom of the frame, but Kellum stranded two runners in scoring position to end the threat. In wrapping up his third victory against New Orleans, the veteran Kellum was vilified in the local press as a bona-fide Pelican killer. His victory had cut slightly into the league leaders' hold on first place.

The date of 31 August was important for all minor league prospects because it marked the occasion when major league clubs declared which players they planned to draft and release. The process directly affected Nashville. Bad news could not have come at a worse time for Kellum. On the heels of giving his team new hope in New Orleans, Kellum learned that Charlie Ebbets announced that Brooklyn had dropped its option on the former Cincinnati star. The mogul also failed to exercise options on Hardy and Duggan, but did offer a 1909 contract to McElveen. Lajoie of Cleveland picked up the rights to Daubert and Sitton, and the St. Louis Browns renewed their interest in Butler. A name surprisingly absent from the list was Bay, whose knee condition was still the subject of great concern. These transactions put $9,000 into Nashville's coffers, but increased public apprehension about the potential for a depleted roster, a normal worry for any successful minor league outfit.⁴

The grandstand and bleachers at Athletic Park were filled to capacity to

September

Mon	Tue	Wed	Thu	Fri	Sat	Sun
	1 @N.O.	2 @N.O.	3 @Mob	4 @Mob	5 @Mob	6
7 Mem (2)	8 Mem	9 L.R.	10 L.R.	11 L.R.	12 L.R.	13
14 Mob	15 Mob	16 Mob	17 N.O.	18 N.O.	19 N.O.	20
21	22	23	24	25	26	27
28	29	30				

Atl = Atlanta
Birm = Birmingham
L.R. = Little Rock
Mem = Memphis
Mob = Mobile
Mont = Montgomery
N.O. = New Orleans
Bold print= @ Nashville
(2) =Double Header

cheer for the Pelicans on the afternoon of 1 September. The freshman Sitton was listed to pitch against a cagey three-year veteran of the Southern Association, Charlie Fritz. Before the game, manager Frank announced that outfielder Ed Manning, a recent acquisition from Birmingham, was injured and unable to play. In his sted the Pelican skipper proposed, tongue-in-cheek, to suit up Charlie Parsons, a veteran of the old Southern League who currently worked in the commercial district. Frank's humor overshadowed a typical problem faced by many teams in the waning days of the season — depleted rosters owing to injury, suspension, or the draft.

The standing-room-only crowd was entertained by Sitton and Fritz. With two outs in the top of the fifth and the game scoreless, Butler hit a grounder that shortstop George Nill fielded cleanly, but Kid hustled down the line and beat the throw to first base. The spectators were incensed by umpire Fitzsimmons' call, just as they had been a day earlier when he had declared Wiseman safe at second base. As soon as play resumed, Butler stole second base and scored on Seabough's clean single to center field. Sitton made the lone run hold up and he struck out the side in dramatic fashion to end the game. Sitton and Fritz had surrendered only five base hits for the entire game and left four runners on base in the classic pitchers duel. New Orleans booted the ball for three errors to equal yesterday's miscues. The story line of the game was about Sitton, however, who mowed down batter after batter in a remarkable ten-strikeout performance. The mighty Pelicans had gone two consecutive games without scoring a run, and the Vols were closing the gap in the standings. The mettle of both teams would be tested in a crucial doubleheader scheduled for the next day.

Excitement could be felt in the Crescent City for the twin bill between the Vols and Pelicans on 2 September. The standing-room-only crowd of 6,600 anticipated a playoff-caliber game, and were not disappointed as the first game offered Duggan versus "The Grand Old Man," southpaw Ted Breitenstein. Breit led the league in winning percentage with an impressive 14–4 record. The afternoon would confirm that both hurlers were in top form.

Duggan ran into brief trouble when catcher Harry Matthews opened the second with a double off the left field wall. Despite the long poke, the lumbering catcher barely beat the relay throw to East at second base. Then Dundon laid down a beautiful bunt in Daubert's direction. Jake fielded the ball, but McElveen, who had also been charging in, did not recover in time to protect his base. The rotund Matty stood only ninety feet from home plate. Now Duggan lost his concentration and issued a base on balls to Nill, loading the bases. During the next at-bat, Hurlburt muffed a pitch and the passed ball allowed Matthews to score uncontested. Two ensuing free passes by Duggan led to a second unearned run. In all, eight Pelicans came to the plate.

At the close of the inning tempers flared as Vols players returned to the bench. Kellum took exception to the manner in which McElveen had reacted to the passed ball that scored Matthews. The veteran southpaw walked up to the team captain, called him a "fathead," and charged that Humpy "didn't know his business." McElveen responded with several well-placed punches to Kellum's face. The Nashville bench quickly separated the brawling teammates, but play was not resumed until Berny "laid down the law good and hard."[5]

After the fracas subsided, the game settled into a battle between two quality pitchers. For the second straight day, Nashville and New Orleans hurlers combined to surrender only five hits. "The Ten-Thousand Dollar Beauty" allowed only four baserunners and lived up to his reputation as the finest veteran pitcher in the league. Almost as impressive, Duggan gave up three hits but added five bases on balls. Had he shied clear of the disastrous second inning, Duggan's performance would have equaled the masterful Breit, but the Pelicans took the opener, 3–0.[6] Hamilton Love questioned whether Hurlburt would be the answer to Nashville's catching problem. "There is an absence of a large amount of ginger when Jack [Hardy] isn't in the game," opined *The Sporting News* correspondent.[7]

Both managers understood the importance of the final game of the twin bill. Berny went with his instincts, and, as usual, selected himself to pitch. He also penciled in a familiar target, Seabough, to do the receiving duties. Frank drew Bill Bartley from his arsenal of proven arms. Both teams produced six baserunners apiece in the seven-inning affair, including a pair of singles by McElveen. The only fireworks occurred in the second when Pelican infielder Augie Dundon was booted by the official for arguing a call. The Vols needed to make their train connection to Mobile, so the game ended in a scoreless tie after seven innings.

The four-game series offers interesting statistical comparisons between the Vols and Pelicans. The numbers reflect how evenly matched both teams were:

	Runs scored	*Hits*	*Strikeouts*	*Scoreless Innings*
Nashville	3	16	18	20
New Orleans	3	12	23	19

The Kellum-McElveen confrontation was not resolved, and it flared again after the game. McElveen and his roommate, Seabough, were returning to their quarters in the St. Charles Hotel to retrieve their luggage when Kellum suddenly appeared in the hallway. "Without preliminary remarks," reported Rice, "Kellum promptly landed a punch hitting McElveen in the face." Both men sported facial bruises as the team boarded a train for its last stop in Mobile. Bernhard stated publicly that he planned to discipline the pugilists for their actions, but qualified his remarks by adding that he considered Kellum and McElveen both "gentlemen and intense competitors." Berny's use of the term "gentlemen" to describe the disagreeing players was deliberate; it was designed to placate the Victorian values of middle-class Nashvillians who might otherwise have taken offense at their unruly behavior. "Under the nerve-wracking strain of a pennant melee like this one in Dixie," editorialized Rice in a similar attempt to gloss over the event, "a few bizarre incidents are bound to break loose."[8]

The Vols and Pelicans parted company with full knowledge that they would meet again in the season finale at Sulphur Dell. The club left town with an African American batboy, who tagged along for the rest of the season as the Vols' "mascot." Nashville rooters also began to pull for other teams that might play a role in knocking off the Pelicans and Turtles. Nashville and Memphis were knotted in a second-place tie, and still within striking distance of first place. "Memphis is the bug-a-boo now," wrote Yancey in the *Banner*.[9] One club slipping out of contention but capable of lending support to Nashville was a team the Vols would not face again — Montgomery. The surprising fourth-place Senators were slated for four games in New Orleans and three more at home against Memphis in the last two series of the season. For the time being, however, the Vols had to dismiss these hypothetical scenarios and focus on their next opponent — a team they would meet seven times in the next two weeks — fifth-place Mobile.

Teams that have nothing to lose in the waning days of a lengthy baseball season are very dangerous opponents, and Mobile was precisely this kind of foe. Due to a backlog of games, the Vols and Sea Gulls prepared for several doubleheaders. Perdue, a true gamer who understood the importance of every contest in September, took the slab. The Tennessean scattered six hits and struck out seven Sea Gulls, but opposing pitcher Gordon Hickman matched his efforts, allowing only five hits while fanning five Vols. The scoreboard showed nothing but zeroes in the ninth inning when Wiseman, the offensive player of the game, turned into the defensive goat by misplaying a leadoff single that rolled between his legs and turned into a double. Perdue then issued a base on balls and clutch single to end the game in a 1–0 loss.

Perdue was shaken by the heartbreaking defeat. When the pitcher reached the bench, he pleaded with Berny to start the second game, too. Berny consented. Nashville manufactured a run in the top of the second when Butler scurried around the bases to score the first Vols run in thirty innings. Given a two-run cushion, Perdue pitched a four-hit shutout and fanned seven Sea Gulls. Seabough had caught Perdue all year, and performed his duties in both games without an error and made fourteen putouts. On the Mobile side, manager Fisher inserted a young outfielder acquired from Shreveport in his first Southern Association contest—future Hall of Famer Zack Wheat.

The eighteen-inning pitching performance of Perdue, while not rare, could only be described as phenomenal; he allowed only one run, ten hits, and struck out fourteen Sea Gulls. Perdue's exploit stands out as one of the highlights in the Vols' season, but as a turning point for the team as well. The victory elevated Nashville to within .007 of the league leading Pelicans, who were experiencing difficulties in Montgomery. Newspaper accounts began to describe the three-way race in terms of percentage points two weeks prior to the conclusion of the season.[10]

The game on 4 September was rained out, so the Nashville nines prepared for their third twin bill in a row the following day. Muddy field conditions caused Kellum difficulty when the first three Sea Gulls—Woodie Thornton, Elmer Benson, and Jud Daley—reached base on safeties. Kellum also failed to properly field a bunt, and Mobile grabbed an early 3–0 lead. Skipper Red Fisher threw for the Sea Gulls, and the Vols jumped on him for ten hits and produced baserunners in every inning. Still, Nashville could muster only one run, and the Mobile manager held onto a 4–1 win.

Berny selected his most rested pitcher, Hunter, to throw game two. For the second game in a row, the Vols broke into double digits (16) in base hits. Only this time *every* Vols player collected at least one hit in the shortened seven-inning contest. The visitors put six runs on the scoreboard in the second and added four tallies in the final three innings to take a commanding ten-run lead. The Sea Gulls went through three pitchers, including shortstop Paul Sentell. Third baseman Elmer Benson filled in for Sentell at shortstop, where he committed five errors. Mobile's defeat held deeper significance for the fourth-place team because they were mathematically eliminated from contention for the league crown.

The final game on the Gulf Coast was the seventh shutout the Vols had been involved in since the beginning of September. The longest road trip of the season was now concluded. Nashville had displayed plenty of firepower but brought home a mediocre 12–12–2 record. "There was no great brilliance nor dash to the trip — just a steady plugging attack," Rice analyzed.[11] The race was as tight as ever with the Vols trailing the Pelicans by half a game and leading the Turtles by the same slim margin.

The Vols were in loose spirits at the Mobile train depot as Perdue and Seabough entertained the passengers with renditions of several popular baseball melodies, including the latest tune — *"Take Me Out to the Ball Game."* The exuberant Vols could also celebrate the news that Tris Speaker had just been sold to the Boston Red Sox. Thankfully, Nashville would not have to face the batting champion when Little Rock made its final visit to Sulphur Dell on 9–12 September. The Nashville Base Ball Club was poised to begin its final thirteen games of the season at home while New Orleans and Memphis went on the road. The September slate broke down as follows:

	Nashville	*New Orleans*	*Memphis*
Labor Day	Memphis	@ Birmingham	@ Nashville
	Little Rock	@ Atlanta	@ Birmingham
	Mobile	@ Montgomery	@ Atlanta
	New Orleans	@ Nashville	@ Montgomery

Labor Day, 1908. The Nashville bug community anxiously awaited the return of their heroes as the sports columnists had been expending a lot of ink on catching the Pelicans and burying the Turtles. It was equally painful for local fans to realize that New Orleans arrived in Birmingham for a series against the last-place Barons, and Memphis was scheduled to visit Slagtown next. Even the most fervent forecaster recognized that Nashville faced an uphill battle to win the crown. And many wondered how the Vols would hold up under the strain of their fourth consecutive doubleheader.

The Nashville-Memphis rivalry ran deeper than commercial or sports boosterism; a genuine dislike existed between players on both teams, owing to a bitter legacy. For instance, in September 1907 Atlanta and Memphis were battling for the crown when the Crackers loaned star pitcher Grant Schopp to Nashville for a crucial series against the Turtles. Memphis did not recover from a pair of defeats in which the ex–Cracker hurler had played a prominent role.[12]

Nashville management announced that the first game of the holiday matchup would begin at noon. Then the stadium would be emptied, and the next crowd would pay for admission for game two. A crowd in excess of 3,500 pushed its way into Sulphur Dell to take part in the matinee with the despised Turtles. The sports editor of the *Memphis Commercial-Appeal* noted that "the town [Nashville] is baseball wild."[13] In his second home appearance, Sitton responded to the thrill of pitching in front of such a boisterous and supportive crowd. "Sitton had everything," said Rice. "His spitter was working up to the mark; his smoke ball had a two-foot jump; and his drop was a loop-the-loop all the way."[14] Both teams missed several scoring opportunities, and the game went into extra innings with the score tied, 1–1. In the top of the twelfth, Sitton tired, and Memphis pitcher Rudy Schwenck delivered the lethal blow, a two-run double. No one doubted Sitton's fortitude following his two-hour performance on the slab. Striking out thirteen Turtles, Sitton "cut loose one of the best pitched games that all this or any other community ever saw," claimed Rice.[15]

The finale began shortly after 2 p.m., and extra space behind a roped-off area on the outfield grass accommodated the overflow crowd. The twine marker extended from the base of the Dump to the clubhouse entrance in right-center to the scoreboard in center to the sulphur spring house in left and hugged the left field line in front of the bleachers as far as third base. An estimated 1,000 knothole fans lined the railroad tracks beyond the right field palisade, and some daring fans climbed trees for a better view of the action. Others hung from windows in the ice house across the street. Duggan took the slab to the roars of a Nashville crowd that "howled like a famished pack of Siberian wolves."[16]

The Vols took advantage of the short outfield porch, owing to the large crowd sitting on the carpet. East, Siegle, McElveen, and Seabough hit routine fly balls that normally would have been caught, but instead fell into the sea of humanity for ground-rule doubles. Every Vols player except Butler made at least one hit off Joe Garrity. The Vols lumped most of their thirteen hits in the second and sixth innings and scored two and four runs respectively. Meanwhile, Duggan scattered eight hits, including a Bill Cranston home run over Bay's head, to salvage game two of the traditional Labor Day doubleheader, 6–3.

The split hurt Memphis on two accounts. First, they lost the services of big first baseman George Carey for the remainder of the season. Carey, whom Rice called "Scoops," had been ailing for about two weeks on account of being hit on the wrist by a pitched ball. Duggan added to Carey's pain when he plunked the hapless Turtle in the exact same spot. Carey's name was now added to the list of players lost for the season — Chappelle, Redmond, and Fox. Second, the Pelicans had swept the Barons to complete an 18–2 series record. The split with Nashville set back Memphis' hopes of overtaking New Orleans.

League Leaders on September 8

New Orleans	68	53	.563
Nashville	66	54	.550
Memphis	67	55	.549

As dawn broke on 8 September, no one knew that this day would be remembered as the beginning of Nashville's storied charge for the league title. The final matchup between Nashville and Memphis established benchmarks in Vols pitching, batting, and fielding that would be repeated on a daily basis over the next two weeks. Berny juggled the Vols' batting order and lineup in preparation for the final encounter with the Turtles. First, he put Hurlburt at catcher for defensive purposes. Seabough had started six out of seven games and needed a break. In a rare shakeup of the pitcher's traditional ninth spot in the batting order, Berny switched Perdue and Hurlburt.

Perdue faced a familiar foe in Savidge, the knuckleballer recently drafted by Cincinnati. Working for the first time since his eighteen-inning stint against Mobile, Perdue hurled what eyewitnesses believe was his most overpowering performance of the year. Ewing had never seen the Tennessean throw so hard, and Rice said that he pitched "the best game of his rural life"—a four-hit shutout with seven strikeouts.[17] Meanwhile, the Vols reached a lofty offensive plateau, stroking fifteen hits. Butler poked four safeties, lacking only a home run to hit for the cycle. His triple in the third inning rolled all the way to the sewage ditch in center field. Daubert stroked home runs in the third and sixth innings—a feat practically unheard of in Southern Association action. "Demon Daubert, the new Home Run Kid," lauded Rice, in recognition of the first baseman's batting feat.[18] Nashville's field work matched its pitching and batting. East and Butler made sterling plays deep in the hole to rob Turtle batters of base hits. On the other side of the diamond, the crippled Turtles kicked the ball around for five errors—three by the normally steady shortstop, Cranston.

The total number of patrons attending the Labor Day doubleheader ranged between 7,000–11,000, depending on the source used. The Memphis newspaper commented that the gate "smashed all baseball records" in the largest Labor Day crowd in league history. The *Commercial-Appeal* approximated the attendance at 9,400.[19]

League Leaders on September 9

New Orleans	69	53	.566
Nashville	67	54	.554
Memphis	67	56	.545

Scrappy Jack was visible in the grandstand selling tickets to a field day and inter-squad game to be held immediately following the regular season on

21 September.[20] The disabled catcher was hoping to raise enough revenue to provide each Vols member (including himself) with a post-season bonus. In an era before incentive clauses, minor leaguers frequently used this type of donation to boost their salaries. Unquestionably, Hardy wanted to cash in on the current wave of team popularity, and build a nest egg that would inspire Vols players to stay in the championship hunt.

Riding a confident wave, the Volunteers prepared for the Speaker-less Little Rock Travelers. In this euphoric moment created by the Labor Day split, Berny proposed a post-season series between the winner of the American Association (either Indianapolis or Louisville), providing the Vols captured the Southern Association flag.

Rice, Yancey, and Ewing lamented the noncompetitive play of Birmingham in the press, but believed the Barons would definitely impact the outcome of the campaign, owing to the number of games remaining to be played against New Orleans and Memphis. The Barons began "to show a yellow streak that would make the Chinese wall look like a picket fence around a hog pen," chided Rice.[21] Memphis, a team still clinging to faint hopes of overtaking the Pelicans themselves, was currently *en route* to Slagtown as New Orleans headed to sixth-place Atlanta, a team that had utterly collapsed.

Without batting champion Tris Speaker, Little Rock had turned into a punchless bunch. The Travelers suited only eleven players, and Finn's pitching staff had been decimated by injury. Kellum took command on the slab, but his teammates looked weary and lacked pep on the diamond. The southpaw opened the door for the Travelers in the fourth inning when he fielded a bunt, but tossed the ball into right field. His attempt to pick off the same runner at second base resulted in the ball rolling to Siegle in center field. The runner scored. Kellum's counterpart, Bill Hart, pitched a first-class game and scattered four hits. Little Rock took a 3–0 lead into the bottom of the ninth when the Vols staged a ferocious comeback. Daubert and Siegle singled and scored on Butler's second triple in two days. Then Seabough slapped a low line drive to center field that froze Butler halfway down the third base line. Speaker's replacement, a newcomer named Blakely, made a marvelous shoestring catch and sent Butler diving back into third. Had Kid been in proper position to tag, Rice predicts he could have walked home for the tying run.[22] Hunter pinchhit for Kellum, but produced the final out in a disappointing 3–2 loss. Elsewhere, the Crackers defeated the Pelicans so the Vols lost no ground to the league leader, but the Turtles thumped the Barons as expected to enter a virtual second-place tie with Nashville.

LEAGUE LEADERS ON SEPTEMBER 10

New Orleans	69	54	.561
Nashville	67	55	.549
Memphis	68	56	.548

Duggan brought his A game to Sulphur Dell for the second game against Little Rock. Prior to the first pitch, a rumor circulated that Pittsburgh, in a fierce battle of its own with the New York Giants for the National League crown, planned to purchase the rights to Duggan and bring him to the Big Show immediately. Whether this hearsay inspired the Hoosier is unknown, but he pitched a gem: "They couldn't have hit him with a Gatling gun," noted Rice.[23] The Vols returned to double-digit form with ten hits, including two safeties each for the first four batters. In the bottom of the sixth, Wiseman singled. Berny signaled for a hit-and-run and the little Doctor raced around the bases to score on East's triple. As it turned out, Duggan needed just one tally. His curveball had plenty of snap and his fastball danced to the plate. Only two Travelers reached base the entire game — one on a base on balls in the second, and the other on a fielding error by McElveen an inning later. The visitors threw a scare as the no-hitter unfolded in the fifth inning when Butler ranged far to his left, snared a grounder deep behind second base, and fired a strike to Daubert to nip the runner in a bang-bang play at the bag. Again, in the ninth, catcher Bob Wood struck a towering fly ball to deep right-center field that looked like a sure base hit. But Wiseman traversed the Dump and snatched the ball out of the air on the dead run. Duggan had spun a no-hitter in less than 90 minutes, and coincidentally against a fellow hurler who owned the league's first no-hitter of the season, Jim Buchanan. The incredible defense of Butler and Wiseman had preserved the rare and marvelous pitching accomplishment.[24]

Despite the sensational 1–0 victory, the Vols found themselves in an unbelievable situation. While the Pelicans were beating the Crackers in Atlanta, Memphis had utterly pulverized "the human punching bag" (Birmingham) in a doubleheader to move percentage points ahead of the Vols—an irony in light of Duggan's near-perfect pitching performance. "The race has reached the sizzling point," announced Rice.[25]

LEAGUE LEADERS ON SEPTEMBER 11

New Orleans	70	54	.565
Memphis	70	56	.566
Nashville	68	55	.553

The game on 11 September promised to be a sunny and warm day as the temperature soared into the upper 80s at game time. After three innings, manager Finn removed aging Pop Eyler after he surrendered five runs on eleven hits. Since the visitors had run out of pitchers, the dubious honor of completing the game fell to catcher Bob Wood. What followed for Nashville was nothing short of sensational. Over the next five innings, the Vols scored fifteen times on nineteen hits. McElveen scored five times and set a Southern Association record, going a perfect 6-for-6.[26] Daubert hit for the cycle; his mammoth home run cleared the right field fence, knocking several spectators out of a crowded sapling. Prior to Daubert's blast, Wood had stationed his right fielder atop the Dump with his back pressed against the wall, but to no avail. Butler, Bay, and Siegle added four hits apiece, including a triple by the shortstop, who was beginning to earn a reputation for banging three-baggers. East hit long balls too — two doubles and a triple. How Seabough avoided hitting the baseball while his teammates pounded twenty-one singles and nine extra-base hits to set a single-game league record (30 base hits) is practically incomprehensible. "Ping-Ping-Crash-Bang-Crash. No, this is not a description of the bombardment of Port Arthur," punned Rice. "It is merely a graphic detail of the slugging feast enjoyed by the locals."[27] Sitton did not let up in light of so much offensive support, and tossed a one-hitter despite committing three fielding errors which led to one unearned run. When the dust had settled on the muggy afternoon, the Vols marched away with a remarkable 20–1 victory. In the past two games, Little Rock had been out hit 40–1! Losses by New Orleans and Memphis allowed the Vols to slip back into possession of second place.

League Leaders on September 12

New Orleans	71	54	.568
Nashville	69	55	.556
Memphis	70	57	.552

Despite two humiliating losses, Bill Hart was given the unenviable task of trying to control Nashville batters for the second time in three days against Perdue. The exuberant fans sweltered in 90-degree heat as the Vols took the field in a rare 3 p.m. start. The offensive pattern of the previous game carried over into this contest, except Nashville's numbers were less gargantuan. Perdue, not as overpowering as Duggan or Sitton, scattered eight hits and allowed one run to score. Balanced hitting took place throughout the lineup, and the Vols batted through the order and scored seven times in the seventh inning. Butler, who was having an incredible two weeks of offensive production, led the way with three hits. Bay, East, and Daubert contributed two hits apiece, resulting in an 11–1 Nashville win.

League Leaders on September 13

New Orleans	72	54	.571
Nashville	70	55	.560
Memphis	71	57	.555

Vols fans reveled in Nashville's demolition of Little Rock, but unruly behavior detracted from the celebration. As the Vols pushed three runs across the plate in the fourth inning of the final game, a fistfight broke out in the bleachers and police arrested several drunken patrons. When the home team plated seven more tallies in the seventh, a mattress hanging from a protective net directly behind home plate inexplicably began to burn. Catcher Wood doused the flames with a bucket of water, but the bedding continued to smolder for the remainder of the game.[28] The over-exhuberance of these spectators points to the fact that the locals were beginning to sense, perhaps for the first time, that their team had a legitimate shot at the 1908 crown. The Little Rock series had been the proof: in four games, the Travelers had been outscored 34–5, out hit 58–16, and outpitched with overpowering performances by Duggan, Sitton, and Perdue. Although the league standings did not change, the Pelicans and Turtles were scheduled to play on Sunday, 13 September — a day off for the Vols. The subsequent Pelican-Turtle losses allowed the idle Vols to gain ground on New Orleans and distance themselves from Memphis.

With the season entering its final week, Rice predicted that Montgomery would play the spoiler role for one team because they would be hosting New Orleans and Memphis. The sportswriter also discussed scheduling options open to Berny based on league rules. Owing to earlier postponements, Nashville's manager could choose to play doubleheaders with Mobile and/or New Orleans based on the outcome of the New Orleans-Montgomery and Memphis-Atlanta series. Berny told Rice that a second twin bill against Mobile might be necessary in order to overtake the Pelicans, but he would avoid a doubleheader with New Orleans at all costs. In an effort to hype the race, President Kuhn ordered the installation of a telegraph line in Sulphur Dell's press box to receive inning-by-inning updates from Montgomery and Atlanta, and construction of a special chalk scoreboard to be mounted against the right field wall to record the progress of the Pelicans and Turtles for the fans. It gave new meaning to Deadball Era baseball to watch the scoreboard. For downtown rooters who could not watch the Vols in person, Western Union agreed to mount a chalkboard slate outside its office to track the progress of all three teams still in the hunt.[29] The city of Nashville was succumbing to pennant fever.

President Kavanaugh added to the excitement with an announcement that a three-game playoff would be held should two teams end deadlocked. The sites, suggested the league mogul, should include the two city's directly involved as well as one neutral site, perhaps his own city of Little Rock.[30] The president also assigned the top two officials on the circuit, Carpenter and Fitzsimmons, to arbitrate the remainder of Nashville's games.

League Leaders on September 14

New Orleans	72	55	.567
Nashville	70	56	.560
Memphis	71	58	.550

As Nashville anxiously awaited the arrival of Mobile, Rice reviewed the city's connection with past Southern Association championships. He informed readers in the *Tennessean* that Nashville had sewn up league titles in 1901 and 1902 on the road, but in 1908 the possibility of such a glorious event would occur at home. "For win or lose," said the articulate Rice, "the local Bug Colony is facing the richest week in its history."[31]

The first game of the Mobile series on 14 September started with a bang. In the opening frame, Siegle tracked down a fly ball in deep center field off the bat of clean-up hitter Paul Sentell to rob the Sea Gull shortstop of a sure three-run home run. The visitors kept the pressure on by jumping to a 2–0 lead the next inning. When Seabough was struck by a foul tip and split the only good finger left on his throwing hand, Hurlburt immediately entered the game. The Vols regained the lead in the third, and Duggan clamped down. The linescore showed nothing but zeroes for the visitors for the rest of the game. Teammates East, McElveen, Siegle, and Butler had three base hits, and McElveen smashed a home run that rattled around in the Dump as part of a string of six consecutive hits and four runs scored in the eighth. In all, the Vols clobbered ten singles, six doubles, and two home runs in the 10–2 victory. Zack Wheat had a terrible time adjusting to the incline in right field.

In other action, the Turtle club experienced off-field excitement on its train ride from Birmingham to Atlanta when another locomotive pulled alongside the Memphis Special and a thirty-minute race ensued. The Turtles' 5–4 loss to the Crackers dropped them from a more important race. A headline in the *Memphis Commercial-Appeal* stated the situation matter-of-factly: PENNANT BOOM IS PUNCTURED.[32]

LEAGUE LEADERS ON SEPTEMBER 15

New Orleans	73	55	.570
Nashville	71	55	.564
Memphis	71	59	.546

Red Fisher had lost seven pitching starts by only one run in 1908 — a statistic that did not impress the Vols. In the first inning, the home team greeted the Sea Gull manager with three consecutive singles and a sacrifice fly to register three runs. "The Awful Swat-Fest Continues," read Rice's headline, led by Daubert's four hits (two doubles) and five RBI.[33] Wiseman and East stroked three hits each in the thirteen-hit attack, and Sitton "splashed his splitter all over the plate" for a three-hitter. The Sulphur Dell crowd thoroughly enjoyed the 8–2 route, but were partially deflated upon learning that New Orleans had handled Montgomery, 7–0, to stay atop the standings. Berny now calculated that a twin bill on the final day of the Mobile series would not take place. If Nashville split the hypothetical doubleheader with Mobile and New Orleans won its single contest, the locals would still be in second place and drop percentage points. Even if they swept the Sea Gulls, the Vols could do no better than enter into a tie with the Pelicans. By dropping both games, Nashville might jeopardize any chance of winning the championship. The risk was simply too great, surmised the Nashville field general. It made better sense for Nashville to take its chances in a winner-take-all three-game series against the pesky Birds. Berny liked the Vols' prospects in a head-to-head encounter since both teams had played well in the last ten games, producing identical 8–2 records.

League Leaders on September 16

New Orleans	74	55	.574
Nashville	72	55	.567

Gordon "The Demon Midget" Hickman had defeated Nashville on three occasions during the season, so there was plenty of concern among the Vols when the final meeting with Mobile commenced on 16 September. The southpaw, also known as "The Featherweight Phenom," did not last long, however. Hickman left his control in the hotel, issuing three bases on balls with the bases loaded in the first inning, and fell behind, 5–0. His wildness continued in the second when Berny's club tacked on two more runs. Undoubtedly angered by his performance, Hickman plucked Bay on his bad knee in the third, and Hunter replaced Deerfoot two innings later. After Hickman's third wild pitch, Lee Garvin stripped off his catcher's gear in frustration and removed himself from the contest. Manager Finn thereupon pulled his ineffective starter, but the Vols went on to score ten runs on thirteen hits. Wiseman and East provided most of the thunder with three-hit performances, and McElveen and Siegle had a pair of safeties. Perdue, accustomed to tremendous run support lately, pitched "with his old-time smoke" and threw as if the game were a scoreless tie. The Pride of Sumner County scattered seven hits, including a solo home run to former Pelican Eddie Sabrie. The Vols found little solace in their one-sided 10–1 victory, however, as New Orleans wrapped up a clean sweep of Montgomery.

The 1908 Southern Association race boiled down to two contenders: the Nashville Vols and New Orleans Pelicans. The winner-take-all face-off was scheduled to begin on 17 September at Sulphur Dell. "This series," proclaimed Yancey, "will be the greatest in the history of baseball in Nashville."[34]

League Leaders on September 17

New Orleans	75	55	.577
Nashville	73	55	.570

Mid-September, 1908. The tables were set. Two teams had survived the grueling season and prepared to face each other on the last weekend of the season in a league publicist's dream. A head-to-head championship weekend in Nashville! Each manager liked the odds of taking two out of three games from their worthy opponent and be crowned league champs. Berny was particularly encouraged by the manner in which his Vols had competed against the Pelicans at the beginning of the September streak.

Several factors contributed to Nashville finding itself in the championship series. First, the thirteen-game homestand was a psychological advantage to Nashville. Second, few professional baseball clubs could match the Vols' offense in the last twelve games. The hot streak began during the Mobile doubleheader on 5 September, continued against Memphis in the Labor Day twin bill, and gathered momentum versus Little Rock and Mobile. The thirty-hit slugfest against Little Rock on 11 September stands as the precise moment when Nashville exercised total domination over its foes. During the twelve-game run, the Vols not only hit for average, but hit with power, too. The club recorded double-digit base hits in eleven out of twelve contests, socked 166 hits (13.8 average per game), and generated 90 runs (7.5 average per game). During the stretch run, the team batted .382 — over .100 above its season average. The middle of the lineup — East, McElveen, Siegle, and Daubert — was particularly deadly. Wiseman and Butler provided support by getting on base, and then stealing them. Finally, the Volunteers had kept pace with the Pelicans, winning nine out of twelve games.

The third factor in the Vols' rise to prominence was solid pitching. Perdue set the tone with his courageous sixteen-inning performance on 3 September. The lesson of sheer determination surely caught the attention of his competitive teammates. Once the Gallatin Squash decided to bear down on an opponent, the result was devastating. And then there was Duggan's no-hitter one week later. Such a near-perfect outing attracted major league interest, and *The Sporting News* and *Sporting Life* carried detailed accounts of the event. Duggan had shown his Nashville teammates that they were unbeatable. Finally, the win-loss record during the momentous run illustrates that most of the pitchers had made positive contributions in the team's success:

Duggan	3–0	Sitton	2–1	Bernhard	No decision
Perdue	3–0	Kellum	0–2	Hunter	1–0

Vols pitchers allowed only 17 runs (1.5 average per game) and 58 hits (5.3 average per game) in 109 innings of work. Although Kellum's numbers were disappointing, the southpaw threw with a sore arm throughout the dog days of summer and never turned down an opportunity to start. Plus, the crafty sidewheeler owned a 3–0 record against the only team that stood between Nashville and the 1908 title — the New Orleans Pelicans.

The outstanding leadership style of manager Bill Bernhard was the fourth and final factor that contributed to the Vols' success. Specifically, he handled the altercation between Kellum and McElveen on 2 September in a manly fashion. Berny, a sage veteran of intense major league campaigns in Philadelphia and Cleveland, understood the pressure under which players performed. The manager accepted the cause of such an outburst as the natural outgrowth of intensity created by a highly charged competitive environment. In his statement on the episode, Berny chastised both parties and promised disciplinary action. In doing so, Berny satisfied the public's Victorian sensibilities concerning rowdy behavior. Then he allowed the issue to quietly die away. But, not only did Berny satisfy the public's need for justice, he also defused a potentially ruinous event in terms of team morale and turned it into a positive for the Nashville Base Ball Club. Some might argue that the team played more focused baseball after the incident, and set the stage for the breakout, which began three days later.

The Nashville–New Orleans championship series was only one baseball venue that came down to the final wire in 1908. Mirroring the Vols, the Richmond Lawmakers of the Virginia State League had risen from a miserable fifth-place finish in 1907 to play in a winner-take-all Labor Day twinkling of instate rival Danville. "The games marked the high point of community interest in seventy-seven years of professional baseball in Richmond," claims baseball historian William Simpson.[35] In this special year of 1908, the major leagues still belonged to the pitchers. Six no-hitters were thrown in the National League, and the American League witnessed four more—including a perfect game twirled by Cleveland ace Addie Joss on 2 October. Ed Walsh won forty games for the White Sox and Christy Mathewson notched thirty-seven victories for the New York Giants. Moreover, the tight races themselves were attracting national attention. In the American and National Leagues, the Detroit Tigers, Chicago White Sox, and Cleveland Indians, and New York Giants, Pittsburgh Pirates and Chicago Cubs, respectively, were locked in three-way battles that were not resolved until the final day of the season. The Cubs and Giants required a playoff game on 8 October to settle the Nationals entree to the World Series.[36] All of these championship races, Nashville included, contributed to make 1908 a unique year—a defining season—that captured the national pastime in the American imagination.[37]

In Nashville, Bernhard had solved the equation that vaulted the Vols into the championship series: a combination of good pitching, solid defense, and timely hitting. These ingredients—along with a self-sacrificing spirit, strong role models, and a team philosophy—forged a team chemistry that guided the Vols through four consecutive doubleheaders. Only three games remained to be played in the campaign. The classic championship atmosphere would provide sports-minded Nashvillians with enough memories to last for decades. "No, there is no circus in town ... no, there hasn't been any fire, either. Why is everybody so excited," asked Yancey in the *Banner*?[38] The city of Nashville had contracted pennant fever. The same sentiment might apply to the nation as well.

CHAPTER 9

The Greatest Game Ever Played in Dixie

"Athletic Park to-day, to-morrow, and Saturday will harbor within its four corners the most numerous, the wildest, and the craziest assortment of frenzied humanity ever gathered together in any baseball lot in Dixie Land," predicted Yancey in the *Banner*.[1] The showdown between the Pelicans and Volunteers had arrived, and the outcome of the three-game series would crown the 1908 Southern Association champion. The encounters promised drama, excitement, and raw emotion, culminating in "the greatest game ever played in Dixie." The contest for the title would be recounted in Nashville for several decades, yet public memory of the event has faded over time and is practically forgotten today, one century later.

A large mob hovered around the Sulphur Dell ticket window at 9 a.m. on game day, waiting to purchase a ticket for admission to the first contest between the Vols and Pels. Mounted constables patrolled through the crowd — a rather strong presence intended to maintain order. The opening game of the series was not just important to the city of Nashville; neighboring communities were sharing in the excitement. Chalkboard details were being set up outside telegraph offices on several town squares in the region to follow the inning-by-inning progress of each game. A large number of visitors arrived at Union Station from the surrounding rural countryside, choking Nashville's trolley lines two hours before game time. The Tennessee State Fair, slated to open on 21 September, contributed to the festive atmosphere in the city, adding to the swelling number of guests. "Interest is at a fever pitch all over the South," noted Yancey in the *Banner*.[2] Well, at least in middle Tennessee.

The morning edition of the *Memphis Commercial-Appeal* ran a player-by-player/position-by-position comparison of the Pelicans and Vols.[3] It is an interesting out-of-town perspective that was duplicated in Atlanta and New Orleans. The predictions were:

First base — Daubert over Tarleton "in every department." The Pelican was a relative unknown, being a recent addition from Cotton States League.
Second base — Dundon gets defensive edge; East is better hitter.
Shortstop — Dexter all over Butler "in every department."
Third base — McElveen and Rohe are "smart and savvy players." The Memphis scribe predicts outcome of series will hinge on play of the third basemen. McElveen hailed from the "twang doodle district of east Tennessee."
Catcher — Seabough seen as class act over Matthews. Hurlburt, the former Turtle, not mentioned.
Pitchers — For New Orleans, Breitenstein is considered the best pitcher on either staff. Bartley and Fritz are respectable and smart.
For Nashville — Kellum is the acknowledged "Bird killer" with 3–0 record over New Orleans. Strength of other Vols pitchers was questioned — Sitton was "inexperienced," Hunter "untested," Duggan "erratic," and Perdue "likely to disappoint all middle Tennessee."
Prediction: New Orleans

While this assessment is relatively accurate, several clarifications are necessary at shortstop, third base, catcher, and pitcher. Dexter had played 55 of 72 games at first base and Butler outhit him by thirty-seven percentage points. Based on game experience and offensive production, the edge should've gone to Kid. McElveen was the league's eleventh-best hitter, outperforming Rohe by forty-three percentage points. In the field, McElveen and Rohe were in a dead heat. Hurlburt ranked first in defense and caught only forty-three contests, but Matthews outhit Big Ed by eighty percentage points. The Pelican receiver deserved the nod. Finally, the critique of Perdue was unreasonable, based on his performance over the last month of the season.[4]

The *Memphis Commercial-Appeal* sportswriter did not analyze specific outfielders, but made a general statement supporting New Orleans. Defensive statistics in the *Spalding Guide* favor Vols outfielders, however. Siegle, the fifth-best defensive outfielder in the league outperformed Lord in center; Wiseman held an edge in experience over newcomer Roy Montgomery, especially in the intangible — how to play in the Dump; and Bay and Rickert played comparable defense in left. Offensively, New Orleans outfielders held a slight advantage. Lord, the second-best hitter in the league (.314), commanded a fifty-two percent lead over Siegle; Bay dominated Rickert by forty percent; Wiseman canceled out his rookie counterpart. Overall, Nashville outfielders held a narrow defensive advantage, and New Orleans outfielders copped offensive honors.[5]

As expected, Berny announced that soft-throwing Kellum would start game one. The southpaw's changes-of-speed had throttled the hard-hitting Pelicans throughout the season. For some inexplicable reason, however, the Nashville manager rescinded his decision shortly before game time and inserted himself in the starting role. It is not known whether Berny had lost confidence in Kellum, owing to his weak performance in September, or the manager simply had more faith in his own ability to pitch the biggest game of the year. Perhaps, Kellum had not thrown since Nashville's last loss on 9 September. Knowing Kellum's competitive nature, it is unlikely that he removed himself from the most important contest of the year. It is more probable that Berny's proven track record of taking the ball in tense situations was the determining factor. Kellum out, Bernhard in.

A capacity crowd of 5,000 fans buzzed in anticipation of the first pitch, and their excitement infected the Vols. Rice thought that the club looked nervous in warm-ups in contrast to the cool looseness projected from the team on the other side of the diamond. As game time approached, the temperature climbed to 86 degrees. The later starting time — 3:30 p.m. — was intended to allow workers from the commercial district an opportunity to attend the game. Carpenter, considered by many baseball people to be the best strike-and-ball man in the league, umpired behind the plate and Fitzsimmons worked the bases. At the appointed time, Carpenter tossed the game ball to Bernhard; the championship series was underway.

Hometown favorite Doc Wiseman opened the bottom of the first inning with a double to the Dump, and scored on a single by McElveen. The Pelicans responded in the top of the second after East juggled a grounder by Charlie Dexter and threw the ball past Daubert for an error. Joe Rickert followed with a bunt single to put two runners aboard. Then Augie Dundon hit a routine grounder to Butler, but the elusive ball went through the shortstop's legs. The second error of the inning allowed Dexter to score. Real damage occurred when rookie Roy Montgomery launched a double to score both Rickert and Dundon. The Vols trailed 3–1.

As Berny's boys struggled with shaky nerves and defense, the Pelicans performed efficiently. "Playing scientific ball and working like a well oiled machine" is the way Rice described them. A gracious Nashville crowd applauded several splendid defensive plays turned by the visitors. Bill Bartley pitched one of the best games of his career, and faced danger only when Daubert led off the third with a triple. Bartley silenced the next Vols batters and stranded the first baseman at third. Rice described "the fast and snappy" 5–1 drubbing as "a clean cut, non-debatable victory" for New Orleans.[6]

Now Nashville trailed New Orleans by 1½ games with two meetings left. The question on everyone's mind was why Berny had not thrown Kellum, but no answer was forthcoming. Diehard Vols fans understood that the team needed to overcome its defensive lapses, rediscover its offense, and pitch at a higher caliber if they expected to raise the championship banner in Nashville. Everything hinged on the Vols sweeping the rest of the way — a lofty challenge. Berny selected Duggan to pitch the crucial second game.

League Standings on September 18

New Orleans	76	55	.580
Nashville	73	55	.566

Nashville readers had come to expect poetic ditties from Rice to describe local sports events. But reporter Allen Johnson composed a piece in the evening *Banner* entitled NEARING THE END. Johnson's doggerel was "a plea to the fans to pull hard for victory and the grand old rag." It added literary hype to the current station of the Nashville Base Ball Club.

> Ye sad-eyed sons of Bugville, hold!
>   Keep down those cringing fears;
> What mean ye slaves?
> The rag still waves
>   Above the Volunteers.
> What matter if Big Bill went down
>   Beneath resounding thumps?
> It takes but two
> To pull us through,
>   Though Bill did get his bumps.
> What matter if poor East went wild,
>   And Butler thought that he
> Was Orville Wright
> And took a flight
>   High o'er the hectic lea?
> The grand old rag still floats in air.
>
>   Ergo — pull hard, ye fans;
> It is not yet
> The one best bet
>   To back the Pelicans.
> East's bludgeon yet may find the sphere
>   (Cheer up, ye Bugville clan),
> Nor cleave the air,
> Creating there
>   A noise like a fan.
> Full many a swatsman oft has failed
>   To swat the spheroid's seam,
> Yet, later, bing!
> Hast sent the thing
>   Beyond the sunset's gleam.
> There's little "Doc" still in the game,
>   With now and then a hit,

While every thump
That finds the dump
　　Sleeps snugly in his mitt.
When Johnny Duggan seeks the slab
　　(To-day he'll do that same),
Let Bugville yell,
For all is well,
　　And Nashville's in the game.
A fighting chance is all we need —
　　Let every rock and crag
Ring o'er and o'er
With Bugville's roar
　　Until we cop the rag.[7]

Johnson's poem employed purple prose reminiscent of Rice's writings, a style very popular in the Victorian age.[8]

Manager Frank fell victim to the second guessers when he overlooked star twirler Breitenstein, and instead chose William "Silver Bill" Phillips to pitch game two. Also known as "Whoa Bill," Phillips had begun his professional career in the late 1880s. He is credited with seventy-one major league victories over a seven-year career primarily with Cincinnati, won thirty-seven games for the Pelicans in 1906 and 1907, and had spent most of the current season in the Cotton States League. Frank had great confidence in Phillips' 40-year-old arm, but Rice and Ewing questioned why Breitenstein, a seventeen-game winner, had not received the nod.[9]

Another sellout crowd filed into Sulphur Dell on 18 September, hoping that the 1908 season would not come to an end for their beloved Vols. For the second straight day, mid-afternoon temperatures again rose to a comfortable 86 degrees with blue skies overhead. In the third, Butler limited a Pelican rally to one run by snagging a grounder deep in the hole and throwing out George Rohe by a step at first base to end the threat. The Vols knotted the score at one apiece moments later on a triple by Butler and sacrifice fly by Hurlburt — Nashville's catcher for the entire championship series. Duggan breezed through the Pelican lineup; on the other hand, "Whoa Bill" was tagged for several extra-base hits, although none of them produced runs until the sixth. In that frame, a costly Pelican error with two outs and a clutch bases-loaded double by East, followed by an RBI single by McElveen, resulted in a three-run outburst for the home team. Daubert added a solo home run that cleared the right field wall in the eighth to seal Nashville's 6–2 victory. Everyone in the Vols batting order reached base with the exception of Hurlburt, yet Big Ed was singled out by two Nashville dailies for stellar work in "calling a brilliant game." Rice boasted that the Pelicans had about as much chance of winning the middle game of the playoffs "as Taft had of carrying Texas" [in the upcoming presidential election].[10]

Knowing Sitton was scheduled to pitch the third and final game, Will

Hamilton asked an appropriate question in the *New Orleans Item:* "Can you remember when the Pelicans have hit a good spitball pitcher with any effect?"[11] One sensed that momentum in the series had shifted to Nashville.

LEAGUE LEADERS ON SEPTEMBER 19

New Orleans	76	56	.576
Nashville	74	55	.569

As the game winded down, several spectators began to collect items to reward Daubert for his tremendous home run. This display of public affection was typical of a bygone sports era. The donations reflected the working-class composition of some of the generous attendees: $27 suit of clothes, three $5 hats, two loads of coal, a barrel of flour, and $50 in cash. Not a bad bonus for a minor league Deadball Era ballplayer.[12]

President Kavanaugh announced that he would attend the championship game on 19 September. Anticipating a large crowd, club president Kuhn requested the loan of 3,000 stadium chairs from Vanderbilt University to be placed along the outfield wall. George A. Dickel, the whiskey magnate from Tullahoma, donated a winner's purse of $100 should the Vols capture the crown. The game promised to be one of historic proportions by almost every indicator; never before in the history of the Southern Association had the championship been decided in head-to-head competition on the last day of the season.

Adding to the drama surrounding the championship game was the contrast between the two pitchers—Breitenstein and Sitton—who both came from opposite ends of the professional spectrum. The 39-year-old Breit was in the twilight of a distinguished career. In the 1890s, he was considered one of the most effective southpaws in the National League, and Breit was still one of the most dominant pitchers in the Southern Association.[13] Sitton, on the other hand, was a fresh talent in his second full season of professional baseball. A bright career in major league baseball seemingly lay ahead as the 25-year-old spitballer was in a position to accomplish the unthinkable — to help two professional baseball franchises win league crowns in the same season. At the conclusion of the game two victory, an exuberant Nashville rooter yelled to manager Frank: "If Sitton is right, he'll beat you." Frank wheeled around and replied: "Breitenstein is always right!"[14] Breit remained the definitive Pelican answer to all of Nashville's hoopla.

Visiting columnist Sam J. Stockard developed an engaging symbolic interpretation of the impending Breit-Sitton clash. "To-day's battle is a contest between youth and age: between a man who has had his day and one whose day has just dawned. It is a contest between the craftiness and experience of a once great pitcher ... and a great pitcher of tremendous physical ability. Sitton is going up and Breitenstein is going down the limelight ladder," noted

Stoddard. The newspaperman also spotted the generational differences presented by the game. "It is youth against age: enthusiasm and confident determination and consciousness of superiority against frazzled-out stars.... Youth triumphs over age. It will be so today if youth backs up youth, and does not forget the main fact — that they are, and of right ought to be, masters of the diamond at Sulphur Dell this afternoon. Determination and grit will win today's battle," concluded Stoddard. Rice interjected that "Sitton was fit to pitch the game of his life."[15]

Thus, the titanic Breit-Sitton matchup was born — youth vs. age, veteran vs. rookie, lefty vs. righty, renowned vs. unknown, favorite vs. underdog. Greek epics and Old Testament narratives come to mind. But this was neither ancient Troy nor Jericho, but 1908 Nashville, Tennessee. Even Rice, with his Vanderbilt education, could not have orchestrated a more grand classical finish to the season.

At noon, most Nashville businesses in the commercial district closed, and downtown streets emptied. A throng of people — a spontaneous movement of humanity — from captains of industry to hourly wage laborers — lit out for Sulphur Dell. Employees refused to work during the game in several stores and factories that chose to remain open. A makeshift scoreboard was erected on Capitol Hill and a man armed with a pair of binoculars supplied updates of the linescore by zeroing in on Sulphur Dell's scoreboard nearly a mile away. Government officials left their offices and congregated on the lawn to cheer at appropriate moments.[16]

In Perdue's hometown, the local newspaper posted an inning-by-inning detail for the citizens to view. By game time, the east side of the Gallatin town square was entirely blocked off to traffic. Friends and neighbors were bursting with pride over the exploits of the homegrown Squash. They chatted about Perdue's pitching exploits in the 17-inning tie on 9 July and the 17-inning iron man performance on 3 September. These Gallatians recognized, with ample justification, that Perdue had made a significant contribution to the Vols' magical rise to success.[17]

The Sulphur Dell ticket windows swung open at 1 p.m., and a large throng of enthusiastic fans rushed to purchase their ducats. Police officers were caught in the middle of the swelling pandemonium, and were unable to preserve any sense of decorum. In less than an hour every seat had been sold despite the fact that the game was not scheduled to commence until 3:30 p.m. A standing-room-only crowd eight people deep lined up behind the roped-off area that encircled the outfield. Special ground rules would be in effect for the game and many Dellians suspected the game would produce a lot of runs, as routine pop flies would fall for ground-rule doubles. An extra squad of constables patrolled the jammed outfield to prevent excited fans from inching the rope forward. A sizable number of African-Americans sat in the bleachers, underscoring the interracial popularity of the Vols.

Reminiscent of an earlier overflow contest, a large contingent of spectators lined the railroad tracks beyond right field, knothole kids peered through the fence, and every window in the nearby icehouse was crammed. Adventuresome fans clung to branches in the infamous tree beyond the right field wall, which resembled a Christmas tree with human ornaments. Over 10,700 paying fans impatiently waited for the first pitch along with an estimated 2,000 nonpaying customers.[18]

Without a doubt, Rice had his thumb on the pulse of the city. "This is the era of the Bug in Nashville," proclaimed the joyous journalist.

> Every man, woman and child capable of feeling is ... bursting with the massive expectation of the moment. It is a chance that reaches a Bug but once in a lifetime. When you cram the full season's conflict into one day's battling — when the worth or value of every play from April through September is sidetracked for one day's conflict — it's easy enough to figure upon the concentrated outburst of enthusiasm and general dippiness that is bound to prevail.[19]

Important local dignitaries were in attendance. President Kuhn sat beside Mayor James S. Brown, who was designated to toss out the game ball to signal the beginning of the contest. Governor Malcolm Patterson followed the game from the state house lawn. The mayor and governor both adroitly claimed to be the Vols' number one fan. Super Fan, Alf Williams, made the same boast from his seat in the band. Only league president Kavanaugh was absent; he was reportedly too ill to travel to Nashville. [20]

The stadium rocked with screaming fans. The noise reached a crescendo as captains McElveen and Rohe exchanged lineup cards at home plate. The official lineup, as drafted by managers Frank and Bernhard, appears below:

New Orleans	Nashville
Roy Montgomery LF	Harry Bay LF
George Rohe 3rd	Julius Wiseman RF
Bris Lord CF	Walter East 2nd
Bob Tarleton 1st	Pryor McElveen 3rd
Charlie Dexter SS	Johnny Siegle CF
Joe Rickert LF	Jake Daubert 1st
Gus Dundon 2nd	Willis Butler SS
Harry Matthews C	Ed Hurlburt C
Ted Breitenstein P	Carl Sitton P

Umpires Carpenter and Fitzsimmons declared everything in order as delirious rooters shouted themselves hoarse in the grandstands.[21]

First Inning

For the third straight day, a bright blue sky welcomed spectator and participant alike with temperatures in the mid–80s at game time. Rice opined that the Vols appeared relaxed during warm-ups while the Pelicans seemed edgy — a reversal of the pregame atmosphere prior to the first playoff.[22] As the Vols burst from the team's bench onto the field to assume their positions, a collective roar from 10,000 throats filled the air. Game time!

Montgomery stepped up to the plate and Sitton prepared to deliver the first pitch. Yancey noticed that "the sudden silence was so intense that a blind man might have thought the park was empty."[23] Then, "the Spitball King" sent the first pitch over for a strike. Unable to pick up the dancing pitch, the rookie sensation proceeded to strike out to register the first out of the championship showdown. George Rohe tapped a slow roller to Daubert, and Bris Lord smashed a grounder to Butler, who fielded the ball cleanly and fired it to Daubert to close the Pelican half of the inning.

Bay had the first look at Breitenstein in the bottom of the first inning, but the veteran pitcher used a sharp breaking ball to produce a groundout to Dundon at second base. Wiseman slugged a long fly ball that landed among patrons in the Dump, and the little Doctor stood atop second base with a ground-rule double. East bounced out to the right side of the infield to advance Wiseman to third. Thunderous applause greeted McElveen as he strode to the plate. The third baseman connected sharply with one of Breit's smoke balls, and it appeared the Vols would notch their first run, but the fleet Rohe cut off the ball as he crossed in front of the shortstop, and tossed it to Tarleton for the third out. The first inning was in the books.

Second Inning

Bob Tarleton, another rookie recently brought up from the Cotton States League, led off the top of the second. The first baseman demonstrated good foot speed in beating out a slow roller to Butler at shortstop. The newest Bird perched on second base when Charlie Dexter grounded out to Daubert. Joe Rickert stepped up to the dish and swatted a swinging bunt down the third base line. Tarleton immediately broke for third base as McElveen charged in. Recognizing he had no chance of gunning down Rickert at first, the third baseman bare-handed the ball and feigned a throw to Daubert. At this crucial moment, Tarleton made perhaps the single greatest mistake in the game as he rounded third base too far. McElveen spun around in a flash, lunged at the braking Tarleton, and tagged him for the second out.[24] The crowd went ballistic with excitement. After Gus Dundon bounced out to Butler deep in the hole at shortstop to end the Pelican threat, the boisterous crowd greeted the

Vols with a monstrous ovation as they ran off the field. Surely, Dundon's poke would have driven in Tarleton.

Siegle opened the Vols half of the inning with a sharp line drive gathered in by rookie right fielder, Montgomery. The lefty Daubert sliced a grounder to Dexter at shortstop, who gobbled it up for the second out. Then Butler, who had been on an offensive tear in the month of September, smashed a hot one that the Pelican shortstop mishandled. Butler failed to advance, however, as Hurlburt grounded out to Pelican captain and third baseman Rohe to bring the inning to a close.

Third Inning

Sitton started the inning in grand style by striking out Harry Matthews, but followed by committing a cardinal error in baseball by walking the opposing pitcher. Now the Pelicans were at the top of the batting order and had their second look at the Vols pitcher. Leadoff batter Montgomery made solid contact, sending a towering fly ball to the outfield, but Siegle tracked it down in front of the rope for the second out. Rohe fanned to end the Pelican third on a whimper. Sitton's spitter was beginning to splatter all around the plate.

In the bottom of the frame, Breitenstein rung up Sitton on three straight pitches. Then Bay lined out sharply to Dexter at shortstop. With two outs and no one on base, "the $10,000 Beauty" pitched around Wiseman, who had clubbed a double in the first inning. The most popular Vols player was stranded on first base, however, when Breit struck out East to set Nashville down.

Fourth Inning

The dangerous Bris Lord struck out to open the Pelican fourth inning. Then the unknown Tartleton ripped his second single of the day past an outstretched Butler. Dexter blistered a similar ball in the vicinity of East, who knocked it down, but the Pelicans threatened with runners at first and second base with only one out. "Diamond Joe" Rickert stepped up to the plate, and the crowd held its collective breathe. Rickert sized up one of Sitton's pitches and crushed it toward East. The charging second baseman speared the bouncing missile, tagged out Dexter, who was heading for second base, and threw over to Daubert to complete the inning-ending double play. East's heady defensive work had turned away the second Pelican opportunity to score the game's first run. Sitton had escaped his last harrowing moment.

McElveen led off the fourth inning with a clean single. In a game that was shaping up to be decided by one run, Siegle squared around to bunt, but sent

Breitenstein's offering right back to the slab. "Red" fielded the ball cleanly and whirled around to force out McElveen at second base. The next batter, Daubert, teed off on a fastball that raced past Dundon. With two Vols aboard, Butler hit a sharp grounder to Rohe, whose momentum carried him toward second base. The Pelican captain fed the ball underhanded to the bag to force out Daubert. With two outs and Vols runners at the corners, it appeared the home team might draw first blood. Standing only 90 feet from paydirt, Siegle implored his catcher to deliver a clutch hit. Instead, Hurlburt grounded out to Rohe to squash the Vols rally. Neither the Vols nor Pelicans had been able to score a run despite two opportunities; outstanding defense and solid pitching had denied each team.

Fifth Inning

Weak-hitting Dundon led off the fifth frame — an unlikely batter to initiate a rally. However, Gus tied into one of Sitton's spitters and blistered "a red hot liner" in the direction of McElveen. The third sacker leaped toward shortstop, and with every ounce of strength, Humpy stretched out parallel to the ground and pawed the frozen rope out of the air with one hand. The crowd roared its approval of the acrobatic play. Nashville's three scribes agreed that McElveen's catch, his second spectacular play of the game, had nipped a potential third Pelican rally in the bud. Then, Matthews grounded out to Butler, Breitenstein received a second free pass, and Montgomery drove a routine line drive to Wiseman to turn away New Orleans. It now was becoming apparent, at the midway point of the game, that a single run might be the difference between victory and defeat.

In the bottom of the fifth inning, Nashville offered little in the way of encouragement as Breitenstein silenced all three Vols batters on infield outs. Sitton and Bay grounded out to Tarleton at first, and Wiseman popped out to Rohe at third. Overpowering pitching had asserted itself and set the tone of the game.

Sixth Inning

Pelican batters swatted helplessly at Sitton's unpredictable spitball and blazing smoke ball. Rohe fouled out to McElveen, and Lord popped out to Butler in shallow left field. Tarleton, the owner of two Pelican hits, was finally retired via the strikeout.

The Nashville nines fared no better in their half of the sixth. East whiffed on one of Breit's benders, and McElveen and Siegle grounded out to shortstop and first base, respectively. The crowd continued to cheer enthusiastically, but a sense of apprehension set in as both teams struggled to take control. To this point, the Pelicans and Vols had only three base hits apiece.

Seventh Inning

Dexter tapped a soft grounder to McElveen, and the Pelicans quickly registered one out in the seventh. Rickert followed with a strikeout, and Dundon concluded the inning with a slow roller back to the slab. Sitton fielded the ball, his weakness, and fired it to Daubert to dispose of little Gus and the Pelicans. Frank's New Orleans squad was noticeably frustrated at the plate, and Sitton was gaining confidence as the game wore on.

In an unusual occurrence, the game was temporarily suspended in mid-inning for a special ceremony to honor the Vols' most popular player. Escorted to second base, Doc Wiseman was awarded a gold pocket watch for eight years of meritous service to Nashville. The timepiece was inscribed: "Presented to Julius A. Wiseman for Efficient Service, Nashville Baseball Club, 1901–1908."[25] Spectators rewarded the little Doctor with waves of applause as he accepted the gift. As Wiseman walked off the field, the New Orleans catcher grabbed the keepsake, tucked it into his hip pocket, and playfully bowed to the crowd as a sign of gratitude for receiving such a fine present.

It is possible that the gift was a veiled bribe to keep Wiseman in a Nashville uniform. Indeed, Doc had been offered a managerial position with several teams in the South Atlantic League. The Macon franchise had contacted him ten days earlier, inquiring into his availability in 1909. Columbus (GA) and Chattanooga expressed similar interest. Even the University of the South, Sewanee, entered the sweepstakes to land the popular Vols member as a coach.[26] Play was resumed at the conclusion of the festivities.

"The bloody seventh" is how Yancey later dubbed the bottom of the seventh inning, but the frame began rather inauspiciously.[27] After Daubert flew out to Dexter at shortstop and Butler hit an unassisted grounder to Tarleton at first, the Vols offense came to life. An unlikely offensive hero, Hurlburt, began the two-out rally with "a crashing single to right field." Then Sitton made weak contact with a pitch that trickled between Tarleton and Dundon for a scratch single. Bay observed that Tarleton held Sitton on at first and Rohe was positioned deep at the other corner; Deerfoot dropped a perfect bunt down the third base line to load the bases. The crowd, sensing the possibilities, mounted a frenzied "huzzah" in the grandstand.[28] Nearly half a century later, Bay recounted that his perfect bunt to load the bases to keep the rally alive in the seventh inning of the '08 championship game was his fondest memory of his entire baseball career.

The game and the season was now in the hands of Julius Augustus Wiseman. Everything hinged on his at-bat. Nerves were tight on both benches.

Ladies in the crowd held their hands in a prayerful position. Men screamed. Little boys and girls jumped up and down in excited anticipation of what might occur next. Then came Breitenstein's offering. The ball seemed to float in slow motion and all eyes shifted to Wiseman as he entered his swing. Crack! The spheroid jumped off his bat. The sizzling line drive barely eluded the outstretched grasp of Dundon and bounced several times before resting in Lord's mitt in center. Hurlburt, the last man to join the Vols, broke for home plate "like an ice wagon" to record the first run of the game. Sitton, known for his foot speed, sprinted for third base. Did Bernhard try to hold him up? No matter. The aggressive pitcher was determined to score and break the game wide open. Meanwhile, the charging outfielder pivoted and sent a low, accurate throw toward home. Blocking the plate with his left leg and bracing his body for a collision, Matthews received Lord's throw just as Sitton was going into a slide, which was more of a controlled fall. The baserunner hit his head on the catcher's outstretched knee. Matthews applied the tag as the pitcher's head fell hard on the rubber dish. "Out," shouted umpire Carpenter, "side's retired." Sitton, overly eager to score, had committed a cardinal baserunning mistake.

The Sulphur Dell crowd was delirious with excitement. Wiseman scurried into second base on the throw—a place he had been ceremoniously toasted only moments ago. As the dust settled, Sitton lay prone across the plate as teammates rushed to his aide. Semiconscious, the Vols carried their fallen pitcher to the bench. The fans lapsed into an eery silence. Berny shouted at Perdue to warm up—and quick. But Sitton revived after several moments and insisted on continuing the game. The crowd welcomed Sitton's courage with spontaneous glee. The Vols led by a slender thread, 1–0.

Eighth Inning

Matthews led off the top of the eighth with a strikeout—the second time he had done so in the game. Breitenstein, probably sensing that time was running out for his team, sent a hot line drive over the bag at third base—a sure double. But McElveen knocked the ball down, recovered beautifully, and threw out Breitenstein in a very close play at first base. The Volunteer captain was the defensive standout for the third time in the contest. Then the keen-eyed Montgomery cracked a ground ball, pulling Daubert away from his bag. This time, an alert Sitton covered first base, and Daubert shoveled him the ball for the third Pelican out.

East drove one of Breitenstein's pitches into the outfield to start the bottom of the eighth—the fourth consecutive single off the New Orleans hurler, a sign that he was tiring. McElveen sacrificed East to second base, where he was stranded on groundouts by Siegle and Daubert.

Ninth Inning

The atmosphere in Sulphur Dell was electric as Sitton strode to the slab to begin the final frame. The Nashville Vols were on the verge of copping the 1908 crown. With adrenaline flowing, Sitton faced the heart of the powerful New Orleans lineup — Rohe, Lord, and Tarleton. Yet the spitballer had not allowed a single Bird to reach base since the fourth. And, how else should a classic championship tilt be decided except by facing the mightiest batters the opponent had to offer?

Rohe stepped into the batter's box to the backdrop of a suddenly hushed stadium. His unselective swings were desperate, however, and Sitton put down the Pelican captain on a groundout to East. The last hopes for the New Orleans Pelicans evaporated on six straight strikes thrown by Sitton. The crowd responded to each strike with increasingly louder applause. When Tarleton whiffed at Sitton's final offering, pandemonium broke loose on the field and in the stands. In less than two hours, the Nashville Volunteers were crowned champions of the Southern Association, and by the slenderest of margins — .002 — a league record that stood for thirty-one years.[29] The linescore on the Sulphur Dell scoreboard stood in silent tribute to the miraculous finish that Nashvillians had just witnessed.[30]

New Orleans	000	000	000	0	3 0
Nashville	000	000	10x	1	8 0

The Nashville team leaped off the team bench and swarmed Sitton on the slab. Within moments, several thousand fans rushed onto the field to join in the victory celebration. The throng "swept away like feathers" six policemen, who were standing on the infield grass to protect the players. Several husky men lifted Sitton onto their shoulders, one woman kissed him, and several hundred grateful spectators shook his hand. Men repeatedly tossed straw hats into the air as the merrymaking continued at a feverish pace. Others partied in the grandstands. One group of revelers raised $100 for Sitton — a bonus for his stellar performance. A small number of unruly fans began tearing up grandstand planks for souvenirs. As the players slowly disappeared through the clubhouse door in right-center, a numb crowd mingled on the lawn of Sulphur Dell for another hour, savoring the moment. In the distance, the city's fire alarms had all been turned on to announce the championship.

As the ballplayers emerged from the stadium, they were escorted by enthusiastic revelers to several nearby restaurants where they were treated to supper. Afterwards, the teammates reconvened at Jack Hardy's cigar shop on the corner of fourth and Union. The presence of the Vols caused a stir in the neighborhood, which attracted many curious onlookers. The growing mob pressed against Hardy's storefront and accidentally broke a large display window. By

7 p.m., the players embarked on a spontaneous parade through downtown streets, tailed by a vast number of admirers. As might be expected, the crowd became hilarious as many straw hats were punched out and rims placed around the necks of favorite players. Noisy pedestrians pushed along the sidewalks with nothing but the champion Vols on their lips. Two hours later, the principal parties were becoming weary, so Jack Hardy procured a wagon and team of horses to carry the players on another impromptu trek up and down Union Street. A brass band led the processional and added much merriment along the route.[31] That evening, Governor Patterson issued a statement: "We should all be proud of the victory," he said. "With the finest heroes, the finest men and women, and now the best baseball team in the South, Tennessee ought to be reasonably satisfied."[32] Ewing had mingled through the streets with the champions into the wee hours of the morning, and noted that "great satisfaction remained" early the next morning.[33]

Following the game, a spirit of generosity fueled by euphoria swept over the Nashville business community. Gentlemen in the Watauga Club raised $50 to present to Doc Wiseman for his timely RBI in "the bloody seventh." Iser Peter Cohen, a clothier and president of the Nashville booster club, offered four dress shirts to each player. Cohen also challenged local merchants to raise additional cash to be presented to the players during the field day benefit on 21 September. The Liberty Mill shipped a barrel of flour to the offseason homes of Daubert and Wiseman. Yancey sponsored "a lofty $1,000 fundraiser" at the *Banner*, but he waged an uphill struggle for the rest of the year. In the end, the sports editor mailed $21.20 drafts to each man.[34]

The Associated Press and Hearst News Service carried accounts of the championship game to the far reaches of the nation, and telegrams of congratulations filled the Nashville press. A sampling of joyous messages included "Congratulations to Captain Humpy," from the *Knoxville Journal and Tribune*. "The darkest horse in the league" had miraculously won the league crown, said Percy Whiting in the *Atlanta Georgian*.[35]

Always the bard and never at a loss for words, Rice wrote a poem that appeared on the editorial page of the *Tennessean* the following day. The doggerel, a parody of Rudyard Kipling's "When Earth's Last Picture is Painted," recapped the impact of the championship on Nashville's public consciousness:

> The tumult and the shouting dies—
> The captains and the teams depart—
> No more they'll hit or sacrifice
> Or round the bases quickly dart;
> We finished first—the One Best Bet—
> Where is the Fan that will forget?[36]

Carmack granted Rice rare front-page status to exhort the details surrounding the championship clash. In words that captured the sentiment of Nashvillians, the Murfreesboro native drafted the following headline: "The Greatest Game Ever Played in Dixie."[37] Neither was the significance of the game lost on Rice's colleague and good friend at the *Banner*. "It is great to be a winner in any kind of race," boasted Yancey. "It is splendid, superb, to finish first in a grand and grueling contest with such a foeman as the New Orleans team of 1908 for the opponent," concluded the team's official scorer.[38]

President Kuhn might have swooned when he counted the gate receipts for the three-game championship series — over $7,000 — which was an astronomical figure by Southern Association standards. Undisclosed revenues were also gleaned from the concession stands. *Sporting Life* calculated the franchise coffers had swelled, owing to larger-than-normal attendance throughout September as well as cash received from major league clubs for optioned players. Once the team accountant had tabulated the season's earnings in December, club secretary Claude Davis announced a staggering figure: the Nashville Base Ball Club had cleared $30,000!

The Nashville organization had hosted more than 140,000 fans (including 20,000 for the final weekend series) at Sulphur Dell in 1908, an increase of over 50,000 from the previous season and a franchise record. The Vols averaged 2,100 patrons per game — and surpassed the minimum mark (1,200) set by management in order to break even. The business of baseball had been good in Nashville and the entire Southern Association as total league attendance surpassed one million paid customers.[39]

A field day and benefit game took place on 21 September at Sulphur Dell with Vols players competing against each other in a wide range of activities. The program included a 50-yard dash between speedsters Hunter, Sitton, Siegle, and Bay; throwing contest featuring the strong arms of McElveen, Perdue, Siegle, Hurlburt, and Hardy; long ball-hitting contest using a fungo bat between McElveen, Hardy, Sitton, and Bernhard; bunt-and-run drill with Hunter, Sitton, and Bay; accurate throwing competition between catchers Seabough, Hardy, and Hurlburt; and circling the bases between East, Sitton, Bernhard, Hunter, Butler, and Wiseman. Then the gates were open to allow the fans to circle the basepaths. A short intra-squad game concluded the carnival-like day. Rice had hoped the community would make a holiday of the occasion and come out to honor the team, but either the nominal admission fee, inclement weather, or lack of interest caused a low turnout. Maybe Nashvillians were exercising the fickle and temporal nature of sport; the Vols season was officially over.

Three days after winning the league championship, most of the Vols had dispersed to their offseason homes. East accompanied Hurlburt on an extended fishing trip down the Mississippi River. Some Nashvillians had seen Wiseman and Butler frolicking on amusement rides at the Tennessee State Fair, but most of the players had already left town. Nashville newspapers supplied readers with the winter locales of the men:

Jake Daubert, Llewellyn, PA
Johnny Duggan, Whiteland, IN
Julius A. Wiseman, Cincinnati, OH
Win Kellum, Big Rapids, MI
Willis Butler, Franklin, PA
Walter East, Akron, OH
Pryor McElveen, Johnson City, TN
Hub Perdue, Gallatin, TN
George Hunter, Harrisburg, PA
Harry Bay, Peoria, IL
Carl Sitton, Pendleton, SC
Ed Hurlburt, Memphis, TN
J. Warren Seabough, Springfield, MO
Johnny Siegle, Urbana, OH

The public continued to have an appetite for the off-field endeavors of their heroes during the offseason. Kellum worked in a Michigan lumber yard, Seabough clerked for a Missouri railroad, Siegle operated a bowling alley in Ohio, Wiseman went back to the Cincinnati post office, Butler enrolled in the University of Tennessee, East studied to pass the Ohio bar exam, Hardy managed his Nashville cigar shop, and Bernhard planned to winter in Nashville and lay plans for the 1909 season.[40]

The most indicative measure of the Vols' regional appeal was manifested in the homecoming celebration afforded to Hub Perdue in Gallatin. One report claims that hundreds of community members met the Sumner County Cyclone at the train depot the night of the great victory. A parade led the local celebrity around the town square as a brass band played "See the Conquering Hero Comes."[41]

There is no question that a mental and physical strain caused by the long season and nail-biting playoff had taken its toll on the players. Writing to Rice a week after the campaign from his home in Pendleton (S.C.), Sitton confided: "I'm all in, down, and out for the time being. The finish of a hard football season is nothing compared to what I went through those last few days at Nashville."[42] Many of Sitton's teammates suffered similarly from fatigue and injuries, and the South Carolinian planned to recoup from the rigors of winning two baseball championships in the same season by assisting the football program at nearby Clemson College.

The thin margin of victory would be subject to discussion and debate for years to come in Rock City. The final league standings appeared in all three Nashville dailies:

FINAL SOUTHERN ASSOCIATION STANDINGS FOR 1908

	W	L	.Pct	GB
Nashville	75	56	.573	—
New Orleans	76	57	.571	½

	W	L	.Pct	GB
Memphis	73	62	.540	4
Montgomery	68	65	.511	8
Mobile	67	67	.500	9½
Atlanta	63	72	.467	14
Little Rock	62	76	.449	16½
Birmingham	53	82	.393	24

Parity played a part in explaining the closeness of the 1908 race. Entering the month of September, the top four finishers all had a legitimate shot at copping the title. A head-to-head chart depicts how evenly each team fared against its opponent.

Comparison Chart—Victories and Defeats

	Nash.	*NO*	*Mem.*	*Mont.*	*Mob.*	*Atl.*	*LR*	*Birm.*	*Won*
Nashville	X	10	11	9	12	13	10	10	75
New Orleans	8	X	7	11	8	11	13	18	76
Memphis	8	11	X	10	12	10	9	13	73
Montgomery	10	8	9	X	7	10	13	12	68
Mobile	6	11	9	11	X	12	9	9	67
Atlanta	6	8	9	10	7	X	12	11	63
Little Rock	9	7	10	8	11	8	X	9	62
Birmingham	9	2	7	6	10	8	11	X	53
Lost	56	57	62	65	67	72	76	82	

The *Tennessean, Banner,* and *American* had taken an active lead in whetting the public's appetite for any newsworthy tidbit concerning the Vols. The year 1908 had represented a breakthrough in the history of Nashville sports journalism as all three broadsheets established a special section devoted to athletics and overseen by a sports editor. Three men chosen to run the sports page, Grantland Rice, Richard Hunter Yancey, and William J. Ewing, Jr., were highly skilled and literate men. Moreover, each man was infected with a large dose of civic pride common to these progressive times. The triumvirate recognized the importance of sport in strengthening the spirit of community in Nashville.

Two national sheets—*The Sporting News* and *Sporting Life*—played an immense role in the nationalization of baseball in the first decade of the new century. Only four days after the Nashville-New Orleans clash, the country was reading about "the Merkle Boner," arguably the most infamous single play in the Deadball Era.[43] The incident, thanks to publicity generated by national and local newspapers, has been forever enshrined in the memory of baseball lore. When vaudevillian Jack Norworth wrote "Take Me Out to the Ball Game" for the Ziegfield Follies in early 1908, his simple lyrics struck a responsive chord that endeared, if not sanctified, the summer game into the cultural folk fabric of America.[44] The summer game had become the beloved darling of sports fans across the land, not just in Dixie.

Out of thousands of minor league seasons that were played in the twentieth century, why were the accomplishments of the 1908 Nashville Vols so significant? The team deserves a place in minor league baseball history as well as Nashville civic history based on how it closed the gap between mediocrity and excellence. Who were the sabermetric contributors who produced a winning margin of only .002? What happened to the franchise in 1909? Did the Nashville boys of '08 establish a Southern Association dynasty? And, whatever happened of the public's awareness of the nail-biting historic game? Does the greatest game ever played in Dixie have a legacy one hundred years after it was played?

CHAPTER 10

Historic Legacy of the 1908 Nashville Vols

Within days of winning the 1908 Southern Association championship, the rostered members on the Volunteers had departed for their offseason homes. The people whom they left behind, the Nashville fans, were afforded an opportunity to revel in the memories of the completed season and entertain hot stove opinions about the coming campaign. Autumn, 1908, ended in a flurry of assassination and civic turmoil in Nashville, however, and the successful baseball season was pushed into comparative obscurity. But the Nashville Base Ball Club did not totally disappear from public awareness. Indeed, the business operation of the franchise continued through the winter months and attracted considerable attention. The most immediate baseball question being asked was whether the 1909 team would be competitive. The question facing readers today, one hundred years after the storybook '08 season, focuses on the historic merits of the greatest game ever played in Dixie.

Nashville's three daily newspapers covered the 1908 World Series between the Detroit Tigers and Chicago Cubs, but any mention of Nashville's championship completely disappeared. Rice, a Vanderbilt alum, immersed himself and his readers in the gridiron exploits of the Commodores and a much-anticipated meeting with the University of Michigan at the end of September. Ewing picked up on bird hunting, skeet shooting, boxing, and horse racing in the *American,* but sports coverage of any kind vanished in the *Banner* until the following spring. This shrinking coverage points to the fact that sports journalism was still in its infancy, and Nashville sports editors were reassigned to other departments in the offseason.

Nashvillians, too, found other diversions. Only two weeks after the baseball season had concluded, Henry Ford introduced the Model T, and middle Tennesseans were smitten with the affordable new automobile. Locally, common folks attended the Tennessee State Fair in record numbers, Al G. Field brought his popular minstrel show to the Vendome, and Ringling Brothers Circus made its annual appearance in the Edgehill district. For the cultured populi, the Nashville stage booked several famous performers throughout October; the Nashville Art Club sponsored an outdoor performance of the Greek tragedy, *Electra;* Mademoiselle Nordica performed in concert at the Ryman Auditorium; and May Robson starred in a stage production at the Vendome. And, of course, October was the traditional moving month for Nashville's high society.[1]

The year 1908 was also an election year, but the presidential campaign between William Howard Taft and William Jennings Bryan hardly attracted much local attention. After all, traditionally the city of Nashville and state of Tennessee were safely within the Democratic Party's camp. State politics, however, had boiled since Edward Ward Carmack's unsuccessful bid to wrestle the governorship from incumbent Malcolm Patterson. The outcome of that gubernatorial primary in the springtime had not resolved the main issue that separated both candidates—Prohibition. Rather, bitter animosities had festered within the state democracy. Carmack kept the partisan temperance issue in front of Nashville readers when he became managing editor of the *Tennessean,* and used his position to belittle rival newspaperman and Patterson supporter Duncan Brown Cooper. The Carmack-Cooper war on words turned violent days after the general election. On 9 November Cooper and his son, Robin, engaged in a shootout with Carmack on a downtown Nashville street, felling the dry editor. The gun battle left Nashvillians numb. The shocking incident led directly to the Tennessee General Assembly passing prohibition legislation in 1909, and erecting a statue of Carmack in front of the state house shortly thereafter. Newspaper coverage of Cooper's trial pushed public memory of the 1908 Nashville Vols into the background as many outraged citizens focused on the more pressing events at hand.[2]

The social and political turmoil engulfing Nashville was of little concern to Berny as he polished plans for the upcoming baseball season. Local baseball fans were relieved when the Nashville manager signed a 1909 contract to manage the club, putting an end to a brief flurry of speculation that he would join the Cleveland staff or some other major league outfit. With his future secure, Berny went about the task of rebuilding the club. In his first official acts, Berny purchased the release contracts of Kid Butler from the St. Louis Browns and Harry Bay from the Cleveland Indians.[3]

Berny attended the minor league draft in mid–October with several notable holes to fill. The Nashville field general announced that the team sought a quality catcher and one or two first-class starting pitchers. He returned with the names of Harry Noyes—a light-hitting but solid defensive third baseman from Hartford, and southpaw Tom Gilroy from San Antonio, who was currently playing winter ball in Mexico.[4]

On 10 November, the day that Nashville was abuzz with sensational accounts of the Carmack-Cooper tragedy, Berny headed to Chicago for the winter meeting of the major leagues, where he hoped to acquire a catcher and first baseman. Everyone expected Daubert to be wearing Cleveland flannels. And Berny had made no secret of his disappointment in Hardy, whose batting average dropped 106 points from the previous year. Rice pointed out that Hardy had used big bats, small bats, batted left-handed, batted right-handed, swung hard, and swung softly throughout the season — all to no avail. In addition, Scrappy Jack carried himself with a haughty arrogance that rubbed Berny the wrong way. Although Seabough fit the program as a substitute and would be retained, Doc's weak throws had cost the club dearly in several key encounters. It was not disclosed until the offseason that Seabough had played the entire '08 season with a broken collarbone.[5]

Berny did not return from the Windy City emptyhanded. James Robertson, a catcher-first baseman on the Wilkes-Barre team, resurfaced on the trading block. The manager also drafted Charlie Tonneman from Springfield in the Western Association on advice from Seabough.[6]

At the Chicago meeting, the Eastern League and American Association petitioned to demote the Southern Association to Class B status or else create a higher level — AA — for themselves. The motion, if implemented, would adversely affect the Southern Association because the proposal would permit the upper classification to draft players from the lower ranks, beginning in 1909. President Kavanaugh, a member of the National Board of Arbitration, lobbied strenuously to squash the uprising, and the challenge took months to resolve.[7]

In mid–December, Nashville hosted the winter meeting of the Southern Association at the Duncan Hotel. Important dignitaries attended the banquet, including Governor Patterson, Mayor Brown, and key businessmen from the Nashville Board of Trade. The league moguls toasted each other for the 1908 attendance record, and delayed a decision to reinstate Otis Stockdale. A rumor, disconcerting to Kavanaugh, claimed that several team owners wished to relocate his struggling Little Rock franchise to Chattanooga. Finally, President Kavanaugh presented the '08 championship banner to President Kuhn, who hung it in the hotel lobby for the duration of the meeting. Later, the cloth trophy graced the window of Kuhn's business establishment until the flag raising ceremony on Opening Day, 1909. Speakers at the love feast included Kavanaugh, Kuhn, Bernhard, and Rice.[8]

Prior to adjourning the business meeting, President Kavanaugh introduced an important matter for general discussion — a flaw in the league's standard operating procedure that dealt with make-up games. Seeing how Franks and Bernhard had manipulated the current system late in the season, Kavanaugh proposed a new policy. The league mogul suggested that every rainout in 1909 should automatically be made up the next day as part of a doubleheader; in the event that the postponed contest was the final game of a series, it must be rescheduled for the very next meeting of the two teams. In this way, every game on the slate would be played. The Memphis franchise was elated with the passage of Kavanaugh's new rule. In 1908, the Turtles had played all of their games, and trailed the Vols by four games. But Nashville had opted not to make up four cancellations in September, including two games in the final week.[9]

Official league statistics for the 1908 season became available at the winter meeting, and Nashville's sports editors grabbed the opportunity to review the Vols' season in greater detail. Following a precedent set by major league journalists, the Nashville triumvirate put their heads together with scribes from Atlanta and New Orleans to create a Southern Association all-star team.[10] They used offensive and defensive categories to formulate the exclusive squads:

	Defensive	*Offensive*
1st Base	George Carey (Memphis)	H. J. Meek (Birmingham)
2nd Base	Augie Dundon (New Orleans)	Bill Cranston (Memphis)
3rd Base	Pryor McElveen (Nashville)	Pryor McElveen (Nashville)
Shortstop	Paul Sentell (Mobile)	Tom Downey (Birmingham)
Outfield	Johnny Siegle (Nashville)	Tris Speaker (Little Rock)
	Joe Collins (Little Rock)	Bris Lord (New Orleans)
	George Winters (Atlanta)	Beals Becker (Little Rock)
Pitcher	Ted Breitenstein (New Orleans)	Elmer Bliss (Montgomery)
Catcher	x x x	J. Warren Seabough (Nashville)
		Harry Matthews (New Orleans)

No one team dominated the all-star selections, just as no one team had overpowered the opposition during the season. Some fine players were also excluded from the subjective list. Players who turned in top performances against Nashville in 1908 but deserve honorable mention include outfielders Carleton Molesworth (Birmingham), Joe Rickert (New Orleans), Archie Persons (Montgomery), Noah Henline (Birmingham); first basemen Ed Gremminger (Montgomery) and Jim Fox (Atlanta); second baseman Otto Jordan (Atlanta); shortstop Joe Pepe (Montgomery); third basemen George Rohe (New Orleans) and Art Hess (Little Rock); catchers Lee Garvin (Mobile) and Rob Wood (Little Rock); pitchers Ralph Savidge (Memphis), Bill Bartley (New Orleans), Jim Buchanan (Little Rock), Anthony Robitaille (Birmingham), and Forest Thomas (Montgomery).

On 13 February, Richard Yancey dropped a bombshell on the Nashville sports community when he suddenly resigned from the *Banner* to become sports editor for the *Chattanooga Times*. Ewing and Rice would miss their press box colleague, and the Vols would have to find a replacement for the experienced official scorer.[11]

President Kuhn was busy in the offseason, too, planning new improvements in the Sulphur Dell facility. The shoe magnate envisioned enlarging the grandstands by a third — an ambitious project. He also wanted to push back the left field wall fifty feet in order to accommodate patrons wishing to watch games from the comfort of their automobiles or carriages. The modification was either a 1909 version of modern day luxury boxes or a remedy to a parking problem around the stadium. Construction crews did push the wall back ten feet to the edge of the Tennessee Central railroad tracks, and the left field incline was leveled. Increasing the outfield area served another purpose; it might generate more inside-the-park home runs. Rice recognized the connection between home run production and fan enjoyment: "Pitcher's battles may appeal to some, and there is still another class of fans who like to deal in the extremely scientific side of the game, but for the big mass of them, give them the long hit, the wild excitement following it, and that is baseball to them."[12] How Rice echoed the modern state of baseball.

Kuhn also ordered an electric scoreboard (a minor league innovation) that recorded strikes, balls, outs, and linescore. The technological innovation was large enough to accommodate the lineup of both teams. When Vols players first saw the scoreboard illuminated during spring training, they joked that Berny would use the bright device to hold night practices. Finally, the owner promised to supply free scorecards to all patrons entering the turnstiles. Kuhn firmly believed that the Vols would repeat as league champions and remain financially solvent in 1909.[13]

In mid–January, Berny felt the normal pressure to sign players to new contracts, but he faced several obstacles. First, he could not count on the return of men who had been drafted by major league clubs: Sitton, McElveen, and Daubert were almost assuredly gone forever. A distressing rumor said Lajoie intended to ship Daubert to Toledo (and not return to Nashville), a story which ultimately proved to be true. Rice sympathized with Berny's struggle to find quality replacements for the Vols: "It's a good deal easier to place the good old Dope on a Big Show team than upon one in the Minor League family.... A team that wins the pennant one season in the Majors is fairly certain to either repeat or at least stick to the running the next. But, the Minors come in only as a tall guess. The club that slips over a pennant winner one season is just as likely to finish seventh as first the next."[14] Could the sportswriter have been professing about Nashville's chances in 1909?

Berny faced another difficulty — holdouts. Duggan had slipped into Nashville in early January wanting to renegotiate his contract. Equally disconcerting were stories coming out of Gallatin. There Perdue was telling folks that Fresno of the outlaw California League was offering him $600 more than Nashville for next season. In addition, Berny was bothered that Perdue was frequenting a pool hall and hustling customers for loose change. Baseball already suffered from unsavory connections between players and gamblers.

Finally, Kellum wrote to say that Bay City in the Michigan League had tendered him a managerial position, and requested his release. The Nashville skipper knew the southpaw would not pass waivers, and a Southern Association foe would surely pick him up. Berny did not relish the thought of facing Kellum in 1909, and so denied the petition.[15] Altogether, Duggan, Ferdue, and Kellum had collected 50 of the Vols' 75 victories. Berny could ill-afford to lose any of these pitchers.

The Nashville rumor mill identified other players allegedly on the move, too. For instance, Hardy was reported for sale, and Mobile showed interest in obtaining the rights to his contract. The Scrappy One was also politicking with former manager Johnny Dobbs, the new skipper of Chattanooga in the SALLY. McCormick had contacted the club asking for reinstatement and release so that he could manage Holyoke in the Connecticut League. The Hardy-McCormick hearsay turned out to be true and Berny granted both men their freedom. Finally, East had passed the Ohio bar exam, and some fans wondered whether the second baseman's baseball career had come to an end.[16] Bernhard mailed player contracts at the beginning of February and scheduled the first day of practice for 15 March. Now it was a matter of wait and see.

Rice followed an interesting personnel shuffle that was taking place in Atlanta. There Billy Smith hired Red Fisher (recently fired by Mobile) and Otto Jordan to assist with the coaching duties. No longer would the Crackers use players to man the coaches boxes, but Fisher and Jordan would fulfill this duty on a regular basis. Rice noted that Smith was employing "the eastern college model," and signified further modernization of the game in the Southern Association.[17]

Berny was not totally consumed with personnel issues during the dreary winter months. He assembled an attractive slate of preseason contests with major league clubs. The slate included Connie Mack's Philadelphia Athletics (26, 27 March), world champion Chicago Cubs (29, 30, 31 March), Boston Red Sox (1, 2 April), Evansville (3, 4 April), Brooklyn Trolley Dodgers (8, 9, 10 April), and St. Paul (12, 13 April).[18]

Heavy rain fell in mid–February and the Cumberland River flooded, filling Sulphur Dell with several feet of water. Rice pointed out that the annual inundation created additional worries besides field maintenance. "Big Show teams are not willing to take a chance on picking Nashville for a spring camping ground as long as the ball park looks like a snap shot of Venice," said the sportswriter.[19] The infield wintered under a blanket of hay, but it had sustained major water damage.

President Kavanaugh released the 1909 Southern Association schedule which, once again, shined favorably on the Vols. The champs opened the season at home against Montgomery, and secured the Fourth of July and Labor Day doubleheaders against Memphis. Hosting the former holiday had eluded Nashville over the past several seasons. Moreover, the Vols would repeat the

'08 slate with thirteen home games in September and close out with New Orleans. The month of July contained twenty-two home games, and August presented the biggest challenge with nineteen away contests.[20]

East surprised prognosticators as the first player to return to Nashville for spring training. On the eve of the first workout, everyone was present except Wiseman and the three pitching holdouts—Duggan, Perdue, and Kellum. Wiseman had earned a reputation over the years as the last to report in the spring and the last to leave in the fall, so his absence was not a point of concern. The pitching trio, on the other hand, was a different matter altogether. A number of new faces were in camp—Noyes, Robertson, Gilroy, Tonneman, and several catching prospects. Charlie Case, a pitcher from the Three I League, showed early promise.

The surface of Sulphur Dell resembled a pond and Berny considered moving the workout site to Vanderbilt or Nashville (Peabody) University. At the last minute, the manager changed his mind and settled for the only patch of dry ground, "an island," near the clubhouse entrance in right-center field. Hundreds of fans turned out to watch the first practice, including a small contingent of ladies as well as young boys who scurried around the sloppy field shagging balls for the players. Several veterans reported overweight, including the outfield duo, Wiseman and Siegle. By the time the Vols took the field in their first competition against Philadelphia on 26 March, only Duggan remained a no-show despite being offered two salary raises.[21]

The weather was wet for the first ten days of training camp, and the Vols spent more time in a local billiard hall than on the field. When Connie Mack's Athletics arrived to kick off the preseason on the chilly afternoon of 26 March, the team had only practiced a handful of times. Over 1,500 fans braved the elements to watch the locals go down, 5–4. The Vols did not fare well against other big league clubs, either. In the final game against the Cubs, a goat offered comic relief after wandering into the stadium from the city dump and had to be chased from the grounds. Berny pitched all nine innings in the meaningless 11–2 affair, and aggravated his sore arm. He would not return to the slab until mid–August. The Vols fared no better against the Red Sox, losing two one-sided games, 9–2 and 10–2.

Nashville finally broke into the winning column with a pair of victories over Evansville, but major league opponents had exposed a number of glaring weaknesses. First, the Vols lacked a quality utility player in the mold of Hunter, who had stuck with Brooklyn. Second, new third baseman Harry Noyes did not hit like McElveen, who also made the Trolley Dodger roster. Third, the rookies on the pitching staff were untested, and Duggan remained a holdout. Tonneman looked good behind the plate and Siegle picked up where he had left off in '08.

Rain showers in early April forced Berny to take his team indoors to play two amateur athletic clubs. The Nashville manager had made a little extra money over the winter officiating the indoor league at the Hippodrome. The Nashville Athletic Club (NAC), champions of the winter league, lost an opening round game to the Vols on 6 April, but bounced back to beat the professionals, 17–16, the next evening. The Vols also defeated the YMCA team twice. Several Vols players complained about sore leg muscles from playing in tennis shoes on the hardwood floors. Throwing the larger and lighter ball also aggravated some arms. Perhaps, the professionals also suffered from bruised egos. Berny canceled the remaining gymnasium contests.[22]

McElveen, Hunter, and the Trolley Dodgers arrived in Nashville at the same time Duggan returned to the Vols. In the opener, Brooklyn won on fireworks provided by McElveen, who launched a Perdue fastball for a home run, and the major leaguers controlled the second game, 7–1. Duggan faced Hunter in the finale on 10 April in a battle of former teammates. The Hoosier did not look sharp, however, as he surrendered four runs to the Dodgers in the first and fifth innings on the way to an 8–4 loss. The Vols had not fared well against big league talent in the preseason—going winless in seven attempts—and Southern Association action would commence in five days. Nashville closed out spring training with a 9–6 victory over St. Paul of the American Association.

Opening Day, 1909. Elaborate plans had been in the works a long time for the presentation of the championship banner to the city, team, and fans. Mayor Brown declared a half-day holiday for city employees and hoped that businesses would follow suit to allow everyone an opportunity to witness the spectacle. A parade of twenty automobiles departed from Public Square at 1:30 p.m., led by super-fan Alf Williams and a marching band from the State Industrial School. The league and team presidents sat in the first vehicle along with Nashville's proud mayor, followed by stockholders of the Nashville Baseball Club.[23] Then the 1909 Vols, comprised of many new faces, filled the remaining autos. Several floats were in the line-of-march to Sulphur Dell.

Once the procession had driven onto the field, Montgomery and Nashville players lined up along their respective basepaths. Each Volunteer was introduced to the audience and was greeted with deafening applause. "Gayly dressed women stood by the hundreds and madly waved their handkerchiefs and cheered," reported Ewing in the *American,* and their loudest demonstration was reserved for Doc Wiseman.[24] For a fleeting moment it was 19 September 1908 all over again. Then Kuhn handed the championship banner to several young girls, who hoisted it on a special flag pole on the outfield wall. No speeches were given, but souvenir pins were distributed to approximately 4,500 fans.[25]

Mayor Brown was escorted to the slab, where he tossed out the ceremonial first pitch to start the 1909 season. The Nashville throng was probably a bit concerned because Montgomery had seen the most success against major league opponents in the recent barnstorming session. And the Senators were picked to do well in league action, too. On the other hand, many lingering questions surrounded Nashville. Would Robertson make the locals forget about Daubert at first base? Was Noyes another McElveen at third? Could Tonneman combine the defense of Hardy and offense of Seabough at catcher? Would the revamped pitching staff with newcomers Gilroy and Case compliment the old hands—Perdue, Kellum, and Duggan? Would there be enough carry over from 1908 to bring another championship to Nashville in 1909? Time would answer each of these questions.

The 1909 season was moments away as Captain East submitted the Vols' lineup card to the officials at home plate:

Bay	LF	Robertson	1st	Noyes	3rd
Wiseman	RF	Siegle	CF	Seabough	C
East	2nd	Butler	SS	Gilroy	P

Montgomery provided ample justification for Nashville's worries as they kept the local fans on the edge of their seats for the entire game. Young southpaw Gilroy was trailing 3–0 in the sixth inning when Berny turned to Duggan in relief. In the bottom of the seventh, the Vols finally broke out of their batting lethargy. With two outs and Noyes on second base and Seabough on first, Bay tapped a grounder to Joe Pepe. The normally sure-handed shortstop misplayed the ball, but hard-charging center fielder Archie Persons picked it up and fired a strike toward home. Pitcher Jake Lively cut off the throw that likely would have cut down Noyes at the plate, and relayed the ball to second base to nab Seabough, who had overrun the bag. Lively's unexpected throw sailed into the outfield and, by the time the right fielder retrieved it near the new flag pole, all three Nashville runners had scored. "Seven thousand voices tore the atmosphere into fragments and made themselves hoarse with shouting. It was electric," reported Ewing.[26] Duggan threw four innings of no-hit ball and the Vols etched a 4–3 "Barnum and Bailey" victory.[27] Perhaps, the new season *would* be as exciting as the 1908 finish.

For two months Nashville clung to a slender lead over Atlanta, largely due to Perdue's incredible 5–0 start. But Bay reinjured his knee in May and played with pain for the remainder of the season. Young Gilroy strained his shoulder and never lived up to expectations. He was released and replaced by ex–Atlantan, Bill Viebahn. In mid-June, Tonneman was hospitalized with a mashed hand, and catching problems returned to haunt the Vols. Ongoing gossip about Berny becoming the manager of the St. Louis Browns, or Washington, or Brooklyn, or Toledo, or Cleveland became a big distraction to the club. Then devastating psychological news came out of Toledo, where the Mud Hens announced that Daubert had been shipped to Memphis. It would be difficult to see the strapping former Vols member in Turtle flannels.

Nashville made a strong showing in late July, sweeping Atlanta, Little Rock, and Mobile to go on a twelve-game winning streak. Then the Crackers won five out of seven head-to-head encounters with the Vols in close, low-scoring games. By 1 September, Atlanta had assumed control in the standings, but Nashville was still within reach of the top. The Vols simply could not keep pace with the Crackers in the last three weeks of the season, although they were not mathematically eliminated until 14 September. When Wiseman joined Perdue for some partying in Gallatin prior to the second-to-last series of the year, Berny removed the popular peruser of the Dump from the lineup for the last six games. Newspapers claimed the little Doctor suffered from a "charlie horse," but it is more likely he suffered from the wrath of Berny. The story of Doc's temporary fall from grace epitomized the collapse of the 1909 Vols. There would be no repeat of the championship in 1909.

FINAL SOUTHERN ASSOCIATION STANDINGS, 1909

Atlanta	87	49	.640	—
Nashville	82	55	.594	5½
Montgomery	76	60	.559	11
New Orleans	73	64	.533	14½
Mobile	64	77	.454	22½
Birmingham	60	79	.429	28½
Little Rock	59	80	.424	29½
Memphis	51	88	.367	37½

What had happened to the Nashville boys in '09? Nothing really drastic went wrong. They won seven more games than 1908. Atlanta simply outplayed Nashville in the final three weeks. Several Vols put up impressive individual numbers, too. Perdue led the league with 23 wins and newcomer Charlie Case added 19 more. But Duggan dropped to 14 wins and Kellum was a disappointment with eight victories. Noyes did not resemble McElveen in the field (.948) or especially at the plate (.216). Tonneman recovered from his midseason injury, hit a robust .312 (fourth in league), and the Red Sox called him up in September. Seabough finished the year as the regular catcher (96 games) and hit a respectable .270. Robertson, ill for the last month of the season, spent a lot of time in the hospital and demanded to be sent back to Wilkes-Barre. In 138 games, East and Butler never missed a contest. Butler improved his batting average to .275 and Wiseman remained consistent at .246. Doc, perhaps still smarting from his earlier tiff with Berny, told Rice he would not be back in 1910, and laid plans to head west for the California League. Wiseman asked for, but did not receive, his release. The trio of Bay-Siegle-Wiseman was simply considered the best outfield in the league. But the magic of '08 was gone. The Nashville franchise would not duplicate its turn-of-the-century successes until the Larry Gilbert era of the 1940s.[28]

So what was so special about the 1908 Nashville Vols? The answer lies in an analysis of the overall team statistics— offense, pitching, and defense. First, the offense. The Vols led the league in extra-base hits (213), triples (65), and trailed only New Orleans with 14 home runs and 144 doubles. Daubert tied for league honors with six home runs. Rice pointed to the consistency of the offense from the top to the bottom of the batting order. In terms of individual stats, McElveen led the team (.284) and Wiseman brought up the rear (.251); only .033 separated the most and least productive of the regular players. Thus, Nashville was a team devoid of an offensive superstar. This meant the men were forced to play scientific baseball in order to manufacture runs. Despite the median batting average of each individual, only one-third of the players in the league hit over .250, a benchmark achieved by ten Vols. The league mean, .237, was surpassed by nearly thirty percentage points.[29] Although there is nothing noteworthy about the .250 range today, the percentage was respectable by Deadball Era standards. The timeliness of Vols hits as well as the total number of extra-base hits is another offensive factor in explaining the Vols' success. Since the league champs were not a flashy lot offensively, the hits they did manage had a more favorable impact on the outcome of their games. In comparison to other teams, the Vols possessed the most efficient and powerful offense. The offensive explosion in September was the culmination of this growing prowess. Base thievery was the only category that did not contribute much in the way of run production. Wiseman led the club with 30 swipes (eighth in league)—on a team that rarely stole bases. A more subtle aspect of the offense concerned the side of the plate each man batted from. In a league dominated by right-handed pitchers and hitters from the right side, the Vols had two left-handed batters in the regular lineup—Daubert and Bay. The team also possessed three switch-hitters in Hunter, Kellum, and Bernhard. This left-handed advantage meant the Vols never worried about domination by right-handed power pitchers. The final team batting statistics are printed below:

	G	AB	R	H	B.A.
McElveen	138	514	66	146	.284
Bay	103	415	45	112	.269
Seabough	96	234	16	90	.269
Siegle	122	428	52	114	.266
Butler	136	480	36	127	.264
Hunter	60	201	33	53	.263
Daubert	138	473	49	124	.262
East	119	464	57	121	.260
Wiseman	138	525	77	132	.251
Hardy	60	194	22	40	.206
Bernhard	15	51	2	10	.196
Hurlburt	46	150	9	28	.186
Kellum	26	78	10	14	.179
Duggan	33	97	17	8	.175
Perdue	34	101	8	16	.159

Pitching was the second key ingredient in the Vols' rise from poorhouse to penthouse in 1908. Unlike team offense, the chart below illustrates that Vols hurlers were far from ordinary. The league ranking was based on winning percentage of the top forty-five active pitchers.

	G	W	L	League Rank by %	PCT.
Duggan	34	19	12	5th	.628
Kellum	24	15	10	6th	.625
Hunter	14	8	5	7th	.615
Sitton	10	6	4	10th	.600
Perdue	32	16	12	15th	.571
Bernhard	14	8	5	21st	.533

These numbers show that Duggan, Kellum, and Perdue were the primary workhorses on the staff. Duggan finished second in league victories (19) behind Memphis' Savidge, and Perdue (16 wins) and Kellum (15 wins) placed tenth and twelfth, respectively. The Gallatin Squash earned intangible bonus points for his perseverance and gutsy performances late in the season; he led the others by example. Like the offense, the Nashville pitchers were grouped together by winning percentages—fifth, sixth, seventh, and tenth; they too overcame the lack of a superstar. In sabermetric terms, Nashville boasted four of the top ten pitchers in the league.

The defense improved steadily throughout the season and marked the third reason for the Vols' success in 1908. The squad recorded 23 errorless games and trailed only Atlanta in that department. While the team did not always play snappy in the field, they were not an inept bunch when it came to applying the leather to the ball. Daubert ranked sixth among active first basemen in errors (19) and third in putouts (1331) while playing the most games (138). East nearly led the league's second basemen with 33 errors, but ranked in the middle of the pack with a .949 fielding average. Butler was the third-best fielding shortstop in the league (.975), but the two players ahead of him participated in less than sixty games. Undoubtedly, Kid was one of the positive defensive surprises in 1908, and demonstrated versatility in games played at second base (55) and shortstop (81). Despite a shaky start in several positions, McElveen ended the campaign by copping top league honors for his coverage of third base (.951), ranked second in games played (132) and putouts (180), and third in assists (287). He had the fewest errors (24) for third basemen with over one hundred games played, and he emerged as the second pleasant defensive surprise. Siegle ranked as the top defender (.989) for outfielders logging over one hundred games, and joined Wiseman in committing only five errors. The outfield trio of Bay, Siegle and Wiseman were the most skilled and quickest in the league. The season-long weak spot—catching—was tied down by Seabough. The other Doc led the league in errors (18) but out-hit (.269) every other backstopper and caught the second-most games (96) — a testimony to his durability at the most injury-prone position on the field. Hardy saw limited duty (36 games) and his poor attitude throughout the season affected his offense (.206) and defense (.964). Hurlburt brought defensive stability behind the plate (3 errors in 67 games), and while his offensive average (.186) was appalling, he is fondly remembered for scoring the lone run in the finale. Finally, Hunter deserves special mention. His numbers are not great — 41 games played in the outfield and eight victories as a pitcher. But no Vols player collected as many meaningful pinch hits, and the southpaw performed his duties with a chronic sore arm. The switch-hitting utility man was, arguably, the most underrated player on the Nashville roster.[30]

So who was the most valuable star on the Vols' pedestrian roster? In an era before such an accolade had become fashionable, the 1908 champions produced an array of candidates. Consider this list of qualifiers:

Wiseman temporary replacement for McCormick at shortstop
skillful defense in the Dump
.500 batting average in the three-game championship series
clubbing the lone RBI in the championship game
quiet leadership
longevity in Nashville–eighth season
popularity with local fans
played in every game
fourth in league in at-bats
second in league in runs scored
eighth in league in stolen bases

McElveen team captain
produced three defensive gems in championship game
solid contact hitter and delivered in the clutch
a Tennessean
played in every game
third in league in base hits
fifth in league in runs scored

Perdue pitched 17-inning no-decision
throwing both ends of doubleheader inspired teammates; major turning point in Vols season
matured into a competitive athlete
usually third base coach
a Tennessean

Honorable Mention:

Daubert solid defense — tall and rangy
showed promise as left-handed power hitter

tied for first in league in home runs
played in every game
fourth in league in sacrifice bunts

Discussions about the most valuable Volunteer on the '08 squad would be debated by local sports fans for years to come.

The name of William Henry Bernhard should not be overlooked when considering key contributors to the '08 season despite the fact that he played in only a handful of games. On a team that boasted no brilliant stars, how did Nashville pull off the championship? Rice offers an answer—Berny. The '08 Vols were "molded into a machine by a leader in whom every member of the squad not only respected, but held as a friend. From him they took the cue that the theory of success was to keep coming back—he had no managerial experience to follow. He set a standard of his own."[31] Another accolade came from the land of the enemy where an observer praised Berny immediately after the season concluded. "Bernhard deserves the honor he attained," said Pelican in *The Sporting News*. "Without any pyrotechnics or hot air ... he won his spurs. He came into the Southern Association unheralded and without a press agent. He did what no other first-year man has ever done in the Southern Association. He won the pennant. His kind are a benefit to any league. He played the game for all it was worth, and played it fair."[32] Berny was universally respected as a player's coach.

There is no denying that the greatest game ever played in Dixie has an historical legacy. It is a fact that the Nashville Vols captured more than the 1908 championship flag; they also captured the imagination of a city and region. In a time before radio and television, the Vols captivated middle Tennesseans, thanks to the able rendering of three colorful sports writers—Rice, Yancey, and Ewing. The hard-working people of Nashville simply identified with this pedestrian team. In an era when heroes were often products of the mass media, the Vols offered a plethora of candidates. Furthermore, the championship game and season elevated the role and purpose of sport in the growing southern urban community; it inextricably ingrained the baseball Volunteers into the folk fabric and popular culture of the city into the 1960s.

Although the big game and the '08 season have slowly faded from public memory, they did reappear sporadically in the decades that followed. In the 1930s, the Southern Association developed a new set of procedures in order to generate more fan excitement: the first-place finishers of the first and second halves of the season met in a playoff to determine the league champion. In September 1934, Nashville and New Orleans squared off once again. In preparation for that tilt, sports editor Fred Russell of the *Banner* reprinted Yancey's inning-by-inning account of the 1908 championship game, complete with the boxscore. Under the headline "Never Will Last Game of 1908 Be Forgotten Here," Russell resurrected the nail-biting contest held nearly three decades earlier. The piece of baseball trivia failed to inspire the home team, however, as New Orleans took three games out of four to win the crown.³³ Two years later, Russell welcomed the beginning of another Southern Association season with a second reprinting of the famous game.³⁴ This time Russell wrote beneath the headline "BASEBALL GAME OF THE CENTURY —1908."

On 8 September 1948, Russell served as master-of-ceremonies for the Larry Gilbert Silver Jubilee Celebration held at the Maxwell House. Gilbert was retiring after thirty-one years as a player, player-manager, and manager in the Southern Association. His baseball resume included the 1914 Miracle Braves of Boston, and a prodigious Southern Association career that began under the tutelage of Johnny Dobbs. Gilbert went on to manage in his hometown of New Orleans, and later Nashville, and won eight league titles. He was singled out as the man most instrumental in rejuvenating Nashville baseball in the 1940s. "Come the year 2000," Russell stated to the audience, "(won't that numeral seem odd to the first letter-writers after midnight, December 31, 1999), I'm certain that some researchers will be going to the newspaper files seeking information about an almost legendary baseball character named Larry Gilbert."³⁵ Gilbert is worthy of scholarly examination, but another baseball topic peaked the interest of a researcher in the late 1990s — the '08 Nashville Vols.

Russell had invited Julius August Wiseman, "the hero of the Dell," to attend the Gilbert tribute as a few old-timers recollected the exploits of Doc in the tricky right field Dump. Doc kindly declined the request, but expressed deep personal feelings to Russell about playing for the Vols. "The old town [Nashville] always brings back many pleasant memories and makes me wish I could live over again the gay nineties and the early 1900s," Wiseman wrote to Russell. "Those were the days." The former right fielder finished with a glowing tribute to the people of Nashville: "I know something of the hospitality and warmheartedness of the old South and I wouldn't trade memories with anyone."³⁶

Two members of the class of '08 did attend the Gilbert luncheon — the Tennesseans, Perdue and McElveen. Perdue entertained the audience with an oral rendition of the 1908 championship game — complete with erroneous information — that Humpy's sensational tag of Tarleton occurred in the ninth inning, and "Johnny" Rickert had hit a hard smash fielded by McElveen and turned into a game-ending double play. The distance of forty years had blurred Perdue's recollection of details surrounding the big game, and he had been an eyewitness to the event. Could the recollection of other Nashvillians have been any clearer? It was becoming obvious that the greatest game ever played in Dixie was slipping from public memory. Perdue did accurately describe the sensational seventh inning, and McElveen opined that Bay's bunt single in that frame was the crucial (and unsung) turning point in the game. In an extremely close call at first base, Bay's perfect (and unexpected) bunt had kept the Nashville rally alive and paved the way for Wiseman's game-winning RBI. Gilbert, himself a friend of Tarleton, stated that the New Orleans first baseman never forgot his baserunning mistake. "I was dumb, *dumb!,*" Tarleton later confided to Gilbert.[37] The audience listened in awe as these relics of Nashville's baseball past reminisced about the greatest game ever played in Dixie.

Since mid-century, the memory of the 1908 Nashville Vols has been practically erased from collective consciousness. In 1962, *American* sports editor Raymond Johnson referenced the contest in one sentence in an article devoted to the career of Doc Wiseman. And then, silence. No more was heard about the team or the players or the game that had established minor league professional baseball in Nashville until 2001. Writing in *The City Paper* (Nashville) on 3 August 2001, Bill Traughber provided an overview of the 1908 championship game in an article entitled "Nashville hosted greatest game played in the South," a sanitized rendition of Rice's original headline.[38]

The greatest game ever played in Dixie was played a century ago, and is worthy of our attention today. But, the narrative should not end with the game itself. Rather, the lives of the men after '08 should also be examined. Whatever happened to Gentleman Jake, the Gallatin Squash, Doc Wiseman, Deerfoot Bay, Berny, and all of the others? Some led long and productive lives. Others met short and tragic ends. While most of the '08 boys became productive members of society, all of them maintained a lifelong connection with the game they loved.

CHAPTER 11

Life After Baseball

Whatever became of the individuals who played key roles in the '08 Nashville season? For all, the life of a professional ballplayer continued for a while. Several reached the lofty heights of the major leagues while most continued to roam in the minors. One thing was certain, however: the time these men would spend in baseball flannels was ultimately numbered. So where did each one go after baseball? What did they do? How did these successful athletes compete in life? Each man's journey is an interesting lifestory through mid-twentieth century America. The remainder of their lives out of baseball should remind us that the private side of our sports heroes is largely a reflection of fundamental values we all share.

Men who tread on baseball diamonds hold a special fascination with Americans. Performing their craft, they are often portrayed in public as characters of mythic proportion. Seldom are they recognized for what they really are — mortal performers who possess exceptional physical talent but who also possess the full range of human strengths and weaknesses. A prosopographical (group) analysis of the men who comprised the '08 Vols highlights this notion and enriches our understanding of who they really were, and what they later became. Most of them took wives and many raised children. The 1908 season did not terminate their baseball careers. Instead, the majority played baseball until about 1915, and stayed connected with the game at various levels for the rest of their lives. Some coached either professional or amateur teams, while others listened to their favorite major league outfit on radio. A surprising number earned college degrees. In terms of employment, many landed civil service jobs and each strove to become productive members of society. A few found politics attractive. Fraternal organizations like the Masons,

Shriners, and American Legion attracted some; church affiliations lured the majority. Some engaged in community volunteerism and several became pillars in their respective communities. A handful of lives ended unexpectedly or tragically, but most lived into their 70s. Finally, a twinge of unfulfilled baseball dreams runs through most of their vignettes. Only three spent any formidable time (5+ years) in the major leagues. The following lifestories are presented in chronological order based on date of death.[1]

President Kavanaugh looked forward to his thirteenth year as chief administrator of the Southern Association.[2] He had laid elaborate plans to host the annual winter league meeting and banquet in Little Rock on the evening of 20 February 1915. Team owners and managers alike shared an abiding respect for Kavanaugh's longevity as league president as well as his hard work in cleaning up the notoriously rough league. "To the squarest man in baseball," toasted C. T. Crawford, in reference to Kavanaugh's fair-mindedness and integrity.[3] It came as a complete shock when Little Rock newspapers reported Kavanaugh's sudden death from acute indigestion the morning following the dinner. City, county, and state offices closed as did public schools on the day of his funeral. The *Arkansas Gazette,* the broadsheet Kavanaugh had managed in the 1890s, closed along with several banks. A color guard of Confederate veterans participated in the graveside ceremony, and accolades were showered upon every aspect of Kavanaugh's life by several orators. Truly the citizens of Little Rock had lost an inspirational and dynamic figure.

Later, local tributes would celebrate Kavanaugh's memory. The Little Rock franchise renamed its baseball stadium Kavanaugh Field, eventually the site of Central High School. Then, city officials approved the naming of Kavanaugh Boulevard in the new Pulaski Heights subdivision. There is no doubt that Kavanaugh would be keenly missed, especially by those who understood his contributions to the Southern Association. Writing on the golden anniversary of the league in *The Sporting News,* Harry Neily reflected on Kavanaugh's eloquence as well as sincerity in doing what was right for the game at the regional and national levels. Kavanaugh's legacy, commented Neily, would forever be his molding the Southern Association into one of the premier minor league circuits in the country.[4] William Marmaduke Kavanaugh, "the squarest man in baseball," is buried in Oakland Cemetery, Little Rock.

When the '08 season ended, Big Ed Hurlburt returned to his Memphis home accompanied by Walter East for an extended fishing trip down the Mississippi River.[5] In the offseason, Berny released the light-hitting catcher, and Big Ed resigned with Memphis. But, Hurlburt appeared in only nineteen games in 1909 before the Turtles cast him off. Then, he retired from baseball altogether to direct his energies in his dry cleaning establishments and real estate speculation. It was suspected that Big Ed also forged ties with illegal gambling and bootlegging operators while a member of the Shelby County Sheriff's Department. Hurlburt had amassed considerable wealth from various sources by 1918.

On the evening of 20 February 1918, Constable Hurlburt deputized his best friend, current roommate and former batterymate with the Turtles, Charlie Shields, to join a raid on a bootlegger's camp in Mullens Station. Accompanied by three other deputies, the party carried out its midnight foray, arrested two men, and confiscated twenty-five cases of moonshine. One of the deputies drove the prisoners to the county jail, while the others went to Hurlburt's cleaning establishment on Popular Avenue ostensibly to wait until dawn, whereupon they would set out to confiscate a boatload of whiskey at Hatchie Chute.

At this point details about events in the early morning hours became muddled. Apparently, the officers played poker and consumed three quarts of contraband booze. Shields later testified that the game of chance was for small stakes—altogether the four men had gambled less than $25. Shortly after 4 a.m., the card game broke up and everyone fell asleep. As the men slumbered, a loud gunshot rang out. Hurlburt leaped out of his chair, and collapsed face down on the floor with a three-inch chest wound. Shields, who had been snoozing directly across from Hurlburt, later believed he accidentally knocked a loaded shotgun off the table, which landed on the floor and discharged its buckshot into the sleeping sheriff. Startled and groggy, Shields raced over to his friend of twenty years and shouted "Get up, Dead-Eye, get up," a nickname referring to Hurlburt's ability to throw out base stealers in his ballplaying days. The police responded quickly to Shields' hysterical telephone call, and noted upon arrival that everyone at Hurlburt's place smelled and acted inebriated. Shields freely admitted to taking 10 to 12 drinks, and that everyone had been imbibing with the exception of Hurlburt. Based on Shields' statement and circumstantial evidence collected at the scene, police captain Gene Hume arrested Shields for the murder of Ed Hurlburt.

Memphians were greeted with a shocking front page headline the next morning: "ED HURLBURT SLAIN, SHOT THROUGH HEART." At his arraignment, Shields proclaimed: "Ed was my best friend I ever had and I would not have killed him intentionally for anything in the world."[6] Although detectives were unable to uncover tangible evidence from the crime scene, Shields remained in custody and the case was turned over to a grand jury, which was in the midst of sorting through allegations of complicity between the sheriff's department and known bootleggers. Actually, the grand jury had already finalized its report and drafted indictments scheduled for release on 22 February—one day after Hurlburt's slaying. The case even reached the desk of state Attorney General Hunter Wilson, owing to its connection with Tennessee's prohibition statute.

The investigation took a twist when Shields implicated county sheriff Mike G. Tate in the card game and consumption of the contraband liquor. The beleaguered chief called the accusation "a damn lie," although he did admit going to Hurlburt's dry goods establishment after the raiders returned to make sure the confiscated whiskey had been properly handled. Tate had recently demanded immediate notification whenever a bootleg operation was in progress and illegal liquor had been rounded up. Tate's name appeared on the homicide report as a witness to the crime, but this information never became public knowledge.

Suspicions surrounding Hurlburt's death heightened when detectives disclosed that the deceased — a man with a reputation for carrying large wads of cash — had only one $20 gold piece in his pocket. Three deputies swore that Big Ed had five gold pieces ($100) in his possession that tragic morning. Hurlburt's lawyer added that an endorsed check in the amount of $460 to cover bail for the two 'leggers was missing. Where, people began to question, had all of the money gone? One possible explanation was that Hurlburt had deposited the cache in his office safe, but no one knew how to open it.

Then an unconfirmed story circulated about Hurlburt's ties with the underworld, alleging that he had invested heavily in illegal slot machines in Memphis, Nashville, Birmingham, and New Orleans and netted over $100,000. The unidentified source claimed Hurlburt had "made several dangerous enemies in this line of work and has been walking on the brink of the grave for two weeks." The source concluded that Big Ed had been "a marked man."[7]

Hurlburt's demise had been the leading topic of conversation on Memphis streets since the news had first broken. One recurring public query centered on Hurlburt's unexplained high success rate in capturing bootleggers which, in turn, led to his mercurial rise within the department. Then, the *Commercial-Appeal* printed a devastating bit of information: ten cases of moonshine from Hurlburt's final raid had never reached headquarters.

The grand jury interviewed five witnesses to Hurlburt's death and found that each one corroborated Shields' original story about the fateful sequence of events. Although the *Commercial-Appeal* had sensationalized the violent episode, the grand jury deliberated only twenty-five minutes and ruled Hurlburt's death an accident. Shields was promptly released after eighty hours in custody, but public concern lingered over the relationship between Memphis policemen and the illegal liquor trade.

Hurlburt's estate created yet more controversy. Big Ed had bequeathed all property to his mother, Sarah, but she had passed away only three weeks earlier. His brother, Charles, was not mentioned in the document, but brother-in-law D. F. Barker of Annawan, Illinois, was identified as executor. Hurlburt's lawyer, Abe Cohn, calculated that the total estate might exceed $350,000, as the deceased had been a pioneer in the city's dry cleaning industry.

The closing chapter of Hurlburt's life left many people, including his family, dissatisfied with the police investigation. When Hurlburt's safe was finally opened, it contained only petty cash and business receipts from the day Big Ed had died. No secret stash of money was uncovered, and the investigation was officially closed. The last player to join the '08 Vols— the man who scored the lone run in the championship game — Big Ed Hurlburt, was the first to pass away. He is buried in Elmwood Cemetery, Memphis.

It is probable that Charlie Shields carried the terrible memory of Hurlburt's last night for the rest of his life. Only a year after Hurlburt's death, the ex–Turtle was shot in the knee by a Memphis patrolman in possible retaliation for his role in the accidental shooting. The tough Shields removed the bullet himself with a pocket knife. In 1924, he became a security officer at the County Fairgrounds, a position he held for over twenty years. Best remembered as the Shelby County Courthouse elevator operator, Shields entertained government officials and patrons with stories from his baseball past and his favorite hobby — catching snakes. The southpaw's fondest recollection from the ballyard was when he struck out nineteen Portland (OR) batters while pitching for Seattle in the old Pacific Coast League in 1905. Charles Jessamine Shields outlived his good buddy, Big Ed Hurlburt, by thirty-five years.[8]

John Dolittle Hardy was not through with baseball even though Berny, the Nashville populous, and Vols management were finished with him following his unproductive 1908 season.[9] The Nashville manager shipped the disgruntled catcher to Mobile early in the offseason. The Scrappy One welcomed the change and caught forty-one games for the Sea Gulls before breaking his arm in June 1909. Given his release, Hardy resurfaced in Columbus (GA) once his arm had mended. Then the last-place Washington Senators, desperate for the services of an experienced catcher to fill in for the injured Gabby Street, signed Hardy to finish the month of September.

The Senators signed Hardy to a 1909 contract extension, but by midsummer he had appeared in only seven games and chirped at rookie manager Jimmy McAleer for more playing time. He finished the season in Montreal, where he slugged two home runs in the final game of the season and resigned with the Canadian club for another year. Things soured in the summer of 1911, and the Royals suspended him. The National Board did not reinstate Hardy until 1914.

Hardy returned to Cleveland, where he founded a real estate company, presided over a mortgage house, and established an investment firm in the Guardian Building. Although these businesses prospered, Jack could not remove baseball from his system. In 1920, he returned to the game in Petersburg (VA), Bradenton (FL), and Bartow (CA). The following year, the wandering catcher played minor league venues in Huron, Joplin, and Omaha. He was under contract with Denver in 1922, but the 45-year-old never returned to the Rocky Mountain city. John Dolittle Hardy, the arrogant and fearsome enforcer of the '08 Vols, suddenly passed away on 20 October 1921. He is buried in Lakewood Park Cemetery, Cleveland, (OH).

In 1964, the 87-year-old widow of Scrappy Jack contacted the National Baseball Hall of Fame Library in Cooperstown, New York. Emma Hardy, then blind, had listened to an appeal by radio broadcaster Mel Allen for old-time ballplayers to send their Deadball Era recollections to Cooperstown before they were forever lost to the public. Emma, who had married Jack in 1903 and briefly shared a Nashville apartment with the Bernhards in 1908, was still a devoted wife and number one fan of Scrappy Jack. She rarely missed any of his games, and kept newspaper clippings, scorecards, and photographs in large scrapbooks. The aging widow complied with Allen's appeal for material, and offered an unsolicited comparison between ballplayers of the 1960s and players from Jack Hardy's era. "Baseball has really turned into a big business [today]," criticized Emma. "When Jack played, it was for fun. Players used to think they were lucky to get paid for it."[10] Mrs. Scrappy Jack outlived her husband by four decades, and commented with obvious affection on her husband's bygone life in baseball.[11]

Everyone associated with Nashville baseball recognized the tremendous potential of Jacob Ellsworth Daubert.[12] Throughout the '08 season, he defended first base like a veteran and his offense improved dramatically. Lajoie invited Daubert for another tryout in 1909, but he was still not satisfied with the young prospect. To Nashville's surprise, the Cleveland manager shipped the lanky first baseman to Toledo, where he hit a disappointing .135 in 35 games. Then, Toledo sent a second shockwave through the Nashville community when it sent him to Memphis.

Daubert finished the '09 season with the Turtles, and his batting eye returned; he led the team with a .314 batting average over 81 games. Despite the team's last-place finish (37½ games out), Daubert's offensive recovery caught the attention of Larry Sutton, who was canvassing ballyards across America as the first major league scout. Sutton reported to Charlie Ebbets that Daubert was "a graceful and powerful player." Forty years later, Frank Graham claimed that Daubert and Zack Wheat were the first finds of the legendary Dodger scout.[13]

In his first season with the Trolley Dodgers, Daubert posted relatively pedestrian numbers (.264 average), but showed promise as a power hitter with eight home runs to rank third in the National League, and fifteen triples to finish fifth. "His power numbers were more attributable to his speed than strength," noted Jim Sandoval.[14] Over the next two seasons, Daubert's average leaped to .307 and .308 when he stroked 176 and 172 hits to rank third and eighth in the league, respectively. Daubert's son revealed much later that his father had kept a little black book describing "the eccentric movements of every pitcher" in the National League. Jake "was a real student of the game," observed George Daubert.[15]

Daubert, a skilled bunter and slap hitter, possessed very quick hands and an agile body. Some contemporaries consider him the finest fielding first baseman in all of baseball. In his early days in Nashville, Daubert was acknowledged as an outstanding bunter. In 1908, he had ranked fourth in sacrifices while batting from the six hole in the lineup — not a typical bunting spot. Grover Alexander later praised Daubert's bunting abilities, and Milton Stock,

Jake Daubert in a Brooklyn Dodgers uniform. (Bain collection, Library of Congress, Prints and Photographs Division, Washington, D.C.)

a fourteen-year third baseman with the Giants, Phillies, Cardinals, and Dodgers, made this lofty observation: "Jake Daubert was the greatest bunter I ever saw. In his prime he could bunt almost at will. I don't know exactly what he did to the ball, but he seemed to put reverse English on it in some way so that it would stop just where he wanted it to stop."[16] Hall of Fame outfielder Max "Scoops" Carey had wished Daubert had batted behind him because Jake "was such a wonderful bunter." Daubert believed the best time to bunt was with two strikes because no one expected it. To prove his point, he once laid down bunts with two strikes in three consecutive games. Daubert concluded that his ability to bunt as well as leg out infield hits increased his on-base hitting proficiency. Had he not developed a chronic leg problem, Daubert felt his career batting average would have been thirty points higher.

In 1913, Daubert established himself as a *bona fide* star in the National League. He won the batting title (.350), and fielded a meticulous .991 with only thirteen errors in almost 1,300 attempts. As a result, sportswriters selected the Brooklyn first baseman for the prestigious Chalmer's Trophy, the predecessor of the MVP Award. Daubert received a 1913 Chalmer's roadster along with American League recipient Walter Johnson, but modestly admitted that he would now have to learn how to drive an automobile.

Daubert shared his innermost thoughts about hitting with *Baseball Magazine* editor Ferdinand Cole Lane, who was assembling similar impressions from over 250 active players for a volume entitled *Batting*. Daubert's comments are a rare glimpse into the mindset of an accomplished Deadball Era hitter. Lane asked the 1913 batting champ how he managed to cop the Chalmer's. "I honestly don't know," responded Daubert.

> It's the hardest thing in the world for me to explain. When I worked in the coal mines they used to do what they called "pound and jumper." That is, one man would hold a heavy iron peg and the rest would swing on it with sledge hammers. If you tried it you probably couldn't hit that peg at all. And yet, men who are used to such work can keep on pounding away with their full strength and never miss, though they hardly have their mind on the job at all. They do the right thing without thinking.[17]

Lane was amazed by Daubert's offensive consistency throughout his career. "Work is the keynote of all baseball success," confided the veteran first baseman. "No player ever yet achieved prominence without the hardest kind of hard work. Baseball is no place for a lazy man. A player must first of all have ability. But ability is not enough. He must have ambition, for unless he strives to succeed he will not succeed. Ambition means hard work."[18] Daubert, acknowledged Lane, was highly esteemed by contemporaries for his intelligence, fine character, likable personality, and prowess on the baseball diamond.

One sportswriter hung an appropriate nickname on Daubert because of his meticulous dress, reputation as a family man, and articulate communication skills. "Gentleman Jake" Daubert was universally respected by family, teammates, sportswriters, and Brooklyn ownership — a rare accomplishment in any baseball era.

As a reward for winning the Chalmer's, Ebbets signed Daubert to a rare three-year contract, which nearly doubled his salary and made him the highest-paid Dodger. The Brooklyn mogul wanted to reward his award-winning first baseman for an outstanding season, but he also feared that Daubert might jump to the new rival Federal League. If Gentleman Jake left the Dodgers, it was believed stars like Wheat and Stengel might soon follow. In other moves to keep Daubert in the Brooklyn fold, Ebbets chose him to be team captain and chief administrator for a barnstorming tour through the South and Cuba in the winter of 1913. Each player received $600 and Daubert earned an additional $1,000 for overseeing the details. While the team was away in the Caribbean, Ebbets selected Wilbert Robinson, a former catcher for Baltimore and currently the pitching coach of the champion New York Giants, to man-

Jake Daubert (far left) receiving his Chalmers roadster for his selection as the Chalmers award recipient for 1913. (Bain collection, Library of Congress, Prints and Photographs Division, Washington, D.C.)

age the Dodgers in 1914. His chief competition for the position? Gentleman Jake Daubert. Uncle Robbie hoped to placate his star first baseman by penciling him in the number two slot of the Dodgers' lineup.

Daubert felt snubbed when Ebbets overlooked him for the Dodgers' managerial position. As expected, the Federal League heavily courted the star first baseman, and Daubert used it as leverage against Ebbets. In the end, Daubert stayed in Brooklyn and again led the N.L. with a .329 batting average, but an award regulation prevented him from repeating as the Chalmer's Trophy recipient.

As it turned out, Ebbets' concerns about Daubert were justified, but for a different reason. In November 1913, Daubert was selected vice president of the Baseball Players Fraternity, an early player's union. The BPF did not overtly challenge the reserve clause — which had evolved into an institutional fixture in baseball — but it did demand that players deserved the right to negotiate with other clubs once they had been released from their contract. The labor union also negotiated for ten days notice before being released unconditionally, full disclosure of terms in the new contract, and the right to refuse sale to a minor league team if other major league clubs were interested in picking up that player. The Fraternity bargained to improve basic working conditions like forcing owners to pay for player uniforms, laundry service, and transportation to spring training. Daubert brought a dynamic style of leadership to the fledgling association, believing in direct negotiations between players and owners. He earned the respect of peers as an unabashed spokesman of player's rights, and one source ranked Daubert "among the most popular players of his time."[19] Owners tread cautiously in his presence.

In 1915 and 1916, Daubert hit .301 and .316, respectively, and led the Dodgers to the National League crown in the latter season. Brooklyn faced the Boston Red Sox in the World Series, led by outfielder Tris Speaker and pitcher Babe Ruth. In the first game, Boston took a five-run lead into the ninth inning when Brooklyn staged a ferocious comeback. With two outs and bases loaded in a one-run game, Red Sox shortstop Everett Scott made a sensational stop on a hard grounder off Daubert to end the game. Gentleman Jake was unimpressive throughout the Series (.176) as Boston pitchers silenced all of the Brooklyn batters. The American Leaguers went on to capture the Series in five games.

In 1917, the relationship between Ebbets and Daubert began to sour. After the Federal League disbanded, Ebbets and other owners saw a golden opportunity to slash salaries, and Daubert's hefty paycheck was a prime target. Indeed, the first baseman had missed twenty-six games to injuries, his fielding suffered a setback, and his batting average plunged to .261. Only 10 of 122 hits went for extra bases.

Events in the final year of the Great War (1918) were the undoing of Daubert's career in the New York borough. In midsummer, Secretary of War Newton Baker announced that, after 1 September, all able-bodied men must either work in a war industry or join the military. This "work or fight" proclamation immediately affected baseball as minor league circuits shut down, and major league owners prepared to comply with Baker's edict. During the season, Daubert had returned to form, batting a robust .308 and leading the league in triples (15).

Always the defender of player rights, Daubert interpreted Baker's policy as a violation of his contract. He notified Ebbets that the federal government could not decree baseball out of existence. Furthermore, Daubert had a signed contract through October, and expected full payment of his salary, which amounted to over $2,100. An angry Ebbets went to the press, saying that Daubert was unpatriotic and greedy. Undeterred by the name-calling, Daubert filed a lawsuit against Ebbets and simultaneously fired off a strong letter to the National Commission. Fearful that Daubert's defection might spread to other players, several team owners pressured Ebbets to settle the matter out of court. The Brooklyn owner reluctantly paid Daubert's wages, but traded his star to Cincinnati for outfielder Tommy Griffith at the 1919 spring meeting.

The move to the banks of the Ohio River favored Daubert as the improved Reds went on to face the Chicago White Sox in the infamous 1919 World Series. Led by Shoeless Joe Jackson, the ChiSox were heavy favorites, but Daubert and the Reds pulled off the upset of the century. The ensuing scandal surrounding White Sox players for allegedly taking bribes to fix the Series shook the national pastime to its core. Daubert produced better numbers in his second World Series appearance with seven base hits and .241 batting average.

Daubert played five more seasons with the Reds in the early 1920s while John McGraw's New York Giants dominated the National League. In 1922, Daubert hit .336 (second personal best), led the league for the second time in triples (22) and games played by a first baseman (156), established a career-high 205 base hits, and fielded a sterling .994. It was arguably his most productive year as a major leaguer.

Jake Daubert was a wealthy man in 1924. Throughout his major league career, he had invested wisely in a wide range of businesses—a pool room, movie house, cigar store, and ice house. For a number of years, Daubert ran a successful coal washing firm in Schuylkill Haven (PA), which netted $25,000 per year. In late 1924 he entertained the idea of retiring as an active player and purchasing the Reading club of the International League. His plans never worked out.

On 24 May 1924, the veteran sustained a serious head injury when he was beaned by St. Louis pitcher Allen Sothoron. He shared his thoughts about the incident with *Baseball Magazine* editor F.C. Lane. "This eighth experience of mine [being hit in the head by a pitch] was the worst of the lot," confided Daubert. "For several hours I couldn't see. And when my sight did return, it kept coming and going like switching an electric light on and off. Besides, blood oozed out of my ears and I developed a first-class headache which lasted for three weeks."[20] Daubert suffered from sleeplessness and blurry vision for the remainder of the season. He appeared in only 102 games—his lowest in fifteen years. As the Giants squared off against the Senators in the 1924 World Series, Daubert entered a hospital suffering from abdominal pains.

On the morning of 9 October 1924, Cincinnatians awakened to a shocking front page headline in the *Times-Star:* "JAKE DAUBERT, REDS' VETERAN CAPTAIN, IS DEAD." When Daubert entered the hospital at the conclusion of the 1924 season, physicians decided to remove his appendix, but the surgery had not gone well and the patient declined rapidly. Four days later, Gentleman Jake passed away from complications surrounding the appendectomy.

The news of Daubert's death stunned the baseball world. Prior to the sixth game of the World Series in Washington, D.C., several veteran players and sportswriters were seen in tears, and a gloom hung over baseball's gala event. Barnstorming teammates led by Edd Roush canceled their tour and promptly returned to Cincinnati. Team President George Herrmann and first-year manager Jack Hendricks were deeply moved. Writing in the *Cincinnati*

Times-Star and reprinted in *The Sporting News,* sportswriter W.A. Phelon commented: "The story of Jake Daubert's life is a glowing page for the strong youth of America to copy," a remark that still touched Jake's son, George, sixty-five years after his father's untimely death.[21] One hundred automobiles transported bereaved family and friends in Daubert's funeral procession. Jacob Ellsworth Daubert — the player with the brightest major league career of any '08 Nashville Vols member — sadly died the youngest at age thirty-nine. He is buried in Barber Cemetery, Pottsville, Pennsylvania.

In a postscript, one of Daubert's attending physicians hypothesized that the beaning incident in May had possibly played a part in the ballplayer's sudden death. In actuality, the physicians had misdiagnosed Daubert's condition. In the late 1980s, George Daubert related that his father's progeny — son, grandson, great grandson and great granddaughter — all suffered from a hereditary malfunction of the spleen, which required its removal. Had doctors taken out Daubert's spleen instead of his appendix, there is the likelihood that he would have survived the surgery.

Daubert has been fondly remembered in the years following his premature death. *The Sporting News* asked one of Jake's old acquaintances to develop a list of the greatest athletes he had ever seen in twenty-one seasons as an umpire in the Southern Association. Old Dan Pfenninger did not hesitate to proclaim Daubert the standout first baseman, based on his ability to catch errant throws, handle a bat, and run the bases. Pfenninger's thoughts were repeated in the early 1950s when the National Association drafted a list of all-star teams for the minor leagues between the years 1901–1951. Daubert's name appeared on the golden teams of the Southern Association and Ohio and Pennsylvania League. Columnist Frank Graham capped the accolades to Daubert in *The Sporting News* article entitled "Maybe Jake Wasn't Better Than Hodges But Many Old Timers Think He Was Tops."[22] It seems Daubert had made a lasting impression on Brooklynites thirty-six years after his Dodger days had ended.

Berny selected Walter East as team captain of the 1909 Nashville Vols, and he remained with the club for two more seasons.[23] He moved on to Montreal (1910), but then reunited with his former skipper, Berny, in Memphis in 1911. A year later, he split time between Atlanta and Kansas City of the Western League. The infielder wrapped up his career as player-manager of Mansfield (Ohio).

East did not achieve the level of baseball success that befell Jake Daubert, but then again he harbored different professional goals. In the winter of 1909, the Buckeye passed the Ohio bar exam, opened a law office in his hometown of Barberton, and later expanded to a second office in Akron with apprentice colleague Lloyd R. Read. Leaving baseball forever in 1912, East devoted the remainder of his life to the practice of law. In the realm of politics, he was defeated twice in the 1920s for municipal court judge and city solicitor. He suddenly died of uremia on 28 August 1930, while on a business trip to Philadelphia. Walter Rufus East — the keeper of the keystone sack who completed the transformation of the '08 Vols infield — is buried alongside his parents in City Cemetery, Coulterville, Illinois.

Few observers doubted that Charles Vedder Sitton would make his mark at the major league level when Cleveland plucked the dazzling spitballer off Berny's roster.[24] Sitton reported to spring training in 1909 determined to challenge ailing Glen Liebhardt for a spot in the starting rotation. But the rookie hurler faced formidable obstacles as the Indians possessed a formidable pitching staff that included Cy Young and Addie Joss. Still, Lajoie gave the South Carolinian every opportunity to make the club. Sitton pitched well in the preseason, including an impressive shutout over Mobile. He made a successful big league debut on 24 April 1909, against Rube Waddell and the St. Louis Browns, and notched a second victory over hard-throwing Walter Johnson of the Washington Senators. Sitton jumped to a 3–0 record, but early concerns arose over his high hits-to-innings-pitched ratio: thirty-two safeties in thirty innings. By midsummer, the new Cleveland manager, Deacon Macguire, relegated Sitton to the bullpen, and had a short hook in his few remaining starts. Sitton stood on a major league mound for the last time on 2 September 1909, against the New York Yankees. He did not finish the game and absorbed a 6–1 loss.

Sitton's lone season in the majors was unimpressive. He appeared in only fourteen games—five as a starter. Opposing batters clobbered fifty hits in as many innings pitched, and Sitton produced as many walks as strikeouts (16). The hurler posted a mediocre 3–2 record, and in the offseason he was optioned to Columbus (OH).

For the next two seasons, Sitton plied the pitching trade in several southern minor league cities, including Atlanta. At the end of 1911, Brooklyn showed mild interest in him, but he failed to make the 1912 roster. So, he returned to the Crackers, where he was reunited with former Vols third baseman, Pryor McElveen. Sitton led the cellar-dwellers in games started (29) and victories (10), but moved on with his brother, Phil, to Troy in the New York State League in 1913. Together, the Sitton brothers played on the upstate team for three years before Carl was traded to Binghamton, where his baseball career came to an end following the 1916 season.

For the next fifteen years, Sitton's life blended into obscurity. He surfaced in the late 1920s as an employee of the California-based Hercules Powder Company, a munitions firm which was venturing into the chemical fertilizer trade. It is likely that Sitton worked as a traveling salesman throughout South Carolina and Georgia. When the Great Depression struck, Sitton resided in the Daniel Ashley Hotel, Valdosta (GA). There, the South Carolinian had become well known to local folks through his stories about his earlier flirtation with baseball fame as a Volunteer, Cracker, and Indian. Like many Americans, he had fallen upon hard times, and lost his job sometime in the summer of 1931.

On the morning of 11 September 1931, Sitton borrowed an automobile from a Valdosta native and drove to the Lowndes County fairgrounds. He parked the vehicle by the baseball diamond, picked up a revolver and placed it to his head. Several hours later, the owner of the car found Sitton slumped over in the front seat dead with the pistol laying at his side. A coroner's inquest held the next day concluded that Sitton had died at his own hand. No motive for the bachelor's suicide was ever determined, although the *Valdosta Times* picked up on the irony of the location of Sitton's death, owing to his well-known baseball exploits. Perhaps, Sitton had been haunted by memories of his unfulfilled baseball dreams; he tragically took his own life less than two weeks before his fiftieth birthday. Carl Vedder Sitton, the pitching hero of the '08 championship game, rests in the Presbyterian Church Cemetery, Pendleton, South Carolina, alongside his parents and several hundred yards away from his boyhood home.

Theo Breitenstein still had forty-three more victories in his aging arm after the championship game in 1908.[25] His record in the Southern Association is a testimony to his endurance as the chart below belies:

		Appearances	*Won-Lost*
1902	Memphis	76	19–14
1903	Memphis	52	17–11
1904	New Orleans	44	15–8
1905	New Orleans	46	21–5
1906	New Orleans	33	21–7
1907	New Orleans	68	5–9
1908	New Orleans	29	17–6
1909	New Orleans	34	13–10
1910	New Orleans	37	19–9
1911	New Orleans	22	11–10
Totals		441	158–89

At the end of his career, Frank elevated Breit to assistant manager, a sign of respect for the aging twirler. Then, he hung up his glove but not his spikes in 1912 as he moved behind the plate for seven more seasons as an umpire in the Southern Association. When the Great War broke out, the 48-year-old attempted to enlist but was twice denied. In 1921, Breitenstein officiated in the Texas League, and then retired from baseball. He returned to his hometown, St. Louis, and found a job in a Ford Motor Company assembly plant. He continued to follow the Browns and Cardinals closely, but the veteran of 830 professional starts harbored biases about the modern game, similar to Jack Hardy. In 1929, Breit told the *St. Louis Post-Dispatch* that he "deplored the modern powder puff tendencies among the modern players." Entitled "When Men Were Bold," Breit's article asserted that current players were simply too pampered.[26]

In the early 1930s, the retired baseball hurler and automobile laborer took a part-time position as groundskeeper at Forest Park Golf and Tennis Club. On the evening of 3 May 1935, Breit suffered a massive heart attack and died on the job. Ironically, his wife of forty years (Ida) had passed away only one week earlier. Theodore P. Breitenstein — the $10,000 Beauty — is buried in St. Peter's Cemetery, St. Louis.

The baseball star of William Henry Bernhard shined bright following the '08 season.[27] Hearsay in national publications predicted that he would soon be tendered a major league managing position. However, he returned to Nashville in 1909, where the Vols finished a close second to Atlanta. Within a year, the Nashville roster didn't even resemble Berny's freshman crew of '08. Only Bay, Wiseman, Perdue, Seabough, and Siegle remained. In the meantime, Berny's primary contact in the major leagues had fallen from managerial grace. Lajoie, the future Hall of Famer, continued to be an outstanding second baseman in the majors until 1916, but he no longer had the authority to recommend his good friend for a job. Then, the Nashville situation deteriorated dramatically in 1910 when the Vols dropped to fifth place, and trailed the champion Pelicans by 23 games. New ownership in Nashville precipitated Berny's flight to Memphis, a treasonous move in the eyes of local fans. Berny remained at the helm of the new Chicks (formerly Turtles) for three years, but the team on the banks of the Mississippi never climbed higher than fourth place.

While maintaining a Memphis residence, Berny managed Salt Lake City in the Pacific Coast League in 1914. The move seemed drastic in a geographic sense because it reached beyond his New York-Pennsylvania-Ohio-Tennessee employment zone. The next season, Chattanooga, the franchise replacement for Little Rock, hired Berny as special instructor to a corps of young pitchers. The aging veteran tossed four games for the Lookouts before being released as the mid–May roster deadline approached. He finished out the season as an umpire alongside Ted Breitenstein and Old Dan Pfenninger, and scouted for Birmingham. The duties of an arbiter probably did not appeal to the long-time manager and he resigned at the end of the season. Then, Salt Lake City inked him to manage two more seasons. In his final professional season (1917), the 46-year-old Bernhard appeared on the mound seven times.

Berny spent the winter of 1916–17 (one of the coldest in recent memory) in the Utah capitol where his wife, Lillian, suddenly took ill and passed away. Her body was transported to Clarence, New York, for internment in the family plot alongside an infant daughter, Marion. Now Berny was cast adrift. The retirement of Lajoie and death of Lillian signaled the severing of his ties with baseball.

Berny's once-promising managerial career had fizzled, and he returned to Memphis to work for the Memphis Term Corporation until 1920. Then he remarried (Lydamae Dills), relocated to Southern California, and became the information chief for the Santa Anita race track. Retiring from that position, the septuagenarian moved to San Diego in 1940 and found a job as a shipping clerk for Stationer's Corporation. When he died from leukemia on 30 March 1949, *The Sporting News* carried a three-paragraph obituary essentially gleaned from his Player Index Card. The *Buffalo Evening News* ran a shorter piece. William Henry Bernhard, the manager who demonstrated marvelous leadership skills and molded the '08 Vols into a champion, is buried in Fillmore Cemetery, Clarence, New York.

At his death, Berny's formidable baseball career seemed forgotten — his nine years in the majors, contribution (with Lajoie) to baseball labor history, and nine seasons as a minor league manager. Yet, in 1976, a sports article in the *Cleveland Plain-Dealer* revisited Berny's most impressive season (1904), when he led the team with twenty-three victories.[28] It also recounted a piece of Indians trivia — the day Strawberry Bill twirled an opening day victory — the first in Cleveland's storied history.

Winford Kellum had resurrected his pitching worth in Nashville in 1908 by dominating New Orleans.[29] He returned in 1909, posted an 8–8 record, and assumed Hunter's role as utilityman in the outfield. His arm did not respond well to double duty, however, and he moved to Wheeling in 1910 but did not play. When Win's career ended, his son, Ford, calculated that Kellum's fifteen-year pitching record stood at 212–150.[30]

Kellum still enjoyed his association with baseball, so he partnered with Breitenstein in 1911 to officiate in the Southern Association. In his rookie season, Kellum experienced several unpleasant run-ins with Atlanta manager Billy Smith. Once Tobacco Billy tried to slug Win while unruly fans pelted him with bottles after an unpopular call. The police added insult to injury by arresting Kellum for disturbing the peace. He retired from umpiring after four seasons and returned to the family farm in Michigan.

In the early 1910s, Kellum purchased a small cottage on Young Lake where he liked to fish with his wife, Frederica, and two children. Next to baseball, Win's greatest passion in life was fishing. Charlie Comiskey was one of his favorite fishing buddies. The owner of the White Sox once bragged to Win that he had landed a 42-pound pike in the Muskegon River. Kellum, not to be outdone, replied that he had landed "a rubber boot and a lumberman's lantern — still lit." When Comiskey challenged Kellum's honesty, Win replied: "You take 40 pounds off that pike and I'll blow the light out of the lantern."[31] Not much of a farmer, Kellum contacted Cincinnati owner Garry Herrmann in 1925, angling for a job. The Reds' owner did not tender one. Yet, the correspondence reveals another influential baseball man that Kellum knew personally.

In his lifetime, Kellum was recognized around Big Rapids for his tireless commitment to youth baseball as a coach and instructor from Little League through Pony League. Once a pitcher for the Big Rapids Independents failed to show up for a game, and Win took the mound at age 55 and tossed a 5–0 no-hitter against Remus. Kellum also took aim at the modern game of baseball with sentiments reminiscent of Hardy and Breitenstein. The southpaw believed "the best brand of ball" was played in the Deadball Era. "We played scientific baseball," said Kellum. "We didn't go for the home run every time up." He disapproved of rules changes that appeared to favor the batter. "If a club doesn't have a home run hitter, they pull the fences in so the balls will go over. Now they are making the strike zone smaller, too," lamented the one-time star.[32] One of Kellum's greatest pleasures was listening to Detroit Tigers radio broadcasts from Briggs Field.

The local *Big Rapids Pioneer* ran a five-segment series on Kellum's life in baseball a year before he passed away. "So this is the Win Kellum story," concluded the *Big Rapids Pioneer*, "a tale of a man who played baseball because he loved the game and not for the money that could be made in it.... Perhaps the facilities were not too good [in early times]. Maybe the ball didn't have as much rubber in it. But the galaxy of stars which studded the diamonds of 45 and 55 years ago need take no bow to today's array of baseball leaders. Just name Mathewson, Wagner, Keeler, Young, Waddell, Lajoie, McGraw, Mack, and yes, somewhere in there — Win Kellum."[33] Kellum, too, seemed aware of his own special place in the history of the sport when he penned his 10,000-word autobiography, which is in the hands of relatives today. The Michigander succumbed to a heart attack on 10 August 1951, while fishing with his son on Young Lake. Winford Ainsley Kellum, the Pelican killer whose occupation was listed on his death certificate as "ball player," is buried in Highland View Cemetery, Big Rapids, Michigan. In a postscript, the Ferris State University baseball diamond was christened "Win Kellum Field" in the 1970s.

Charlie Ebbets plucked McElveen off the '08 Nashville roster following his breakout season.[34] Humpy appeared in his first major league game on 26 April 1909, against the Phillies. Over the course of the season, he demonstrated versatility as a utilityman by appearing at third base (37), shortstop (10), second base (5), first base (5), and outfield (13). He fielded .948 — a decent average for a journeyman bouncing between several positions. His batting average dipped to .198, however, and he struck out 10 percent of the time.

McElveen fared no better in his sophomore season with Brooklyn. His offensive average improved only slightly (.225) and he fielded a consistent .943 as a backup to third baseman Ed Lennox. McElveen repeated at every infield position, including one stint as catcher. Humpy's slow start in 1911 forced the Dodgers to replace him with light-hitting Eddie Zimmerman, and he faced Slim Sallee of the St. Louis Cardinals in his final major league plate appearance on 4 June 1911. Then Ebbets shipped him to Montgomery, where he played 81 games and rediscovered his batting eye (.276).

Back in familiar southern surroundings, the 31-year-old McElveen continued to decline. In 1912, he split time between sixth-place Montgomery and last-place Atlanta. Reunited with former '08 teammates East and Sitton on the Crackers, all three were destined to play their final Southern Association season together. McElveen hung on for three more seasons in Beaumont, Knoxville, and Shreveport to wrap up his professional career.

In the twilight of his playing days, McElveen resumed his affiliation with Carson-Newman College, where he coached basketball and baseball. During his five-year tenure, he mentored individuals such as future football coaching legend Dana X. Bible in two basketball seasons that produced only one loss, and Tennessee Supreme Court Justice Hamilton Sands Burnett in baseball. He also instructed younger brother Lee in baseball and represented the coaches on the college's athletic council. In the 1920s, he opened a grocery store close to campus.

Coaching a small college program and operating a dry goods establishment were not going to make McElveen a rich man. Eventually he went to work for the American Zinc Company, but baseball remained close to his heart. Perhaps the highest public kudos he received came from Volunteer and Dodger teammate Jake Daubert. In August, 1911, Gentleman Jake authored an article in *Baseball Magazine* entitled "The Greatest Play I Ever Saw." In the selection, Daubert recounted McElveen's cunning defensive gem to nab Tarleton at third base in the '08 championship game.[35] In 1948, Humpy also appeared at the Larry Gilbert celebration in Nashville and attended a Vols game to honor former players. Pryor Mynatt McElveen, the team captain of the '08 Vols, died in Pleasant Hill, Tennessee, on 27 October 1951, after a long battle with lung disease. He is buried in West View Cemetery, Jefferson City, Tennessee.

Doc Seabough was at the height of his baseball career in 1908.[36] He played three more seasons in Nashville and followed Berny to Memphis for two more. After two years in Omaha of the Western Association, Doc hung up his catching gear forever.

During the offseason, Seabough always returned to Springfield, where he worked as a clerk in the mechanical department of the St. Louis and San Francisco Railway. By the early 1930s he was promoted to chief clerk. He was prominent in the employee's union and charter member and president of the Men's Club. The latter organization met at monthly social gatherings in the Springfield Auditorium, and it was not uncommon for several hundred people to attend. Still the former catcher could not divorce himself altogether from the game he had played for twelve seasons. In the early 1920s, he organized the Springfield Midgets and helped create the Western Association with franchises in Topeka, Hutchinson, Springfield, Joplin, Bartlesville, Okmulgee, Muskogee, Ardmore, and Fort Smith. He presided over the league for seven years. In 1930, he organized the Frisco System Baseball League in company towns sprouting up along the route. He served as deacon of the Temple Baptist Church and belonged to the Masons. A lifelong resident of Springfield,

Seabough passed away on 10 November 1951, from a heart attack. James Warren Seabough — the reliable reserve catcher of the '08 Vols— is buried in Eastlawn Cemetery, Springfield.

Harry Bay was a fan favorite from the instant he put on a Nashville uniform, and he remained a consistent offensive and defensive player for three more seasons despite being hampered by his bum knee. A year after Bernhard departed for Memphis, Bay decided to try his own hand as a minor league player-manager, working mostly in the Three-I League: Bloomington (1912), Madison (1913–1914), Mason City (1915), Rock Island (1916), and Alton (1917).

When Bay retired from baseball, he returned to his hometown, Peoria, to work as a state automobile license examiner. He was best remembered locally, however, as secretary and later switchboard operator for the Peoria Fire Department. Learning about Bay's position, Connie Mack sent a congratulatory note: "I bet you're the first one at every fire," noted Mack whimsically. "Such speed as you had will never be forgotten."[37]

Bay's life as a musician was held in high esteem. "His fame as a trumpet virtuoso almost equaled that of his big league ball playing," claimed the *Peoria Journal*.[38] For years, Bay was a featured soloist with the Peoria Municipal Band, and he regularly accompanied the local Shriners marching band and American Legion stage band. He also formed his own dance band, which entertained at numerous local functions.

On 3 July 1938, Bay was invited to Cleveland to participate in an old-timers game. Representing the "Immortal Naps," Bay joined former teammates Nap Lajoie, Dusty Rhoads, Cy Young and Ed Walsh to face a team made up of the 1920 world champion squad — Tris Speaker, Stan Coveleski, Joe Sewell, and John "Duster" Mails. Bay soaked up the thunderous applause of an adoring major league crowd for the last time. On 20 March 1952, Bay passed away several days after slipping on an icy sidewalk. The official cause of death was a coronary occlusion. Harry Elbert Bay, the bunter extraordinaire and baserunner with speed to burn, is buried alongside his wife, who preceded him in death, at Parkview Cemetery, Peoria.

Over eleven seasons, the career of Doc Wiseman personified classic virtues of hard work, loyalty, and dedication; his record with Nashville is an incredible one[39]:

Year	GP	AB	R	H	B.A.
1901	96	375	91	125	.333
1902	126	490	111	119	.243
1903	115	433	59	121	.279
1904	140	518	78	134	.258
1905	126	463	52	119	.257
1906	110	478	51	121	.252
1907	142	534	85	138	.258

Year	GP	AB	R	H	B.A.
1908	138	525	77	132	.251
1909	132	460	62	110	.239
1910	142	495	47	134	.270
1911	134	467	59	104	.223
Totals	1401	5238	772	1357	.259

It is possible that Wiseman's minor league career had caught the attention of big leaguers. In the first decade of the twentieth century, many major league clubs swung through Nashville on their way north. Once, Doc threw out a New York Giant at first base from right field and received praise from manager John McGraw. In another instance, Cincinnati native Miller Huggins chuckled that Doc might have made a good major leaguer if only he could have "gained one hundred pounds and grown a foot." Law school classmates, Wiseman and Huggins later attended meetings of a Cincinnati organization called Ballplayers of Yesterday — a group dedicated to raising money for local ex-ballplayers who had fallen on hard times.[40]

Wiseman's presence would surely be missed when he retired at the end of 1911 at age thirty-four. His batting eye had faded and he knew the time had come to hang up his spikes for good. And the handsome Little Doc would be missed in Nashville social circles for more than his baseball exploits. "He fondly remembered well the gatherings of friends and supporters on the banks of the Cumberland, where beer flowed and songs were sung," recounts Doc's son, Don. "Doc played an eight-string mandolin in those days and he did not want for company."[41] When grandsons Tom and Andrew rummaged through Doc's old trunk while cleaning out the attic several years ago, they uncovered a trove of letters and postcards addressed to "the hero of the Dell" from an array of lady admirers across the South.

Doc had always returned to Cincinnati in the offseason to work in the Cincinnati post office. He also assisted his father in selecting and managing rental properties, residential as well as commercial. The real estate market in turn-of-the-century Cincinnati was bursting, and Dr. Sam entered the speculation by financing frame houses in a new subdivision off Eastern Avenue. He also purchased tracts of land in Orlando (FL). It is likely that Julius took a direct role in procuring these properties, owing to his understanding of real estate law, and later managing the sizable holdings.

On 8 July 1912, the Nashville Base Ball Club invited Wiseman to return to receive a gift of appreciation for his years of service to the Vols. Doc Wiseman Day was scheduled the following day at Sulphur Dell, and a rumor circulated that the former right fielder would play in the contest. Heavy rain caused postponement of the event, so *Banner* sports editor Jack Hopper Nye escorted the former star around town.

On 10 July, Doc sat on the player's bench in front of a packed stadium as the home team jumped to an early lead over a familiar foe — the New Orleans Pelicans. In the middle of the fifth inning, umpire Win Kellum temporarily halted the contest to allow Al Fremont to present a "blushing and embarrassed" Wiseman a handsome Masonic diamond ring. Doc thanked the audience and then the game was resumed. The locals went on to a 3–1 victory, but the real winners that afternoon were the Vols fans and Julius Augustus Wiseman. Doc's presence reminded Nashvillians of more successful times since the current product languished eighteen games out of first place.

From the early 1900s until the mid–1920s, Cincinnati's municipal government employed Doc in several departments. Besides the post office, the city directory listed him as a clerk for the street department and another duty required a detailed knowledge of railroad schedules. His children were amazed at his encyclopedic memory concerning timetables and his identification of different types of locomotives and freight shipments that rumbled past their Delta Avenue doorstep.[42]

Doc remained close to his parents over the years. When his mother fell ill and declined rapidly, Doc decided not to enlist in the first call for volunteers in the Great War. He later confided to a close friend that her death in October 1917 was the single most traumatic event of his life. When Dr. Sam passed away in 1924, Julius and Cash inherited considerable assets. Cash moved to Florida, perhaps to administrate properties there. Investing (but not speculating on margin) in the stock market, Doc's fortune began to multiply.

Doc moved into the Delta Avenue house, and rented the downstairs to a practicing physician. In the mid–1920s, he began to court Mildred Messemer— daughter of the local druggist — a pretty girl who had attracted his attention years earlier. Although twenty-four years his junior, Mildred married the man she called "Jay," a derivative of his two initials, in August 1927. Three children — James (b. 20 August 1928), Jeanne (b. 19 November 1929), and Donald (b. 13 January 1931) — were the result of their union.

The 1930s were busy times around the Wiseman household. Three youngsters demanded a lot of attention and Doc willingly provided it. The 50-year-old father doted over his children, playing games with the kids on the parlor floor and taking them to romp around nearby Ault Park. The family took long automobile excursions to Florida and short hops to local points of historical interest. Each sibling remembers "Papa" fondly as a stern but fair man.[43]

Doc never shared stories about his exploits on the Sulphur Dell diamond with his children, but he did impart a wealth of baseball knowledge to his sons, Jim and Don. Etched in both of their minds were lessons of a father's fetish for the proper way to throw and hit a baseball. With fingers bent from so many years of rugged play, Doc would take his boys to the field across the street and hit fungos, demonstrate proper fielding and throwing mechanics, and drill, drill, drill. Doc lived by a simple maxim and he used baseball to teach it to his kids: "If it's worth doing at all, it's worth doing well."[44] One of Doc's favorite aphorisms, reflected oldest son Jim, was "excellence."

Doctorius Wiseman took formal education very seriously, and through his deep understanding of the classics, he instructed his children on time-honored values such as hard work (industriousness) and strength of character (integrity). Toward the end of his life, Doc wrote a letter to his son, Jim, who was preparing to graduate from Washington and Jefferson College and enter the University of Cincinnati Medical School. The missive encapsulated the elder Wiseman's code about living an ethical life: "Anything to be done at this end of the line will always be done promptly and correctly. Be careful to hold up your end as well. You won't get any place without hard work. The harder you work, the easier things will become. Don't get careless. You are now a man and about to graduate from college with a B.A. degree. People will expect close to perfection from you, so when you even write a letter or do anything else, get as close to perfection as you can. It all adds up to reputation, even the smallest of things, and that counts more than you can at present realize." Doc signed the letter "Your pardner" to underscore the close father-son relationship.[45]

Doc never lost his passion for the game of baseball. Throughout his life, he enjoyed listening to radio broadcasts of Cincinnati Reds games. His daughter, Jeanne, remembers that he would nervously turn off the set in the late innings if the game was too close. As an athlete-alumnus of the University of Cincinnati, Doc received a lifetime pass to all university sporting events, which he followed with a special zeal.

Wiseman retired from business altogether in the 1940s. Following in his father's footsteps, Doc served as a Republican precinct chairperson — a tradition he traced to his friendship with William Howard Taft. He took pleasure in tossing horseshoes with neighbors on long summer evenings and taking leisure on his Ohio River houseboat. As Wiseman entered his seventieth year, he accepted the title of vice president of a neighborhood building and loan association — the last business venture of his life.

In the late 1940s, physicians diagnosed Wiseman with arteriosclerosis, and on 3 April 1953, he succumbed to congestive heart failure in the Delta Avenue house that had witnessed his birth nearly seventy-six years earlier. News of his death spread in a flurry of newspaper obituaries. In Nashville, sports editor Fred Russell wrote a tribute in his *Side Lines* column, reminding a younger generation of Vols fans that Nashville had never seen a "bank shot artist" quite like him — a billiard reference to Wiseman's excellent play in the Dump. Russell also interviewed Doc's last manager, Bill Schwartz, who added that the popular outfielder was "one of the finest characters I ever knew in baseball, a real quiet person who always gave his best performance." Well-known baseball figure Larry Gilbert esteemed Doc's style of play in a letter to a Wiseman family member. *The Sporting News* reprinted a passage from the

1913 *Reach Guide*, which predicted that Wiseman's record of longevity and games played with one club in the Southern Association would likely never be broken. Julius Augustus Wiseman, "the hero of the Dell," is entombed in Laurel Cemetery, Cincinnati.[46]

Mike McCormick may seem like an undeserving candidate for a vignette of important member of the '08 Nashville Vols, but his impact through desertion resulted in necessary changes that led directly to the team's ultimate success.[47] Blackballed for the remainder of 1908, Dude resurfaced in Holyoke (1909), and St. Paul (1910). He wandered to the West Coast in 1913 to play for Portland in the old Pacific Coast League, and closed his baseball career as player-manager at New Haven (1914).

McCormick did not abandon the game when his playing days were over. He scouted for the Chicago Cubs and Brooklyn Dodgers in the late 1910s. Then he found employment as a maintenance man and attendant at the Hudson County (N.J.) government garage. Dude participated in local Democratic Party affairs as a precinct committeeman and participated in Second Ward Regular Democratic Club activities for many years.

Like several former Nashville Vols, McCormick followed local big league baseball — in his case the Brooklyn Dodgers. In 1936, he sent a letter to National League president Ford Frick requesting a free season pass, which was being granted to all ten-year veterans of the major leagues. Frick denied the petition based on the fact that Dude had not done the math — he had played only one season.[48] Mike McCormick, the sore-headed, error-prone deserter on the '08 Vols, died from cardiac disease in the heart of his boyhood Horseshoe district on 18 November 1953. He is buried in Holy Name Cemetery, Jersey City.

In 1911, Grantland Rice left Nashville again to accept an offer by Franklin Adams to operate the sports desk at the *New York Daily Mail*.[49] The transplanted Tennessean immediately ingratiated himself to local readers with an eloquent piece about Giants manager John McGraw. Three years later, Granny jumped to the *New York Tribune* with the promise that his column would go into national syndication. By 1917, Rice had garnered a national following, but when President Woodrow Wilson called for all able-bodied Americans to work or fight, he enlisted as a private in the 115th Field Artillery — a National Guard unit from Tennessee. The U.S. Army reassigned him to the staff of *Stars and Stripes*.

At the conclusion of the Great War, Rice returned to the *Tribune*, where his notoriety soared to new heights. By the 1920s, he was the most recognizable sports commentator in the country. He interviewed a wide range of sports celebrities such as Babe Ruth, Jack Dempsey, and Bobby Jones, and his column covered major events of the era from college football to boxing, golf, baseball, and horse racing. In 1930, Rice crossed over to the *New York Sun*, where he remained for twenty years. During this time he worked in other communication mediums as well. For instance, Rice was the first to provide play-by-play radio coverage of a World Series game in 1921, wrote feature articles in the expanding magazine industry, edited *American Golfer,* and prepared the annual All-America college football team for *Collier's*. Later, Rice narrated weekly newsreels in a piece entitled *Sportslight*.

When the *Sun* closed in the early 1950s, Granny migrated to the *New York Mirror*. He counted as colleagues an amazing array of sports journalists — Ring Lardner, Heywood Broun, Damon Runyon, Arthur Daley, Jimmy Cannon, and Fred Russell. The protégé, Russell, boasted that his mentor [Rice] was "the most widely read and respected American sports writer of the first half of the twentieth century."[50] Yet, Granny had outlived his reputation as "the dean of American sportswriters" as some critics chided that his poetic style was anachronistic — the product of old-fashioned Victorian principles that had glorified sport and athletes, hyped the importance of teamwork, and elevated sportsmanship to unrealistic levels. In truth, Rice probably agreed with this assessment. He never was able to shed his naive optimism for and admiration of the world of sports. It is ironic that the confrontational Jimmy Cannon captured these unique qualities best. "The music Grantland Rice made was small but it filled his life," eulogized Cannon. "The great sports writer [Rice] .... didn't seem old because he held onto the illusions of his youth. The dream remained pure and glowed with an obsolete splendor because of his faith in the goodness of men. ... He cherished decency above all and searched for it in the characters of those he knew. It was often hard to find but Granny didn't become discouraged. It was his failing that he judged all of us according to his own standards and there were few such as Grantland Rice...."[51] Cannon believed that Rice was an American original who influenced every sports columnist who came after him. "All of us in this generation ... are improved because we borrowed some of his techniques," concluded the scribe. "Few handle the language with as much grace. Many of us croak because we can't sing. Grantland Rice could sing!"[52]

In his poem entitled *Driftwood*, Rice wrote autobiographically about his own nomadic life as a newspaperman. One melancholy passage stanza reads:

> We know how far we've wandered from the dim, old-fashioned highways,
> We meant to come a little way, as fledglings test their power,
> And then to seek the old home nest around the nearest turn ...
>
> And so we stumbled out dim trails, still dreaming and still hoping
> That we might find the long lost turn, some day, that wandering home....[53]

Rice had wandered far from his beloved middle Tennessee to pursue his career. Henry Grantland Rice, the literary voice and public conscience of the '08 Nashville Vols, died in New York City on 14 July 1954. He is buried in Woodlawn Cemetery in the Bronx.

Kid Butler remained a Volunteer until the end of the 1909 season, and then he blazed a long trail through the minors.[54] Officially the property of

Toledo, he spent three years bouncing back and forth between the Mud Hens and Portland (OR) in the old Pacific Coast League. He returned to the Southern Association in 1913 to cover shortstop for Berny's final season in Memphis. Going west again, Butler landed in Spokane (1914) and player-manager in Victoria, British Columbia (1915). His wanderings extended from Wichita to St. Joseph and San Antonio prior to America's entry into the Great War. When the San Antonio franchise disbanded owing to the work or fight announcement, Butler joined the U.S. Army and was assigned to the 144th Field Artillery. Comprised mostly of Californians, his Grizzly Division saw action in France. Following his military discharge, Butler made his home in Richmond, California, and returned to play for San Antonio (1919), Sacramento (1920), Portland (1921), and two Canadian clubs—London and Brantford (1922).

It is unclear what form of employment Butler pursued immediately following his playing days, but he eventually reconnected with baseball. In 1929, he scouted the California region for the St. Louis Browns, and switched allegiances to the Cleveland Indians in 1942. He retired from baseball altogether in 1949.

Butler was a charter member of the Fresno and Richmond Posts of the American Legion. He also belonged to the 144th Field Artillery Association, the Professional Baseball Association of Los Angeles, and International Brotherhood of Teamsters. He retired as assistant manager of the Richmond (CA) Housing Authority. Willis Everett Butler, the key ingredient to the '08 Vols infield, died from a heart ailment on 22 February 1964. The Richmond Post officiated at his funeral at Golden Gate National Cemetery, San Bruno, California.

John Duggan amassed an unimpressive four-year record in Nashville: 9–19 (1906), and 8–10 (1907), 17–12 (1908), 14–13 (1909).[55] His standout year—the '08 championship season—led to a tryout with Pittsburgh the following spring, but nothing developed. Duggan suffered from chronic arm fatigue beginning in 1909, so as he never stuck with any minor league franchise more than a month after leaving Nashville—Indianapolis (1910), Trenton (1911), Mobile (1912), Decatur and Bloomington (1913), Appleton (1914), and Freeport (1915). He turned briefly to coaching baseball at Wabash College in 1913.

After baseball, Duggan plied the grocery trade in Whiteland (IN) for four years. In the mid-1920s, he lived in Pleasant, Johnson County, Indiana, where he worked as a rural mail carrier. After thirty-four years as a postal employee, he retired to Coral Gables, Florida, in the early 1960s. He died there on 20 April 1964. John Duggan, the inconsistent Hoosier who fired a no-hitter in '08, is buried in Flagler Memorial Park, Miami.

George Hunter joined the Trolley Dodgers' camp in 1909, but his major league career was short lived.[56] He lost his debut on 4 May against the Boston Braves to a familiar Southern Association foe—former Memphis ace Bill Chappelle. Over the course of the season Hunter compiled a 4–10 record, but he had the second-lowest ERA on the team — 2.46. The entire Brooklyn pitching staff struggled and manager Harry Lumley used seven starters who combined for only 55 wins. The adaptable Hunter appeared more frequently in the outfield — 23 times, but he batted only .228. Ebbets gave Hunter only one opportunity to prove his worth in 1910, and then released him to Montreal.

Wilkes-Barre purchased Hunter's contract, but a chronic sore arm from his Nashville experience combined with a leg injury in 1911 relegated the switch-hitter to the outfield. Elmira picked up Hunter midway through 1913 and he retired from the New York State League team four years later. In a last hurrah, he suited up for Steelton in the old Bethlehem Steel League and then retired for good.

Hunter, like Duggan, found steady employment with the U.S. Postal Service in Harrisburg (PA), and he retired in 1956 after twenty-seven years of service. On 11 January 1968, he passed away from bronchial pneumonia at age eighty. George Henry Hunter, the versatile utilityman on the '08 Vols, is buried at Rolling Green Memorial Park, Camp Hill, Pennsylvania.

Johnny Siegle's most productive year in Nashville occurred in 1908, when he struck for 114 base hits on the way to a .262 batting average.[57] His numbers dipped to 103 safeties and a .212 batting average the next season, and in an injury-plagued year (1910), he appeared in only 102 games and batted .203. Birmingham picked the outfielder off waivers in 1911, but there is no evidence that he ever wore a Barons uniform. With everyday playing behind him, Siegle turned to managing Gadsden (1912), Urbana and Akron (1913), and Huntington (W.Va.) (1914). He occasionally penciled himself into the lineup, but by 1915 the 40-year-old had washed out of baseball.

During his playing days, Johnny always wintered in Urbana and managed a bowling alley. Bigger things awaited Siegle in 1917 when he was elected sheriff of Champaign County. Four years later, he became Urbana's postmaster — a position he held for twelve years. He completed his tenure in public service as a member of the Champaign County Board of Elections for seventeen years. A staunch Republican like Wiseman, Siegle sat on the GOP Executive Committee at the state level. He was also extremely active in Masonic affairs and achieved high office. A member of the Urbana First Presbyterian Church for fifty years, Deacon Siegle volunteered as the church treasurer for twenty years.

John Herbert Siegle, the pivot man in the fastest outfield in the '08 Southern Association, passed away on 12 February 1968, from congestive heart failure three days after fracturing his hip. At age 93, Siegle earned the distinction of being the oldest member of the '08 Vols at time of death. He is buried in Oak Dale Cemetery, Urbana, Ohio.

There is no question that Berny's arrival in Nashville in 1908 reversed the baseball fortunes of Hub Perdue.[58] The Gallatin Squash improved the follow-

Hub Perdue in a Boston Braves uniform. (Bain collection, Library of Congress, Prints and Photographs Division, Washington, D.C.)

ing year and his 23 victories led the Southern Association. In 1910, his numbers dropped off (12–17), but the doormat Boston Braves were convinced that Perdue could bolster their sagging pitching staff.

Perdue began his rookie season in Boston on 19 April 1911, and finished with a 6–10 record (4.98 ERA). Not one of the Braves pitchers had generated more than eight wins and together they combined for only 44 victories; the hapless team trailed the champion New York Giants by 54 games. Perdue fared a little better in 1912 with a 13–16 record (3.80 ERA), and he ranked first in home runs allowed, fourth in hits and earned runs, and sixth in bases on balls. The Braves improved by eight wins but still trailed the Giants by 52 games while the crosstown Red Sox captured the American League title.

Perdue's finest season in the majors was in 1913. Under his third manager in as many years, Perdue led the Braves with a 16–13 record and an impressive 3.26 ERA. His fun-loving antics did not impress the rookie skipper, however. George Stallings had warned Perdue to take his at-bats seriously, but in his first plate appearances of the season, the jester struck out batting right-handed, and then left-handed. In his third attempt, Hub took two called strikes from the right side, changed over, and looked at the third strike from the left side. Stallings fumed, and from that moment on the manager and hurler did not get along. Fred Russell later opined that Perdue had clowned his way off the Braves' roster. While the team improved to 69 victories and rose to the middle of the National League standings, Stallings had bigger plans for Boston's future and they did not include Hub Perdue.

Perdue started slowly in 1914 and when his record sunk to 2–5, Stallings acted. He traded his happy-go-lucky hurler, who had bulked up to 200 lbs., to the St. Louis Cardinals for infielder George "Possum" Whitted and outfielder Ted Cather. Perdue was not exactly sent into baseball exile when he landed with the Cardinals. For much of the season, Miller Huggins' club had battled the Giants for supremacy of the National League. Perdue joined a successful rotation — Slim Sallee (18 wins / 6 saves) and Bill Doak (20 wins / league-leading 1.72 ERA). Perdue was less impressive — an 8–8 record but he carded a career-best 2.82 ERA. The Cardinals finished in third place, thirteen games behind Perdue's former teammates, "the Miracle Braves." When asked what he had gotten (implying cash) from his years in Boston, Hub replied in typical comic fashion: "I got smart!"[59]

Prior to his departure for St. Louis in 1915, Marion Perdue sat down with his big league son and had a serious talk. The elder Perdue noted with disappointment how Hub had always managed to squander his big league paychecks; so, he proposed a wager. If Hub could come home at the end of the season with any money whatsoever, he would match it. Hub returned to Gallatin penniless at the end of the season, but before going home, he paid a visit to the bank on the town square and took out a $3,000 loan. Pleased beyond all understanding at Hub's newfound thriftiness, the overjoyed father equaled the amount as promised. Then, Hub returned to the bank and repaid his short-term loan.

Hub's baseball world had turned upside-down in 1915 when he irritated an old elbow injury, and his production dropped drastically. Fifty years later, the happy-go-lucky pitcher confided that he had originally chipped the elbow in 1909, but did not seek medical attention to repair it until two years later; by then it was too late. Perdue went 6–12 and his ERA ballooned to 4.26, almost two points above his closest teammate. But, shades of the old Gallatin Squash returned on 15 August when Perdue pitched two-plus innings of winning relief against the New York Giants in the first game of a doubleheader, and then tossed seven innings in the nightcap to earn his second victory of the day. But such bravado was too late to save his career. The Cardinals released the Tennessean on 30 September 1915.

Perdue landed in Louisville, but he returned to the Southern Association in 1917, where he pitched remarkably well for sixth-place Chattanooga — a 15–10 record (1.95 ERA) in 217 innings. The following season he reunited with manager Johnny Dobbs and outfielder Larry Gilbert in New Orleans, where he registered the most league wins (12) in the war-shortened season. Two years later, at age 37, Perdue wrote his name into the Southern Association record book when he finished the 1919 season with an incredible 1.56 ERA — a mark that still stands. Allowing only 45 earned runs in 260 innings of work, Perdue coasted to a 17–12 record. When asked to identify his proudest accomplishment in baseball, Perdue pointed to the ERA record.[60]

Nashville was ecstatic when Perdue, one of the heroes of '08, returned to the Vols in 1920. Unfortunately, his elbow flared up, production dropped by over one hundred innings, and his record plummeted to 5–13. Yet, Perdue was selected player-manager for the next season. Great expectations were placed upon him in 1921 to restore the Vols to prominence. He failed to enforce team discipline, however, and was fired after a disappointing 62–90 mark, and 41½ games behind Memphis. Perdue's Southern Association experience had spanned nine seasons in which he amassed a 111–93 record. Perdue hung around the minors in Shreveport (1922) and Charlotte (1923), but he had lost his effectiveness as a player.

In retirement, he was briefly employed in Ferd Kuhn's shoe store, but he soon returned to the family farm on Scottsville Pike outside Gallatin. Later, he won election as Sumner County Clerk and held the post for twelve years. Throughout his life, Hub reveled in reminiscences about the bygone era of the spitball. "Baseball experts of the period agree that Perdue might have been a great pitcher," asserted *The Sporting News*, "if he had taken himself and his work more seriously."[61] The pride of Sumner County passed away in Gallatin on 31 October 1968, on an evening set aside for youthful costumed hijinx. The 83-year-old would have appreciated the irony of the date. Herbert Rodney Perdue, the homegrown Tennessee workhorse and last of the '08 Vols to pass away, is buried in Bethpage Cemetery, Sumner County, Tennessee, surrounded by generations of his ancestors.

Sulphur Dell continued to house minor league baseball until 1963. The park's trademark — its bizarre right field configuration — continued to attract attention throughout the decades. A young Montgomery outfielder named Casey Stengel once joked that he had laid a bunt down the first base line that carried for a home run. Famed *New York Times* sports columnist Arthur Daley could not believe what he saw in his first visit to the Dell in the 1930s. "I've heard about it [the Dump] all my life," said the Yankee scribe, "and I still don't believe it."[62] Near mid-twentieth century, Volunteer slugger Charlie Workman admitted that he loved roaming in right field: "It's a short distance to everything ... infield, dugouts, clubhouse, fans — and the hospital."[63]

In the mid–1920s, the strategy of the game had shifted from scientific baseball and playing for one run to the modern version which stressed power and the long ball. Thus, new ownership spearheaded by Nashville lumberman Stanley Horn called for renovating the rickety stadium with its unrealistic short right field porch, which lay within easy range of mediocre batters. At first, Horn's group searched for a new location, but when a suitable site was not found, they decided to dismantle the entire ballpark. Plans called for the infield to be turned completely around so that home plate was moved from the northeast to the southwest corner. A complex drainage system was installed beneath the playing surface, new grandstands with a seating capacity of 7,000 were erected, and a 16 foot wall enclosed the outfield. Rainy weather and the annual floods of the Cumberland River slowed construction, but the remodeled facility was ready for occupancy in 1927.

Two indelible traces from the old yard could not be erased: the original base paths remained faintly visible in the new outfield grass as did the former home plate area, owing to the olden days remedy of using oil to disperse rain puddles. Grass never did grow on the spot where Bay, McElveen, and Daubert had once dug in.

Another round of improvements to Sulphur Dell took place in the winter of 1930–31 when a tall screen was mounted atop the outfield wall from right to right center field. Perhaps the greatest technological innovation since the electric scoreboard in 1909 was the introduction of night baseball on 18 May 1931, a novelty that Fred Russell believes saved minor league baseball in Nashville.

Nashville continued to be a popular stop for major league teams as they played their way north at the conclusion of spring training. In the 1920s, the Bronx Bombers paid frequent visits to Sulphur Dell. On one memorable occasion in 1926, Lou Gehrig blasted one of the longest home runs ever seen at the Dell, planting it off the wall in straight away center field. Three years later, Babe Ruth entertained local fans while chasing a wild hare that had snuck under the right field fence. Yankee exhibitions were so important to the city's economy and image that the mayors always ordered a temporary halt to burning refuse in the real dump in an effort to quell obnoxious odors that locals compared to a smoldering mattress. In Ruth's final appearance (1934), the fire chief came up with an aggressive plan to douse the flames using fire engines, and then the Vols snapped the Yankees win streak at seventeen games in a smoky haze.

Great moments in Vols team history were recorded at the Dell throughout the decades. One of the greatest occurred on 11 July 1916, when Vols pitcher Tom Rogers threw the only perfect game in stadium history. His 2–0 shutout overshadowed a great performance by Chattanooga Lookout pitcher Jim "Lefty" Allen, who tossed a one-hitter. The umpires on that occasion were Old Dan Pfenninger and Ted Breitenstein. Rogers (1916) joined Duggan as the only Nashville hurlers ever to throw a no-hitter at Sulphur Dell. In 1925, Johnny Bates hit safely in 46 consecutive games for another nostalgic memory. In the early 1930s, the Nashville Elite Giants used the facility for several seasons in the old Negro league. Over the years, Sulphur Dell hosted a variety of famous barnstormers, including Ted Williams, Warren Spahn, Johnny Sain, Lefty Gomez, and Chuck Connors (*The Rifleman*). LBJ politicked and Max Patkin, the clown prince of baseball, entertained there.

12-17-26

WILES
NASHVILLE, TENN.

J. B. Hanson Co.
Contractors and Engineers
Nashville Baseball Stadium

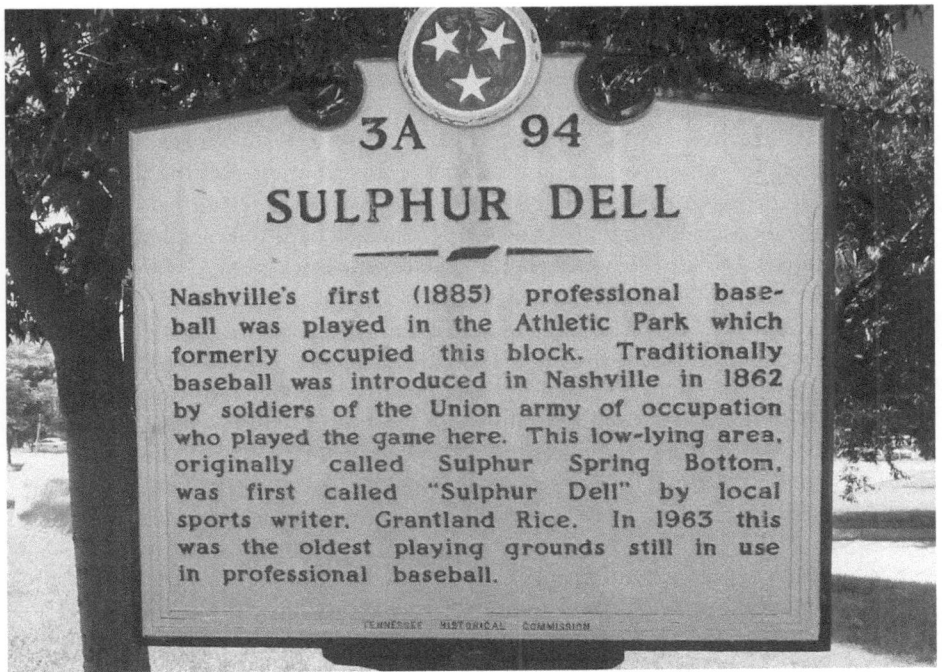

This historical marker stands at the original location of home plate at Sulphur Dell, where the Vols won the 1908 Southern Association championship.

By mid-century, the Nashville Vols franchise had won nine Southern Association pennants in Sulphur Dell—1901, 1902, 1908, 1916, 1940, 1943, 1944, 1948, 1949. Larry Gilbert had captured four of the flags during his managerial career, which spanned the 1940s. From 1915–1950, the Vols drew 4.3 million fans. The largest gate (14,502) occurred on Opening Day, 1932, and the smallest crowd (21) showed up on 10 September 1937. WSM, "the air castle of the South," carried the first Vols game on radio, but Larry Munson of WKDA was the announcer most associated with Nashville baseball.

By the late 1950s, the Southern Association was struggling for financial survival. The Vols had became a public-owned corporation in 1959, but the league folded three years later. In 1963, Nashville joined the SALLY, and Sulphur Dell held the distinction as the oldest operational baseball park in the country when the last game was played there on 8 September 1963.

In October, 1964, the Sulphur Dell Speedway group, headed by country

Opposite: Sulphur Dell renovation in 1926. The old infield and pitcher's rubber are on the far right. (Courtesy of the Tennessee State Library and Archives, Nashville, TN.)

music star Faron Young, bought the property and planned to construct a quarter-mile stock car track. In the meantime, the stadium hosted rock 'n' roll concerts. Little Stevie Wonder, Dionne Warwick, James Brown, Gladys Knight, and B.B. King along with other personalities, such as wrestler Gorgeous George, entertained crowds in the historic ballyard. Sulphur Dell was razed in 1966, and today its location is the site of a state government parking lot on the east side of Bicentennial Capitol Mall. The Tennessee Historical Commission unveiled an historic marker and fountain where the original stadium once stood. Aging historian and one-time team owner Stanley Horn gave an oration.

At the time, few local citizens seemed to care about the loss of Sulphur Dell. Fred Russell refused to allow the public's recollection of the stadium to completely fade away, however. In 1970, he addressed the Tennessee Historical Society on the history of Sulphur Dell, and in his eighty-eighth year, the retired icon wrote a column entitled "Too bad historic Sulphur Dell not here for State Bicentennial."[64] For people like Russell, the memory of Sulphur Dell was simply too ingrained in Nashville sports culture to be forgotten.

Today, there is an electronic effort afoot to remember Sulphur Dell. An internet website, www.sulphurdell.com, contains a link called "I remember..." which is filled with personal reminiscences about the old park. One individual described Vols games at the Dell as a multi-sensory experience. "You just don't see 'em like that anymore: Sulphur Dells and Dads," noted a former patron. Another contributor captured the emotion of the defunct ballyard:

> The last day I was with my dad before he passed away in the summer of 2000 we drove to the site of Sulphur Dell. What made me want to pull into the parking lot was when he saw the old Atlantic Ice house that stood behind right field. He had just told me that he once got a ball out of the gutter there when he was a kid. I could tell he was excited to see the old site of Sulphur Dell, so I pulled into the State parking lot and stopped about where I figured the pitcher's mound was. He said he had many great memories as a child himself as a part-time batboy and as a spectator. I told him I can sit here and look around and ... sort of see the old infield in my mind, the noise, and I even seemed to begin smelling that old cigar and pipe smell. We were quiet when we pulled out of the lot and were both smiling with those wonderful memories that we had just shared together for the last time.[65]

Sentimental memories of old ballparks like Sulphur Dell have always had a way of bringing families into closer relationship. Our emotional attachment to these recollections explains, in part, why the game of baseball is so deeply rooted in the American folk fabric.

Fred Russell was born in Nashville on 27 August 1907, to John and Mabel Russell. When he was only six weeks old his parents moved to Wartrace in rural Bedford County, where is father plied the trade of a traveling salesman. Shortly after a memorable trip to see a Vols game, Russell's family returned to the city where young Fred enrolled in Duncan Preparatory School. The studious lad spent much time reading the sports columns in the daily newspapers, memorizing the baseball poetry of Grantland Rice, and attending Vols games. Russell fondly remembered Boy's Day — held every Monday — when youngsters were admitted at no charge to the bleachers. "One of my earliest remembered thrills after moving back to Nashville," said Russell, "was the day at old Sulphur Dell when Clarence Jonnard let me carry his shin guards and protector into the park and take them to the dugout. ... All the kids would vie for the favor of the Vols."[66]

Russell entered Vanderbilt University in 1923, where he pitched and played second base for the Commodores. Later he enrolled in law school and passed the Tennessee Bar Exam six months after graduation, but he did not like the legal trade. So, in 1929, he joined the staff of the *Nashville Banner*, where he was assigned the police beat, Vanderbilt football, and local sports in general. "I'd always imagined sports writing must be the greatest life in the world," Russell later admitted.[67] Within a year, the hard-working reporter had risen to sports editor — a position he held for the next 39 years.

Russell forged a career practically unmatched in journalism. He combined thorough knowledge and care to detail, and possessed a lively writing style and pleasing personality. Associates remember Russell as tough and demanding but fair. He possessed a marvelous sense of humor and enjoyed practical jokes. Subjects liked Russell because he took a genuine interest in them as people. He deeply admired Grantland Rice and the pair became lifelong friends. Some observed that Rice and Russell had developed a quasi father-son relationship over the years.

Russell wasn't even one year old when the Nashville Vols participated in one of the most exciting finishes in Southern Association history. He later learned about the miraculous '08 championship from newspaper clippings in the *Tennessean, American, and Banner,* as well as from oral tradition. Although Russell did not possess first-hand knowledge about the '08 Vols, he was personally responsible for keeping their championship game alive in the 1930s with two reprints of Yancey's original play-by-play account in the *Banner*. And he personally knew the Tennessee stars — Hub Perdue and Pryor McElveen.

The lapse of time played tricks on Russell's memory as he struggled to remember details about the '08 season in an interview on 7 April 1999.[68] The kindly nonagenarian recalled only vague pieces about Perdue, McElveen, and Wiseman, and he did not recollect the '08 campaign or championship game at all. And naturally so. It is safe to say that, on the dawn of the twenty-first century, the dean of Nashville sports journalism had forgotten more about Volunteer baseball than most people had ever known. Fred McFerrin Russell passed away on 26 January 2003, at age 96 — an American original — just like his closest friend, Granny Rice. He is buried in Mt. Olivet Cemetery, Nashville.

They're all gone now — Berny, Gentleman Jake, Kid, Humpy, Scrappy Jack, Deerfoot, Big Ed, Win, the Gallatin Squash, Sitton, and the popular sandy-haired outfielder named Doc, who combed the Dump with pinpoint precision. But, it wouldn't take much for one to lean back and reminisce about that balmy September afternoon a century ago... at the precise moment when the little Doctor stepped up to the dish, the crowd holding its collective breath... Breit's delivery from the slab... the whip-like crack echoing from Wiseman's bat, the fans spontaneously erupting into cheers as Hurlburt chugged for home... and three sportswriters bug-eyed with anticipation in the wooden press box atop the grandstand. Perhaps Rice had already formulated the words he would use to capture this precise moment in Nashville sports history. And for those who know about the Vols and their sensational climax to the '08 season, perhaps it really was the greatest game ever played in Dixie.

Appendix A:
Players' Careers

Based on player contract cards on file at the National Baseball Hall of Fame Library, Cooperstown, New York, and *The Sporting News Archive*, St. Louis, Missouri. Major League experience is listed in bold type.

Harry Elbert Bay (Deerfoot)

1897	Peoria	1908	Nashville
1898	Lincoln/Rock Island/Troy	1909	Nashville
1899	Detroit/Marion	1910	Nashville
1900	Indianapolis	1911	Nashville
1901	Indianapolis/**Cincinnati**	1912	Bloomington (manager)
1902	**Cincinnati/Cleveland**	1913	Madison
1903	**Cleveland**	1914	Madison
1904	**Cleveland**	1915	Mason City
1905	**Cleveland**	1916	Mason City/Rock Island
1906	**Cleveland**	1917	Alton
1907	**Cleveland**		

William Henry Bernhard (Strawberry Bill)

1897	New York State League	1904	**Cleveland**
1898	New York State League	1905	**Cleveland**
1899	**Philadelphia** (N.L.)	1906	**Cleveland**
1900	**Philadelphia** (N.L.)	1907	**Cleveland**
1901	**Philadelphia** (A.L.)	1908	Nashville (manager)
1902	**Cleveland**	1909	Nashville (manager)
1903	**Cleveland**	1910	Memphis (manager)

1911   Memphis (manager)
1912   Memphis (manager)
1913   Southern Association (umpire)
1914   Salt Lake City (manager)
1915   Chattanooga (manager/umpire)
1916   Southern Association (umpire)
1917   Salt Lake City (manager)

Willis Everett Butler (Kid)

1904   Toledo/Augusta (GA)
1905   Toledo/Youngstown
1906   Toledo/Akron
1907   Akron/Toledo/**St. Louis** (A.L.)
1908   Nashville
1909   Nashville
1910   Tulsa/Seattle
1911   Seattle/Salt Lake City/Portland
1912   Portland/New Orleans
1913   Memphis
1914   Spokane
1915   Victoria (Canada) (manager)
1916   Victoria (manager)
1917   St. Joseph/San Antonio
1918   Served in World War 1
1919   San Antonio
1920   Sacramento
1921   Portland
1922   London/Brantford (Canada)
1929–1941   **St. Louis** (A.L.) (scout)
1942–1949   **Cleveland** (scout)

Jacob Ellsworth Daubert (Gentleman Jake)

1907   Kane/Marion
1908   Nashville
1909   Toledo/Memphis
1910   **Brooklyn**
1911   **Brooklyn**
1912   **Brooklyn**
1913   **Brooklyn**
1914   **Brooklyn**
1915   **Brooklyn**
1916   **Brooklyn**
1917   **Brooklyn**
1918   **Brooklyn**
1919   **Cincinnati**
1920   **Cincinnati**
1921   **Cincinnati**
1922   **Cincinnati**
1923   **Cincinnati**
1924   **Cincinnati**

Johnny Duggan

1905   Vincesnnes
1906   Nashville
1907   Nashville
1908   Nashville
1909   Nashville
1910   Indianapolis
1911   Trenton
1912   Mobile
1913   Wabash College (coach)
       Decatur/Bloomington
1914   Appleton
1915   Freeport

Walter Rufus East

1904   Akron
1905   Akron
1906   Akron
1907   Akron
1908   Little Rock/Nashville
1909   Nashville
1910   Buffalo/Montreal
1911   Montreal/Memphis
1912   Atlanta/Kansas City
1913   Mansfield

John Dolittle Hardy (Scrappy Jack)

1902	Ft. Wayne	1910	**Washington**/Montreal
1903	Los Angeles/Ft. Wayne/**Cleveland**	1911	Montreal
1904	Ft. Wayne	1912	
1905	Ft. Wayne/Sharon	1913	
1906	Nashville	1920	Petersburg/Bradenton/Bartow
1907	Nashville/**Chicago** (N.L.)	1921	Huron/Joplin/Omaha/Denver
1908	Nashville	1922	Denver
1909	Mobile/Columbus/**Washington**		

Jack Hess (Heinie)

1904	Springfield	1908	Nashville/Raleigh
1905	Springfield	1909	Northhampton/Lawrence
1906	Springfield	1910	Northhampton
1907	Springfield	1911	New Britain/Roanoke

George Henry Hunter

1906	Wilkes-Barre	1911	Wilkes-Barre/Rochester
1907	Wilkes-Barre/Buffalo/Wilkes-Barre	1912	Wilkes-Barre
1908	Nashville	1913	Wilkes-Barre/Elmira
1909	**Brooklyn**/Montreal/Wilkes-Barre	1914	Elmira
		1915	Elmira
1910	Montreal	1916	Elmira
		1917	Elmira

Edward Leroy Hurlbut (Big Ed)

1901	Spokane	1906	Memphis
1902	Spokane	1907	Memphis/Atlanta
1903	Seattle	1908	Atlanta/Nashville
1904	Memphis	1909	Nashville/Memphis
1905	Memphis		

Henry Augustus Jansing (Swede)

1901	Vancouver (B.C.)	1907	out of baseball
1902	Vancouver (B.C.)	1908	Nashville/Memphis
1903	Seattle	1909	Oakland
1904	Montgomery	1910	Tacoma/Hoquiam
1905	Nashville	1911	Hoquiam/Tacoma
1906	Nashville	1912	Tacoma/Boise/Tacoma

Winford Ansley Kellum (Win)

1895	Quincy	1899	Indianapolis
1896	Montgomery	1900	Indianapolis
1897	Indianapolis	1901	**Boston** (A.L.)/New Orleans
1898	Indianapolis	1902	Indianapolis

1903	Indianapolis	1909	Nashville
1904	**Cincinnati**	1910	Wheeling
1905	**St. Louis** (N.L.)/Toledo	1911	Southern League (umpire)
1906	Indianapolis	1912	Southern League (umpire)
1907	Indianapolis	1913	Southern League (umpire)
1908	Nashville	1914	Southern League (umpire)

Michael J. McCormick (Dude)

1901	Waterbury	1909	Holyoke
1902	Holyoke	1910	Toledo/St. Paul
1903	Holyoke	1911	St. Paul
1904	**Brooklyn**	1912	St. Paul
1905	Holyoke (player-manager)	1913	Portland
1906	Holyoke (player-manager)	1914	New Haven (player-manager)
1907	Nashville	1915	**Chicago** (N.L.) (scout)
1908	Nashville/suspended		**Brooklyn** (scout)

Pryor Mynatt McElveen (Humpy)

1904	Carson-Newman College	1910	**Brooklyn**/Atlanta
1905	Carson-Newman/Meridian	1911	**Brooklyn**/Atlanta
1906	Knoxville/Jacksonville	1912	Atlanta
1907	Nashville	1913	Atlanta/Beaumont
1908	Nashville	1914	Knoxville/Portsmouth
1909	**Brooklyn**/Montgomery	1915	Shreveport

Herbert Rodney Perdue (The Gallatin Squash)

1905	Vincennes	1915	**St. Louis** (N.L.)
1906	Vincennes	1916	Louisville
1907	Nashville	1917	Chattanooga
1908	Nashville	1918	New Orleans
1909	Nashville	1919	New Orleans
1910	Rochester	1920	Wichita Falls/Nashville
1911	**Boston** (N.L.)	1921	Nashville (manager)
1912	**Boston** (N.L.)	1922	Shreveport/Wichita Falls
1913	**Boston** (N.L.)	1923	Charlotte
1914	**Boston** (N.L.)/**St. Louis** (N.L.)		

James Warren Seabough (Doc)

1904	Pittsburg (KS)	1910	Nashville
1905	Springfield	1911	Nashville
1906	Springfield	1912	Nashville/Memphis
1907	Montgomery	1913	Memphis
1908	Nashville	1914	Ogden/Omaha
1909	Nashville	1915	Omaha

Johnny Herbert Siegle

1899	Dayton/Columbus/Grand Rapids	1907	Cincinnati/Indianapolis
1900	Ilion (New York State League)	1908	Nashville
1901	Ilion (New York State League)	1909	Nashville
1902	Ilion (New York State League)	1910	Nashville
1903	Ilion (New York State League)	1911	Birmingham
1904	Coach at Columbia University	1912	Gadsden (manager)
1905	Coach at Columbia University	1913	Urbana/Akkron
1906	Cincinnati/Indianapolis	1914	Huntington (WVa.) (manager)

Carl Vedder Sitton

1901	Clemson College	1910	Columbus/**Brooklyn**/Atlanta
1902	Clemson College	1911	Atlanta
1903	Clemson College	1912	Atlanta
1906	Spartanburg	1913	Troy
1907	Jacksonville	1914	Troy
1908	Jacksonville/Nashville	1915	Troy/Binghamton
1909	**Cleveland**	1916	Binghamton

Bill Sorrell

1908	Nashville/Waco	1911	Jackson (manager)
1909	Shreveport	1912	Meridian/Ft. Worth
1910	Jackson (manager)	1913	New Orleans

Julius Augustus Wiseman (Doc)

1896	Mobile	1905	Nashville
1897	University of Cincinnati	1906	Nashville
1898	New Orleans	1907	Nashville
1901	Nashville	1908	Nashville
1902	Nashville	1909	Nashville
1903	Nashville	1910	Nashville
1904	Nashville	1911	Nashville

Stanley Lewis Yerkes

1901	**Baltimore/St. Louis (N.L.)**	1905	Buffalo
1902	**St. Louis (N.L.)**	1906	Buffalo
1903	**St. Louis (N.L.)**/Buffalo	1907	Nashville
1904	Buffalo	1908	Nashville/Galveston

Theodore P. Breitenstein (Breit)

1891	Grand Rapids/**St. Louis (AA)**	1896	**St. Louis (N.L.)**
1892	**St. Louis (N.L.)**	1897	**Cincinnati**
1893	**St. Louis (N.L.)**	1898	**Cincinnati**
1894	**St. Louis (N.L.)**	1898	**Cincinnati**
1895	**St. Louis (N.L.)**	1899	**Cincinnati**

1900	**Cincinnati**	1911	New Orleans (assistant manager)
1901	**St. Louis** (N.L.)/St. Paul	1912	Southern Association (umpire)
1902	Memphis	1913	Southern Association (umpire)
1903	Memphis	1914	Southern Association (umpire)
1904	New Orleans	1915	Southern Association (umpire)
1905	New Orleans	1916	Southern Association (umpire)
1906	New Orleans	1917	Southern Association (umpire)
1907	New Orleans	1918	Southern Association (umpire)
1908	New Orleans	1921	Southwestern League/Texas League (umpire)
1909	New Orleans		
1910	New Orleans (assistant manager)		

Appendix B: Linescores for the Vols' 1908 Season

The linescores have been modernized so as not to confuse the reader. In the Deadball Era, the linescore appearing beneath the box score in newspapers sometimes put the home team on the top line, regardless of whether they batted first or last. Sometimes the winning team was put on top regardless of whether they batted first or last. And, sometimes the newspaper accounts put a "0" in the 9th inning instead of an "X" even if the team didn't come to bat. The format for linescoring was all a matter of preference chosen by the sports editor.

Game 1 April 16

        Nashville   010 000 000   1 2 1
        Atlanta   210 000 00x   3 7 1

(WP: Ford; LP: Sorrell 0–1) Ump: Pfenninger. Attendance: 6,000. Time: 1:50 (Attendance figures and length of game information are occasionally unavailable)

Game 2 April 17

        Nashville   000 200 001   3 5 1
        Atlanta   000 000 000   0 4 3

(WP: Duggan 1–0; LP: Castleton) Ump: Pfenninger. A: 3,000. T: 1:45

No Decision April 20

        Montgomery   000 000 120 000 000   3 6 1
        Nashville   020 000 001 000 000   3 15 1

(Thomas vs. Hunter) Ump: Brown. A: 4,400. T: 2:40

236   Appendix B

Game 3   April 21
        Montgomery   020 001 110   5 10 1
        Nashville   010 000 000   1 6 4
(WP: Van Ada; LP: Sorrell 0–2) Ump: Brown. A: 2,000. T: 1:45

Game 4   April 22
        Montgomery   030 002 010   6 12 3
        Nashville   000 400 010   5 6 3
(WP: Cristall; LP: Duggan 1–1) Ump: Brown. A: 1,500. T: 1:10

Game 5   April 23
        Montgomery   000 010 100   2 3 0
        Nashville   000 100 03x   4 11 1
(WP: Perdue 1–0; LP: Helm) Ump: Brown. A: 1,500. T: 1:32

Game 6   April 25
        Birmingham   000 000 000   0 7 1
        Nashville   000 000 30x   3 7 3
(WP: Hess 1–0; LP: Robitaille) Ump: Brown. A: 3,000. T: 1:40

Game 7   April 27
        Birmingham   001 300 020   6 6 2
        Nashville   000 100 06x   7 9 4
(WP: Hunter 1–0; LP: McNeal) Ump: Brown. A: 1,500. T: 1:45

Game 8   April 28
        Birmingham   200 100 000   4 9 0
        Nashville   000 000 100   1 10 4
(WP: Fleharty; LP: Duggan 1–2) Ump: Brown. A: 1,500. T: 1:36

Game 9   April 29
        Nashville   100 000 000   1 7 2
        Montgomery   000 011 20x   4 14 1
(WP: Thomas; LP: Perdue 1–1) Ump: Pfenninger. T: 1:55

Game 10   April 30
        Nashville   100 000 000   1 5 3
        Montgomery   200 000 02x   4 9 1
(WP: Stackpole; LP: Hess 1–1) Ump: Pfenninger.

Game 11   May 1
        Nashville   000 000 032   5 8 1
        Montgomery   000 000 000   0 5 4
(WP: Kellum 1–0; LP Merriman) Ump: Pfenninger. T: 1:55

Game 12   May 2
        Nashville   000 001 000   1 7 3
        Montgomery   101 100 00x   3 8 4
(WP: Duggan 2–2; LP: McNeal) Ump: Pfenninnger. T: 1:35

Game 13   May 4
        Nashville   003 000 000   3 8 1
        Birmingham   010 010 000   1 10 4
(WP: Duggan 2–2; LP: McNeal) Ump: Brown. T: 1:30

Game 14 May 7
        Nashville   100 000 000   1 2 2
        Birmingham   010 101 01x   4 12 1
(WP: Tumer; LP: Perdue 1–2) Ump: Brown. A: 450. T: 1:56

Game 15 May 8
        Atlanta   000 002 020   4 7 0
        Nashville   100 000 000   1 6 1
(WP: Ford; LP: Hess 1–2) Ump: Brown. T: 1:45

Game 16 May 9
        Atlanta   000 001 000   1 9 1
        Nashville   000 010 10x   2 5 0
(WP: Kellum 2–0; LP: McKenzie) Ump: Brown. A: 1,500. T: 1:37

Game 17 May 11
        Atlanta   101 000 000   2 4 0
        Nashville   201 010 00x   4 8 2
(WP: Yerkes 1–0; LP: Cummings) Ump: Brown. A: 1,500. T: 1:57

Game 18 May 12
        Atlanta   050 000 001   6 8 1
        Nashville   010 400 000   5 7 2
[WP: Ford; Perdue (7), LP: Duggan (2) 2–3] Ump: Brown. A: 2,000. T: 2:30

Game 19 May 14
        Nashville   000 400 200   6 6 2
        Memphis   100 001 000   2 8 2
(WP: Duggan 3–3; LP: Chappelle) Umps: Fitzsimmons, Carpenter. T: 1:40

Game 20 May 15
        Nashville   111 001 100   5 7 0
        Memphis   000 000 100   1 5 0
(WP: Hess 2–2; LP: Savidge) Umps: Fitzsimmons, Carpenter. T: 1:30

Game 21 May 16
        Nashville   011 000 001   3 5 1
        Memphis   100 010 000   2 7 1
(WP: Hunter 2–1; LP: Garrity) Umps: Fitzsimmons, Carpenter. T: 1:45

Game 22 May 18
        Nashville   100 120 001   5 9 1
        Little Rock   000 120 000   3 5 3
(WP: Perdue 2–2; LP: Connelly) Ump: Fitzsimmons. T: 1:40

Game 23 May 19
        Nashville   000 100 000   1 6 3
        Little Rock   200 000 01x   3 6 4
(WP: Hart; LP: Kellum 2–1) Ump: Fitzsimmons. T: 1:50

Game 24 May 20
        Nashville   000 010 0   1   4 3
        Little Rock   200 053 x   10 15 3
[WP: Eyler; LP: Hess (5) 2–3; Yerkes (2)] Ump: Fitzsimmons. T: 1:25

No decision   May 21
    Nashville   000 000 000 000 0   0 6 0
    New Orleans 000 000 000 000 0   0 7 3
(Duggan vs. Ryan) Umps: Carpenter, Brown. T: 2:35

Game 25 May 22
    Nashville   000 000 100   1 5 5
    New Orleans 001 010 02x   4 6 0
(WP: Bartley; LP: Hunter 2–2) Ump: Brown. T: 1:40

Game 26 May 23
    Nashville   100 000 000   1 2 5
    New Orleans 000 120 43x 10 15 3
(WP: Guese; LP: Perdue 2–3) Ump: Brown. T: 1:58

Game 27 May 24
    Nashville   000 000 000   0 6 1
    New Orleans 011 002 01x   5 7 1
(WP: Bartley; LP: Hess 2–4) Ump: Brown. T: 1:40

Game 28 May 25
    Nashville   000 001 000 1   2 8 3
    Mobile   000 001 000 0   1 8 2
(WP: Kellum 3–1; LP: Torrey) Ump: Carpenter. T: 1:50

Game 29 May 26
    Nashville   000 040 240 10 12 4
    Mobile   100 030 000   4 7 7
[Yerkes (6), WP: Duggan (3) 4–3; LP: Beeker] Ump: Carpenter. T: 2:20

Game 30 May 29
    Memphis   000 100 000   1 6 3
    Nashville   051 000 12x   9 16 1
[WP: Hunter (8) 3–2, Duggan (1); LP: Garrity] Ump: Fitzsimmons. A: 3,000. T: 1:45

Game 31 May 30 (first game of doubleheader)
    Memphis   000 000 000 000 1   1 15 2
    Nashville   000 000 000 000 0   0 7 1
(WP: Savidge; LP: Duggan 4–4) Ump: Fitzsimmons. A: 4,000. T: 2:14

Game 32 May 30 (second game of doubleheader)
    Memphis   020 003 0   5 7 1
    Nashville   110 000 0   2 6 4
(WP: Chapelle; LP: Hess 2–5) Ump: Fitzsimmons. T: 125

Game 33 May 31
    Nashville   000 100 000   1 4 2
    Memphis   002 001 01x   4 10 0
(WP: Shields; LP: Perdue 2–4) Ump: Pfennninger. T: 1:50

Game 34 June 1
    Memphis   100 000 000   1 7 4
    Nashville   001 020 00x   3 5 1
(WP: Kellum 4–1; LP: Garrity) Ump: Fitzsimmons. A: 1,500. T: 1:35

Game 35 June 2
        New Orleans   000 100 022   5 11 1
        Nashville   000 000 020   2 11 1
[WP: Guese; LP: Yerkes (8+) 1-2, Duggan (1)] Ump: Carpenter. A: 1,800. T: 1:45

Game 36 June 4
        New Orleans   001 000 010   2 8 3
        Nashville   200 000 001   3 11 0
[Perdue (8), WP: Duggan 5-4; LP: Clark] Ump: Carpenter. A: 1,500. T: 1:57

Game 37 June 5
        New Orleans   000 000 011   2 6 3
        Nashville   400 010 00x   5 8 0
(WP: Duggan 6-4; LP: Bartley) Ump: Carpenter. A: 1,800. T: 1:30

Game 38 June 6
        Mobile   200 001 200   5 15 1
        Nashville   000 000 020   2 8 2
(WP: Beeker; LP: Kellum 4-2) Ump: Pfenninger. A: 2,800. T: 1:57

Game 39 June 8
        Mobile   000 000 010   1 7 4
        Nashville   212 000 12x   8 17 2
(WP: Perdue 3-4; LP: Torrey) Ump: Pfenninger. A: 1,400. T: 1:33

Game 40 June 9
        Mobile   010 101 000   3 8 0
        Nashville   000 000 001   1 5 2
(WP: Stockdale; LP: Yerkes 1-3) Ump: Pfenninger. A: 1,500. T: 1:34

Game 41 June 10
        Mobile   000 000 000   0 5 0
        Nashville   000 002 10x   3 9 1
(WP: Duggan 7-4; LP: Beeker) Ump: Pfenninger. A: 1,200. T: 1:40

Game 42 June 11
        Little Rock   202 000 004   8 13 1
        Nashville   200 000 000   2 9 2
(WP: Eyler; LP: Bernhard 0-1) Ump: Brown. A: 1,599. T: 1:47

Game 43 June 12
        Little Rock   000 000 000   0 4 4
        Nashville   001 003 12x   7 11 2
(WP: Perdue 4-4; LP: Walters) Ump: Brown. A: 1,200. T: 1:40

Game 44 June 13
        Little Rock   303 010 001   8 11 1
        Nashville   000 000 100   1 7 2
(WP: Eastman; LP: Kellum 4-3) Ump: Brown. A: 1,500. T: 1:50

Game 45 June 15
        Birmingham   001 010 031   6 13 2
        Nashville   000 000 000   0 3 0
(WP: Robitaille; LP: Duggan 7-5) Ump: Carpenter. A: 1,100. T: 1:31

Game 46 June 16
  Birmingham   010 200 000   3 8 2
  Nashville   200 200 100   5 11 2
(WP: Perdue 5-4; LP: Turner) Ump: Carpenter. A: 1,300. T: 1:47

Game 47 June 17
  Birmingham   000 000 000   0 7 2
  Nashville   000 400 02x   6 7 0
(WP: Kellum 5-3; LP: Robinson) Ump: Carpenter. A: 1,500. T: 1:32

Game 48 June 18
  Montgomery   000 000 010   1 8 2
  Nashville   101 001 02x   5 8 5
(WP: Bernhard 1-1; LP: Cristall) Ump: Carpenter. A: 1,500. T: 1:35

Game 49 June 19
  Montgomery   000 000 002   2 4 0
  Nashville   002 010 40x   7 11 1
(WP: Duggan 8-5; LP: Guese) Ump: Carpenter. A: 1,500. T: 1:45

Game 50 June 20
  Montgomery   000 000 000   0 6 5
  Nashville   110 200 40x   8 9 1
(WP: Perdue 6-4; LP: Juul) Ump: Carpenter. A; 3,000 T: 1:53

Game 51 June 22
  Nashville   000 121 001   5 9 1
  Atlanta   020 100 100   4 8 2
[Yerkes (3), WP: Kellum (6) 6-3; LP: Schopp] Umps: Carpenter, Brown. T: 2:00

Game 52 June 23 (first game of doubleheader)
  Nashville   200 020 000   5 7 1
  Atlanta   000 010 000   1 6 0
[WP: Perdue 7-4; LP: Cummings (1), Johns (8)] Umps: O'Brien, Carpenter. T: 1:55

Game 53 June 23 (second game of doubleheader)
  Nashville   000 000 100   1 4 3
  Atlanta   000 120 01x   4 5 0
(WP: Castleton; LP: Duggan 8-6) Umps: O'Brien, Carpenter. T: 2:02

Game 54 June 24
  Nashville   000 000 000   0 3 2
  Atlanta   003 001 10x   5 11 1
(WP: Ford; LP: Bernhard 1-2) Ump: Carpenter. T: 1:30

Game 55 June 25
  Nashville   000 000 102   3 7 3
  Montgomery   010 000 21x   4 6 2
(WP: Guese; LP: Kellum 6-4) Ump: Fitzsimmons. T: 1:35

Game 56 June 26
  Nashville   000 001 000   1 3 3
  Montgomery   010 001 00x   2 7 1
(WP: Thomas; LP: Perdue 7-5) Ump: Fitzsimmons. T: 1:35

Linescores for the Vols' 1908 Season 241

Game 57 June 27 FORFEIT LOSS
        Nashville   110 100 0   3 6 0
        Montgomery   010 001 0   2 5 2
(WP: Duggan 9–6; LP: McCafferty) Ump: Fitzsimmons. T: 1:10

Game 58 June 30
        Atlanta   000 000 100   1 2 2
        Nashville   000 102 00x   3 8 2
[Hunter (1), WP: Duggan (8) 10–6; LP: Ford] Ump: O'Brien. A: 1,500. T: 1:35

Game 59 July 1
        Atlanta   000 000 000   0 3 0
        Nashville   011 030 00x   5 8 1
(WP: Perdue 8–5; LP: Schopp) Ump: O'Brien. A: 1,600. T: 1:53

Game 60 July 3
        Nashville   200 000 300   5 8 3
        Birmingham   000 000 200   2 4 2
[WP: Kellum 7–4; LP: McNeal (2), Robinson (7)] Ump: O'Brien. T: 2:00

Game 61 July 4
        Nashville   010 000 004   5 7 1
        Birmingham   200 000 000   2 7 2
[WP: Duggan 11–6; LP: Bauer (8+), Raub (1)] Ump: O'Brien. A: 1,500. T: 2:10

Game 62 July 5
        Nashville   100 000 000   1 2 2
        New Orleans 010 000 001   2 8 2
(WP: Clark; LP: Perdue 8–6) Ump: O'Brien. T: 1:43

Game 63 July 6
        Nashville   200 000 000   2 6 0
        New Orleans 000 000 000   0 3 1
(WP: Kellum 8–4; LP: Breitenstein) Ump: O'Brien. T: 1:27

Game 64 July 7
        Nashville   010 002 000   3 10 2
        New Orleans 000 000 100   1 6 2
(WP: Duggan 12–6; LP: Bartley) Ump: O'Brien. T: 1:47

No decision July 9
        Nashville   000 000 000 000 000 00   0 9 2
        Mobile   000 000 000 000 000 00   0 8 0
(Perdue vs. Torrey) Ump: Carpenter. T: 2:52

Game 65 July 10
        Nashville   000 000 110 1   3 8 4
        Mobile   000 101 000 0   2 4 1
[WP: Hunter 4–2; Beeker (9), LP: Gaskill] Ump: Carpenter. T: 2:07

Game 66 July 11
        Nashville   000 010 000   1 4 2
        Mobile   000 002 00x   2 2 0
(WP: Hickman; LP: Kellum 8–5) Ump: Carpenter. T: 1:35

Game 67 July 12
    Nashville   010 004 010   6 9 1
    Mobile   000 200 001   3 6 7
(WP: Bernhard 2-2; LP: Gaskill) Ump: Carpenter. T: 1:50

No decision July 13
    Nashville   200 100 000 000 0   3 9 1
    Little Rock   030 000 000 000 0   3 13 1
(Perdue vs. Eyler) Umps: Wood, Hardy. T: 2:10

Game 68 July 14
    Nashville   000 010 000   1 7 1
    Little Rock   000 001 03x   4 10 1
(WP: Hart; LP: Hunter 4-3) Ump: Hale. T: 1:50

Game 69 July 15 (first game of doubleheader)
    Nashville   000 000 010   1 3 2
    Little Rock   000 000 002   2 9 2
(WP Eastman; LP: Duggan 12-7) Umps: Moran, Hale. T: 1:30

Game 70 July 15 (second game of doubleheader)
    Nashville   100 100 030   5 7 0
    Little Rock   000 101 011   4 15 4
(WP: Kellum 9-5; LP: Buchanan) Umps: Moran, Hale. T: 140

Game 71 July 17
    Nashville   002 000 000 01   3 11 0
    Memphis   000 020 000 00   2 8 2
(WP: Perdue 9-6; LP: Chappelle) Ump: Moran. T: 2:00

Game 72 July 18
    Nashville   100 001 310   6 11 2
    Memphis   000 000 001   1 5 3
(WP: Bernhard 3-2; LP: Shields) Ump: Moran. T: 1:30

Game 73 July 20
    Little Rock   100 000 000 000 00   1 4 2
    Nashville   000 100 000 000 01   2 9 1
(WP: Duggan 13-7; LP: Neuer) Ump: Carpenter. A: 3,000. T: 2:10

Game 74 July 21
    Little Rock   020 001 000   3 9 0
    Nashville   000 000 000   0 4 3
(WP: Buchanan; LP: Perdue 9-7) Ump: Carpenter. T: 1:37

Game 75 July 22
    Little Rock   000 031 211   8 13 4
    Nashville   019 020 03x   15 20 5
[WP: Hunter 5-3; LP: Eyler (7+), Buchanan (1)] Ump: Carpenter. T: 2:22

Game 76 July 23
    Mobile   200 000 000   2 6 0
    Nashville   000 000 000   0 6 5
(WP: Hickman; LP: Kellum 9-6) Ump: Carpenter. T: 1:40

Linescores for the Vols' 1908 Season

Game 77 July 25
    Mobile   010 100 000   2   8   1
    Nashville   001 020 10x   4 13   3
(WP: Perdue 10–7; LP: Torrey) Ump: Carpenter. A: 1,800. T: 1:40

Game 78 July 26
    Nashville   100 000 000 000 1   2   6   0
    Memphis   000 000 001 000 0   1   5   1
(WP: Bernhard 4–2; LP: Garrity) Ump: Brown. T: 2:20

Game 79 July 27
    New Orleans   000 000 001   1   7   0
    Nashville   001 001 01x   3 10   1
(WP: Kellum 10–6; LP: Bartley) Ump: Pfenninger. A: 3,000. T: 1:30

Game 80 July 28
    New Orleans   100 006 000   7   9   2
    Nashville   000 010 031   5 12   0
(WP: Clark; LP: Hunter 5–4) Ump: Pfenninger. A: 3,500. T: 1:55

Game 81 July 29
    New Orleans   000 000 000   0   5   4
    Nashville   110 000 000   2   8   3
(WP: Bernhard 5–2; LP: Fritz) Ump: Pfenninger. A: 2,500. T: 1:30

Game 82 July 30
    Memphis   000 010 220   5   8   2
    Nashville   000 001 001   2   8   1
[WP: Garrity (8+), Savidge (1); LP: Perdue (7) 10–8, Bernhard (2)] Ump: Pfenninger. A: 2,000. T: 1:45

Game 83 July 31
    Memphis   000 100 000   1   7   0
    Nashville   000 000 000   0   5   1
(WP: Savidge; LP: Duggan 13–8) Ump: Pfenninger. A: 1,800. T: 1:27

Game 84 Aug. 1
    Memphis   000 000 000   0   6   0
    Nashville   200 100 00x   3   9   0
(WP: Kellum 111–6; LP: Schwenck) Ump: Pfenninger. A: 3,500. T: 1:25

Game 85 Aug. 3
    Birmingham   101 010 120   6 14   0
    Nashville   000 000 101   2   7   1
(WP: Bauer; LP: Perdue 10–9) Ump: Carpenter. A: 1,400. T: 1:52

Game 86 Aug. 4
    Birmingham   020 000 000   2   5   8
    Nashville   100 040 55x   15 18   3
(WP: Hunter 6–4; LP: Robitaille) Ump: Carpenter. A: 2,000. T: 1:50

Game 87 Aug. 5 (first game of doubleheader)
    Birmingham   000 000 100   1 10   5
    Nashville   312 130 30x   13 18   3
(WP: Kellum 12–6; LP: Ford) Ump: Carpenter. A: 2,000. T: 1:50

Game 88 Aug. 5 (second game of doubleheader)
          Birmingham   001 011 200   5 7 2
          Nashville   001 011 010   4 12 0
   (WP: Turner; LP: Duggan 13-9) Ump: Carpenter. T: 1:30

Game 89 Aug. 6
          Atlanta   000 000 000   0 6 2
          Nashville   120 000 30x   6 11 2
   (WP: Bernhard 6-2; LP: Radabaugh) Ump: Pfenninger. A: 2,000. T: 1:45

Game 90 Aug. 7
          Atlanta   000 001 000   1 4 2
          Nashville   100 010 00x   2 5 3
   (WP: Sitton 1-0; LP: Maxwell) Umps: Pfenninger, Brown. A: 3,500. T: 1:27

Game 91 Aug. 8
          Atlanta   000 000 000   0 4 0
          Nashville   100 001 00x   2 5 0
   (WP: Hunter 7-4; LP: Viebahn) Umps: Pfenninger, Brown. T: 1:25

Game 92 Aug. 10
          Montgomery   100 000 000   1 8 3
          Nashville   002 210 01x   6 10 3
   (WP: Duggan 14-9; LP: Bliss) Umps: Pfenninger, Brown. A: 2,400. T: 1:40

Game 93 Aug. 11
          Montgomery   101 010 000   3 6 2
          Nashville   100 000 000   1 6 5
   (WP: Guese; LP: Kellum 12-7) Umps: Pfenninger, Brown. T: 1:27

Game 94 Aug. 12
          Montgomery   000 000 000   0 7 0
          Nashville   010 000 00x   1 4 2
   (WP: Bernhard 7-2; LP: Thomas) Umps: Pfenninger, Brown. A: 2,500. T: 1:25

Game 95 Aug. 13
          Nashville   100 010 000   2 5 1
          Atlanta   001 002 02x   5 9 2
   (WP: Viebahn; LP: Hunter 7-5) Umps: Brown, Pfenninger. T: 1:23

Game 96 Aug. 14 (first game of doubleheader)
          Nashville   100 000 004   5 7 0
          Atlanta   000 010 000   1 4 4
   (WP: Sitton 2-0; LP: Ford) Umps: Pfenninger, Brown. T: 1:40

Game 97 Aug. 14 (second game of doubleheader)
          Nashville   020 000 000   2 5 2
          Atlanta   000 000 003   3 5 1
   (WP: Johns; LP: Duggan 14-10) Umps: Brown, Pfenninger. T: 1:50

Game 98 Aug. 15
          Nashville   000 000 003   3 5 1
          Atlanta   000 000 100   1 9 1
   (WP: Kellum 13-7; LP: Maxwell) Umps: Pfenninger, Brown. T: 1:45

Game 99 Aug. 17
        Nashville   000 002 001   3 6 3
        Montgomery   005 000 03x   8 10 0
(WP: Thomas; LP: Sitton 2-1) Umps: Carpenter, Brown. T: 1:40

Game 100 Aug. 18
        Nashville   010 080 002   11 13 0
        Montgomery   100 040 010   6 11 6
(WP: Perdue 11-9; LP: Juul) Umps: Brown, Carpenter. T: 2:00

Game 101 Aug. 19
        Nashville   001 000 113   6 8 1
        Montgomery   000 020 001   3 7 1
(WP: Bernhard 8-2; LP: Guese) Umps: Brown, Carpenter. T: 1:40

No decision Aug. 20
        Nashville   000 000 001 000 00   1 7 2
        Birmingham   001 000 000 000 00   1 7 1
(Duggan (8), Perdue (6) vs. Bauer) Umps: Brown, Carpenter. T: 2:35

Game 102 Aug. 21 (first game of doubleheader)
        Nashville   200 000 0   2 5 0
        Birmingham   020 031 x   6 9 3
(WP: Ford; LP: Kellum 13-8) Umps: Brown, Carpenter. T: 1:40

Game 103 Aug. 21 (second game of doubleheader)
        Nashville   010 001 2   4 5 0
        Birmingham   000 131 x   5 8 2
(WP: Robinson; LP: Sitton 2-2) Umps: Brown, Carpenter. T: 1:30

Game 104 Aug. 22 (first game of doubleheader)
        Nashville   010 000 200   3 9 1
        Birmingham   000 001 000   1 9 1
[Hunter (6), WP: Perdue (3) 12-9; LP: Robitaille] Umps: Brown, Carpenter. T: 2:00

Game 105 Aug. 22 (second game of doubleheader)
        Nashville   000 000 00   0 4 3
        Birmingham   421 000 0x   7 12 1
[WP: Fleharty; LP: Perdue (1⅔) 12-10, Daubert (5⅔)] Umps: Brown, Carpenter. T: 1:45

Game 106 Aug. 24
        Nashville   000 010 000   1 11 2
        Little Rock   000 100 001   2 7 3
(WP: Eyler; LP: Bernhard 8-3) Ump: Pfenninger. T: 1:40

Game 107 Aug. 25
        Nashville   100 012 100   5 11 0
        Little Rock   000 000 003   3 6 3
(WP: Duggan 15-10; LP: Eastman) Ump: Pfenninger. T: 1:35

Game 108 Aug. 26 (first game of doubleheader)
        Nashville   001 002 001   4 11 4
        Little Rock   000 000 000   0 4 1
(WP: Perdue 13–10; LP: Buchanan) Ump: Pfenninger. T: 1:40

Game 109 Aug. 26 (second game of doubleheader)
        Nashville   000 110 100   3 8 2
        Little Rock   000 200 000   2 5 1
(WP: Kellum 14–8; LP: Hart) Ump: Pfenninger. T: 1:35

Game 110 Aug. 28
        Nashville   000 000 100   1 6 1
        Memphis   000 110 00x   2 8 1
(WP: Schwenck; LP: Sitton 2–3) Umps: Brown, Fitzsimmons. T: 1:55

Game 111 Aug. 29
        Nashville   000 000 001   1 9 2
        Memphis   010 020 11x   5 13 1
(WP: Savidge; LP: Bernhard 8–4) Umps: Brown, Fitzsimmons. T: 1:40

No decision Aug. 30
        Nashville   010 000 000 100 0   2 13 2
        Memphis   000 010 000 100 0   2 7 0
(Duggan (7), Perdue (6) vs. Kieber (11), Garrity (2⅓) Umps: Brown, Fitzsimmons. A: 5,000. T: 2:25

Game 112 Aug. 31
        Nashville   000 000 020   2 5 2
        New Orleans   000 000 000   0 4 3
(WP: Kellum 15–8; LP: Bartley) Umps: Fitzsimmons, Brown. A: 3,300. T: 1:50

Game 113 Sept. 1
        Nashville   000 010 000   1 3 1
        New Orleans   000 000 000   0 2 3
(WP: Sitton 3–3; LP: Fritz) Umps: Brown, Fitzsimmons. A: 3,500. T: 1:43

Game 114 Sept. 2 (first game of doubleheader)
        Nashville   000 000 000   0 2 0
        New Orleans   021 000 00x   3 3 1
(WP: Breitenstein; LP: Duggan 15–11) Umps: Fitzsimmons, Brown. A: 6,600. T: 1:40

No decision Sept. 2 (second game of doubleheader)
        Nashville   000 000 0   0 6 0
        New Orleans   000 000 0   0 3 0
(Bernhard vs. Bartley) Umps: Brown, Fitzsimmons. T: 1:25

Game 115 Sept. 3 (first game of doubleheader)
        Nashville   000 000 000   0 5 1
        Mobile   000 000 001   1 6 2
(WP: Hickman; LP: Perdue 13–11) Umps: Wheeler, Pfenninger. T: 1:54

Linescores for the Vols' 1908 Season

Game 116 Sept. 3 (second game of doubleheader)
        Nashville   011 000 00   2 6 1
        Mobile   000 000 00   0 4 3
(WP: Perdue 14–11; LP: Hixon) Umps: Pfenninger, Wheeler. T: 1:25

Game 117 Sept. 5 (first game of doubleheader)
        Nashville   000 010 000   1 10 2
        Mobile   300 010 00x   4 8 1
(WP: Fisher; LP: Kellum 15–9) Umps: Wheeler, Pfenninger. T: 1:28

Game 118 Sept. 5 (second game of doubleheader)
        Nashville   060 012 1   10 16 0
        Mobile   000 000 0   0 4 7
[WP: Hunter 8–5; LP: Beeker (1⅓), Killian (4⅓), Sentell (1⅓)] Umps: Wheeler, Pfenninger. T: 1:31

Game 119 Sept. 7 (Labor Day, first game of doubleheader)
        Memphis   010 000 000 003   4 8 0
        Nashville   010 000 000 000   1 10 2
(WP: Schwenck; LP: Sitton 3–4) Umps: Moran, Clarke. A: 3,500. T: 2:30

Game 120 Sept. 7 (second game of doubleheader)
        Memphis   001 100 100   3 8 1
        Nashville   020 004 00x   6 13 2
(WP: Duggan 16–11; LP: Garrity) Umps: Moran, Clarke. A: 7,500. T: 1:50

Game 121 Sept. 8
        Memphis   000 000 000   0 4 5
        Nashville   105 201 10x   10 15 0
[WP: Perdue 15–11; LP: Savidge (3), Kieber (3), Willis (2)] Umps: Moran, Wheeler. T: 1:50

Game 122 Sept. 9
        Little Rock   000 210 000   3 7 2
        Nashville   000 000 002   2 7 4
(WP: Hart; LP: Kellum 15–10) Umps: Moran, Wheeler. T: 1:45

Game 123 Sept. 10
        Little Rock   000 000 000   0 0 0
        Nashville   000 001 00x   1 10 1
(WP: Duggan 17–11; LP: Buchanan) Umps: Moran, Wheeler. T: 1:29

Game 124 Sept. 11
        Little Rock   000 010 000   1 1 3
        Nashville   203 403 26x   20 30 4
[WP: Sitton 4–4; LP: Eyler (3), Wood (5)] Umps: Moran, Wheeler. T: 1:57

Game 125 Sept. 12
        Little Rock   001 000 000   1 8 3
        Nashville   000 300 71x   11 11 0
(WP: Perdue 16–11; LP: Hart) Umps: Moran, Wheeler. T: 1:30

Game 126 Sept. 14
                Mobile   020 000 000   2 8 2
                Nashville   012 021 04x   10 18 2
(WP: Duggan 18-11; LP: Beeker) Umps: Fitzsimmons, Carpenter. T: 1:50

Game 127 Sept. 15
                Mobile   000 010 001   2 3 2
                Nashville   302 010 20x   8 13 1
(WP: Sitton 5-4; LP: Fisher) Umps: Carpenter, Fitzsimmons. T: 1:30

Game 128 Sept. 16
                Mobile   000 000 100   1 7 0
                Nashville   520 002 01x   10 13 1
[WP: Perdue 17-11; LP: Hickman (3), Killian (5)] Umps: Carpenter, Fitzsimmons. T: 1:35

Game 129 Sept. 17
                New Orleans 030 000 110   5 9 0
                Nashville   100 000 000   1 9 2
(WP: Bartley; LP: Bernhard 8-5) Umps: Carpenter, Fitzsimmons. A: 5,000. T: 1:45

Game 130 Sept. 18
                New Orleans 001 000 001   2 7 3
                Nashville   001 003 11x   6 11 2
(WP: Duggan 19-11; LP: Phillips) Umps: Carpenter, Fitzsimmons. A: 5,000. T: 1:30

Game 131 Sept. 19 (for Southern League championship)
                New Orleans 000 000 000   0 3 1
                Nashville   000 000 10x   1 8 0
(WP: Sitton 6-4; LP: Breitenstein) Umps: Carpenter, Fitzsimmons. A: 10,700. T: 1:42

Appendix C: Should Jake Daubert Be in the Hall of Fame?

How is Jake Daubert's major league career evaluated? How is he best remembered? Today the ultimate measure of a player's worth is determined by induction into the Baseball Hall of Fame in Cooperstown, New York. But what constitutes a "HoF" career? Bill James tackles this difficult question in a thought-provoking book, *Whatever Happened to the Hall of Fame? Baseball, Cooperstown, and the Politics of Glory.* James believes the Hall of Fame never established consistent criteria for membership into baseball's elite fraternity of stars. In the early years, the Permanent Committee made choices based on the preferences of baseball commissioner Kenesaw Mountain Landis. Daubert received two votes in the second year of elections (1937), and one vote in 1938, 1939, 1951, and 1952.[1]

Daubert's best chance of selection rested with the Veterans Committee. But James argues that this committee failed to scour the sport in its early years. Furthermore, James argues that the Veterans were prone to favoritism; by the time it began to look seriously at late nineteenth and early twentieth century players, too many worthy candidates had fallen through the cracks. Another strike against Daubert was his position; first basemen have always had difficulty reaching the hallowed halls of Cooperstown.[2]

Whether there is substance to Daubert supporters is open to conjecture, but there is intriguing statistical and narrative evidence in his favor. Some relevant information is listed below:

- Career .303 batting average
- Over 100 hits in all of his fifteen seasons
- Season average over .300 in ten seasons
- National League MVP once
- Led National League in batting average twice
- Led National League in triples twice
- Played on two pennant winners
- Chosen team captain for every team he played on
- Slugged a career-high 205 hits when he was 38 years old (three fewer than Pete Rose and 45 more than Ty Cobb)
- Set two National League records for most sacrifice bunts in a doubleheader (6) and a single game (4)
- Still holds National League record for most career sacrifice bunts (392)

How do Daubert's career numbers compare over time? In an effort to give validity to Hall of Fame comparisons from different eras, James recognizes Daubert as a good to very good player, but probably not a great one. The sabermetrician identifies a candidate worthy of admission as one who amasses 35 points (100 is perfect) in his quantatative system.[3] Daubert received 22 points for the following accomplishments:

- 6 points for career batting average of .303 (1 point for each .005 over .275, plus an additional 1 point if the career average is over .300).
- 4 points for career slugging average of .401 (1 point for each .025 above .300).
- 5 points for 2,326 base hits (1 point for every 150 hits above 1,500).
- 3 points for 1,117 career runs scored plus 1,117 runs in 2,014 games (1 point for each 100 runs scored in excess of 900, plus 1 point if player scored one run for every two games played).
- 1 point for 623 bases on balls (1 point for every walk in excess of 500).
- 2 points for 251 stolen bases (1 point for every 100 swipes).
- 1 point for career first baseman.

In another quantitative study, *Ranking Baseball's Elite*, A. W. Laird contends that Daubert is the eleventh-best first baseman of all-time. His evaluation places Daubert's ahead of Hall of Famers' Rod Carew (#15), Ernie Banks (#19), and Willie McCovey (# 32).[4] James and Laird compare Daubert's career most favorably to Keith Hernandez.

In 2002, Bill James and Jim Henzler collaborated on a book entitled *Win Shares*, with the goal of improving upon the mathematical theories and formulas presented in *Whatever Happened to the Hall of Fame*? Their new methodology calculated the number of victories each player generated for his team, and thereby determined an individual's worth to that team through "win shares" based on the team's overall number of victories. Defensive and pitching statistics were also factored into the results.[5] James and Henzler conclude that Daubert's value in the decade of 1910–1919 was 182 points to rank 21st in the National League. Despite playing only five seasons in the 1920s, the first baseman dropped to 81 points with an individual rank of 149th.[6] Daubert accumulated 263 points for his career, the same as Gil Hodges and Don Mattingly. While most of his points were earned for offense (229), Daubert ranked eleventh among first basemen for overall defense. Daubert's defensive grade (B+) places him behind Keith Hernandez (A) and John Olerud (A+).[7]

Does this analysis of Daubert's career merit his entrance into Cooperstown? For sure, it makes for interesting hot stove discussion. One thing is certain: Daubert seems to have been more highly regarded by contemporaries than he is today.

Chapter Notes

Chapter 1

1. Jennifer M. Bartlett, Charles P. Stripling, and Fred. M. Prouty, *Historical and Archaeological Investigations of the Site of the Tennessee Bicentennial Mall, 40DV469, Davidson County* (Nashville: Tennessee Department of Environment and Conservation, Division of Archaeology, 1995): 11, 35.
2. See entry on Sulphur Dell in Carroll Van West, ed., *The Encyclopedia of Tennessee History and Culture* (Nashville: Tennessee Historical Society and Rutledge Hill Press, 1998): 896–897.
3. Allison Caveglia Barash, "Base Ball in the Civil War," *The National Pastime; A Review of Baseball History* 21 (2001): 18.
4. See Fred Russell, "Grantland Rice Gave It a Name... Sulphur Dell," *Nashville Magazine* (Feb. 1957): 1; Bartlett, Stripling, and Prouty, *Historical and Archaeological Investigations*, 35. The Nashville Athletic Club (N.A.C.) defeated the Phoenix club, 58–29, to even the three-game series, but went on to lose the championship game. See Bill Traughber, "Baseball Stirred Passions in Nashville after War," in *City Paper* (Nashville), 1 April 2003.
5. See remarks of Joe Hatcher in *Nashville Tennessean*, 22 January 1978.
6. Bartlett, Stripling, and Prouty, *Historical and Archaeological Investigations*, 6; Van West, *The Encyclopedia of Tennessee History and Culture*, 896; Bill O'Neal, *The Southern Association: Baseball in Dixie, 1885–1994* (Austin, TX: Eakin Press, 1994): 5; Walter T. Durham, *Nashville: The Occupied City* (Nashville: Tennessee Historical Society, 1985): xv; Bill Traughber, "The Nashville Seraphs, 1895," in *The National Pastime: A Review of Baseball History* 23 (2003): 57–59.
7. Van West, *The Encyclopedia of Tennessee History and Culture*, 47.
8. Bill O'Neal, *The Southern Association: Baseball in Dixie, 1885–1994* (Austin, TX: Eakin Press, 1994): 2; Russell, "Grantland Rice Gave It A Name," 1.
9. Benjamin G. Rader, *Baseball: A History of America's Game* (Urbana: University of Illinois Press): 16.
10. Steven A. Riess, *City Games: The Evolution of American Urban Society and the Rise of Sports* (Urbana: University of Illinois Press, 1989): 65.
11. For more on the problems faced by organized baseball in the period between 1880–1900, see Steven A. Riess, *Touching Base: Professional Baseball and American Culture in the Progressive Era* (Westport, CT: Greenwood Press, 1980); Riess, *City Games: The Evolution of American Urban Society and the Rise of Sports* (Urbana: University of Illinois Press, 1989); Neil J. Sullivan, *The Minors: The Struggles and the Triumphs of Baseball's Poor Relation from 1876 to the Present* (New York: St. Martin's Press, 1990); Harold Seymour, *Baseball: The Early Years* (New York: Oxford University Press, 1960); Mark Okkonen, *Baseball Memories, 1900–1909: An Illustrated Chronicle of the Big Leagues' First Decade* (New York: Sterling Publishing Co., 1992); David Nemec, *The Beer*

and *Whiskey League: The Illustrated History of the American Association — Baseball's Renegade Major League* (New York: Lyons and Burford, 1994); Rader, *Baseball: A History of America's Game,* 7–89; O'Neal, *The Southern Association,* 1–19; Ida Clyde Clark, *Nashville: A Complete Historical Guide to the City* (Nashville: n.p., 1912): 189–190.

12. Seymour, *Baseball: The Early Years,* 275–277. Rader, *Baseball: A History of America's Game,* 63–87; David Nemec, *The Beer and Whiskey League: The Illustrated History of the American Association — Baseball's Renegade Major League* (New York: Lyons and Burford, 1994): 68; O'Neal, *The Southern Association,* 4. Two notable omissions from the reforms necessary to modernize the game included the computation of earned run average (1912) and runs batted in (1920). Paul Dickson, *The Joy of Keeping Score: How Scoring the Game Has Influenced and Enhanced the History of Baseball* (New York: Walker and Co., 1996): 86–87.

13. See Rader, *Baseball: A History of America's Game,* 87–88; Seymour, *Baseball: The Early Years,* 280–282; *The Baseball Encyclopedia: The Complete and Definitive Record of Major League Baseball,* 9th edition (New York: Macmillan Co., 1993): 6. For a closer examination of McGraw's coaching style and its impact upon Wilbert Robinson, see Jack Kavanaugh and Norman Macht, *Uncle Robbie* (Cleveland: Society for American Baseball Research, 1999): 11–41.

14. Seymour, *Baseball, The Early Years,* 282–283.

15. *Ibid.;* Rader, *Baseball: A History of America's Game,* 64, 88.

16. *Ibid.,* 88–89; Seymour, *Baseball, The Early Years,* 279–284; Nemec, *The Beer and Whiskey League,* 28–29. For an interesting photographic look at equipment used by Deadball Era players, Gwen Aldridge and Bret Wills, *Baseball Archaeology: Artifacts from the Great American Pastime* (San Francisco: Chronicle Books, 1993).

17. For a thorough examination of baseball's evolution as an organized sport, David Q. Voigt, *American Baseball,* 3 vols. (Norman, OK: University of Oklahoma Press, 1966–1983); *The Baseball Encyclopedia,* 3–13.

18. The reserve clause allowed the owner to continue an option on a player after the contract had ended. The club could terminate a contract within 30 days of notice or trade the rights of the player to another team. By signing a contract, the player gave up his right to negotiate individually with another team. With the advent of a minor league system in the 1880s, owners expanded the clause, which allowed them to send injured players to an unaffiliated team for rehabilitation. See Seymour, *Baseball, The Early Years,* 106–107; Sullivan, *The Minors,* 9; *Baseball Encyclopedia,* 4.

19. Rader, *Baseball: A History of America's Game,* 20; Nemec, *The Beer and Whiskey League,* 15–22. The new league also scheduled Sunday games, and lowered the price of admission to 25 cents.

20. Seymour, *Baseball: The Early Years,* 105.

21. Seymour, *Baseball, The Early Years,* 119–120.

22. Sullivan, *The Minors,* 27.

23. Nashville failed to field a team in 1888, 1889, or 1892, and the league temporarily shut down in 1890 and 1891. See Wright, *The Southern Association in Baseball,* 5–76; Traughber, "The Nashville Seraphs, 1895," 57–59; O'Neal, *The Southern Association,* 298–299.

24. *The Baseball Encyclopedia,* 6; Seymour, *Baseball: The Early Years,* 309–314; Rader, *Baseball: A History of America's Game,* 70–81.

25. O'Neal, *The Southern Association,* 20–21.

26. Seymour, *Baseball: The Early Years,* 314–315; Sullivan, *The Minors,* 38; Rader, *Baseball: A History of America's Game,* 79.

27. Seymour, *Baseball: The Early Years,* 315.

28. League presidents from the Western League, Eastern League, Three-I League, New York State League, Pacific Northwest League, Western Association, and New England League were present. The Southern Association, California League, North Carolina League, and Connecticut League all sent letters of support. Sullivan, *The Minors,* 44; Lloyd Johnson and Miles Wolff, eds. *The Encyclopedia of Minor League Baseball: The Official Record of Minor League Baseball* (Durham, N.C.: Baseball America, Inc., 1993): 103.

29. Johnson and Wolff, eds., *The Encyclopedia of Minor League Baseball,* 103; Seymour, *Baseball, The Early Years,* 317; Rader, *Baseball: A History of America's Game,* 81; Sullivan, *The Minors,* 44; Johnson and Wolff, eds., *The Encyclopedia of Minor League Baseball,* 103.

30. O'Neal, *The Southern Association,* 21–22; Tim Darnell, *Southern Yankees: The Story of the Atlanta Crackers* (n.p.: 1995): 41; Sullivan, *The Minors,* 58.

31. Johnson and Wolff, eds., *The Encyclopedia of Minor League Baseball,* 103; Riess, *Touching Base,* 14; Seymour, *Baseball: The Early Years,* 317–323.; Rader, *Baseball: A History of America's Game,* 81; *The Encyclopedia of Baseball,* 6; Sullivan, *The Minors,* 39, 44–45.

32. A tremendous amount of family information was obtained in an eight-hour interview with Dr. James A. Wiseman, Dr. Donald E. Wiseman, Mrs. Jeanne Wiseman Groenke,

and Mrs. Helen Wiseman in Cincinnati, Ohio, on 4–5 April 2004. Also see Donald E. Wiseman, "Julius Augustus 'Doc' Wiseman (1877–1953): The Hero of the Dell," (unpublished family genealogy); Darl L. Stephenson, *Headquarters in the Brush: Blazer's Independent Union Scouts* (Athens, Ohio: Ohio University Press, 2001); Patricia L. Faust, ed., *Historical Times Illustrated Encyclopedia of the Civil War* (New York: Harper & Row, 1986): 510–511; Certificate of Death, Julius Augustus Wiseman, Ohio Department of Health; Wright, *The Southern Association*, 63, 70, 78, 84, 96, 101, 109, 115, 121, 124, 131, 140, 145; *The Burnet Woods Echo*, 10, 24 May, 14 June 1897, Blegin Library Archives, University of Cincinnati, Cincinnati, OH; James A. Wiseman to John A. Simpson, 27 January, 2, 9 February 2004 in possession of the author; Simon, ed., *Deadball Stars of the National League*, 355–357; *Nashville Tennessean and the Nashville American*, 10, 11 July 1912; *Banner*, 8–11 July 1912; Russell, *Vols Feats*, 18; *Cincinnati City Directory, 1909–1927*; J.A. Wiseman to Jim Wiseman, 12 Nov. 1949, Larry Gilbert to M.C. Saunders, 15 April 1953, in possession of Dr. James A. Wiseman, Cincinnati, OH; *Banner*, 9, 10 April 1953; *The Sporting News*, 22 April 1953.

33. Wiseman, "The Hero of the Dell," 2, 4, 6; Wiseman Interviews, 4–5 April 2004.

34. *Ibid*.

35. Wiseman, "The Hero of the Dell," 5, 19; Wiseman Interviews, 4–5 April 2004.

36. *The Burnet Woods Echo*, 14 June 1897, Blegin Library Archives, University of Cincinnati, Cincinnati, OH.

37. Seven Nashville batters hit over .300 in that opening season. *Spalding's Official Baseball Guide, 1902* (New York: American Sports Publishing Co., 1902): 159; O'Neal, *The Southern Association*, 21–22, 283; Fred Russell and George Leonard, *Vol Feats: Records, History and Tales of the Nashville Baseball Club in the Southern Association, 1901–1950* (Nashville: Nashville Banner Press, 1950): 18; Edward Michael Ashenback, *Humor Among the Minors: True Tales from the Baseball Brush* (Chicago: M. A. Donohue and Co., 1911): 108.

38. Seymour, *Baseball, The Early Years*, 295.

39. For more on the growing conflict between the voices of tradition and change in the early twentieth century South, see William A. Link, *The Paradox of Southern Progressivism, 1880–1930* (Chapel Hill: University of North Carolina Press, 1992): 53–54. Recent examinations of Sabbatarianism in the major leagues is Charlie Bevis, *Sunday Baseball; The Major Leagues' Struggle to Play Baseball on the Lord's Day, 1876–1934* (Jefferson, N.C.: McFarland Press, 2003); Jon David Cash, *Before They Were Cardinals: Major League Baseball in Nineteenth Century St. Louis* (Columbia: University of Missouri Press, 2002), 63; Riess, *Touching Base*, 121, 138, 141.

40. Riess, *Touching Base*, 141.

41. Quoted in Link, *The Paradox of Southern Progressivism*, 117.

42. "William K. Kavanaugh," *Pulaski County Historical Review* 16 (March 1968): 9–13; *Arkansas Gazette*, 22 February 1915; *Arkansas Democrat*, 22 Feb. 1915; *TSN*, 21 May 1936.

43. *Arkansas Democrat*, 22 Feb. 1915.

44. Darnell, *Southern Yankees*, 41; O'Neal, *The Southern Association*, 22, 28, 33, 308; Russell and Leonard, *Vols Feats*, 44.

45. See *Arkansas Gazette*, 22 February 1915; *The Sporting News*, 21 May 1936. In the ten seasons between 1901–1910, New Orleans finished in the top half of the league nine times, Atlanta eight times, and Memphis six times, those three clubs were considered the elite teams in the Southern Association. Through the 1907 season, Memphis led the league in total victories with 513, followed by New Orleans with 493. Nashville led all teams with three championships. O'Neal, *The Southern Association*, 300–301; *Tennessean*, 16 March 1908.

46. See Mark G. Manuel, "That Ball's on the Queer!," *The Baseball Research Journal* 26 (1997): 116.

47. Darnell, *Southern Yankees*, 44.

48. Mark Garfield Manuel was a great competitor on the New Orleans pitching staff for years. In 1907, he pitched both games of a doubleheader against Birmingham and won by identical scores of 1–0, and earned the nickname "Iron Man." He played two seasons in the major leagues and established his name in official baseball scoring history when he was removed from a game in the eighth inning and his team regained the lead in the bottom of the frame. Thereafter, the starting pitcher and not the reliever earned the win. See Arthur O. Schott, *70 Years with the Pelicans, 1887–1957* (n.p.: 1992 reprint): 45; *The Baseball Encyclopedia*, 2052; Donald Dewey and Nicholas Acocella, *The Biographical History of Baseball* (New York: Carroll and Graf Publishers, Inc., 1995): 287.

49. Manuel, "That Ball's on the Queer!," 116.

50. *Ibid.*, 114–117; *New Orleans Times-Picayune*, 16 June 1906.

51. See newspaper clipping dated 21 July 1906, in Theodore P. Breitenstein, Vertical File, A. Bartlett Giamatti Research Center, National Baseball Hall of Fame Library, Cooperstown, NY.

52. See Riess, *Touching Base*, 4–5, 13. For

similar analysis of the progressive era and its impact upon baseball, see Marc Okkonen, *Baseball Memories, 1900–1909: An Illustrated Chronicle of the Big Leagues' First Decade* (New York: Sterling Publishing Co., 1992): 1.

53. Statistics are derived from the 1910 census. See Don H. Doyle, *New Men, New Cities, New South: Atlanta, Nashville, Charleston, Mobile, 1860–1910* (Chapel Hill: University of North Carolina Press, 1990): 15. Okkonen points out that the national population increased 21 percent in the first decade of the twentieth century. Okkonen, *Baseball Memories*, 1. During the same time, attendance at major league baseball games doubled. See Riess, *City Games*, 197.

54. Riess, *City Games*, 69, 214; Riess, *Touching Base*, 4–5, 26, 38; Okkonen, *Baseball Memories*, 2.

55. Rader, *Baseball: A History of America's Game*, 26. For a similar analysis on the role of civic boosterism between St. Louis and Chicago, see Cash, *Before They Were Cardinals*, 10.

56. Riess, *Touching Base*, 18–19.

57. See Riess, *City Games*, 35, 68,199; Riess, *Touching Base*, 49, 75–76; Doyle, *New Men, New Cities, New South*, 19; Rader, *Baseball: A History of America's Game*, 30.

58. For more on the sporting news explosion and its importance to baseball, see *Baseball Encyclopedia*, 6; Okkonen, *Baseball Memories*, 5, 8; Riess, *Touching Base*, 16; Okkonen, *Baseball Memories*, 8; Dickson, *The Joy of Keeping Score*, 35.

59. See Riess, *City Games*, 66; Riess, *Touching Base*, 6–7.

60. Riess, *Touching Base*, 6–7, 14.

61. Rader, *Baseball: A History of America's Game*, 82.

62. See Lawrence S. Ritter, *The Glory of Their Times: The Story of the Early Days of Baseball Told by the Men Who Played It* (New York: Morrow, 1984 reprint): 33. Ritter interviewed 26 major league ballplayers in 1966 who had played between 1900–1930. These fascinating vignettes are important primary accounts of life in the days of the Deadball Era.

63. *Tennessean*, 20 Sept. 1908.

Chapter 2

1. O'Neal, *The Southern Association*, 21, 300; Johnson and Wolff, eds., *The Encyclopedia of Minor League Baseball*, 114; Wright, *The Southern Association in Baseball*, 118–122.

2. For game accounts, *Nashville Tennessean*, 15 Sept. 1907; *Nashville Banner*, 16 Sept. 1907; *Nashville American*, 16 Sept. 1907. Hereafter, these dailies will be referred to as *Tennessean, Banner,* or *American*. The *Banner*, an evening newspaper, did not publish on Saturday nor did the *Tennessean* publish on Sunday in 1908. In the earliest version of this book, every paragraph that contained game information was footnoted with the three dailies as well as two national publications, *The Sporting News* and *Sporting Life*. Such notes have been removed for brevity, but the reader should be aware that local newspaper coverage usually appeared one day after each game was played. Occasionally the *Banner* provided same-day coverage and carried Saturday contests in the Monday edition, owing to its weekend publication schedule.

3. For more on Breitenstein's career, *The Baseball Encyclopedia*, 24, 1722; J. Thomas Hetrick, *Chris Von der Ahe and the St. Louis Browns* (Lanham, MD: Scarecrow Press, Inc., 1999): 100, 135–136, 157, 160, 193–194; Nemec, *The Beer and Whiskey League*, 228; Seymour, *Baseball: The Early Years*, 277, 300–301; Dewey and Acocella, *The Biographical History of Baseball*, 12; Theodore P. Breitenstein, Vertical File, A. Bartlett Giamatti Research Center, National Baseball Hall of Fame Library, Cooperstown, N.Y.; Bill James, *Whatever Happened to the Hall of Fame?: Baseball, Cooperstown, and the Politics of Glory* (New York: Firestone Books, 1995): 266.

4. Rice emerged at an opportune moment when sportswriting was becoming more important in American culture. He brought respectability to a profession that, until 1907, had a rather seedy image. Charles Fountain, *Sportswriter: The Life and Times of Grantland Rice* (New York: Oxford University Press, 1993): 3–7, 33–57, 62–86, 90; Riess, *Touching Base*, 15.

5. For league statistics see *Spalding's Baseball Guide, 1908* (New York: American Sports Publishing Co., 1909): 233; *Tennessean*, 15, Dec. 1907. For a collection of baseball guides, Grantland Rice Collection, Special Collections, Jean and Alexander Heard Library, Vanderbilt University, Nashville, TN.

6. Thirty-one-year-old Dobbs played outfield for five years in the majors (1901-1905). Later, he posted the second-longest managerial stint in Southern Association history with almost every team before retiring in 1933. He oversaw 1,841 wins and directed five league champions. O'Neal, *The Southern Association*, 32; *The Baseball Encyclopedia*, 842.

7. *Tennessean*, 15 Sept. 1907.

8. *Ibid*.

9. *Tennessean*, 22 Sept. 1907. For Southern Association attendance see *Spalding's Baseball Guide, 1908*, 229–231. For general comments about the growth of baseball at the turnstiles,

Okkonen, *Baseball Memories*, 1; Rader, *Baseball: A History of America's Game*, 85; *Encyclopedia of Baseball*, 6; Riess, *Touching Base*, 40.

10. Sam Crawford and Jimmy Austin in Ritter, *Glory of Their Times*, 65, 87; Riess, *Touching Base*, 156.

11. Okkonen, *Baseball Memories*, 10–11; Rader, *Baseball: A History of America's Games*, 33; Nemec, *The Beer and Whiskey League*, 28–29.

12. Nashville Base-ball Association, State of Tennessee, Secretary of State, Charter of Incorporation, Book U-7: 108–109; *Nashville City Directory, 1907*; Doyle, *Nashville in the New South*, 200; Waller, *Nashville, 1900–1910*, 165, 316.

13. Waller, *Nashville, 1900–1910*, 89, 114; *American*, 25 Jan. 1908; *Nashville City Directory, 1908*: 190, 199, 442, 583, 693, 731; *Nashville City Directory, 1909*: 325, 473, 620, 738; *Who's Who in Tennessee: A Biographical Reference Book of Notable Tennesseans of Today* (Memphis: Paul and Douglass, 1911): 408, 450; Ilene J. Cornwell, *Biographical Directory of the Tennessee General Assembly*. 3 vols. (Nashville: Tennessee Historical Commission, 1988): 3: 678–679; Will T. Hale and Dixon L. Merritt, *A History of Tennessee and Tennesseans: The Leaders and Representative Men of Commerce, Industry and Modern Activity*. 4 vols. (Chicago: Lewis Publishing Co., 1913): 4: 889–890, 1044; Austin P. Foster and Albert H. Roberts, *Tennessee Democracy: A History of the Party and Its Representative Members — Past and Present*, 4 vols. (Nashville: Democratic Historical Association, 1940): 3: 806–811; J. T. Moore, *The Volunteer State, 1769–1923*, 2 vols. (Nashville: S. J. Clarke Publishing Co., 1923): 2: 778–779.

14. *American*, 29 Feb. 1908.

15. *Tennessean*, 22 Dec. 1907. Cross retired in 1908 after a distinguished twenty-one-year career in the majors as a catcher and third baseman. The son of Austro-Hungarian immigrants, Cross finished with a .292 career batting average in 2,275 games, one of the first players to reach the coveted plateau of 2,000 hits. Frederick Ivor-Campbell, *Baseball's First Stars* (Cleveland: Society for American Baseball Research, 1996): 42; *Baseball Encyclopedia*, 802–803.

16. *The Sporting News*, 9 Jan. 1908; *Sporting Life*, 4 Jan. 1908. Hereafter, the national weeklies are referred to as *TSN* and *SL*. Again, citation of these two sources for each game has generally been removed to reduce the overabundance of notes. A general rule, however, is that box scores and accompanying articles normally appeared approximately two weeks after the contest was played.

17. *Tennessean*, 31 Dec. 1907; *Banner*, 1 Jan. 1908.

18. *American*, 22 Jan. 1908. For Voorhees' two-year career in the majors, *The Encyclopedia of Baseball*, 2315.

19. *TSN*, 23 Jan. 1908.

20. *Tennessean*, 30 Dec. 1907.

21. *SL*, 11 Jan. 1908.

22. *Ibid.*; *Banner*, 1 January 1908. Yancey became sports editor, and later followed his father as managing editor of the *Banner* in 1922. Active in the local, state, and national Democratic Party, Yancey was a close advisor to Senator Kenneth McKellar, campaigned for Woodrow Wilson and Franklin D. Roosevelt, worked in Washington, D.C. during the FDR administration, and directed the Federal Housing Administration in Memphis. Yancey Family, Vertical file, Tennessee State Library and Archive, Nashville, TN; *Who's Who in Tennessee: A Biographical Reference Book of Notable Tennesseans of Today* (Memphis: Paul and Douglass, 1911): 416.

23. *American*, 22 March 1908.

24. *TSN*, 9 Jan. 1908.

25. *Tennessean*, 19 Jan. 1908.

26. *Tennessean*, 22 Jan. 1908. New Orleans was in the middle of renovating its stadium for the 1908 season. For a discussion of Nashville stadium renovation plans, see *Tennessean*, 22 Sept. 1907, 28 Dec. 1907, 31 Dec. 1907.

27. Riess, *Touching Base*, 51, 92–92. Also see Riess, *City Games*, 214; Rader, *Baseball: A History of America's Game*, 85. For more on the import connection between the location of trolley routes and urban expansion in Nashville, Doyle, *New Men, New Cities, New South*, 190.

28. See Michael Benson, *Ballparks of North America: A Comprehensive Historical Reference to Baseball Grounds, Yards, and Stadiums, 1845 to Present* (Jefferson, N.C.: McFarland, 1989): 14; Riess, *Touching Base*, 92; Riess, *City Games*, 214; O'Neal, *The Southern Association*, 37; Darnell, *Southern Yankees*, 14, 47.

29. *American*, 1 Jan 1908, 3 March 1908, 12 March 1908.

30. Rader, *Baseball: A History of America's Game*, 32; Riess, *City Games*, 213, 217; Riess, *Touching Base*, 94–96.

31. Riess, *City Games*, 219.

32. *Tennessean*, 14 Jan. 1908; *Banner*, 15 Jan. 1908; J. D. Brown, "The Name Stuck," *Nashville Tennessean Magazine*, 12 April 1947; Russell, "Grantland Rice Gave It a Name... Sulphur Dell," *Nashville Magazine* (Feb. 1957); Fountain, *Sportswriter*, 39.

33. *Tennessean*, 22, Jan. 1908. Madame Emma Calve, a singer billed as the world's greatest prima donna, performed at the Ryman Audi-

torium on 17 January 1908. Waller, *Nashville, 1900–1910*, 330.

34. Similar names were picked for major league diamonds—Ebbets Field and Sportsman's Park to name two. Rader, *Baseball: A History of America's Game*, 86.

35. Philip J. Lowry, *Green Cathedrals: The Ultimate Celebration of all 273 Major League and Negro League Ballparks* (New York: Addison-Wesley Publishing Co., 1992):184–5; Benson, *Ballparks of North America*, 245; O'Neal, *The Southern Association*, 37–39; *Encyclopedia of Tennessee History and Culture*, 896; Sulphur Dell, Vertical File, William Waller Collection, Special Collections, Jean and Alexander Heard Library, Vanderbilt University, Nashville, TN; Jennifer M. Bartlett and Charles P. Stripling, Fred. M. Prouty, *Historical and Archaeological Investigations of the Site of the Tennessee Bicentennial Mall, 40DV469, Davidson County* (Nashville: Tennessee Department of Environment and Conservation, Division of Archaeology, 1995): 35–38; Edward Michael Ashenback, *Humor Among the Minors: True Tales from the Baseball Brush* (Chicago: M.A. Donohue and Co., 1911): 148.

36. *Tennessean*, 19 April 1908.

37. Ashenback, *Humor Among the Minors*, 148.

38. *Tennessean*, 17 Feb. 1908; *Banner*, 17 Feb. 1908; *American*, 17 Feb. 1908.

39. In 1908, Southern states normally celebrated Decoration Day on the birth date of Jefferson Davis, 3 June. The Southern Association doubleheader slated for the last weekend in May marked the quarter-point in the season—an important measure for teams to assess initial success. Eventually, Memorial Day twin bills became the single most popular date in baseball. Riess, *City Games*, 224.

40. *Banner*, 17 Feb. 1908, 24 Feb. 1908; *American*, 17, 22, 23 Feb. 1908; *TSN*, 20, 27 Feb. 1908.

41. *TSN*, 20 Feb. 1908; *Banner*, 4 Feb. 1908; *American*, 22, 23 Feb. 1908; *TSN*, 27 Feb. 1908.

42. *American*, 22, 23 Feb. 1908; *TSN*, 27 Feb. 1908.

43. *Banner*, 24 Feb. 1908.

44. *TSN*, 20, 27 Feb. 1908; *American*, 22, 23 Feb. 1908.

45. *American*, 4 Feb. 1908.

46. *Tennessean*, 14 Feb. 1908.

47. *Banner*, 15 Feb. 1908.

48. Yancey's plea was acknowledged as teams went by the following nicknames beginning in 1908: Atlanta Crackers, Birmingham Barons, Little Rock Travelers, Memphis Turtles (Chicks in 1911), Mobile Sea Gulls, Montgomery Senators, New Orleans Pelicans, and Nashville Vols. O'Neal, *The Southern Association*, 85.

49. See *Banner*, 18 Feb. 1908; *Tennessean*, 17 Feb. 1908; *American*, 21 Feb. 1908. The suggestion of Rocks refers to limestone deposits upon which Nashville was built and the city's nickname dating from before the Civil War, Rock City.

50. Rice used cute euphemisms for fans like "bugs," "bug brigade," and "bug family." *Tennessean*, 18 Feb. 1908; Fountain, *Sportswriter*, 117.

51. *Tennessean*, 29 Feb. 1908; *Banner*, 29 Feb. 1908; *American*, 29 Feb. 1908.

52. *Tennessean*, 1 March 1908.

Chapter 3

1. See Waller, *Nashville*, 1900–1910, 330–335.

2. *Ibid.* For more on the tragic gubernatorial campaign of 1908, see William R. Majors, *Editorial Wild Oats: Edward Ward Carmack and Tennessee Politics* (Macon, GA: Mercer University Press, 1984); Van West, ed., *Encyclopedia of Tennessee History and Culture*, 124–125, 207; James Summerville, *The Carmack-Cooper Shooting: Tennessee Politics Turned Violent* (Jefferson, N.C.: McFarland, 1994).

3. *American*, 31 Dec. 1907; *Tennessean*, 3, 24 Jan. 1908; *Banner*, 9 Jan. 1908.

4. *Tennessean*, 3, 24, 26, 28 Jan. 1908.

5. "Dope" was slang in the turn-of-the-century referring to inside sports information or opinion. See Paul Dickson, *The New Dickson Baseball Dictionary* (New York: Harcourt Brace and Co., 1999): 142.

6. *Banner*, 9, 17, 21, 31 Jan. 1908; 14 Feb. 1908.

7. *American*, 15 Jan. 1908.

8. See *TSN*, 23 Jan. 1908; *American*, 15, 25, 30 Jan. 1908; 1 Feb. 1908.

9. Jack Dolittle Hardy file, Player Career Index, The Sporting News Archive, St. Louis, MO.; John D. Hardy Vertical File, National Baseball Hall of Fame Library, Cooperstown, N.Y.; *Cleveland Plain-Dealer*, 21 Oct. 1921; Cleveland City Directory, 1921, 1399.

10. *Tennessean*, 26 Jan. 1908.

11. *American*, 14 Feb. 1908; *Tennessean*, 14 Feb. 1908; *TSN*, 20 Feb. 1908. Arthur Francis Nichols (Meikle) played in 241 games over six seasons (1898–1903) with the Cubs and Cardinals as a catcher and first baseman. *Encyclopedia of Baseball*, 1291.

12. See *Diamond Jubilee—Bicentennial, Mossy Creek-Jefferson City, 1788–1976* (n.p.: 1976) in Carson-Newman Library archive, Carson-Newman College, Jefferson City, TN.; Chris Jones, "It Gets Foggy at Mossy Creek; the

Origin and Development of Intercollegiate Athletics at Carson-Newman College," (unpublished research paper, 1974): 200, in Carson-Newman Library archive, Carson-Newman College, Jefferson City, TN; Wright, *The Southern Association*, 121, 124, 144, 153–54; *Baseball Encyclopedia*, 1213, 167, 170; Pryor M. McElveen, Player Career Index, *The Sporting News Archive*, St. Louis, MO; Catalogue of Carson and Newman College, 1917–1918 (Jefferson City: Tennessee Litho Company, 1917): 63; Isaac Newton Carr, *History of Carson-Newman College*, vol. 1 (Jefferson City: n.p., 1959): 262, 264, 266; *The Orange and Blue* (Carson-Newman College newspaper) 1 March 1917, 15 April 1917, 1 May 1917, 1 April 1920; Jake Daubert, "The Greatest Play I Ever Saw," *Baseball Magazine* (August, 1911): 15; *Knoxville News-Sentinel*, 28 Oct. 1951.

13. See *Tennessean*, 3, 7, 11, 14 March 1908; *TSN*, 6 Feb. 1908. Kellum, no stranger to Nashville fans, had pitched for New Orleans in 1901. When a deal fell through to send the southpaw to Newark in 1908, Indianapolis traded him to Nashville for Buttons Briggs. *TSN*, 9 Jan., 26 March 1908.

14. "The Win Kellum Story" in *Big Rapids (MI) Pioneer*, 10–14 July 1950, 11 Aug. 1951, 30 Sept. 1967, 1 May 1976; 12th U.S. Census, 1900 (Michigan); 14th U.S. Census, 1920 (Michigan); Wright, *The Southern Association*, 63, 79–80, 131–32; *The Baseball Encyclopedia*, 1987, 2466; Winford A. Kellum, Player Career Index, *The Sporting News* Archive, St. Louis, MO; Ford Kellum to Gerald E. Wensloff, 12 Feb. 1976 in Win Kellum file, River Street Park Collection, Big Rapids Library, Big Rapids, MI.; Certificate of Death, Michigan Department of Health, Winford Ansley Kellum; *TSN*, 22 Aug. 1951.

15. *Big Rapids Pioneer*, 10 July 1950.

16. *TSN*, 20 Feb. 1908.

17. See Sullivan, *The Minors*, 56.

18. See *Banner*, Feb. 29, 1908; *Tennessean*, 26 Jan. 1908; *American*, 23 Feb. 1908; *TSN*, 6 Feb. 1908. Most newspapers of the day anglicized the name of the Russian-born pitcher as "Crystal." *Encyclopedia of Baseball*, 960, 1790.

19. For Franks' complete interview, *TSN*, 26 March 1908.

20. See *Tennessean*, 6, 10, 13, 17 March 1908; *Banner*, 7, 12 March 1908; *American*, 17, 18 March 1908. Phillips's antics were similar to Mike "Nuf Sed" McGreevey and his Royal Rooters in Boston. See Ritter, *Glory of Their Times*, 27. Other minor league teams boasted similar super fans. The 1908 Richmond squad had "Bleacher Jim" Orange, King of the Rooters. William S. Simpson, Jr., "1908: The Year Richmond Went 'Baseball Wild,'" *Virginia Cavalcade* 26 (Spring 1977): 187.

21. *Tennessean*, 18 March 1903.

22. *Baseball Encyclopedia*, 727; Willis Everett Butler, Player Career Index, *The Sporting News* Archive, St. Louis, MO; Wright, *The Southern Association*, 158; *Richmond Independent*, 24, 25 Feb. 1963.

23. *Tennessean*, 19 March 1903.

24. *American*, 19 March 1908.

25. *American*, 23 March 1908.

26. *American*, 26 March 1908; *Tennessean*, 26 March 1908; *Banner*, 26 March 1908; *TSN*, 2 April 1908. Bernhard's first lineup and substitutions were:

1. Decker CF	7. McCormick SS
2. Wiseman RF	8. Seabough C
3. Jansing 3rd	Harcy C
4. McElveen LF	Kerr C
5. Morse 1st	9. Sitton P
6. Butler 2nd	Sorrell P

27. Mrs. H.P. Sitton, *Houses of Old Pendleton*, unpublished manuscript in Special Collections, Clemson University Library, Clemson, South Carolina; Emma J. Sitton, *Some Early Pendleton History*, unpublished manuscript in Special Collections, Clemson University Library, Clemson, South Carolina; Sitton Family File, Pendleton District Historical Society, Pendleton, South Carolina; R.W. Simpson, *History of Old Pendleton District with a Genealogy of the Leading Families of the District* (Easley, S.C.: Southern Historical Press, 1978 reprint), 12–20, 220; *The Oconeean* (Clemson University yearbook), 1903 in Special Collections, Clemson University Library, Clemson, South Carolina; *Spalding Guide*, 1908, 213–214; *Tennessean*, 7, 12, 21 June 1909; *Banner*, 12 March 1909; *American*, 21 July, 5, 7, 21, 24 Aug., 3 Sept. 1909; *Encyclopedia of Baseball*, 2247; Carl Vedder Sitton file, Player Career Index, *The Sporting News* Archive, St. Louis, MO.; *Southern Association in Baseball*, 153–54; *Valdosta Daily Times*, 11–12 Sept. 1931; Certificate of Death, Bureau of Vital Statistics, C. Vedder Sitton, Georgia State Board of Health, 1931; *Keowee (S.C.) Courier*, 16 Sept. 1931.

28. *Tennessean*, 20 April 1908. The American Association and Eastern League, the other Class A leagues, were allowed 18 rostered players per team. *American*, 20 May 1908.

29. *TSN*, 2 April 1908.

30. *Tennessean*, 1 April 1908; *American*, 1 April 1908; *Banner*, 1, 9 April 1908. Dr. J. E. Nelius treated Vol players for a variety of muscle ailments.

31. Nashville's city league was scheduled to begin play on 2 May. The teams included Cheek-Neal, Nashville Athletic Club (N.A.C.),

Cumberland Telephone, YMCA, East Nashville, and West Nashville. Games were played at Peabody Field and Sulphur Dell when the Vols were on the road. See *American*, 2 May 1908.

32. Michael J. McCormick file, A. Bartlett Giamatti Research Center, Cooperstown, N.Y.; Michael J. McCormick, Player Career Index, *The Sporting News* Archive, St. Louis, MO.; *Baseball Encyclopedia*, 1209; Jersey City Journal, 19 Nov. 1953;

33. Much of the original Horseshoe district was demolished to construct the access ramps to the Holland Tunnel. What remains today is known locally as "the Island."

34. *American*, 8 April 1908.

35. *Baseball Encyclopedia*, 1047, 1959; George Hunter, Player Career Index, *The Sporting News Archive*, St. Louis, MO.; George Henry Hunter file, A. Bartlett Giamatti Research Center, Cooperstown, N.Y.; *Harrisburg Patriot*, 12 Jan. 1968.

36. *Tennessean*, 10 April 1908. Also see *American*, 10 April 1908; *Banner*, 10 April 1908.

37. See Okkonen, *Baseball Memories*, 12.

38. "Old Dan," or "Vinegar Dan" as fans called him, had officiated games in the Southern Association, beginning in 1903, and maintained a continuous association with the league for twenty-one years. See *TSN*, 6. Nov. 1924.

39. Ford played seven seasons in the majors with the New York Yankees (1909–1913) and Buffalo in the Federal League (1914–1915). He allegedly pitched with sandpaper tucked inside his glove to scuff the baseball. In 1920, the emery ball was outlawed along with the spit ball. *Encyclopedia of Baseball*, 1859.

40. For box score information and interviews, see *Tennessean*, 17 April 1908; Banner, 14, 17 April 1908; *American*, 17 April 1908; *TSN*, 23 April 1908; *SL*, 2 May 1908.

41. John Duggan file, A. Bartlett Giamatti Research Center, Cooperstown, N.Y.; Johnny Duggan, Player Career Index, *The Sporting News* Archive, St. Louis, MO; [Franklin-Greenwood, Indiana] *Daily Journal* , 21 March 1975; John Duggan file, Franklin College Alumnus Biographical Sketch, Alumni Office, Franklin (IN) College; Office of Vital Statistics, State of Florida.

42. *Tennessean*, 18 April 1908; *Banner*, 18 April 1908; *American*, 18 April 1908; *TSN*, 23 April 1908; *SL*, 2 May 1908.

Chapter 4

1. Harold C. Evans, "Baseball in Kansas, 1867–1940," *Kansas Historical Quarterly* 9 (1940): 175–192; J. Warren Seabough, Player Career Index, *The Sporting News Archive*, St. Louis, MO; Wright, *The Southern Association*, 121, 124, 131, 140, 145, 154, 159; *TSN*, 23, Oct. 1924; Johnson and Wolff, eds., *Encyclopedia of Minor League Baseball*, 163, 165; *Springfield* (MO) *News and Leader*, 10, 11 Nov. 1951.

2. In a related piece of Southern Association trivia, Atlanta and Mobile hook up for a game in 1910 designed to speed up play. The Sea Gulls notched a 2–1 victory in a contest that took only 32 minutes. See Sullivan, *The Minors*, 57.

3. Interview with Fred Russell, 7 April 1999, Nashville, Tennessee; Hub Perdue file, A. Bartlett Giamatti Research Center, Cooperstown, N.Y.; Hubbard Perdue, Player Career Index, *The Sporting News* Archive, St. Louis, MO.; *TSN*, 16 Nov. 1963; *Baseball Encyclopedia*,174, 175, 178, 182, 1181, 2155; *Tennessean*, 2 April 1998; 13 May 1962; *Banner*, 1 Nov. 1968; Wright, *The Southern Association*, 122, 124, 132, 140, 187, 191, 197, 199, 208, 214; *Gallatin Examiner*, 7 Nov. 1968.

4. Persons had a tremendous series, batting 9-for-13 with seven stolen bases.

5. Waller, *Nashville, 1900–1910*, 322; O'Neal, *The Southern League*, 308.

6. *Tennessean*, 26 April 1908.

7. Birmingham released its out-of-shape first sacker four days later. Meek, who also answered to the nickname of "Jumbo," reportedly tipped the scales at 245 lbs.

8. *Baseball Encyclopedia*, 1465; John Herbert Siegle, Player Career Index, *The Sporting News* Archive, St. Louis, MO.; Urbana (OH) *Citizen*, 13 Feb. 1968; Wright, *The Southern League*, 124, 131, 140, 145; John H. Siegle file, A. Bartlett Giamatti Research Center, Cooperstown, N.Y.

9. See *American*, 27 April, 1908; Sullivan, *The Minors*, 52.

10. *Tennessean*, 30 April 1908. The schedule did not favor the eastern teams in the league—Nashville, Atlanta, Montgomery, and Birmingham—in the month of May. The reverse would be true in the month of June. The scheduling format meant that it would take until 1 July before the standings balanced out.

11. The Slag Pile was replaced in 1910 with Rickwood Field. Benson, *Ballparks of North America*, 33; O'Neal, *The Southern Association*, 37.

12. *Tennessean*, 9 May 1908.

13. *TSN*, 28 May 1908.

14. *Banner*, 20 May 1908; 23 June 1908; *Tennessean*, 17 May 1908.

15. *Tennessean*, 14 May 1908.

16. John A. Simpson, "Harry Bay" in *Amer-*

ican League Stars of the Deadball Era (Dulles, Va.: Potomac Books): 647–648; Harry Bay, Player Career Index, *The Sporting News* Archive, St. Louis, MO.; Harry Elbert Bay file, A. Bartlett Giamatti Research Center, Cooperstown, N.Y.; *Baseball Encyclopedia*, 648; *Peoria Journal*, 21 March 1952; Scott Longert, *Addie Joss; King of the Pitchers* (Cleveland: Society for American Baseball Research, 1998): 50; Russell Schneider, *The Cleveland Indians Encyclopedia* (Philadelphia: Temple University Press, 1996): 254; *TSN*, 2 April 1952; *Reach Guide*, 1910, 274; 1911, 284; 1912, 240; Wright, *The Southern League*, 113, 140, 145; *Peoria Daily Record*, 7 Feb. 1939.

17. Clipping in Harry Bay, Player Career Index, *The Sporting News* Archive, St. Louis, MO.

18. *TSN*, 14 May 1908. See John Simpson, "Harry Bay," in *Deadball Stars of the American League*, 647–648.

19. *American*, 19, 24 May 1908; *Tennessean*, 30 May 1908.

20. *Banner*, 9 June 1908.

21. See Benson, *Ballparks of North America*, 224; O'Neal, *The Southern League*, 38; In 1915 the stadium was rebuilt and renamed Russwood Park. The wooden stadium burned down in 1960, and its location today is a medical center. For more on the rich baseball heritage in Memphis, see Paul R. Coppock, *Memphis Sketches* (Memphis: Memphis and Shelby County Libraries, 1976): 60–61; Helen M. Coppock and Charles W. Crawford, *Paul R. Coppock's Mid-South.* 3 (1976–1978). The Paul R. Coppock Publication Trust, n.d.: 96–99; William D. Miller, *Memphis During the Progressive Era, 1900–1917* (Memphis: Memphis State University Press, 1957): 34.

22. *Banner*, 28 May 1908.

23. *American*, 18 May 1908; *SL*, 30 May 1908.

24. Savidge's new pitch and how it was thrown is explained in *SL*, 9 May 1908.

25. *Tennessean*, 17 May 1908.

26. William Franklin Hart went on to pitch for eight seasons in the major leagues between 1886–1901 where he received the nickname "Uncle Billy." He finished his professional career in the Southern Association, mostly with Little Rock (1907–1910), then retired from the game at the age of 44. See O'Neal, *The Southern League*, 3; *Encyclopedia of Baseball*, 1920.

27. *Tennessean*, 21 May 1908; *American*, 21 May 1908; *Banner*, 21 May 1908; *TSN*, 21 May 1908; *SL*, 30 May 1908.

28. Benson, *Ballparks of North America*, 248; O'Neal, *The Southern League*, 38.

29. *Tennessean*, 24 May 1908.

30. *Ibid.*

31. *American*, 24 May 1908; *Banner*, 25 May 1908.

32. *Tennessean*, 25 May 1908.

33. *Tennessean*, 25 May 1908; *American*, 25 May 1908; *Banner*, 27 May 1908. See Frank's comments in *TSN*, 26 March 1908.

34. *Tennessean*, 28 May 1908.

35. "Caught in the Act of Farming," *Chicago Daily Tribune*, 18 Aug. 1908.

Chapter 5

1. *American*, 17, 18, 23 May 1908; *Banner*, 19 May 1908; *TSN*, 28 May 1908; *SL*, 28 May 1908.

2. *TSN*, 28 May 1908; *SL*, 6 June 1908; *American*, 12 July 1908.

3. *TSN*, 28 May 1908; *SL*, 25 July 1908, 8 Aug. 1908.

4. *American*, 14 April 1908, 11 May 1908; *Banner*, 25 May 1908; *SL*, 13 June 1908, 8 Aug. 1908. In late August, Little Rock, Mobile, and Montgomery all played home make-up games on Sundays.

5. *American*, 8 June 1908.

6. *Tennessean*, 30 May 1908; *American*, 28, 30 May 1908; *Banner*, 30 May 1908.

7. Paul Dickson asserts that the knuckleball was first used by Detroit's Ed Summers. Savidge drew Southern Association acclaim for throwing the pitch in the same season. See Paul Dickson, *The New Dickson Baseball Dictionary* (New York: Harcourt Brace and Company, 1999): 194.

8. *American*, 11 May 1908; O'Neal, *The Southern League*, 39.

9. *Tennessean*, 3 June 1908.

10. *Tennessean*, 5 June 1908.

11. Rice's analysis, a crude attempt to develop a statistic to define pitching performance, anticipated Earned Run Average (ERA). See *Tennessean*, 6 June 1908.

12. Otis Hinkley Stockdale had pitched for Washington, Boston, and Baltimore in the National League between 1893 and 1897. *The Baseball Encyclopedia*, 2271.

13. For complete coverage of the Stockdale scandal, see *Tennessean*, 3–18 June 1908.

14. *Tennessean*, 4 June 1908.

15. *SL*, 13 June 1908.

16. *Tennessean*, 18 June 1908; *American*, 15 June 1908; *SL*, 13 June 1908.

17. *SL*, 13 June 1908.

18. *TSN*, 25 June 1908.

19. The board of directors upheld their earlier decision on the Stockdale matter at a special meeting held on 30 August 1908 in Memphis. See *Banner*, 31 August 1908.

20. *Tennessean*, 10 June 1908; *American*, 10 June 1908; *Banner*, 10 June 1908; *TSN*, 18 June 1908; *SL*, 20 June 1908.

21. *Tennessean*, 11 June 1908.

22. *SL*, 20 June 1908.
23. *American*, 14 June 1908.
24. *American*, 14 June 1908.
25. *Tennessean*, 14 June 1908.
26. *Tennessean*, 14 June 1908.
27. *American*, 15 June 1908.
28. *Tennessean*, 17 June 1908.
29. *Banner*, 16 June 1908.
30. *Ibid.*
31. *Tennessean*, 16 June 1908; Fountain, *Sportswriter: The Life and Times of Grantland Rice*, 92–95.
32. *TSN*, 25 June 1908.
33. *Banner*, 18 June 1908.
34. Wiseman was no stranger to the infield. A shortstop at the University of Cincinnati in 1896–97, he played shortstop twenty-six times in 1906 and second base nine times in 1907. Wright, *The Southern Association*, 84, 96, 115, 121.
35. For the meaning of "Humpy" or "Humpy-dumpty," see Dickson, *The New Dickson Baseball Dictionary*, 265.
36. *Tennessean*, 18 June 1908.
37. *Tennessean*, 21 Sept. 1908.

Chapter 6

1. *American*, 19 June–8 July 1908.
2. *Tennessean*, 21 June 1908.
3. *Banner*, 23 June 1908.
4. *Tennessean*, 24 June 1908.
5. *Akron Beacon Journal*, 17, 24 Dec. 1908, 30 Aug. 1930; Walter East, Player Contract Cards, National Baseball Hall of Fame Library, Cooperstown, N.Y.; Walter East file, Player Career Index, *The Sporting News Archive*, St. Louis, MO.; *The Southern Association in Baseball*, 153; *U.S. Census, 1930, Ohio*; <FamilySearch.org>.
6. See Stanley Yerkes to Garry Herrmann, 17 September 1908; William Bernhard to Stanley Yerkes, 3 September 1908 in Stanley Lewis Yerkes, Vertical File, A. Bartlett Giamatti Research Center, National Baseball Hall of Fame Library, Cooperstown, N.Y.
7. *Tennessean*, 28 June 1908; *American*, 28 June 1908; *Banner*, 29 June 1908; *TSN*, 2 July 1908; *SL*, 11 July 1908. When the board of directors met on 30 August in Memphis to discuss the event, the Southern Association upheld the forfeit despite protests from Bernhard. *Banner*, 31 August 1908; *TSN*, 27 Aug. 1908.
8. *Tennessean*, 29 June 1908; *American*, 29 June 1908; *Banner*, 29 June 1908.
9. *Banner*, 1 July 1908.
10. *Tennessean*, 1 July 1908; *American*, 1 July 1908; *Banner*, 1 July 1908; *TSN*, 9 July 1908; *SL*, 11 July 1908. O'Brien played for Nashville in 1894.
11. *Tennessean*, 2 July 1908; *American*, 2 July 1908; *Banner*, 2 July 1908; *TSN*, 9 July 1908; *SL*, 18 July 1908. Hurlburt announced his retirement three weeks later and returned to his home in Memphis. See *TSN*, 23 July 1908; *SL*, 1 August 1908.
12. *Tennessean*, 3 July 1908.
13. See *American*, 12 July 1908.
14. *The Baseball Encyclopedia*, 24, 1722; J. Thomas Hetrick, *Chris Von der Ahe and the St. Louis Browns* (Lanham, MD: Scarecrow Press, 1999): 100, 135–136, 157, 160, 193–4; Nemec, *The Beer and Whiskey League*, 228; Seymour, *Baseball: The Early Years*, 277, 300–01; Dewey and Acocella, *The Biographical History of Baseball*, 12; Theodore P. Breitenstein Vertical File, A. Bartlett Giamatti Research Center, National Baseball Hall of Fame Library, Cooperstown, N.Y.; Bill James, *Whatever Happened to the Hall of Fame?: Baseball, Cooperstown, and the Politics of Glory* (New York: Firestone Books, 1995): 266; Ted Breitenstein file, Player Career Index, *The Sporting News Archive*, St. Louis, MO; Wright, *The Southern Association in Baseball*, 86, 92, 100, 106, 114, 119, 125, 133, 138, 144; *St. Louis Post-Dispatch*, 4 May 1935.
15. *American*, 7 July 1908; *Banner*, 7 July 1908; *TSN*, 16 July 1908; *SL*, 18 July 1908.
16. *Tennessean*, 8 July 1908; *Banner*, 8 July 1908.
17. *Banner*, 9, 11 July 1908.
18. Monroe Park was located on the corner of Ann and Tennessee Streets. It possessed lofty dimensions—406 feet to straight away center field. Later, the field became known as Hartwell Field. See O'Neal, *The Southern League*, 92, 200.
19. *Banner*, 10 July 1908; *TSN*, 16 July 1908.
20. *Banner*, 10 July 1908; *Tennessean*, 10 July 1908.
21. See Russell, *Vols Feats*, 40.
22. *Tennessean*, 15 July 1908.
23. *Tennessean*, 13 July 1908; *American*, 13 July 1908; *Banner*, 13 July 1908; *TSN*, 23 July 1908; *SL*, 25 July 1908.
24. *Tennessean*, 16 July 1908.
25. See *TSN*, 16 July 1908.
26. *TSN*, 16 July, 1908; *Tennessean*, 18 July 1908.
27. See *SL*, 25 July 1908; *TSN*, 16 July, 1908; *Tennessean*, 18 July 1908.
28. *Tennessean*, 16 July 1908. O'Brien was promptly replaced by Wheeler, an official from the Three-I League.
29. See *American*, 26 July 1908.

Chapter 7

1. *TSN*, 30 July 1908; *SL*, 1 August 1908.
2. *Tennessean*, 21 July 1908.

3. Reprinted from *Atlanta Journal* in *Tennessean*, 18 August 1908.
4. *Tennessean*, 21 July 1908.
5. *American*, 21 July 1908.
6. *Tennessean*, 21 July, 1908.
7. *Tennessean*, 22 July, 1908.
8. *Ibid.*
9. *American*, 23 July 1908.
10. *Tennessean*, 23 July, 1908.
11. For conflicting reports on Duggan's absence, see *Tennessean*, 23 July, 1908; *American*, 23 July 1908; *Banner*, 23 July 1908; *TSN*, 30 July 1908; *SL*, 1 August 1908.
12. For more on Sitton's rising stock with the Vols, *Tennessean*, 10, 24 July 1908; *Banner*, 24, 25 July 1908.
13. *Banner*, 18 July 1908; *Tennessean*, 24 1908; Okkonen, *Baseball Memories, 1900–1909*, 4.
14. *Tennessean*, 29 July, 1908; *American*, 29 July 1908; *Banner*, 29 July 1908; *TSN*, 6 August 1908; *SL*, 8 August 1908.
15. *Tennessean*, 30 July 1908.
16. *Tennessean*, 30 July 1908.
17. *Banner*, 29 July 1908.
18. *American*, 30 July 1908. Wiseman attracted quite a following in other cities on the southern circuit as well. Many enamored young ladies took the liberty of writing brief letters and postcards expressing their affection for him. See documents in the private collection of Dr. James A. Wiseman, Cincinnati, Ohio.
19. For more on the Duggan-Sitton situation, see *TSN*, 30 July, 6 August 1908; *SL*, 8 August 1908.
20. *Tennessean*, 2 August 1908.
21. *Banner*, 4 August 1908.
22. *Tennessean*, 4 August, 1908.
23. *Ibid.*
24. *Tennessean*, 6 August 1908.
25. *American*, 6 August 1908.
26. *Tennessean*, 6 August 1908.
27. *American*, 8 August 1908.
28. *Tennessean*, 12 August 1908.
29. *Tennessean*, 13 August 1908.
30. *Banner*, 14 August 1908.
31. *American*, 16 August 1908.
32. *American*, 19 August 1908.
33. *Tennessean*, 25 August 1908.
34. *Tennessean*, 21 August 1908; *Banner*, 21 August 1908; *American*, 21 August 1908; *TSN*, 27 August 1908; *SL*, 29 August 1908.
35. *Banner*, 22 August 1908.
36. *TSN*, 20 August 1908.
37. *Tennessean*, 26 August 1908.
38. *Memphis Commercial-Appeal*, 21–26 Feb. 1918; Wills, Probate Court of Shelby County, Tennessee, 31 January, 3 May, 7 Nov. 1918; Report of Homicide, # 389, Police Department, City of Memphis, Tennessee. Wright, *The Southern Association*, 87, 99, 109, 112, 118, 129, 135.
39. *Banner*, 26 August 1908.
40. *Tennessean*, 27 August 1908.

Chapter 8

1. *Tennessean*, 6 Sept. 1908. With one month to go in the major league season four teams battled for the American League crown and three teams competed for the National League honor.
2. Majors, *Editorial Wild Oats*, 138–140.
3. *Tennessean*, 31 August 1908.
4. *Tennessean*, 1 Sept. 1908. *TSN*, 3 Sept. 1908. Pittsburgh took an option on Johnny Duggan ten days later. For a rundown on the Vols destined to report to major league camps in the spring of 1909, *Banner*, 14 Sept. 1908.
5. For Rice's coverage of the incident, *Tennessean*, 4 Sept. 1908.
6. In a sobering case of vigilantism in the Jim Crow South, a macabre story came out of Memphis where Breitenstein had taken ill prior to an August pitching start after witnessing the lynching of a Negro. The incident was a stark reminder of the pervasive racism facing African Americans in the turn-of-the-century South. *Banner*, 9 August 1908.
7. *TSN*, 3 Sept. 1908.
8. *Tennessean*, 4 Sept. 1908.
9. *Banner*, 4 Sept. 1908.
10. *Tennessean*, 6 Sept. 1908; *Banner*, 7 Sept. 1908; *American*, 6 Sept. 1908; *TSN*, 10 Sept. 1908; *SL*, 19 Sept. 1908.
11. *Tennessean*, 7 Sept. 1908.
12. See *American*, 7 Sept. 1908.
13. *Memphis Commercial-Appeal*, 8 Sept. 1908.
14. *Tennessean*, 8 Sept. 1908.
15. *Tennessean*, 8 Sept. 1908.
16. *Tennessean*, 8 Sept. 1908.
17. *American*, 9 Sept. 1908; *Tennessean*, 9 Sept. 1908.
18. *Tennessean*, 9 Sept. 1908.
19. *Memphis Commercial-Appeal*, 9 Sept. 1908.
20. *Banner*, 9 Sept. 1908.
21. *Tennessean*, 9 Sept. 1908. See a follow up editorial critical of Birmingham's lackluster play on 11 Sept. 1908.
22. *Tennessean*, 10 Sept. 1908.
23. *Tennessean*, 11 Sept. 1908.
24. Duggan's no-hitter was the first of three in the initial fifty years of the Vols franchise. Russell, *Vols Feats*, 20.

25. *Tennessean*, 11 Sept. 1908.
26. By 1950, the six-hit performance of McElveen had been duplicated three times in Volunteer history — by Zack Smith (1932), Doug Taitt (1936), and Hal Boguskie (1948). Russell, *Vols Feats*, 23.
27. *Tennessean*, 12 Sept. 1908.
28. *Tennessean*, 13 Sept. 1908.
29. *Tennessean*, 12, 15, 16 Sept. 1908.
30. *Tennessean*, 16 Sept. 1908.
31. *Tennessean*, 12 Sept. 1908.
32. *Memphis Commercial-Appeal*, 15 Sept. 1908.
33. *Tennessean*, 16 Sept. 1908.
34. *Banner*, 17 Sept. 1908.
35. See William S. Simpson, Jr., "1908: The Year Richmond Went 'Baseball Wild,'" *Virginia Cavalcade* 26 (Spring 1977): 184–191.
36. See Okkonen, *Baseball Memories*, 228.
37. See David W. Anderson, *More Than Merkle: A History of the Best and Most Exciting Baseball Season in Human History* (Lincoln: University of Nebraska Press, 2000); Gordon H. Fleming, *The Unforgettable Season: 1908* (New York: Bison Books, 2006).
38. *Banner*, 17 Sept. 1908.

Chapter 9

1. *Banner*, 19 Sept. 1908.
2. *Banner*, 19 Sept. 1908.
3. *Memphis Commercial-Appeal*, 19 September 1908. The chart below is a summation of the sportswriter's predictions.
4. For a comprehensive list of individual player statistics, see *Spalding Guide*, 1909, 182–185.
5. *Spalding Guide*, 1909, 182–185.
6. *Tennessean*, 18 Sept. 1908.
7. *Banner*, 18 Sept. 1908.
8. See *Nashville, City Directory*, 1908, 1909, 1910 (Nashville: Marshall, Bruce, Polk).
9. *Tennessean*, 19 Sept. 1908; *American*, 19 Sept. 1908.
10. *Tennessean*, 19 Sept. 1908.
11. See *Tennessean*, 19 Sept. 1908.
12. *Banner*, 19 Sept. 1908.
13. See Theodore P. Breitenstein, Vertical File, A. Bartlett Giamatti Research Center, National Baseball Hall of Fame Library, Cooperstown, N.Y.
14. *Tennessean*, 19 Sept. 1908.
15. See *Tennessean*, 19 Sept. 1908.
16. *American*, 19, 20 Sept. 1908; *Tennessean*, 20 Sept. 1908.
17. *Tennessean*, 21 Sept. 1908.
18. *Tennessean*, 20 Sept. 1908.
19. *Tennessean*, 20 Sept. 1908.
20. *Tennessean*, 20, 21 Sept. 1908. Alfred Williams, the president of Harris-Davis Company was a familiar sight at most home games. For personal information, see *Nashville City Directory*, 1909 (Nashville: Marshall, Bruce, Polk, 1909):1205.
21. It is coincidental that William Carpenter and Dan Fitzsimmons, both former officials in the National League, lived in Rochester, N.Y. in the offseason along with other Southern Association officials — Augie Moran and Dan Pfenninger. See *American*, 16 Feb. 1909; *Banner*, 16 Feb. 1909.
22. *Tennessean*, 20 Sept. 1908.
23. The *Banner* carried a detailed inning-by-inning description of the game. Sports editor Yancey had been the Vols' official scorer for the season. See *Banner*, 20 Sept. 1908.
24. A modern scorekeeper would have given Rickert a fielder's choice (FC) in the official book, but Yancey recorded a base hit.
25. See *Tennessean*, 21 Sept. 1908.
26. See R.C. Morgan to J.A. Wiseman, 11, 18 September 1908; K.M.D. Lynne to J. A. Wiseman, 8 July 1909, in possession of James A. Wiseman, Cincinnati, OH.
27. *Banner*, 21 Sept. 1908.
28. *Tennessean*, 20 Sept. 1908; *Peoria Journal*, 21 March 1952.
29. In 1939, the top three teams in the Southern Association were separated by only .001, Chattanooga (.567), Memphis (.556), and Nashville (.556). See Wright, *The Southern Baseball Association*, 339–340.
30. For play-by-play details of the championship game, see Yancey's coverage in the *Banner*, 21 Sept. 1908. Also see, *Tennessean*, 20 Sept. 1908; *TSN*, 24 Sept. 1908; *SL*, 3 Oct. 1908.
31. *Banner*, 21 Sept. 1908.
32. *Banner*, 21 Sept. 1908.
33. *American*, 20 Sept. 1908.
34. *Banner*, 24 Sept. 1908; 16 Jan. 1909.
35. See *Tennessean*, 20 Sept. 1908.
36. *Tennessean*, 20 Sept. 1908; Waller, *Nashville, 1900–1910*, 71. For Kipling's 1892 poem, see Rudyard Kipling, *A Kipling Pageant* (New York: The Literary Guild, 1935): 877–878.
37. *Tennessean*, 20 Sept. 1908.
38. *Banner*, 21 Sept. 1908.
39. *SL*, 10 Oct. 1908; *Tennessean*, 12 Dec. 1908; *TSN*, 17 Dec. 1908.
40. See *Tennessean*, 20, 21 Sept. 1908; *American*, 2 Oct. 1908; *Banner*, 16 Jan. 1909.
41. *Tennessean*, 22 Sept. 1908.
42. *Tennessean*, 30 Sept. 1908.
43. On 23 September 1908, New York Giants first baseman Fred Merkle was guilty of a base-running gaffe that wound up costing his team the pennant when he ran off the field following

an apparent game-winning hit without touching the second base. Rader, Baseball, 93–94; Ritter, Glory of Their Times, 105.
44. Rader, Baseball, 83.

Chapter 10

1. For a rundown of the Nashville social calendar for 1908, Waller, Nashville, 1900–1910, 334–335.
2. See Summerville, The Carmack-Cooper Shooting: Tennessee Politics Turned Violent (Jefferson, N.C.: McFarland, 1993).
3. American, 4 Oct. 1908; Tennessean, 2 Oct. 1908; TSN, 15 Oct. 1908
4. Tennessean, 16 Oct. 1908; American, 18 Oct. 1908; TSN, 23 Oct. 1908.
5. Banner, 19 March 1909.
6. Tennessean, 19 Nov., 7 Dec. 1908; American, 10 Nov. 1908; TSN, 10 Dec. 1908.
7. Tennessean, 7 Jan. 1909; American, 11, 19 Nov. 1908; 3 Jan. 1909; Banner, 4 Jan. 1909.
8. Tennessean, 15, 16 Dec. 1908; American, 14, 15 ,16 Dec. 1908; TSN, 24 Dec. 1908.
9. Tennessean, 16, 17 Dec. 1908; American, 16 Dec. 1908; TSN, 24 Dec. 1908.
10. American, 6 Dec. 1908.
11. Banner, 13 Feb. 1909.
12. Tennessean, 30 Dec. 1908.
13. TSN, 10 Dec. 1908, 7 Jan. 1909; Banner, 16 Feb., 22 March 1909; American, 2 Mar. 1909.
14. Tennessean, 31 Jan. 1909.
15. Tennessean, 6 Jan., 12 March 1909; Banner; TSN, 18 March 1908.
16. Tennessean, 5 Feb. 1909; American, 10 Jan., 1 Feb. , Feb. 26 1909; Banner, 29, Dec. 1908, 23 Jan., 26 Feb. 1909; TSN, 25 March 1909. Kuhn sold Hardy at the end of February, but Mobile released him two months into the season.
17. Tennessean, 12 Dec. 1908.
18. Banner, 8 March 1909.
19. Tennessean, 13 Feb., 3 March 1909; Banner, 12 Feb. 1909.
20. See Tennessean, 17, 24 Feb. 1909; American, 17, 23 Feb. 1909; Banner, 23 Feb. 1909.
21. Tennessean, 15, 16, 18, 23 March 1909; Banner, 15, 16, 18 March 1909; American, 16, 23 March 1909.
22. American, 6, 7 April 1909; Banner, 1, 6, 7, 8 April 1909.
23. The stockholders included J. P. Connor, W. W. Taylor, W. G. Hirsig, L. G. Durr, Chris Haury, R. L. Bolling, James B. Carr, Dave Lowenheim, I. S. Morse, and W. H. Fletcher. American, 16 April 1909.
24. American, 16 April 1909.
25. Tennessean, 15–16 April 1909; Banner, 15 April 1909; American, 16 April 1909; TSN, 1 April 1909.
26. American, 16 April 1909.
27. Tennessean, 16 April 1909; Banner, 16 April 1909; American, 16 April 1909.
28. For individual statistics, Spalding Guide, 1909. Up to mid-century, the Vols won league crowns in 1901, 1902, 1908, 1916, 1940, 1943, 1948, and 1949. O'Neal, The Southern League, 300–306; Johnson and Wolff, eds., The Encyclopedia of Minor League Baseball, 117.
29. Montgomery and Memphis produced six hitters above .250 — the closest competitors to the Vols. Spalding Guide, 1909, 183.
30. For offensive, defensive and pitching statistics used above, Spalding Guide, 1909, 182–185.
31. Tennessean, 21 Sept. 1908.
32. TSN, 1 Oct. 1908.
33. Banner, 18 Sept. 1934.
34. Banner, 12 April 1936.
35. Banner, 9 Sept. 1948.
36. J.A. Wiseman to Fred Russell, [n.d] 1948, in possession of James A. Wiseman, Cincinnati, OH.
37. Banner, 9 Sept. 1948.
38. The City Paper (Nashville), 3 Aug. 2001.

Chapter 11

1. A comprehensive bibliographic citation is tendered when each personality is introduced.
2. "William K. Kavanaugh," Pulaski County Historical Review 16 (March 1968): 9–13; Arkansas Gazette, 22 February 1915; Arkansas Democrat, 22 Feb. 1915; TSN, 21 May 1936.
3. See Arkansas Gazette, 22 February 1915.
4. TSN, 21 May 1936.
5. Memphis Commercial-Appeal, 21–26 Feb. 1918; Wills, Probate Court of Shelby County, Tennessee, 31 January , 3 May, 7 Nov. 1918; Report of Homicide, # 389, Police Department, City of Memphis, Tennessee; Wright, The Southern Association, 87, 99, 109, 112, 118, 129, 135.
6. Memphis Commercial-Appeal, 21 Feb. 1918.
7. Memphis Commercial-Appeal, 24 Feb. 1918.
8. Shields died in Memphis on 27 August 1953. See Memphis Commercial-Appeal, 28 August 1953.
9. Jack Dolittle Hardy file, Player Career Index, The Sporting News Archive, St. Louis, MO.; John D. Hardy Vertical File, National Baseball Hall of Fame Library, Cooperstown, N.Y.; Cleveland Plain-Dealer, 21 Oct. 1921; Cleveland City Directory, 1921, 1399.

10. See Emma Hardy's comments in *Akron Beacon Journal*, 20 April 1964.

11. See Emma Hardy to Lee Allen, 14 March, 26 May 1964 in John D. Hardy Vertical File, A. Bartlett Giamatti Research Center, National Baseball Hall of Fame Library, Cooperstown, N.Y.

12. Jake E. Daubert file, Player Career Index, *The Sporting News Archive*, St. Louis, MO.; Jacob Ellsworth Daubert Vertical File, National Baseball Hall of Fame Library, Cooperstown, N.Y.; Jim Sandoval, "Jacob Ellsworth Daubert," in Tom Simon, ed. *Deadball Stars of the National League* (Washington, D.C.: Brassey, Inc., 2004): 293–295; *The Call*, Schuyllkill Haven, PA., 10 July 1997; Wright, *The Southern Association*, 135; *TSN*, 16 Oct., 6 Nov. 1924,15 Aug. 1954; Robert W. Creamer, *Stengel; His Life and Times* (Lincoln: University of Nebraska Press, 1984): 50–51, 71–6, 115, 120–1; *The Baseball Encyclopedia*, 194–5, 816, 2413, 2697; Jack Kavanaugh and Norman Macht, *Uncle Robbie* (Cleveland: Society for American Baseball Research, 1999): 54, 61–5, 105–7; John Thorn and Pete Palmer *Total Baseball* (New York: Warner Books): 766; Donald Dewey and Nicholas Acocella, *The Biographical History of Baseball* (New York: Carroll and Graf Publishers, 1995): 105; F.C. Lane, *Batting* (Cleveland: Society for American Baseball Research, 2001 reprint): 6, 21, 56–7, 82–4,139–140, 167; *Cincinnati Times-Star*, 9 Oct. 1924; *New York Times*, 11 Aug. 1929; Brooklyn Spectator, 16 Nov. 1994; *Spalding's Official Base Ball Guide, 1925*, 344; Robert L. Finch, L.H. Addington, Ben M. Morgan, eds., *The Story of Minor League Baseball in the United States with Particular Reference to its Growth and Development in the Smaller Cities and Towns of the Nation— The Minor Leagues; The Record of Championship Performances From 1901-1952* (Columbus, Ohio: Stoneman Press, 1952): 642, 648.

13. *TSN*, 15 Aug. 1954.

14. Sandoval, "Daubert," 293.

15. Clipping with George Daubert quote in *New York Post*, 3 July 1989 in Jacob Ellsworth Daubert Vertical File, National Baseball Hall of Fame Library, Cooperstown, N.Y.

16. Quoted in F.C. Lane, *Batting* (Cleveland: Society for American Baseball Research, 2001 reprint): 56–57.

17. Quoted in Lane, *Batting*, 6.

18. Quoted in Lane, *Batting*, 21.

19. Clipping quote from *Biographical Dictionary of American Sports*, in Jacob Ellsworth Daubert Vertical File, National Baseball Hall of Fame Library, Cooperstown, N.Y.; John W. Smith, "Jake Daubert Struck Blow for Ballplayers' Rights," in Jacob Ellsworth Daubert Vertical File, National Baseball Hall of Fame Library, Cooperstown, N.Y.

20. In F.C. Lane, *Batting* (Cleveland: Society for American Baseball Research, 2001 reprint): 139–140.

21. See *Cincinnati Times-Star*, 9 Oct. 1924; *TSN*, 16 Oct. 1924.

22. *TSN*, 15 Aug. 1954.

23. *Akron Beacon Journal*, 17, 24 Dec. 1908, 30 Aug. 1930; Walter East, Player Contract Cards, National Baseball Hall of Fame Library, Cooperstown, N.Y.; Walter East file, Player Career Index, *The Sporting News Archive*, St. Louis, MO.; *The Southern Association in Baseball*, 153; *U.S. Census, 1930, Ohio*; <FamilySearch.org>.

24. Mrs. H.P. Sitton, *Houses of Old Pendleton*, unpublished manuscript in Special Collections, Clemson University Library, Clemson, South Carolina; Emma J. Sitton, *Some Early Pendleton History*, unpublished manuscript in Special Collections, Clemson University Library, Clemson, South Carolina; Sitton Family File, Pendleton District Historical Society, Pendleton, South Carolina; R.W. Simpson, *History of Old Pendleton District with a Genealogy of the Leading Families of the District* (Easley, S.C.: Southern Historical Press, 1978 reprint), 12–20, 220; *The Oconeean* (Clemson University yearbook), 1903 in Special Collections, Clemson University Library, Clemson, South Carolina; *Spalding Guide, 1908*, 213–214; *Tennessean*, 7, 12, 21 June 1909; *Banner*, 12 March 1909; *American*, 21 July, 5, 7, 21, 24 Aug., 3 Sept. 1909; *Encyclopedia of Baseball*, 2247; Carl Vedder Sitton file, Player Career Index, *The Sporting News Archive*, St. Louis, MO.; *Southern Association in Baseball*, 153–54; *Valdosta Daily Times*, 11–12 Sept. 1931; Certificate of Death, Bureau of Vital Statistics, C. Vedder Sitton, Georgia State Board of Health, 1931; *Keowee (S.C.) Courier*, 16 Sept. 1931.

25. *The Baseball Encyclopedia*, 24, 1722; J. Thomas Hetrick, *Chris Von der Ahe and the St. Louis Browns* (Lanham, MD: Scarecrow Press, 1999): 100, 135–136, 157, 160, 193–4; Nemec, *The Beer and Whiskey League*, 228; Seymour, *Baseball: The Early Years*, 277, 300–01; Dewey and Acocella, *The Biographical History of Baseball*, 12; Theodore P. Breitenstein Vertical File, A. Bartlett Giamatti Research Center, National Baseball Hall of Fame Library, Cooperstown, N.Y.; Bill James, *Whatever Happened to the Hall of Fame?: Baseball, Cooperstown, and the Politics of Glory* (New York: Firestone Books, 1995): 266; Ted Breitenstein file, Player Career Index, *The Sporting News Archive*, St. Louis, MO; Wright, *The Southern Association in Baseball*, 86, 92, 100, 106, 114, 119, 125, 133, 138, 144; *St. Louis Post-Dispatch*, 4 May 1935.

26. See clipping in Theodore P. Breitenstein file, A. Bartlett Giamatti Research Center, Cooperstown, N.Y.

27. William H. Bernhard, Player Contract Card, A. Bartlett Giamatti Research Center, Cooperstown, N.Y.; William H. Bernhard, Player Career Index, *The Sporting News Archive*, St. Louis, MO.; Wright, *The Southern Association in Baseball*, 131, 140, 146, 151, 159, 173; *Chattanooga Daily Times*, 6, 7 May 1915; Carlos Bauer, *An Encyclopedia of the Old Pacific Coast League, 1903–1957*, vol. 3 (New York: Baseball Press Books, 2003): 796; *Salt Lake City Herald-Republican*, 20 Feb. 1917; *Cemetery Records, Town of Clarence, New York*, Historical Society of the Town of Clarence, N.Y.; *San Diego City Directories*, 1940–1948; *Memphis City Directory* (Memphis, R.L. Polk, 1911–1920); *TSN*, 6 April 1949; *Buffalo Evening News*, 31 March 1949.

28. Clipping in William Henry Bernhard file, A. Bartlett Giamatti Research Center, National Baseball Hall of Fame Library, Cooperstown, N.Y.

29. "The Win Kellum Story" in *Big Rapids* (MI) *Pioneer*, 10–14 July 1950, 11 Aug. 1951, 30 Sept. 1967, 1 May 1976; 12th U.S. Census, 1900 (Michigan); 14th U.S. Census, 1920 (Michigan); Wright, *The Southern Association*, 63, 79–80, 131–32; *The Baseball Encyclopedia*, 1987, 2466; Winford A. Kellum, Player Career Index, *The Sporting News Archive*, St. Louis, MO; Ford Kellum to Gerald E. Wensloff, 12 Feb. 1976 in Win Kellum file, River Street Park Collection, Big Rapids Library, Big Rapids, MI; Certificate of Death, Michigan Department of Health, Winford Ansley Kellum; *TSN*, 22 Aug. 1951.

30. *Big Rapids* (MI) *Pioneer*, 1 May 1976.

31. *Big Rapids* (MI) *Pioneer*, 11 August 1951.

32. *Big Rapids* (MI) *Pioneer*, 13, 14 July 1950.

33. *Big Rapids* (MI) *Pioneer*, 14 July 1950.

34. See *Diamond Jubilee — Bicentennial, Mossy Creek–Jefferson City, 1788–1976* (n.p.: 1976) in Carson-Newman Library archive, Carson-Newman College, Jefferson City, TN.; Chris Jones, "It Gets Foggy at Mossy Creek; the Origin and Development of Intercollegiate Athletics at Carson-Newman College," (unpublished research paper, 1974): 200, in Carson-Newman Library archive, Carson-Newman College, Jefferson City, TN; Wright, *The Southern Association*, 121, 124, 144, 153–54; *Baseball Encyclopedia*, 1213, 167, 170; Pryor M. McElveen, Player Career Index, *The Sporting News Archive*, St. Louis, MO; *Catalogue of Carson and Newman College, 1917–1918* (Jefferson City: Tennessee Litho Company, 1917): 63; Isaac Newton Carr, *History of Carson-Newman College*, vol. 1 (Jefferson City: n.p., 1959): 262, 264, 266; *The Orange and Blue* (Carson-Newman College newspaper) 1 March 1917, 15 April 1917, 1 May 1917, 1 April 1920; Jake Daubert, "The Greatest Play I Ever Saw," *Baseball Magazine* (August, 1911): 15; *Knoxville News-Sentinel*, 28 Oct. 1951.

35. Jake Daubert, "The Greatest Play I Ever Saw," *Baseball Magazine* (August, 1911): 15.

36. Harold C. Evans, "Baseball in Kansas, 1867–1940," *Kansas Historical Quarterly* 9 (1940): 175–192; J. Warren Seabough, Player Career Index, *The Sporting News Archive*, St. Louis, MO; Wright, *The Southern Association*, 121, 124, 131, 140, 145, 154, 159; *TSN*, 23 Oct. 1924; Johnson and Wolff, eds., *Encyclopedia of Minor League Baseball*, 163, 165; [Springfield] *Leader and Press*, 10 May 1960; 14th U.S. Census, 1930; *The Frisco Employee's Magazine*, 1925–1935.

37. *Peoria Journal*, 21 March 1952.

38. *Peoria Journal*, 21 March 1952.

39. A tremendous amount of family information was obtained in an eight-hour interview with Dr. James A. Wiseman, Dr. Donald E. Wiseman, Mrs. Jeanne Wiseman Groenke, and Mrs. Helen Wiseman in Cincinnati, Ohio, on 4–5 April 2004. Also see Donald E. Wiseman, "Julius Augustus 'Doc' Wiseman (1877–1953): The Hero of the Dell," (unpublished family genealogy); Darl L. Stephenson, *Headquarters in the Brush: Blazer's Independent Union Scouts* (Athens, Ohio: Ohio University Press, 2001); Patricia L. Faust, ed., *Historical Times Illustrated Encyclopedia of the Civil War* (New York: Harper & Row, 1986): 510–511; Certificate of Death, Julius Augustus Wiseman, Ohio Department of Health; Wright, *The Southern Association*, 63, 70, 78, 84, 96, 101, 109, 115, 121, 124, 131, 140, 145; *The Burnet Woods Echo*, 10, 24 May, 14 June 1897, Blegin Library Archives, University of Cincinnati, Cincinnati, OH; James A. Wiseman to John A. Simpson, 27 January, 2, 9 February 2004 in possession of the author; Simon, ed., *Deadball Stars of the National League*, 355–357; *Nashville Tennessean and the Nashville American*, 10, 11 July 1912; *Banner*, 8–11 July 1912; Russell, *Vols Feats*, 18; *Cincinnati City Directory, 1909–1927*; J.A. Wiseman to Jim Wiseman, 12 Nov. 1949, Larry Gilbert to M.C. Saunders, 15 April 1953, in possession of Dr. James A. Wiseman, Cincinnati, OH; Banner, 9, 10 April 1953; *TSN*, 22 April 1953.

40. James A. Wiseman to John A. Simpson, 27 January, 2, 9 February 2004 in possession of the author.

41. Wiseman, "The Hero of the Dell," 14.

42. Wiseman Interviews, 4–5 April 2004.

43. Wiseman Interviews, 4–5 April 2004.

44. James A. Wiseman to John A. Simpson, 9 February 2004 in possession of the author.
45. J.A. Wiseman to Jim Wiseman, 12 Nov. 1949, in possession of Dr. James A. Wiseman, Cincinnati, OH.
46. Russell, Vols Feats, 18; Larry Gilbert to M.C. Saunders, 15 April 1953, in possession of Dr. James A. Wiseman, Cincinnati, OH; *Banner,* 9, 10 April 1953; *TSN,* 22 April 1953. Dr. James A. Wiseman, the source of so much Doc Wiseman material, passed away on 24 July 2004.
47. Michael J. McCormick file, A. Bartlett Giamatti Research Center, Cooperstown, N.Y.; Michael J. McCormick, Player Career Index, *The Sporting News Archive,* St. Louis, MO.; *Baseball Encyclopedia,* 1209; *Jersey City Journal,* 19 Nov. 1953;
48. See Mike McCormick to Ford Frick, 26 April 1936; Ford Frick to Mike McCormick, 30 April 1936, in Michael J. McCormick file, A. Bartlett Giamatti Research Center, Cooperstown, N.Y.
49. Fountain, *Sportswriter,* 33–109, 289–90; Louise Davis, "At the Top, But Dreaming Still" in *Nashville Tennessean Magazine,* 6 Feb. 1947; *Tennessee Encyclopedia of History and Culture,* 795–796; *Nashville Tennessean,* 6 Feb. 2003.
50. *Tennessee Encyclopedia of History and Culture,* 796.
51. Reprinted in Fountain, *Sportswriter,* 289.
52. Fountain, *Sportswriter,* 290.
53. In Davis, "At the Top, But Dreaming Still," *Nashville Tennessean Magazine,* 6 Feb. 1947.
54. *Baseball Encyclopedia,* 727; Willis Everett Butler, Player Career Index, *The Sporting News Archive,* St. Louis, MO; Wright, *The Southern Association,* 158; *Richmond Independent,* 24, 25 Feb. 1963.
55. John Duggan file, A. Bartlett Giamatti Research Center, Cooperstown, N.Y.; Johnny Duggan, Player Career Index, *The Sporting News Archive,* St. Louis, MO; [Franklin-Greenwood, Indiana] *Daily Journal,* 21 March 1975; John Duggan file, *Franklin College Alumnus Biographical Sketch,* Alumni Office, Franklin (IN) College; Office of Vital Statistics, State of Florida.
56. *Baseball Encyclopedia,* 1047, 1959; George Hunter, Player Career Index, *The Sporting News Archive,* St. Louis, MO.; George Henry Hunter file, A. Bartlett Giamatti Research Center, Cooperstown, N.Y.; *Harrisburg Patriot,* 12 Jan. 1968.
57. *Baseball Encyclopedia,* 1465; John Herbert Siegle, Player Career Index, *The Sporting News Archive,* St. Louis, MO.; *Urbana (OH) Citizen,* 13 Feb. 1968; Wright, *The Southern Association,* 124, 131, 140, 145; John H. Siegle file, A. Bartlett Giamatti Research Center, Cooperstown, N.Y.
58. Interview with Fred Russell, 7 April 1999, Nashville, Tennessee; Hub Perdue file, A. Bartlett Giamatti Research Center, Cooperstown, N.Y.; Hubbard Perdue, Player Career Index, *The Sporting News Archive,* St. Louis, MO.; *TSN,* 16 Nov. 1963; *Baseball Encyclopedia,* 174, 175, 178, 182, 1181, 2155; *Tennessean,* 2 April 1998; 13 May 1962; *Banner,* 1 Nov. 1968; Wright, *The Southern Association,* 122, 124, 132, 140, 187, 191, 197, 199, 208, 214; *Gallatin Examiner,* 7 Nov. 1968.
59. Interview with Fred Russell, 7 April 1999, Nashville, Tennessee; *Tennessean,* 2 April 1998.
60. *TSN,* 16 Nov. 1963, in Hubbard Perdue file, *The Sporting News Archive,* St. Louis, MO.
61. See *TSN,* 16 Nov. 1963.
62. Quote in Russell, *Bury Me in an Old Press Box,* 100.
63. Quote in Russell, *Bury Me in an Old Press Box,* 26.
64. *Banner,* 15 Feb. 1996.
65. See contribution of Mike Allen in <www.sulphurdell.com>.
66. *Tennessean,* 28 January 2003.
67. *Ibid.* For more on Russell's illustrious career, see *Who's Who in the South and Southwest, 1997–1998* (New Providence, N.J.: Marquis, 1998): 786.
68. Interview with Fred Russell, 7 April 1999, Nashville, TN.

Appendix C

1. See Bill James, *Whatever Happened To The Hall of Fame?; Baseball, Cooperstown, and the Politics of Glory* (New York: Firestone Books, 1995): 28, 31, 34, 46; Thorn and Palmer, eds., *Total Baseball,* 519.
2. Bill James, *Whatever Happened To The Hall of Fame?; Baseball, Cooperstown, and the Politics of Glory* (New York: Firestone Books, 1995): 50, 121, 157, 166.
3. For a specific breakdown of James' cliometrics, see *Whatever Happened To The Hall of Fame?,"* 174–175.
4. For a breakdown of Daubert's career, see A. W. Laird, *Ranking Baseball's Elite; An Analysis Derived from Player Statistics, 1893–1987* (Jefferson, N.C.: McFarland, 1990): 60–69.
5. For a detailed explanation, see Bill James and Jim Henzler, *Win Shares* (New York: STATS Publishing, 2002) 2–3, 14–16.
6. Here is a breakdown of Daubert's "win shares":

Year	Win Shares	Rank on team	Team	Year	Win Shares	Rank on team	Team
1910	17	5th	Brooklyn	1921	12	8th	Cincinnati
1911	20	2nd	"	1922	24	1st	"
1912	17	2nd	"	1923	13	10th	"
1913	17	3rd	"	1924	8	13th	"
1914	19	5th	"	15 seasons	263 points	5.0 average worth	
1915	27	1st	"				
1916	21	3rd	"				
1917	12	9th	"				
1918	15	3rd	"				
1919	17	7th	Cincinnati				
1920	24	3rd	"				

See James and Henzler, *Win Shares,* 297–319.

7. Check Daubert's point totals, ranking, and comparison with other players in James and Henzler, *Win Shares,* 140, 495, 501, 506, 595, 658.

Bibliography

Primary Sources

Books and Pamphlets

Ashenback, Edward Michael. *Humor Among the Minors: True Tales from the Baseball Brush.* Chicago: M. A. Donohue and Co., 1911.
Cincinnati City Directory, 1909–1927.
Clark, Ida Clyde. *Nashville: A Complete Historical Guide book to the City.* Nashville: n.p., 1912.
Foster, John B., ed. *Spalding's Official Base Ball Record, 1909.* New York: American Sports Publishing Co., 1909.
Hale, Will T. and Dixon L. Merritt. *A History of Tennessee and Tennesseans: The Leaders and Representative Men of Commerce, Industry and Modern Activity.* 4 vols. Chicago: Lewis Publishing Co., 1913.
Lane, F. C. *Batting.* Cleveland: Society for American Baseball Research, 2001 reprint of 1925 volume.
Memphis City Directory. Memphis: R. L. Polk and Co., 1918.
Nashville City Directory, Nashville: Marshall, Bruce, and Polk Co., 1907–1909.
Spalding's Official Base Ball Rule Book, 1908. New York: American Sports Publishing Co., 1908.
Who's Who in Tennessee: A Biographical Reference Book of Notable Tennesseans of Today. Memphis: Paul and Douglass, 1911.

City Directories

Memphis City Directory, 1911–1920.
Nashville City Directory, 1907–1910.

San Diego City Directory, 1940–1948.

Manuscripts and Other Unpublished Material

A. Bartlett Giamatti Research Center, National Baseball Hall of Fame Library, Cooperstown, New York

Player contract cards   *Vertical files*
Harry Bay   Harry Elbert Bay
William H. Bernhard   William Henry Bernhard
Willis Butler   Theodore P. Breitenstein
John Duggan   Jacob Ellsworth Daubert
Walter R. East   John D. Hardy
John D. Hardy   George Henry Hunter
George H. Hunter   Winford Ansley Kellum
Stanley Yerkes   Michael J. McCormick
                                      Pryor Mynatt McElveen
                                      John H. Siegle
                                      Carl Vedder Sitton
                                      Stanley Lewis Yerkes

Clemson University Library, Special Collections, Clemson, S.C.
Sitton, Emma J. *Some Early Pendleton History,* unpublished manuscript.
Sitton, Mrs. H.P. *Houses of Old Pendleton,* unpublished manuscript.
The Oconeean (Clemson yearbook) 1903.

Franklin (Indiana) College Alumni Office
Franklin College Alumnus Biographical Sketch, John Duggan File.

Jean and Alexander Heard Library, Vanderbilt University, Nashville
Grantland Rice Collection.
William Waller Collection.

Historical Society of the Town of Clarence, N.Y.
Vertical file of Bernhard family.

Pendleton District Historical Society, Pendleton, S.C.
Sitton Family file.

Tennessee State Library and Archive, Nashville
Vertical files
Fred Russell
Sulphur Dell
Yancy family

The Nashville Room, Public Library of Nashville and Davidson County, Nashville
Vertical files
James Stephens Brown
Sports—Sulphur Dell Ball Park

***The Sporting News* Library and Archive, St. Louis**
Player contract cards
Harry Bay   Winford A. Kellum
William H. Bernhard   Michael J. McCormick
Ted Breitenstein   Pryor M. McElveen
Willis Everett Butler   Hubbard Perdue
Jake E. Daubert   James Warren Seabough
Johnny Duggan   John Herbert Siegle
Walter East   Carl Vedder Sitton
John Dolittle Hardy   William Sorrell
John (Jack) Hess   Julius A. Wiseman
George Hunter   Stanley Yerkes
Henry Jansen

Newspapers and Periodicals

Akron Beacon Journal, 1930.
Arkansas (Little Rock) Gazette, 1915.
Baseball Magazine, 1908–1909.
Big Rapids (Mich.) Pioneer, 1950–1951, 1967, 1976.
Boston Globe, 1940.
Buffalo Evening News, 1949.
Chattanooga Daily Times, 1915.
Chicago Daily Tribune, 1908.
Cincinnati Times-Star, 1924, 1953.
Cleveland Plain-Dealer, 1921.
Daily Journal, Franklin, Indiana, 1975.
Gallatin (Tenn.) Examiner, 1968.
Harrisburg (Pa.) Patriot, 1968.
Jersey City (N.J.) Journal, 1953.
Keowee (S.C.) Courier, 1931.
Knoxville News-Sentinel, 1951.
Memphis Commercial-Appeal, 1908, 1918, 1953.
Nashville American, 1907–1909.
Nashville Banner, 1907–1968.
Nashville Tennessean, 1907–2001.
Nashville Tennessean and the Nashville Banner, 1912.
New Orleans Times Picayune, 1908.
Salt Lake City Herald-Republican, 1917.
Spalding's Official Base Ball Record, 1900–1925.
Sporting Life, 1907–1909.
Springfield (Mo.) Leader and Press, 1960.
St. Louis Post-Dispatch, 1935.
The Burnet Woods Echo (University of Cincinnati), 1897.
The Call, Schuykill Haven, Pa., 1997.
The Frisco Employee's Magazine, 1925–1935 (St. Louis and San Francisco Railway).
The Orange and Blue, Carson-Newman College, Jefferson City, Tenn., 1920.
The Sporting News, 1907–1949.
Urbana (Ohio) Citizen, 1968.
Valdosta Times, 1931.

Public Records and Proceedings

Bartlett, Jennifer M., Charles P. Stripling, and Fred. M. Prouty. *Historical and Archaeological Investigations of the Site of the Tennessee Bicentennial Mall, 40DV469, Davidson County*. Nashville: Tennessee Department of Environment and Conservation, Division of Archaeology, 1995.
Secretary of State, State of Tennessee Charter of Incorporation, Nashville Base-ball Association (1905).
U.S. Census, Population, 1880–1930.

Secondary Sources

Articles

Barash, Allison Caveglia. "Base Ball in the Civil War." *The National Pastime; A Review of Baseball History* 21 (2001): 17–19.
"Baseball Stirred Passions in Nashville after War," *The City Paper* (Nashville), 1 April 2003.
Beck, Ken. "Sulphur Dell Sights, Smells Linger On." *Nashville Banner Panorama*, 18 Sept. 1977.
Brown, J.D. "The Name Stuck." *Nashville Tennessean Magazine*, 12 April 1947.
Davis, Louise. "At the Top, But Dreaming Still: Grantland Rice." *Nashville Tennessean Magazine*, 6 Feb. 1949.
Evans, Harold C. "Baseball in Kansas, 1867–1940." *Kansas Historical Quarterly* 9 (1940): 175–192.
Jones, Chris. "It Gets Foggy at Mossy Creek; the Origin and Development of Intercollegiate Athletics at Carson-Newman College." Research paper, Carson-Newman Library, Jefferson City, Tennessee, 1974.

Manuel, Mark G. "The Ball's on the Queer!" *The Baseball Research Journal* 26 (1997): 114–117.

Neel, Roy. "Never a Dull Moment: Veteran Sportswriter Fred Russell." *Vanderbilt Alumnus* 61 (1975): 12, 39–41.

Russell, Fred. "Grantland Rice Gave It A Name... Sulphur Dell." *Nashville Magazine* (Feb. 1957).

Simpson, John A. "Harry Bay," in David Jones, ed. *Deadball Stars of the American League.* Dulles, Va.: Potomac Books, 2006: 647–648.

Simpson, Jr., William S. "1908: The Year Richmond Went 'Baseball Wild.'" *Virginia Cavalcade* 26 (Spring 1977): 184–192.

"The Nashville Seraphs, 1895," *The National Pastime; A Review of Baseball History* 23 (2003): 57–59.

Traughber, Bill. "Nashville Hosted Greatest Game Played in South," *The City Paper* (Nashville), 3 August 2001.

"William M. Kavanaugh." *Pulaski County (AR) Historical Review* 16 (March 1968): 9–13.

Books and Pamphlets

Aldridge, Gwen, and Bret Wills. *Baseball Archaeology: Artifacts from the Great American Pastime.* San Francisco: Chronicle Books, 1993.

Anderson, David W. *More Than Merkle: A History of the Best and Most Exciting Baseball Season in Human History.* Lincoln: University of Nebraska Press, 2000.

Bauer, Carlos. *An Encyclopedia of the Old Pacific Coast League, 1903–1957,* vol. 3. New York: Baseball Press Books, 2003.

Benson, Michael. *Ballparks of North America: A Comprehensive Historical Reference to Baseball Grounds, Yards and Stadiums, 1845 to Present.* Jefferson, N.C.: McFarland, 1989.

Bevis, Charlie. *Sunday Baseball; The Major Leagues' Struggle to Play Baseball on the Lord's Day, 1876–1934.* Jefferson, N.C.: McFarland, 2003.

Carr, Isaac Newton. *History of Carson-Newman College.* Jefferson City, TN: Carson-Newman College, 1959.

Cash, Jon David. *Before They Were Cardinals: Major League Baseball in Nineteenth-Century St. Louis.* Columbia: University of Missouri Press, 2002.

Coppock, Helen M., and Charles W. Crawford. *Paul R. Coppock's Mid-South.* 3 (1976–1978). The Paul R. Coppock Publication Trust, n.d.

Coppock, Paul R. *Memphis Sketches.* Memphis: Friends of Memphis and Shelby County Libraries, 1976.

Cornwell, Ilene J. *Biographical Directory of the Tennessee General Assembly.* 3 vols. Nashville: Tennessee Historical Commission, 1988.

Creamer, Robert W. *Stengel: His Life and Times.* Lincoln: University of Nebraska Press, 1984.

Darnell, Tim. *Southern Yankees: The Story of the Atlanta Crackers.* n.p., 1995.

Dewey, Donald, and Nicholas Acocella. *The Biographical History of Baseball.* New York: Carroll and Graf Publishers, Inc., 1995.

Diamond Jubilee — Bicentennial, Mossy Creek-Jefferson City, 1788–1976 (n.p.: 1976), in Carson-Newman Library archive, Carson-Newman College, Jefferson City, TN.

Dickson, Paul. *The Joy of Keeping Score: How Scoring the Game Has Influenced and Enhanced the History of Baseball.* New York: Walker and Co., 1996.

_____. *The New Dickson Baseball Encyclopedia.* New York: Harcourt Brace and Co., 1999.

Doyle, Don H. *Nashville in the New South, 1880–1930.* Knoxville: University of Tennessee Press, 1985.

_____. *New Men, New Cities, New South; Atlanta, Nashville, Charleston, Mobile, 1860–1910.* Chapel Hill: University of North Carolina Press, 1990.
Durham, Walter T. *Nashville: The Occupied City.* Nashville: Tennessee Historical Commission, 1985.
Faust, Patricia L., ed., *Historical Times Illustrated Encyclopedia of the Civil War.* New York: Harper & Row, 1986.
Finch, Robert L., L. H. Addington and Ben M. Morgan, eds. *The Story of Minor League Baseball: A History of the Game of Professional Baseball in the United States with Particular Reference to its Growth and Development in the Smaller Cities and Towns of the Nation.* Columbus, OH: Stoneman Press, 1952.
Fleming, Gordon H. *The Unforgettable Season: 1908.* New York: Bison Books, 2006.
Foster, Austin P., and Albert H. Roberts. *Tennessee Democracy: A History of the Party and Its Representative Members — Past and Present.* Nashville: Democratic Historical Association, 1940.
Fountain, Charles. *Sportswriter: The Life and Times of Grantland Rice.* New York: Oxford University Press, 1993.
Goodwin, Doris Kearns. *Wait till Next Year: A Memoir.* New York: Simon and Schuster, 1997.
Hetrick, J. Thomas. *Chris Von der Ahe and the St. Louis Browns.* Lanham, MD: Scarecrow Press, Inc., 1999.
Hoobler, James A. *Cities Under the Gun: Images of Occupied Nashville and Chattanooga.* Nashville: Rutledge Hill Press, 1986.
Ivor-Campbell, Frederick. *Baseball's First Stars.* Cleveland: Society for American Baseball Research, 1996.
James, Bill. *Whatever Happened to the Hall of Fame?: Baseball, Cooperstown, and the Politics of Glory.* New York: Firestone Books, 1995.
_____ and Jim Henzler. *Win Shares.* Morton, Ill.: STATS, Inc., 2002.
Johnson, Lloyd, and Miles Wolff, eds. *The Encyclopedia of Minor League Baseball: The Official Record of Minor League Baseball.* Durham, N.C.: Baseball America, Inc., 1993.
Kavanagh, Jack, and Norman Macht. *Uncle Robbie.* Cleveland: Society for American Baseball Research, 1999.
Kipling, Rudyard. *A Kipling Pageant.* New York: The Literary Guild, 1935.
Laird, A. W. *Ranking Baseball's Elite: An Analysis Derived from Player Statistics, 1893–1987.* Jefferson, N.C.: McFarland, 1990.
Lee, Bill. *The Baseball Necrology: The Post-Baseball Lives and Deaths of Over 7,600 Major League Players and Others.* Jefferson, N.C.: McFarland, 2003.
Link, William A. *The Paradox of Southern Progressivism, 1880–1930.* Chapel Hill: University of North Carolina Press, 1992.
Longert, Scott. *Addie Joss: King of the Pitchers.* Cleveland: Society for American Baseball Research, 1998.
Lowry, Philip J. *Green Cathedrals: The Ultimate Celebration of All 273 Major League and Negro League Ballparks.* New York: Addison-Wesley Publishing Co., 1992.
Majors, William R. *Editorial Wild Oats: Edward Ward Carmack and Tennessee Politics.* Macon, GA: Mercer University Press, 1984.
Marquis Who's Who: Who's Who in the South and Southwest, 1997–1998. Silver Edition. New Providence, N.J.: Marquis, 1998.
Miller, William D. *Memphis During the Progressive Era, 1900–1917.* Memphis: Memphis State University Press, 1957.
Moore, J. T. *The Volunteer State, 1769–1923.* Nashville: S. J. Clarke Publishing Co., 1923.
Nemec, David. *The Beer and Whiskey League: The Illustrated History of the American Association — Baseball's Renegade Major League.* New York: Lyons and Burford, 1994.

Okkonen, Marc. *Baseball Memories, 1900–1909: An Illustrated Chronicle of the Big Leagues' First Decade.* New York: Sterling Publishing Co., 1992.
O'Neal, Bill. *The Southern League: Baseball in Dixie, 1885–1994.* Austin, TX: Eakin Press, 1994.
Rader, Benjamin G. *Baseball: A History of America's Game.* Urbana: University of Illinois Press, 1992.
Reddick, David B., and Kim M. Rodgers. *The Magic of Indianapolis Indians Baseball: 1887–1987.* Indianapolis: Indians, Inc., 1988.
Riess, Steven A. *City Games: The Evolution of American Urban Society and the Rise of Sports.* Urbana: University of Illinois Press, 1989.
_____. *Touching Base: Professional Baseball and American Culture in the Progressive Era.* Westport, CT: Greenwood Press, 1980.
Ritter, Lawrence S. *The Glory of Their Times: The Story of the Early Days of Baseball Told by the Men Who Played It.* New York: Morrow Publishers, 1984 reprint.
Russell, Fred. *Bury Me in an Old Press Box.* New York: A. S. Barnes and Co., 1957.
Russell, Fred, and George Leonard. *Vol Feats: Records, History and Tales of the Nashville Baseball Club in the Southern Association, 1901–1950.* Nashville: Nashville Banner Press, 1950.
Schneider, Russell. *The Cleveland Indians Encyclopedia.* Philadelphia: Temple University Press, 1996.
Schott, Arthur O. *70 Years With the Pelicans, 1887–1957.* n.p., 1992.
Seymour, Harold. *Baseball: The Early Years.* New York: Oxford University Press, 1960.
Simon, Tom, ed. *Deadball Stars of the National League.* Washington, D.C.: Brassey's, Inc., 2004.
Simpson, R. W. *History of Old Pendleton District with a Genealogy of the Leading Families of the District.* Easley, S.C.: Southern Historical Press, 1978 reprint.
Stephenson, Darl L. *Headquarters in the Brush: Blazer's Independent Union Scouts.* Athens, Ohio: Ohio University Press, 2001.
Sullivan, Neil J. *The Minors: The Struggles and the Triumphs of Baseball's Poor Relation from 1876 to the Present.* New York: St. Martin's Press, 1990.
Summerville, James. The *Carmack-Cooper Shooting: Tennessee Politics Turned Violent.* Jefferson, N.C.: McFarland, 1994.
Tennessee Historical Markers. Nashville: Tennessee Historical Commission, 1980.
The Baseball Encyclopedia: The Complete and Definitive Record of Major League Baseball, 9th edition. New York: Macmillan Company, 1993.
Thorn, John, and Pete Palmer, eds. *Total Baseball.* New York: Warner Books, 1989.
Turkin, Hy, and S. C. Thompson. *The Official Encyclopedia of Baseball.* Jubilee Edition. New York: A. S. Barnes and Co., 1951.
Van West, Carroll, ed. *The Tennessee Encyclopedia of History and Culture.* Nashville: Tennessee Historical Society and Rutledge Hill Press, 1998.
Voigt, David Q. *American Baseball.* Norman, OK: University of Oklahoma Press, 1966–1983.
Waller, William. *Nashville, 1900 to 1910.* Nashville: Vanderbilt University Press, 1972.
Wills II, Ridley. *Touring Tennessee: A Postcard Panorama, 1898–1955.* Franklin, TN: Hillsboro Press, 1999.
Wright, Marshall D. *The Southern Association in Baseball, 1885–1961.* Jefferson, N.C.: McFarland, 2002.

Unpublished Material

Wiseman, Donald E.. "Julius Augustus "Doc" Wiseman (1877–1953): The Hero of the Dell" (unpublished family geneaology).

Northen, Hub 136
Noyes, Harry 179–80, 184, 187
Nye, Jack Hopper 213

O'Brien, John (Chewing Gum)(umpire) 39, 83–84, 106, 110; failure to report for game 113; resignation 116
O'Leary, Dan 76

Patterson, Malcolm R. 45, 179–80; at championship game 166; statement 173
Peitz, Heinie 109
Pepe, Joe 23, 64, 101, 104, 186
Perdue, Herbert or Hub (The Gallatin Squash) 27, *28*, *59*, 68, *220*; acquaintance of Fred Russell 227; attended Larry Gilbert Silver Jubilee (1948) 192; background and professional career 65–66; death and burial 222; erratic performances 88; hijinx 136; leads league in wins (1909) 187; major and minor league career after 1908 219–22; off season holdout 182; overwork 127, 130; pitched both ends of double-header 147; player's career index 232; relief successes 139; role as reliever 72; sets Southern Association record for lowest ERA 221–22; seventeen inning non-decision 111–12; six game winning streak 102; Sumner County Clerk 222; Vols' manager (1921) 222
Perry, Clayton 64, 130
Persons, Archie *28*, 64, 68, 94, 103, 133, 134, 186
Pfenninger, Dan (Vinegar Dan)(umpire) 39, 60, 123–24, 208, 223; reminisces about Daubert 205; works championship series 161
Phillips, Bill (Silver Bill) 163
Ponce de Leon Park (Atlanta) 35, opening day (1908) ceremonies 59
Powell, Abner 13, 16
Prohibition (temperance) issue in Tennessee politics 45

Radabaugh, Roy 128
Rader, Benjamin G. 9
Rapp, Barbara 15
Reach Guide 23
Reagan, Pat 66; difficulties in the Dump 130
Red Elm Park (Memphis) 76
Redmond, Harry 86; injury 125; loss of 138
Reserve Clause 11, 13
Rice, Henry Grantland *29*; background, education, and early career 27; championship game poem 173; coins "it's how you played the game" phrase 96; coins "the Greatest Game" phrase 25; death and burial 217; *Driftwood* (poem) 217; importance to Nashville journalism 176; Jimmy Cannon tribute 217; journalistic career after 1908 216–17; national fame 217; preseason analysis of rostered Nashville players 45–46; World War I experience 216

Rickert, Joe (Diamond Joe) 79, 160–61
Riess, Steven G. 9, 36
Robertson, Jim 50, 180, 187
Robitaille, Joseph (Chick) 66, 95, 127
Rohe, George 79, 89, 143, 160, 163; in championship game 167–72
Roush, Edd 204
Rowdyism 115–16, 153–54
Russell, Fred: background and newspaper career 226–28; comments on Wiseman's death 215; death and burial 227–28; efforts to maintain public memory of Sulphur Dell 226; friendship with Grantland Rice 227; on Hub Perdue 221; on importance of night baseball in Nashville 223; master of ceremonies for 1948 Gilbert reception 192; protege of Rice 217; reprints Yancey's 1908 box score and narrative of championship game twice in 1930s *Banner* articles 191–92
Ryan, Jack (Gulfport Jack) 79
Ryan, Jimmy 63, 84, 103, 105; firing of 130
Ryman Auditorium 44

Sabbatarianism 3, 18, 84–85
Sabrie, Eddie 111
Sallee, Slim 210, 221
Sargent, Gordon B. ix
Savidge, Ralph (the Human Whipcord) 76, 86, 124–25, 139, 150
Schopp, Grant 72, 106, 148
Schwartz, Bill: tribute to Wiseman 215
Schwenck, Rudy (Iron Man) 138, 149
Scientific baseball 2, 7, 85; explanation 10–11
Seabough, James Warren 45, 57, *59*, 137; all-star selection 181; background and professional career 64; death and burial 212; defensive problems 72, 81, 92, 141; hand injury 155; minor league career after 1908 211; player's career index 232; president of Western (baseball) Association and Frisco System Baseball League 211; railroad career 211–12; shoulder injury discovered 180
Sentell, Paul 122, 147, 155; all-star selection 181
Shields, Charlie 86, 117; involvement with death of Hurlburt 196; life after baseball 198
Siegle, Johnny *59*, 69, 70; all-star selection 181; background and professional career 56; death and burial 219; fraternal 219; religious affiliations 219; injury 114; minor league player/manager career after 1908 219; player's career index 233; political career 219; popularity 129; postmaster 219; purchased contract 58; steady performance 121, 130
Sitton, Carl Vedder, 49, *59*; background and professional career 54–54; and Cleveland 206; contrast with Breitenstein in championship game 164–65; debut 129; drafted by Cleveland 143; fielding weakness 134, 153; key role in championship game 167–72;

minor league career after 1909 206; player's career index 233; recalled 127; released to Jacksonville 58; return to Nashville 121; tragic death and burial 207
Sitton, Phil 132, 206
Sloan, J.A.G. 35
Smith, Carlos (The Human Giraffe) 128
Smith, William (Tobacco Billy) 20, *40*, 59, 90, 102, 209; institutes system of paid base coaches for 1909 183
Sorrell, Bill 27, *28*, 46; player's career index 233
Southern Association: classification 14; creation 13; early qualities 3; final 1907 standings 26; folds 225; predictions of 1908 championship series 160; problems of rowdyism, gambling, and Sabbatarianism 18; tight 1908 race 2, 133, 136; umpire shortage 115
Southern League, founding of (1885) 7, 8
Spalding's Guide 23
Speaker, Tris 78, 94, 136, 203, 212; all-star selection 181; sold to Boston Red Sox 148; top major league prospect in Southern Association 113
Sporting Life 23
The Sporting News 23
Sportsman's Park (New Orleans) 78–79
Stallings, George 13, 220
Stark, Monroe 115
Stengel, Casey 38, 222
Stockard, Sam J.: comparison of Breitenstein-Sitton matchup 164–65
Stockdale, Otis 32, 89–91, 93, 180; banned from baseball 91
Stockdale Scandal 89–91, 99
Street, Gabby 198
Sulphur Dell 52, *224*, *225*; championship game day 165–66; championship series 159; demolishion 226; electric scoreboard installed 181; enlargement of left field (1909) 182; flooding 183; historical sketch (1909–1963) 222–26; intimate and odd configurations 38; naming 36–37, 68; new chalk scoreboard 154; non-sports venues 226; opening day 63; opening day (1909) ceremonies 185; origin of the Dump 38; overflow crowds 149; sentimental memories 226; victory celebration 172
Sulphur Springs Bottom 7, 24
Sutton, Larry, scout for Charlie Ebbets 199

Taft, William Howard 16, 179, 215
"Take Me Out to the Ball Game" 148, 176–77
Tarleton, Bob 160; in championship game 167–72; recollects baserunning mistake in championship game 192–93
Tate, Mike G. 196
Taylor, Walter 90–91
Thomas, Forrest 104, 130, 134
Thornton, Woodie 93, 147

Tonneman, Charlie 180, 187
Torrey, Clarence 111
Traughber, Bill 193
Tyne, Thomas James 32

Vanderbilt University *29*; baseball at 9; loan of chairs by 164
Vaughn, Harry (father) 48, 66; firing of 85
Vendome 44, 179
Victorian prose: unique baseball terminology 3
Viebahn, Bill 129, 131, 132; traded to Vols 186
Von der Ahe, Chris 109
Voorhees, Henry (Cy) 34

Waddell, Rube 206
Walsh, Ed 158, 212
Walters, Lewis 66
Ward, John M. 12
Wells, Robert (Kid) 27, *28*
West End Park (Little Rock) 78
Wheat, Zack 147, 155, 199
Whiting, Percy 90–91, 173
Williams, Alf 51, 122, 166, 185
Winters, George 71; all-star selection 181; loss of 131
Wiseman, Donald E. viii, 213, 214
Wiseman, James A. v, viii, ix, 214
Wiseman, Julius Augustus (Doc) *17*, *28*, *59*; all-league selection (1907) 30; base stealing abilities 94; business interests 213; childhood and public schooling 15–16; Cincinnati municipal employment 214; Cincinnati neighborhood 16; complete Nashville career statistics 212–13; death and burial 215–16; Doc Wiseman Day at Sulphur Dell (1912), appearance by 213–14; early professional career 16; family background 15; family life 214–15; Fred Russell's tribute 215; high school, club and university baseball career 16; invited to Larry Gilbert Silver Jubilee (1948) 192; joins Nashville club 18; key role in championship game 170–71; law school training 16; lifetime pass to University of Cincinnati sporting events 215; nickname 16; player's career index 233; popularity in Nashville 38, 45, 46, 53, 124; posthumous accolades 215–16; special award during championship game 170; stock investments 214; temporary move to shortstop 97
Wiseman, Samuel Vinton 15
Wood, Bob 152, 154
Wormser, Mose 94

Yancey, Richard Hunter, Jr. 26; gambling concerns on Vols 110–11; importance 176; official scorer of Vols 174; resigns to become sports editor of *Chattanooga Times* 181; selected sports editor of *Nashville Banner* 34
Yerkes, Stanley 45, 46, 48, 68, 71, 78, 87, 93, 102; release of 103, 233

www.ingramcontent.com/pod-product-compliance
Ingram Content Group UK Ltd.
Pitfield, Milton Keynes, MK11 3LW, UK
UKHW041928140426
5217IPUK00014B/367